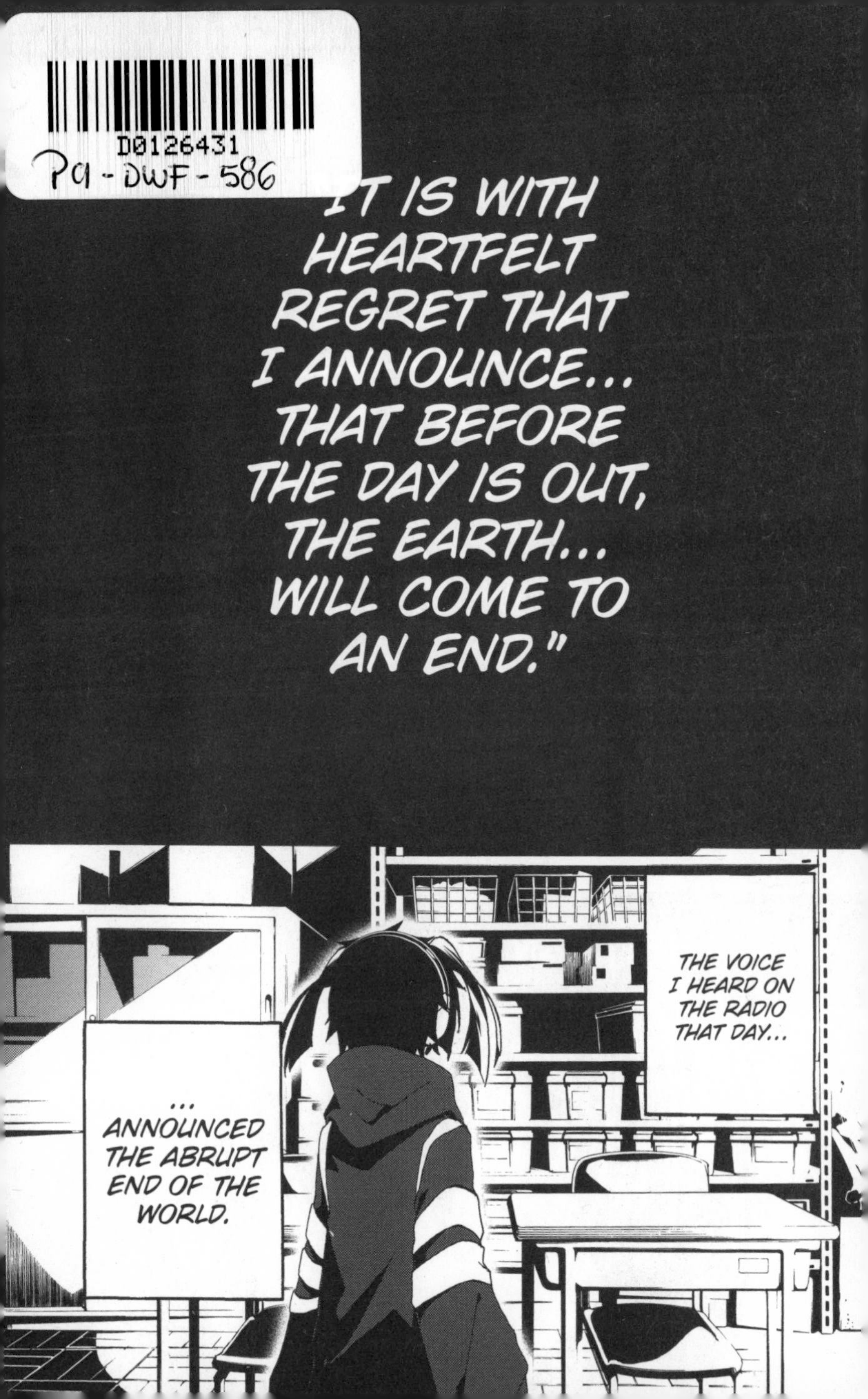
"IT IS WITH HEARTFELT REGRET THAT I ANNOUNCE... THAT BEFORE THE DAY IS OUT, THE EARTH... WILL COME TO AN END."
THE VOICE I HEARD ON THE RADIO THAT DAY...
...ANNOUNCED THE ABRUPT END OF THE WORLD.

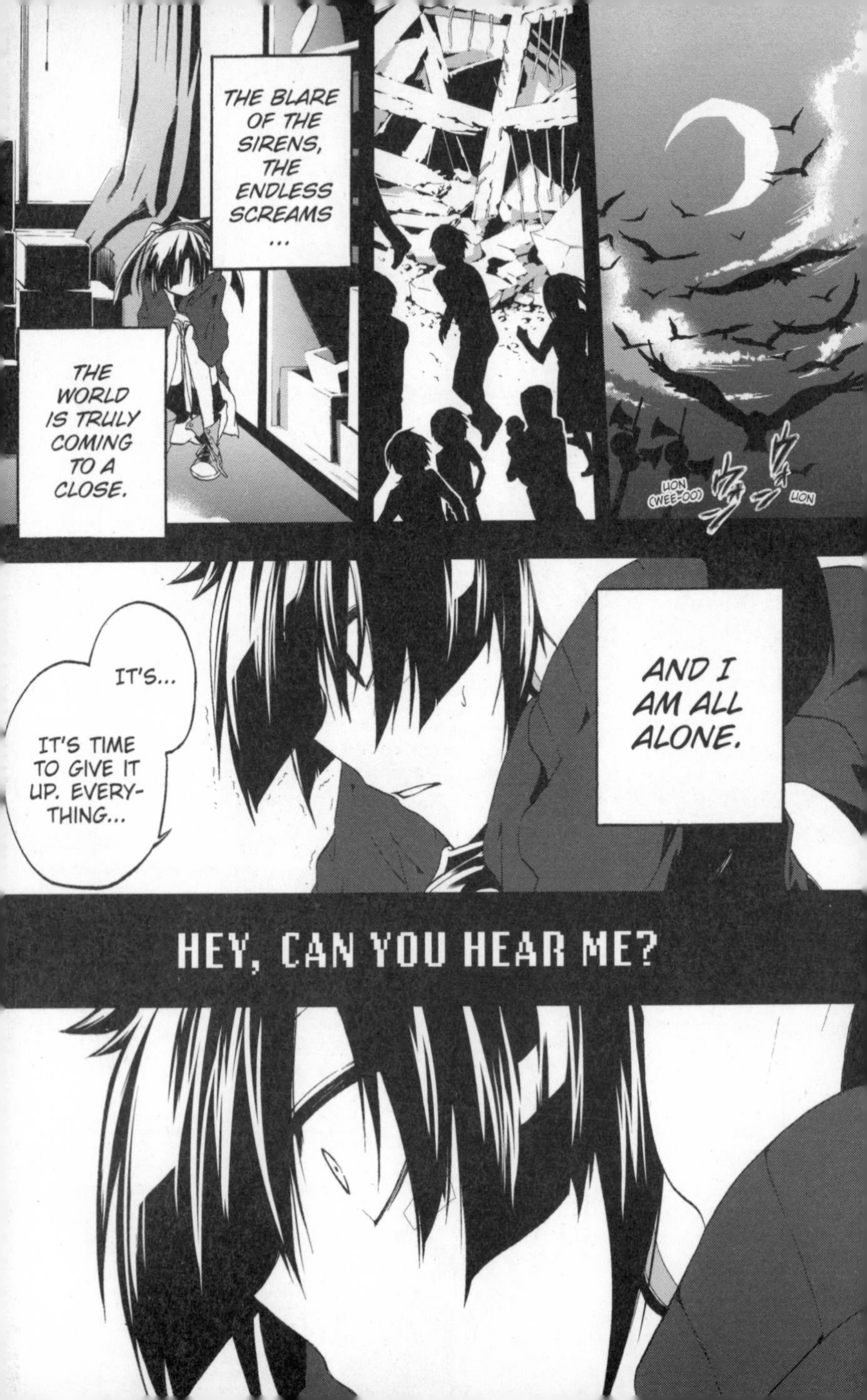
UON
UON (WEE-OO)
THE BLARE OF THE SIRENS, THE ENDLESS SCREAMS ...
THE WORLD IS TRULY COMING TO A CLOSE.
AND I AM ALL ALONE.
IT'S...
IT'S TIME TO GIVE IT UP. EVERY-THING...
HEY, CAN YOU HEAR ME?

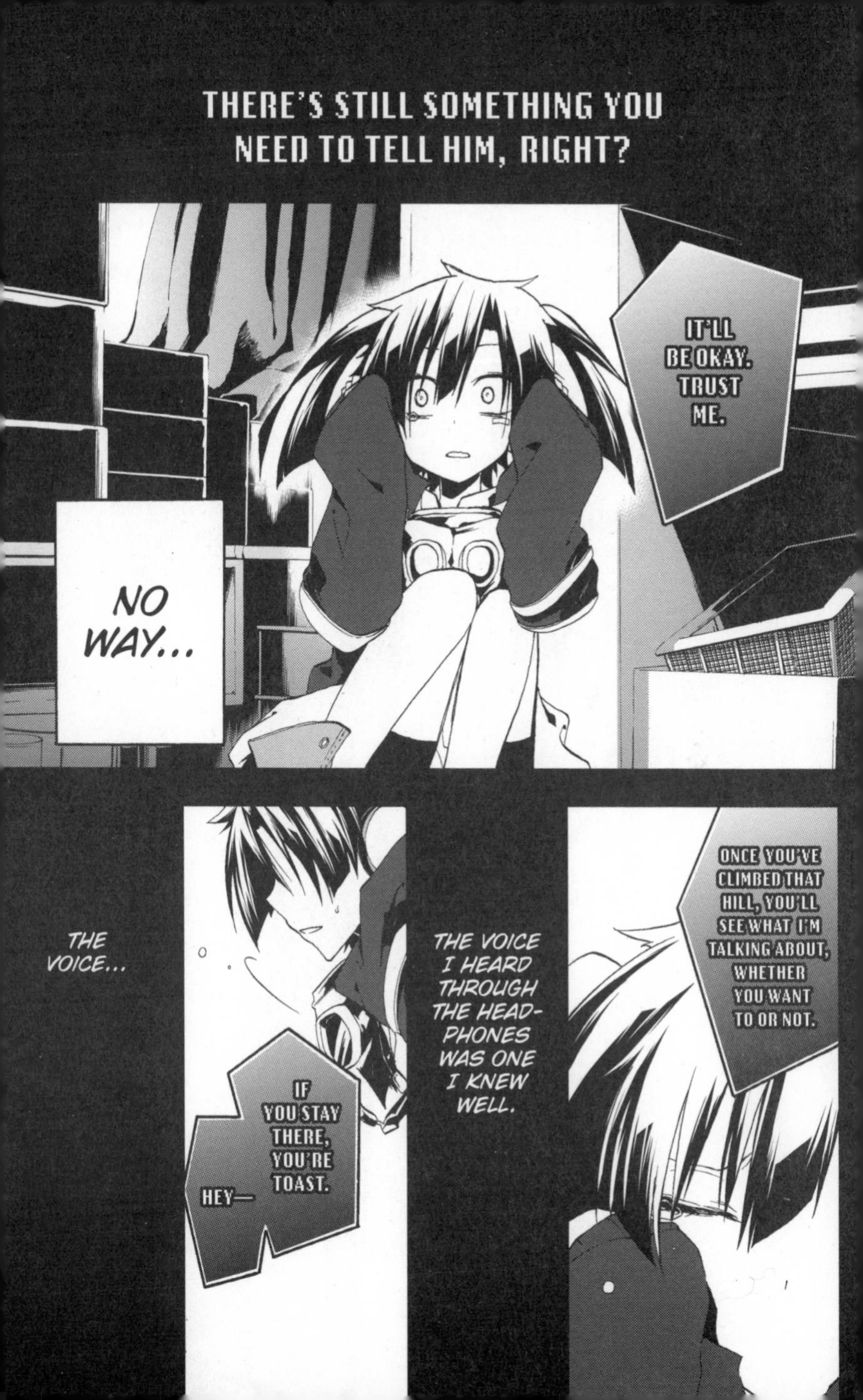
THERE'S STILL SOMETHING YOU NEED TO TELL HIM, RIGHT?
IT'LL BE OKAY. TRUST ME.
NO WAY...
ONCE YOU'VE CLIMBED THAT HILL, YOU'LL SEE WHAT I'M TALKING ABOUT, WHETHER YOU WANT TO OR NOT.
THE VOICE I HEARD THROUGH THE HEAD-PHONES WAS ONE I KNEW WELL.
IF YOU STAY THERE, YOU'RE TOAST.
HEY—
THE VOICE...

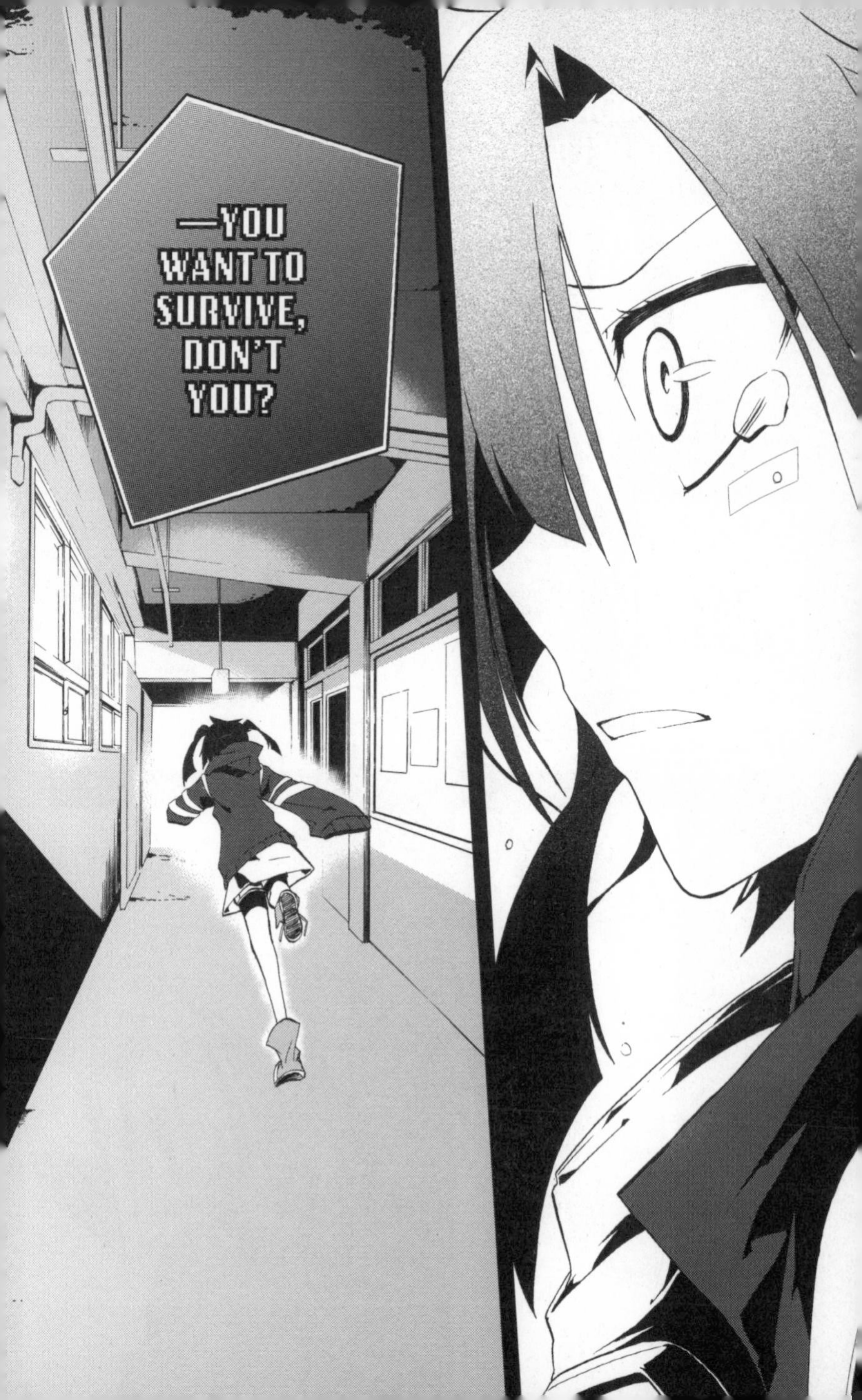
—YOU WANT TO SURVIVE, DON'T YOU?

...WAS NONE OTHER THAN MY OWN.

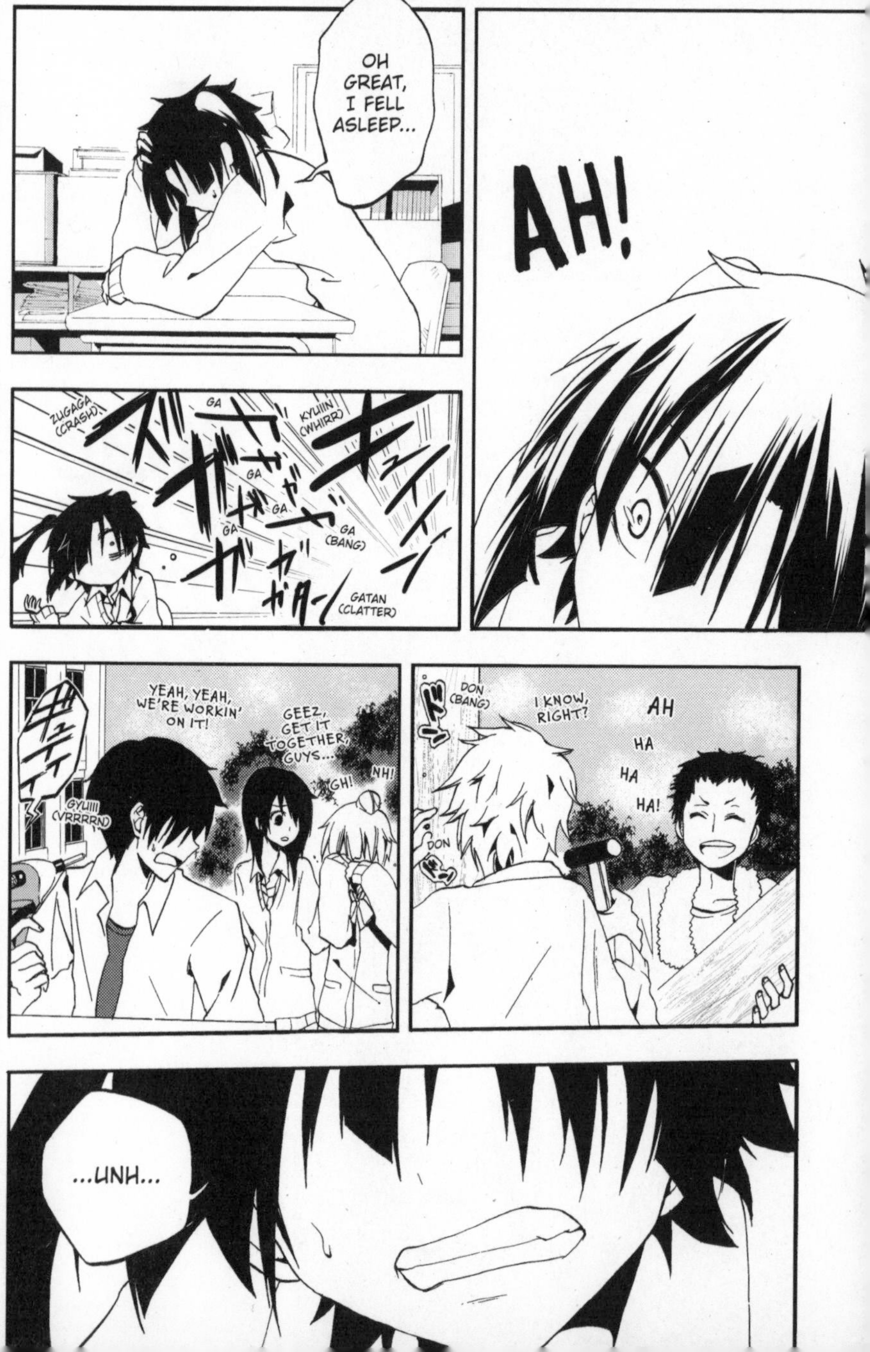
AH!
OH GREAT, I FELL ASLEEP...
KYUIIN (WHIRR)
GA
ZUGAGA (CRASH)
GA
GA
GA (BANG)
GA
GATAN (CLATTER)
DON (BANG)
I KNOW, RIGHT?
AH HA HA HA!
DON
GEEZ, GET IT TOGETHER, GUYS...
NH!
GH!
YEAH, YEAH, WE'RE WORKIN' ON IT!
GYUIII (VRRRRN)
...UNH...

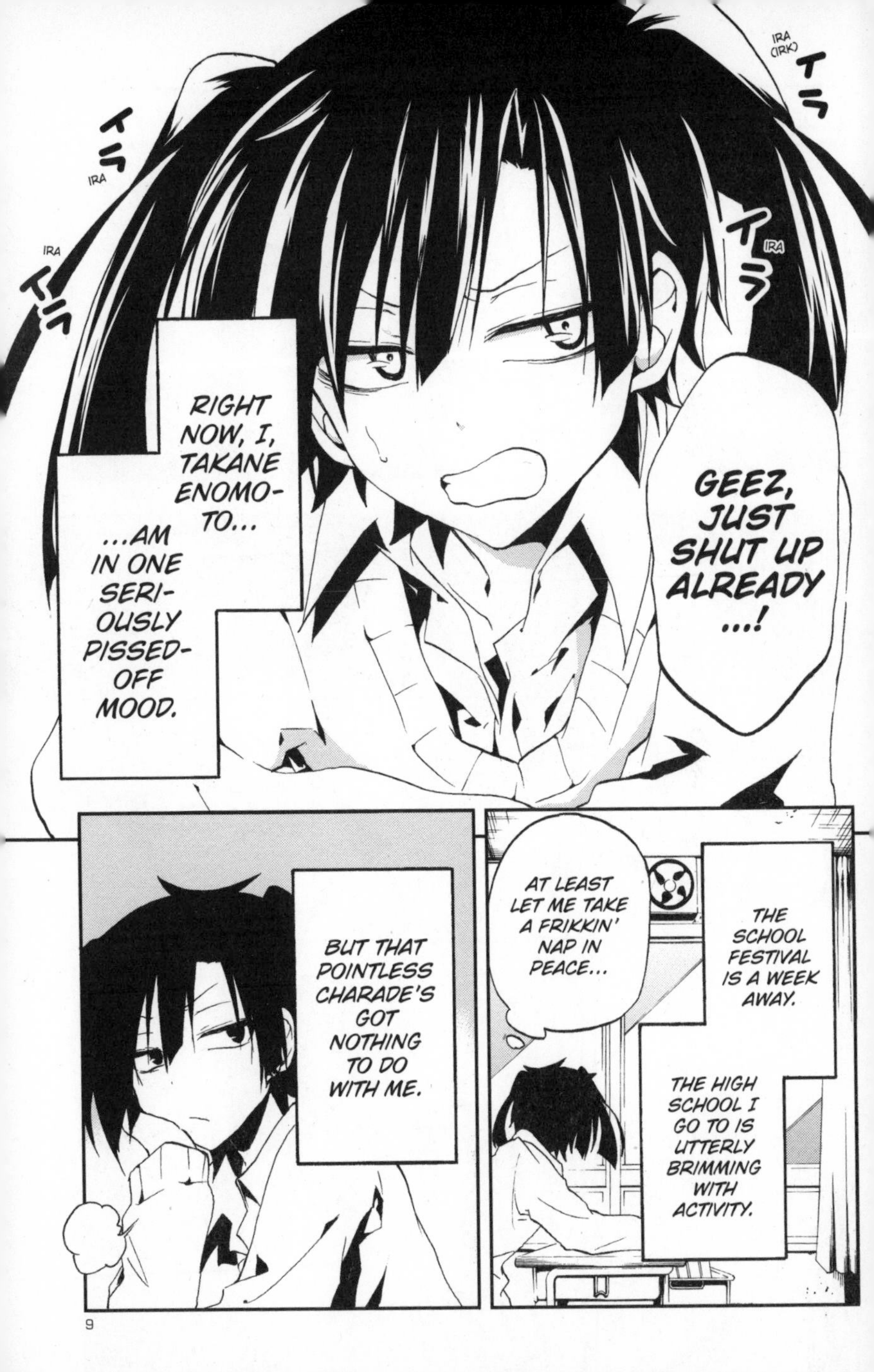
IRA (IRK)
IRA
GEEZ, JUST SHUT UP ALREADY ...!
RIGHT NOW, I, TAKANE ENOMOTO...
...AM IN ONE SERIOUSLY PISSED-OFF MOOD.
IRA
IRA
THE SCHOOL FESTIVAL IS A WEEK AWAY.
THE HIGH SCHOOL I GO TO IS UTTERLY BRIMMING WITH ACTIVITY.
AT LEAST LET ME TAKE A FRIKKIN' NAP IN PEACE...
BUT THAT POINTLESS CHARADE'S GOT NOTHING TO DO WITH ME.

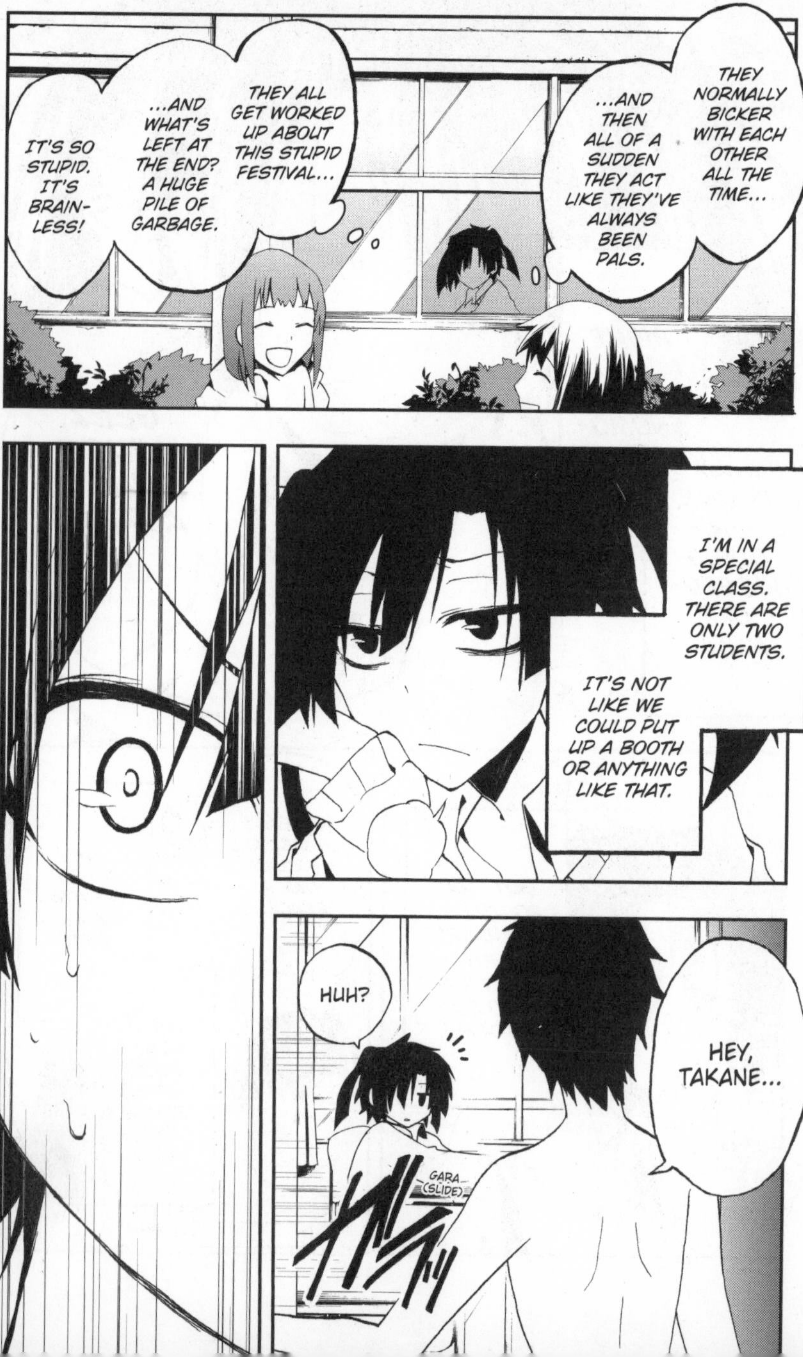
THEY NORMALLY BICKER WITH EACH OTHER ALL THE TIME...
...AND THEN ALL OF A SUDDEN THEY ACT LIKE THEY'VE ALWAYS BEEN PALS.
THEY ALL GET WORKED UP ABOUT THIS STUPID FESTIVAL...
...AND WHAT'S LEFT AT THE END? A HUGE PILE OF GARBAGE.
IT'S SO STUPID. IT'S BRAIN-LESS!
I'M IN A SPECIAL CLASS. THERE ARE ONLY TWO STUDENTS.
IT'S NOT LIKE WE COULD PUT UP A BOOTH OR ANYTHING LIKE THAT.
HEY, TAKANE...
HUH?
GARA (SLIDE)

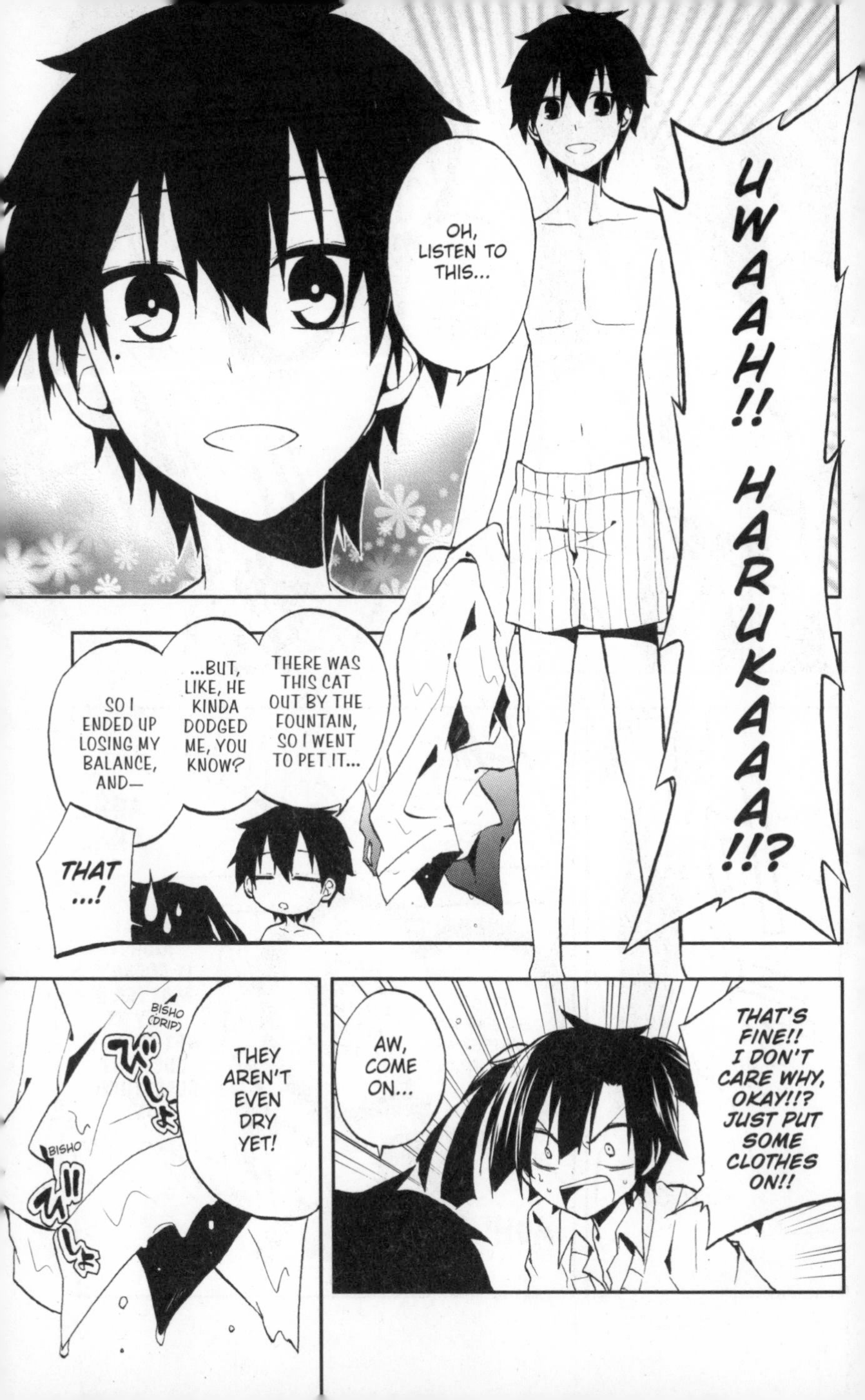
UWAAAH!! HARUKAAAA!!?
OH, LISTEN TO THIS...
THERE WAS THIS CAT OUT BY THE FOUNTAIN, SO I WENT TO PET IT...
...BUT, LIKE, HE KINDA DODGED ME, YOU KNOW?
SO I ENDED UP LOSING MY BALANCE, AND—
THAT...!
THAT'S FINE!! I DON'T CARE WHY, OKAY!!? JUST PUT SOME CLOTHES ON!!
AW, COME ON...
BISHO (DRIP)
THEY AREN'T EVEN DRY YET!
BISHO

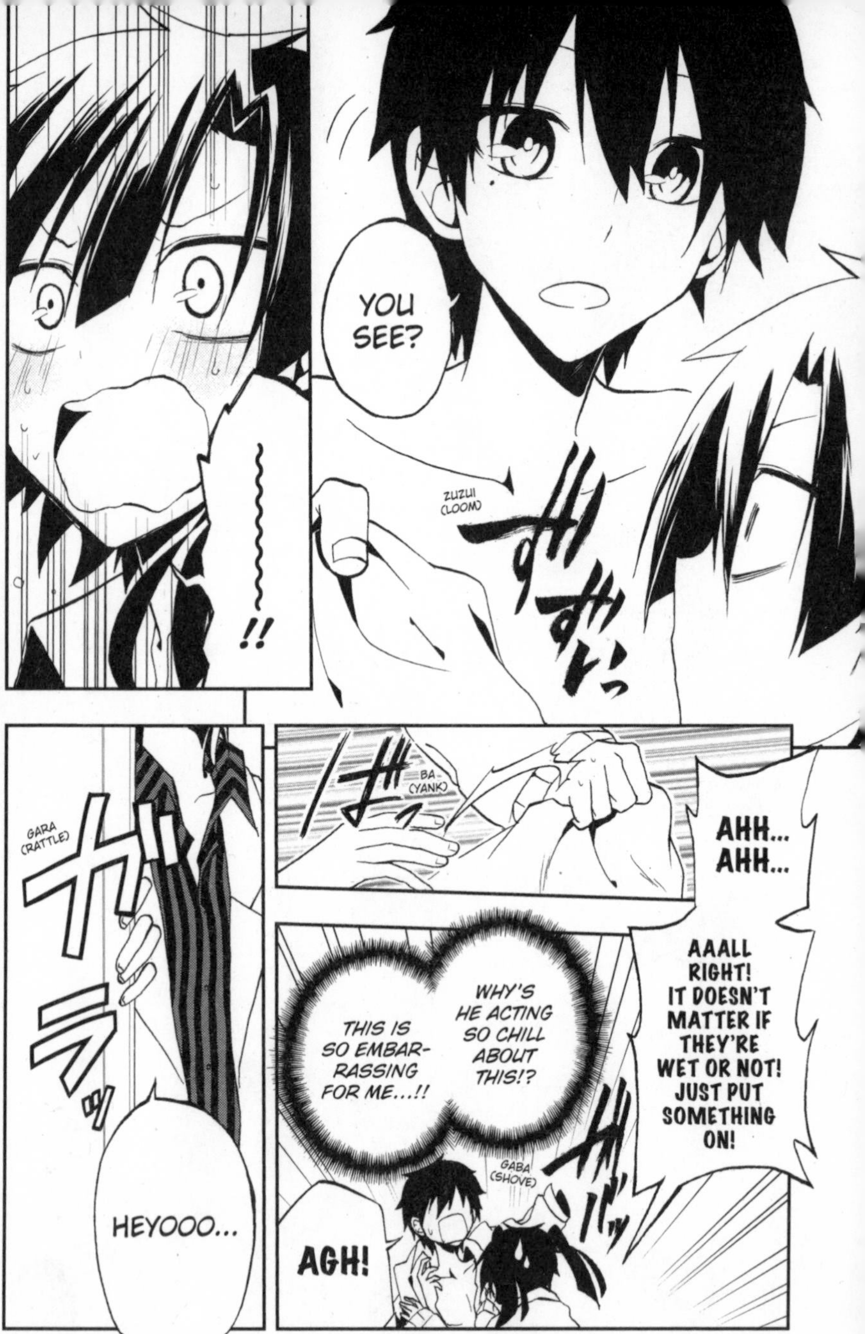
YOU SEE?
ZUZUI (LOOM)
~~~~!!
BA (YANK)
AHH... AHH...
AAALL RIGHT! IT DOESN'T MATTER IF THEY'RE WET OR NOT! JUST PUT SOMETHING ON!
WHY'S HE ACTING SO CHILL ABOUT THIS!?
THIS IS SO EMBAR-RASSING FOR ME...!!
GABA (SHOVE)
AGH!
GARA (RATTLE)
HEYOOO...
~~~~

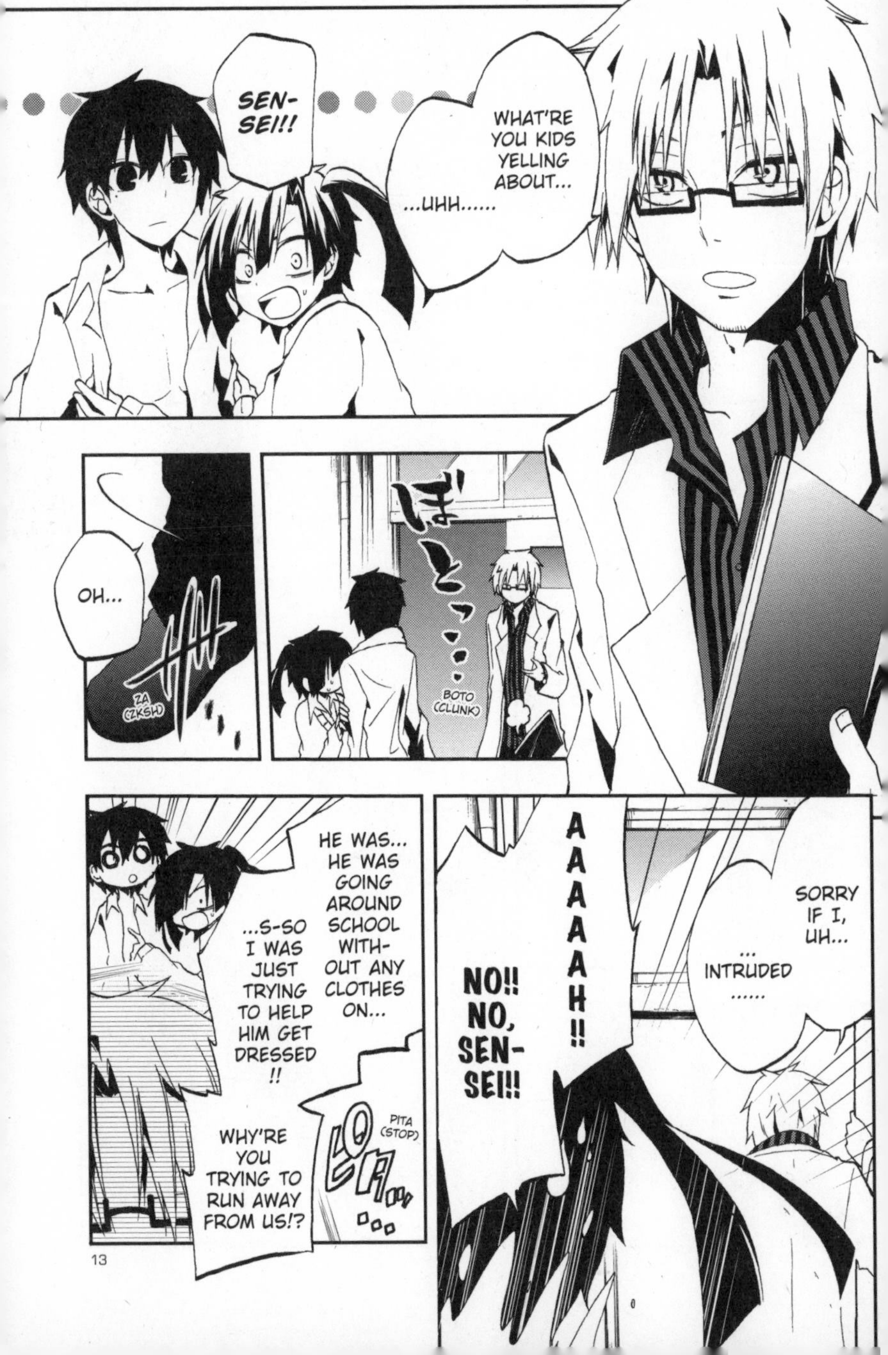
WHAT'RE YOU KIDS YELLING ABOUT...
...UHH......
SEN-SEI!!
BOTO (CLUNK)
OH...
ZA (ZKSH)
SORRY IF I, UH... ...INTRUDED......
AAAAAAH!!
NO!! NO, SEN-SEI!!
HE WAS... HE WAS GOING AROUND SCHOOL WITH-OUT ANY CLOTHES ON...
...S-SO I WAS JUST TRYING TO HELP HIM GET DRESSED!!
PITA (STOP)
WHY'RE YOU TRYING TO RUN AWAY FROM US!?

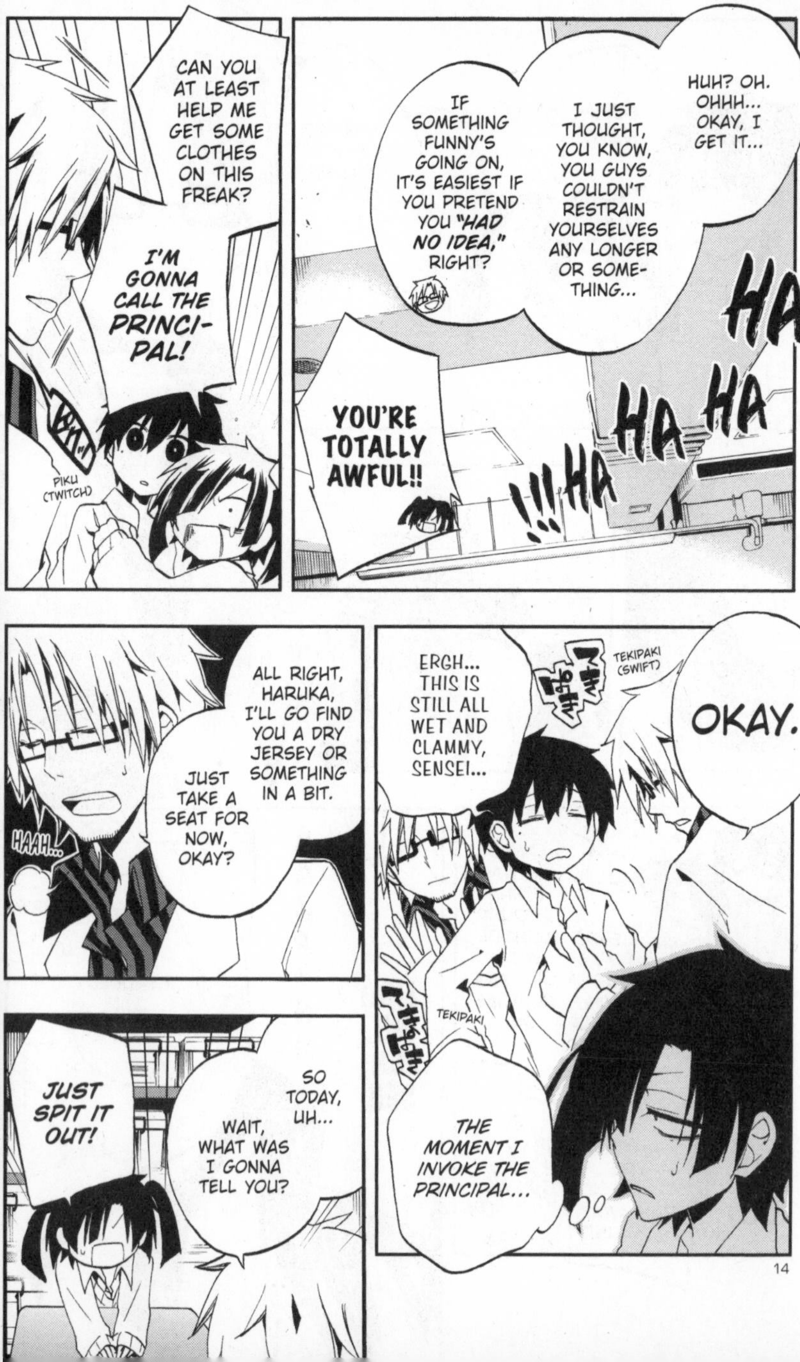
HUH? OH. OHHH... OKAY, I GET IT...
I JUST THOUGHT, YOU KNOW, YOU GUYS COULDN'T RESTRAIN YOURSELVES ANY LONGER OR SOME-THING...
IF SOMETHING FUNNY'S GOING ON, IT'S EASIEST IF YOU PRETEND YOU "HAD NO IDEA," RIGHT?
HA HA HA HA
!!!
YOU'RE TOTALLY AWFUL!!
CAN YOU AT LEAST HELP ME GET SOME CLOTHES ON THIS FREAK?
I'M GONNA CALL THE PRINCI-PAL!
PIKU (TWITCH)
OKAY.
TEKIPAKI (SWIFT)
ERGH... THIS IS STILL ALL WET AND CLAMMY, SENSEI...
TEKIPAKI
THE MOMENT I INVOKE THE PRINCIPAL...
ALL RIGHT, HARUKA, I'LL GO FIND YOU A DRY JERSEY OR SOMETHING IN A BIT.
JUST TAKE A SEAT FOR NOW, OKAY?
HAAH...
SO TODAY, UH...
WAIT, WHAT WAS I GONNA TELL YOU?
JUST SPIT IT OUT!

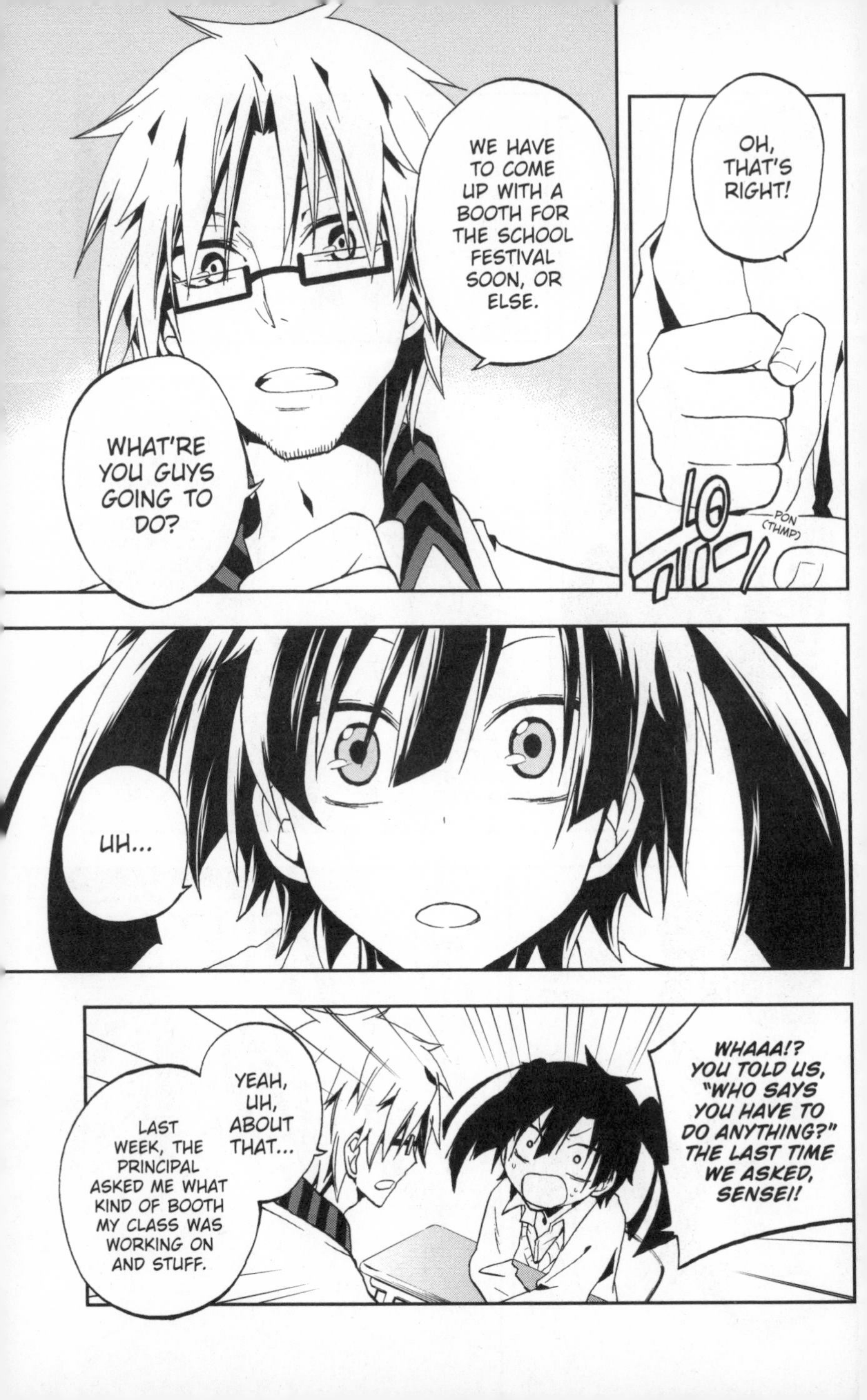
OH, THAT'S RIGHT!
PON (THMP)
WE HAVE TO COME UP WITH A BOOTH FOR THE SCHOOL FESTIVAL SOON, OR ELSE.
WHAT'RE YOU GUYS GOING TO DO?
UH...
WHAAA!? YOU TOLD US, "WHO SAYS YOU HAVE TO DO ANYTHING?" THE LAST TIME WE ASKED, SENSEI!
YEAH, UH, ABOUT THAT...
LAST WEEK, THE PRINCIPAL ASKED ME WHAT KIND OF BOOTH MY CLASS WAS WORKING ON AND STUFF.

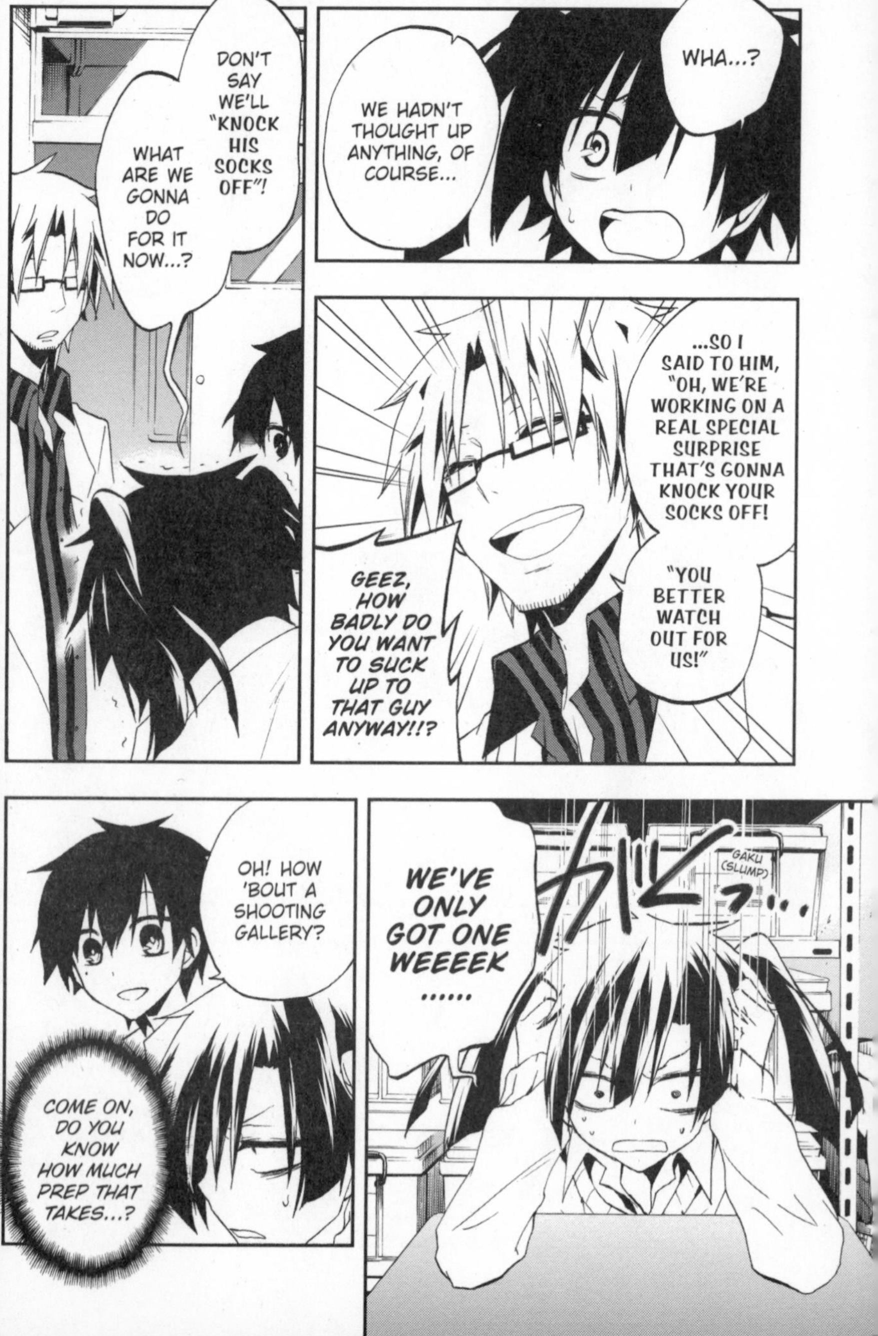
WHA...?
WE HADN'T THOUGHT UP ANYTHING, OF COURSE...
...SO I SAID TO HIM, "OH, WE'RE WORKING ON A REAL SPECIAL SURPRISE THAT'S GONNA KNOCK YOUR SOCKS OFF!
"YOU BETTER WATCH OUT FOR US!"
GEEZ, HOW BADLY DO YOU WANT TO SUCK UP TO THAT GUY ANYWAY!!?
DON'T SAY WE'LL "KNOCK HIS SOCKS OFF"!
WHAT ARE WE GONNA DO FOR IT NOW...?
GAKU (SLUMP)
WE'VE ONLY GOT ONE WEEEEK ......
OH! HOW 'BOUT A SHOOTING GALLERY?
COME ON, DO YOU KNOW HOW MUCH PREP THAT TAKES...?

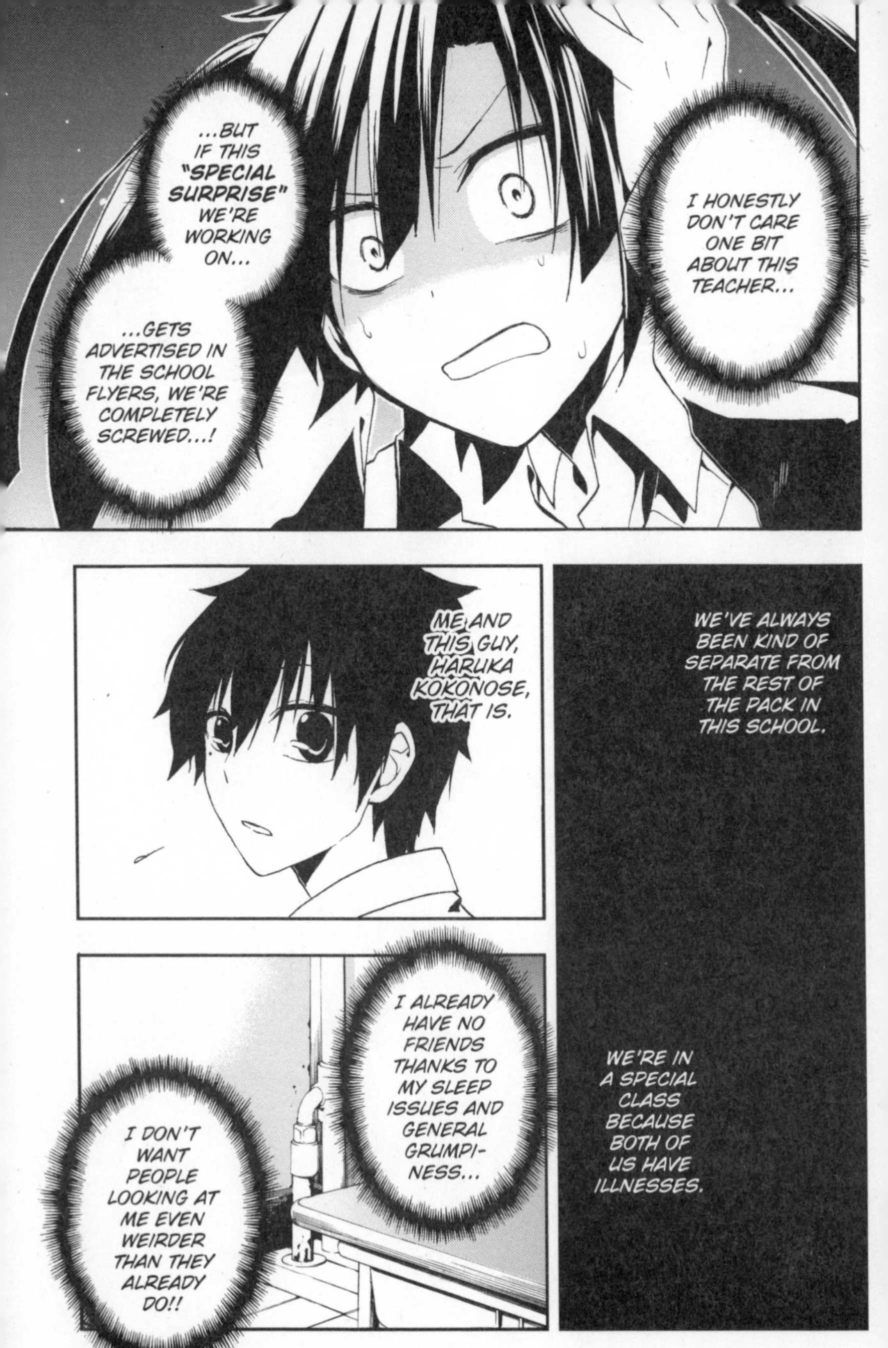
I HONESTLY DON'T CARE ONE BIT ABOUT THIS TEACHER...
...BUT IF THIS "SPECIAL SURPRISE" WE'RE WORKING ON...
...GETS ADVERTISED IN THE SCHOOL FLYERS, WE'RE COMPLETELY SCREWED...!
WE'VE ALWAYS BEEN KIND OF SEPARATE FROM THE REST OF THE PACK IN THIS SCHOOL.
WE'RE IN A SPECIAL CLASS BECAUSE BOTH OF US HAVE ILLNESSES.
ME AND THIS GUY, HARUKA KOKONOSE, THAT IS.
I ALREADY HAVE NO FRIENDS THANKS TO MY SLEEP ISSUES AND GENERAL GRUMPI-NESS...
I DON'T WANT PEOPLE LOOKING AT ME EVEN WEIRDER THAN THEY ALREADY DO!!

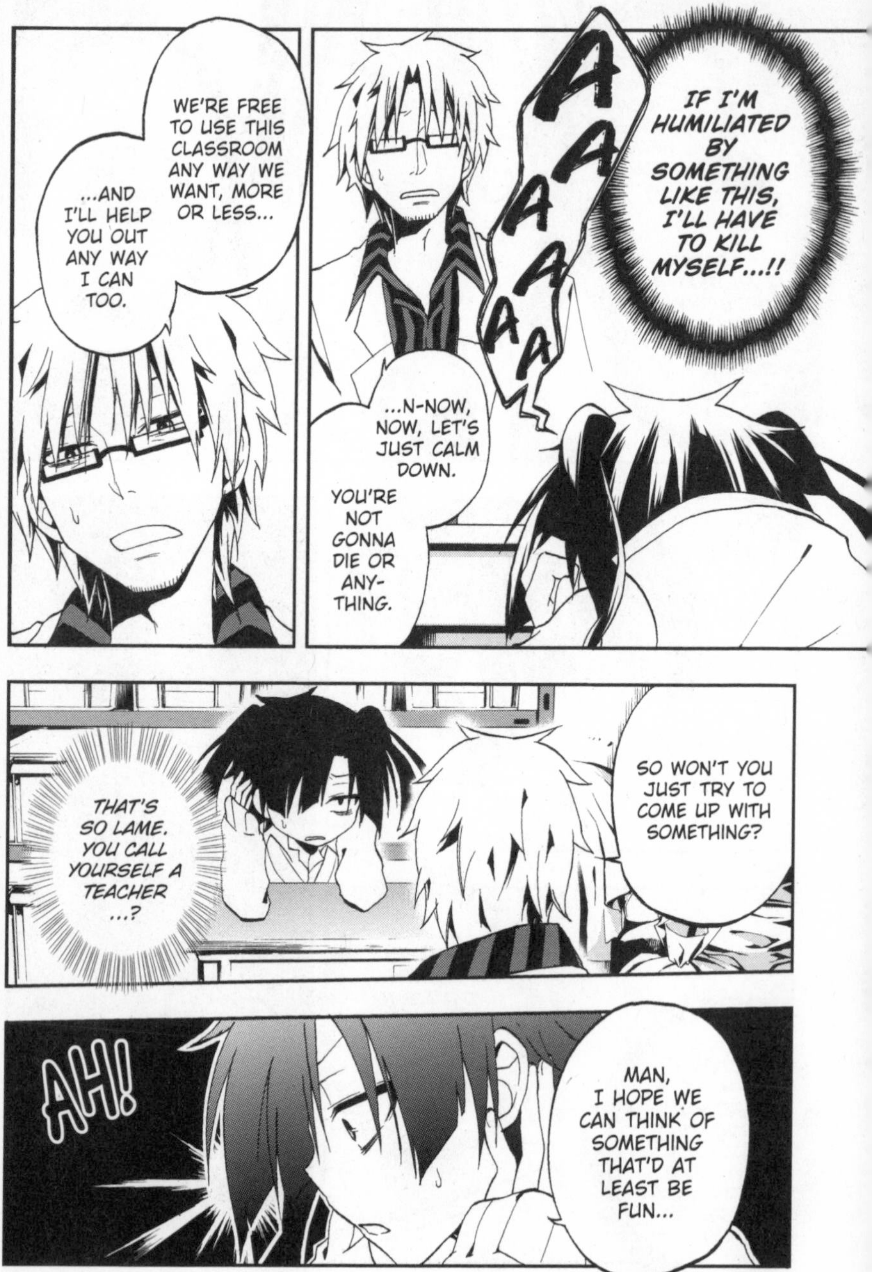
IF I'M HUMILIATED BY SOMETHING LIKE THIS, I'LL HAVE TO KILL MYSELF...!!
AAAAAAA
...N-NOW, NOW, LET'S JUST CALM DOWN.
YOU'RE NOT GONNA DIE OR ANY-THING.
WE'RE FREE TO USE THIS CLASSROOM ANY WAY WE WANT, MORE OR LESS...
...AND I'LL HELP YOU OUT ANY WAY I CAN TOO.
SO WON'T YOU JUST TRY TO COME UP WITH SOMETHING?
...
THAT'S SO LAME. YOU CALL YOURSELF A TEACHER ...?
MAN, I HOPE WE CAN THINK OF SOMETHING THAT'D AT LEAST BE FUN...
AH!

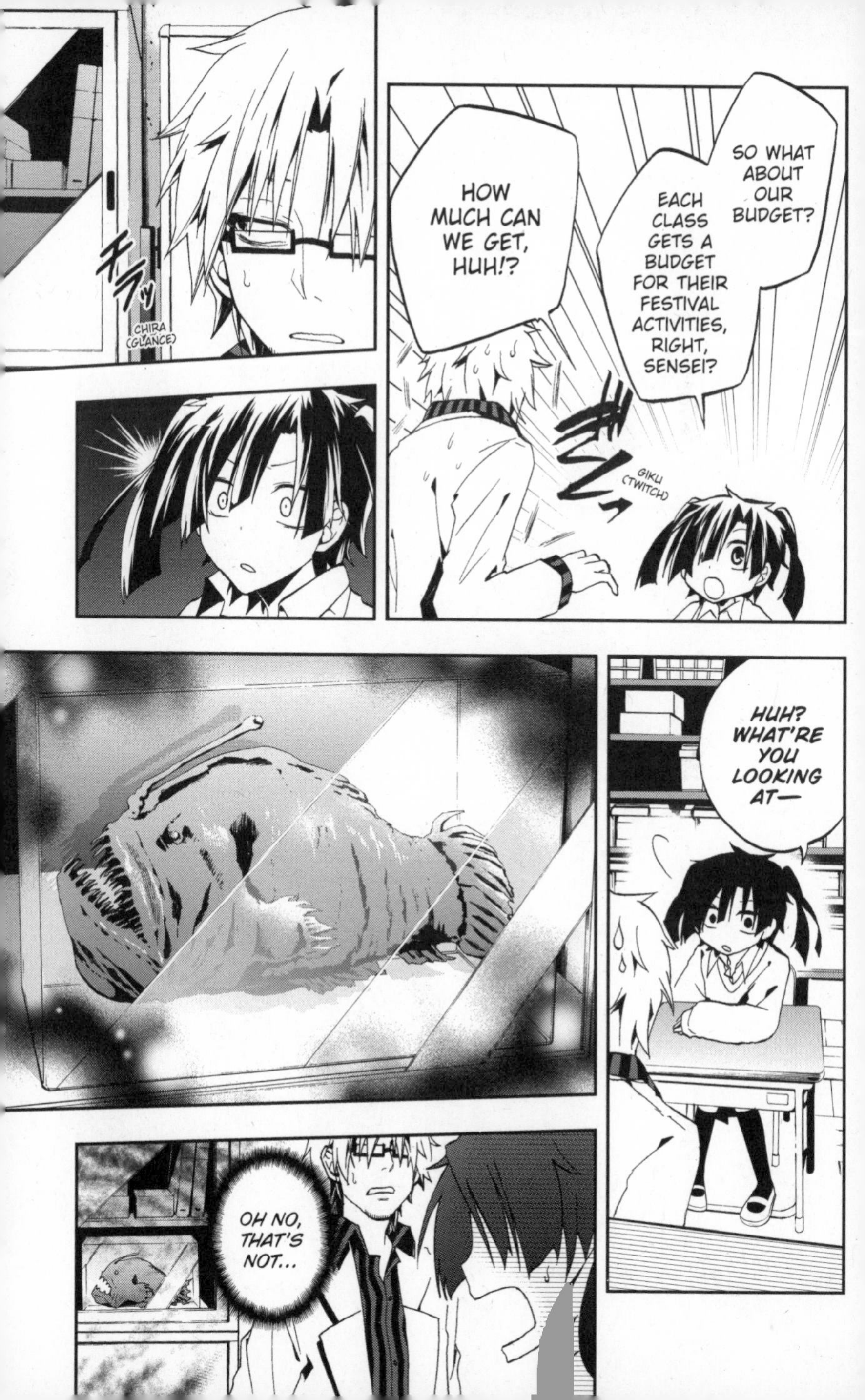
SO WHAT ABOUT OUR BUDGET?
EACH CLASS GETS A BUDGET FOR THEIR FESTIVAL ACTIVITIES, RIGHT, SENSEI?
HOW MUCH CAN WE GET, HUH!?
GIKU (TWITCH)
CHIRA (GLANCE)
HUH? WHAT'RE YOU LOOKING AT—
OH NO, THAT'S NOT...

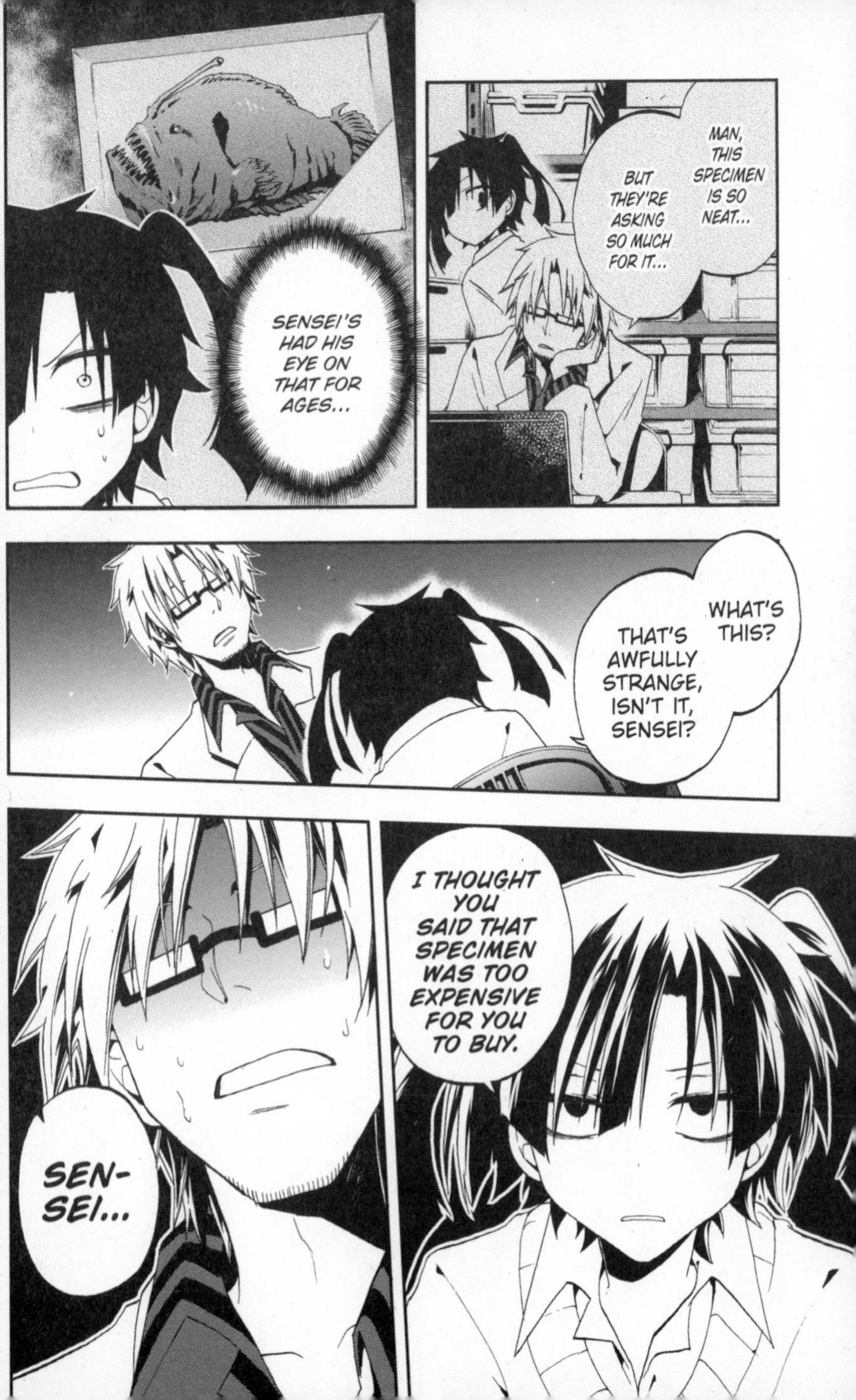
MAN, THIS SPECIMEN IS SO NEAT...
BUT THEY'RE ASKING SO MUCH FOR IT...
SENSEI'S HAD HIS EYE ON THAT FOR AGES...
WHAT'S THIS?
THAT'S AWFULLY STRANGE, ISN'T IT, SENSEI?
I THOUGHT YOU SAID THAT SPECIMEN WAS TOO EXPENSIVE FOR YOU TO BUY.
SEN-SEI...

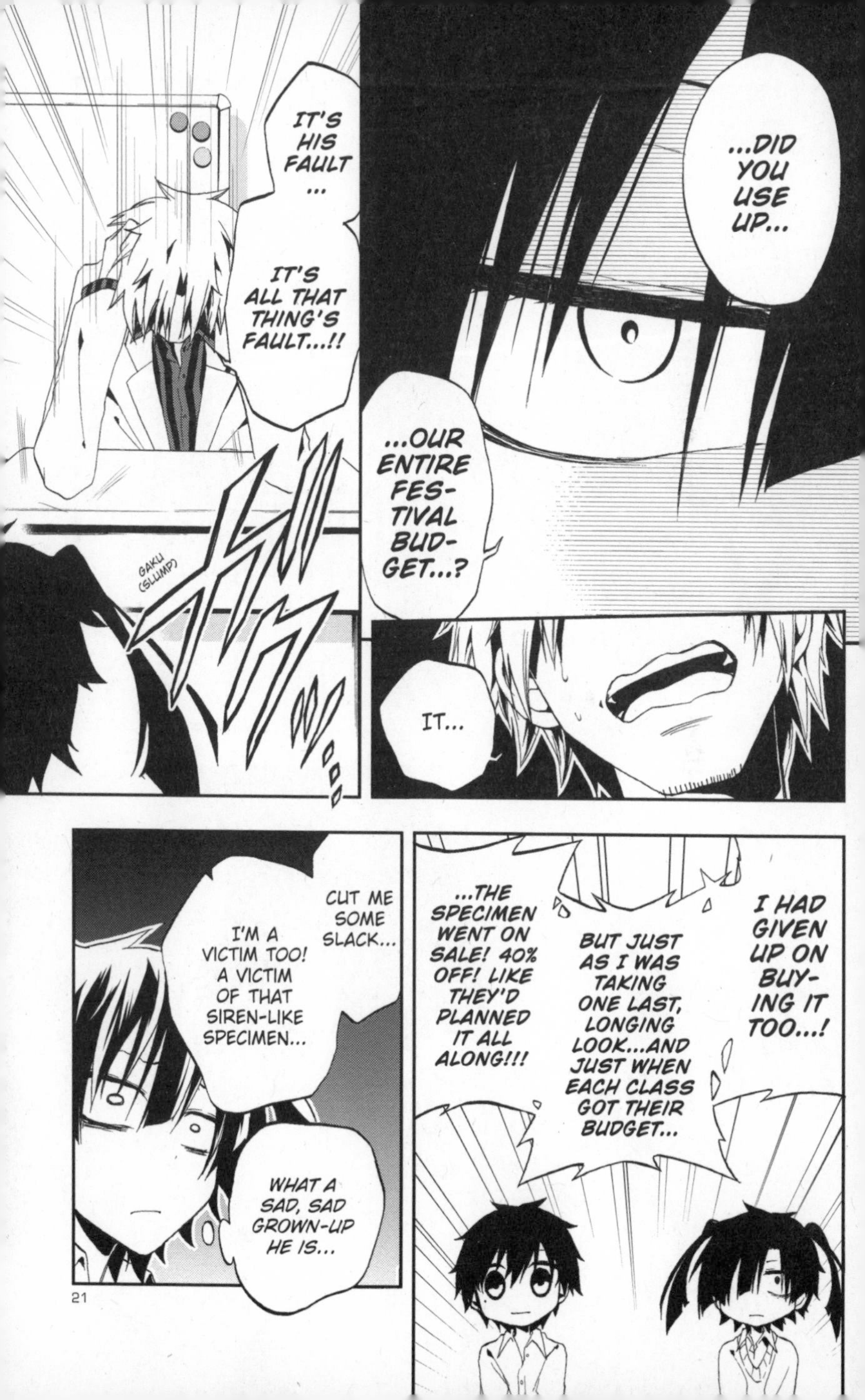
...DID YOU USE UP...
...OUR ENTIRE FESTIVAL BUDGET...?
IT...
IT'S HIS FAULT...
IT'S ALL THAT THING'S FAULT...!!
GAKU (SLUMP)
I HAD GIVEN UP ON BUYING IT TOO...!
BUT JUST AS I WAS TAKING ONE LAST, LONGING LOOK...AND JUST WHEN EACH CLASS GOT THEIR BUDGET...
...THE SPECIMEN WENT ON SALE! 40% OFF! LIKE THEY'D PLANNED IT ALL ALONG!!!
CUT ME SOME SLACK...
I'M A VICTIM TOO! A VICTIM OF THAT SIREN-LIKE SPECIMEN...
WHAT A SAD, SAD GROWN-UP HE IS...

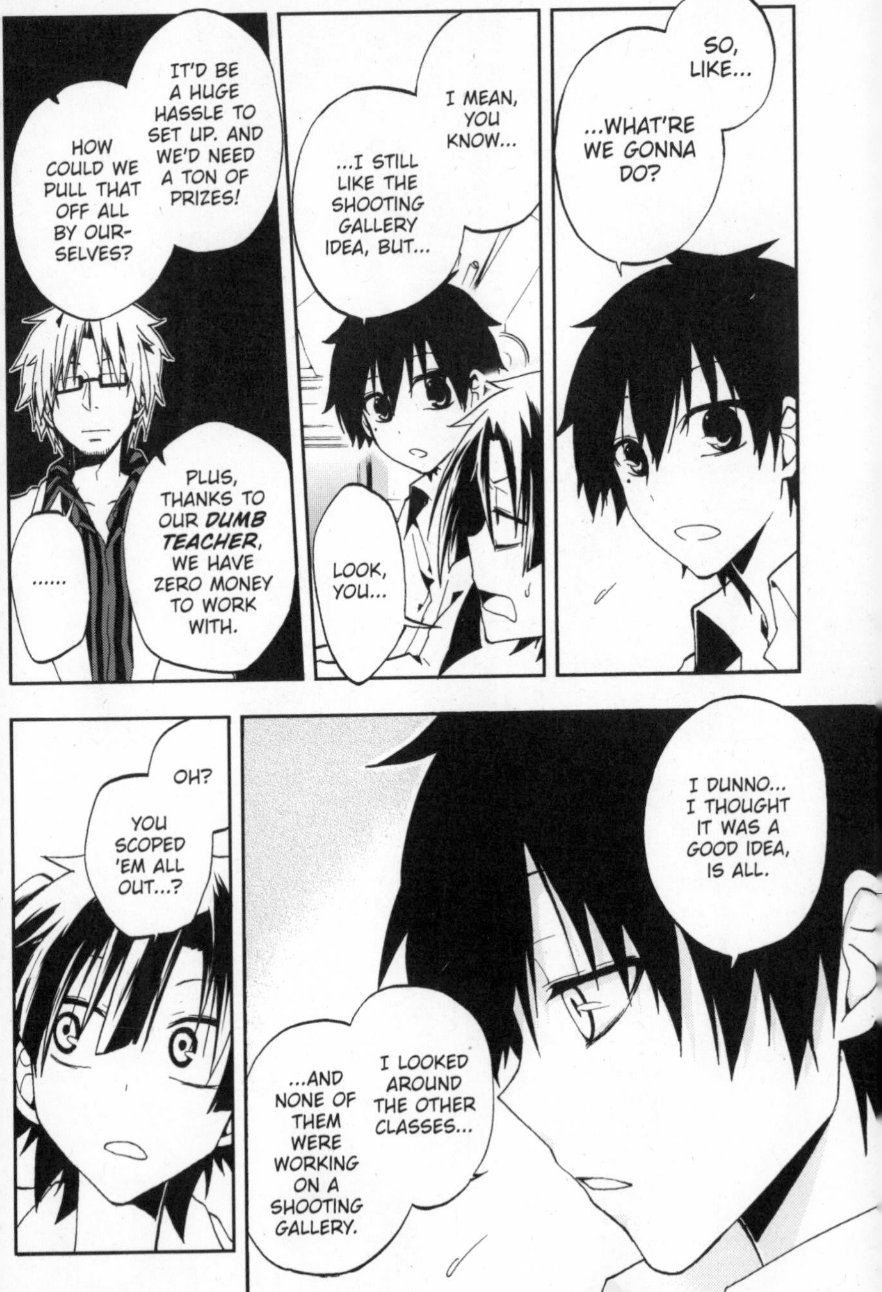
SO, LIKE...
...WHAT'RE WE GONNA DO?
I MEAN, YOU KNOW...
...I STILL LIKE THE SHOOTING GALLERY IDEA, BUT...
LOOK, YOU...
IT'D BE A HUGE HASSLE TO SET UP. AND WE'D NEED A TON OF PRIZES!
HOW COULD WE PULL THAT OFF ALL BY OUR-SELVES?
PLUS, THANKS TO OUR *DUMB TEACHER*, WE HAVE ZERO MONEY TO WORK WITH.
......
I DUNNO... I THOUGHT IT WAS A GOOD IDEA, IS ALL.
I LOOKED AROUND THE OTHER CLASSES...
...AND NONE OF THEM WERE WORKING ON A SHOOTING GALLERY.
OH?
YOU SCOPED 'EM ALL OUT...?

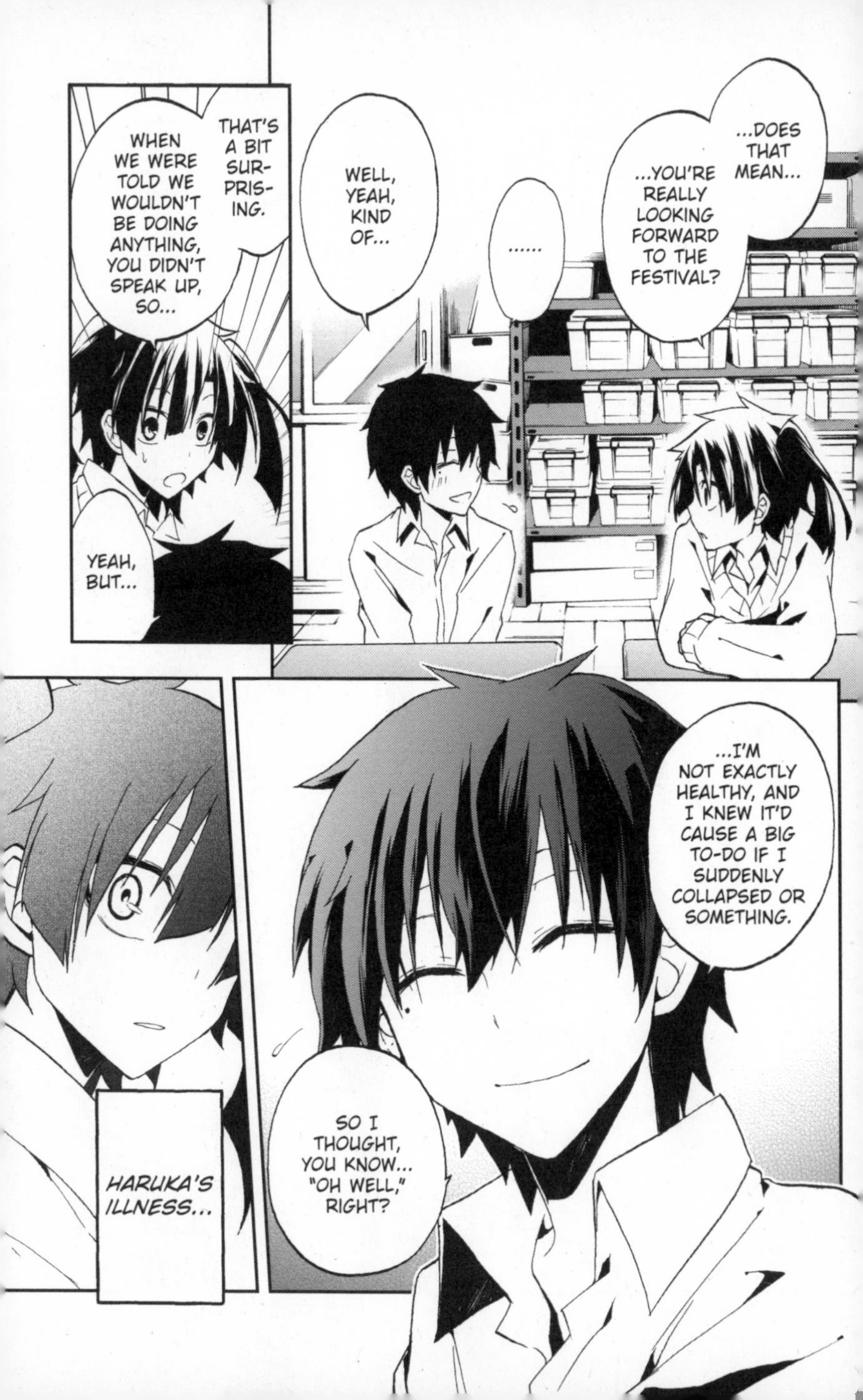
...DOES THAT MEAN...
...YOU'RE REALLY LOOKING FORWARD TO THE FESTIVAL?
......
WELL, YEAH, KIND OF...
THAT'S A BIT SUR-PRIS-ING.
WHEN WE WERE TOLD WE WOULDN'T BE DOING ANYTHING, YOU DIDN'T SPEAK UP, SO...
YEAH, BUT...
...I'M NOT EXACTLY HEALTHY, AND I KNEW IT'D CAUSE A BIG TO-DO IF I SUDDENLY COLLAPSED OR SOMETHING.
SO I THOUGHT, YOU KNOW... "OH WELL," RIGHT?
HARUKA'S ILLNESS...

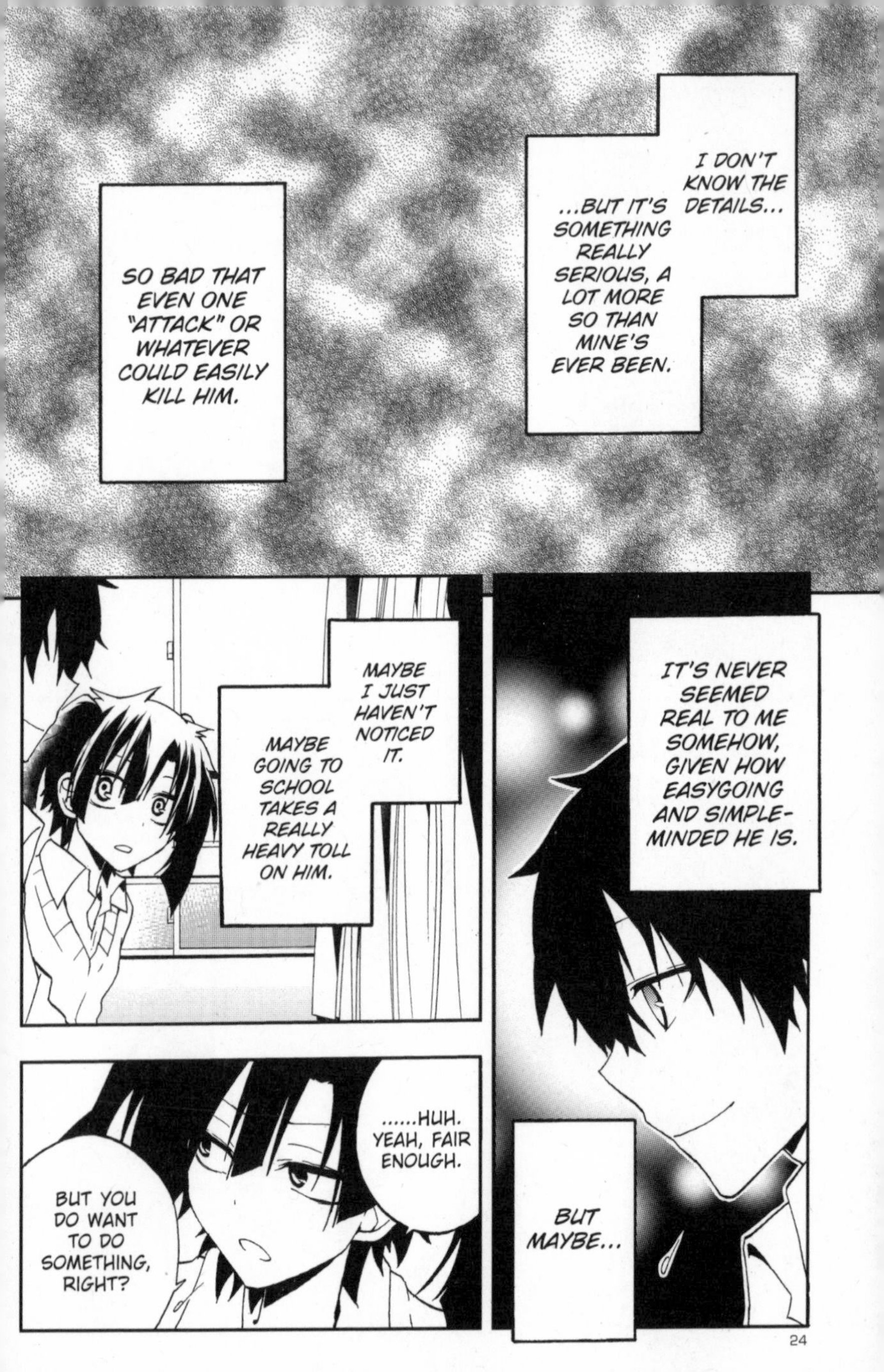
I DON'T KNOW THE DETAILS...
...BUT IT'S SOMETHING REALLY SERIOUS, A LOT MORE SO THAN MINE'S EVER BEEN.
SO BAD THAT EVEN ONE "ATTACK" OR WHATEVER COULD EASILY KILL HIM.
IT'S NEVER SEEMED REAL TO ME SOMEHOW, GIVEN HOW EASYGOING AND SIMPLE-MINDED HE IS.
BUT MAYBE...
MAYBE I JUST HAVEN'T NOTICED IT.
MAYBE GOING TO SCHOOL TAKES A REALLY HEAVY TOLL ON HIM.
......HUH. YEAH, FAIR ENOUGH.
BUT YOU DO WANT TO DO SOMETHING, RIGHT?

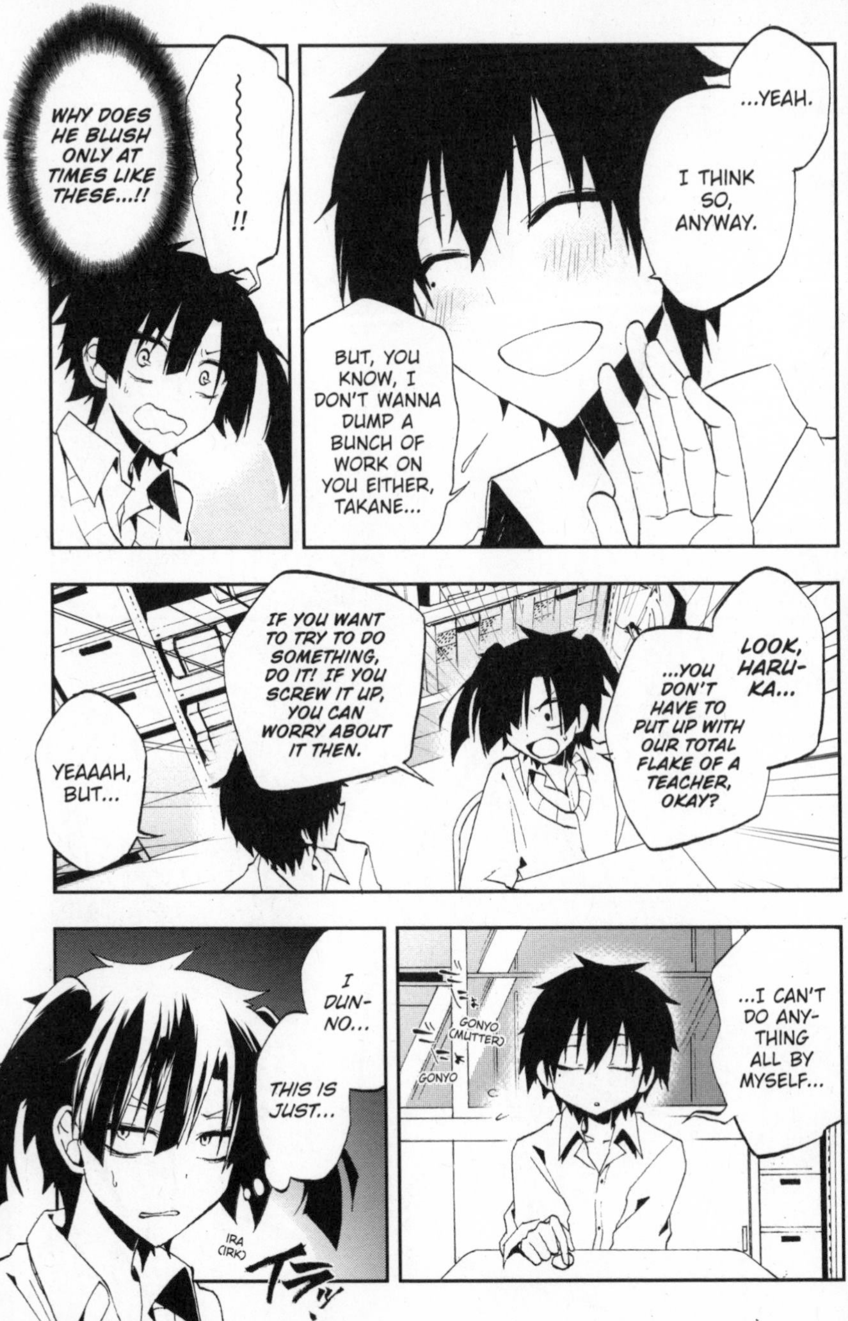
...YEAH.
I THINK SO, ANYWAY.
BUT, YOU KNOW, I DON'T WANNA DUMP A BUNCH OF WORK ON YOU EITHER, TAKANE...
~~~~~~~~!!
WHY DOES HE BLUSH ONLY AT TIMES LIKE THESE...!!
LOOK, HARUKA...
...YOU DON'T HAVE TO PUT UP WITH OUR TOTAL FLAKE OF A TEACHER, OKAY?
IF YOU WANT TO TRY TO DO SOMETHING, DO IT! IF YOU SCREW IT UP, YOU CAN WORRY ABOUT IT THEN.
YEAAAH, BUT...
...I CAN'T DO ANYTHING ALL BY MYSELF...
GONYO (MUTTER)
GONYO
I DUNNO...
THIS IS JUST...
IRA (IRK)
~~~~~~~~

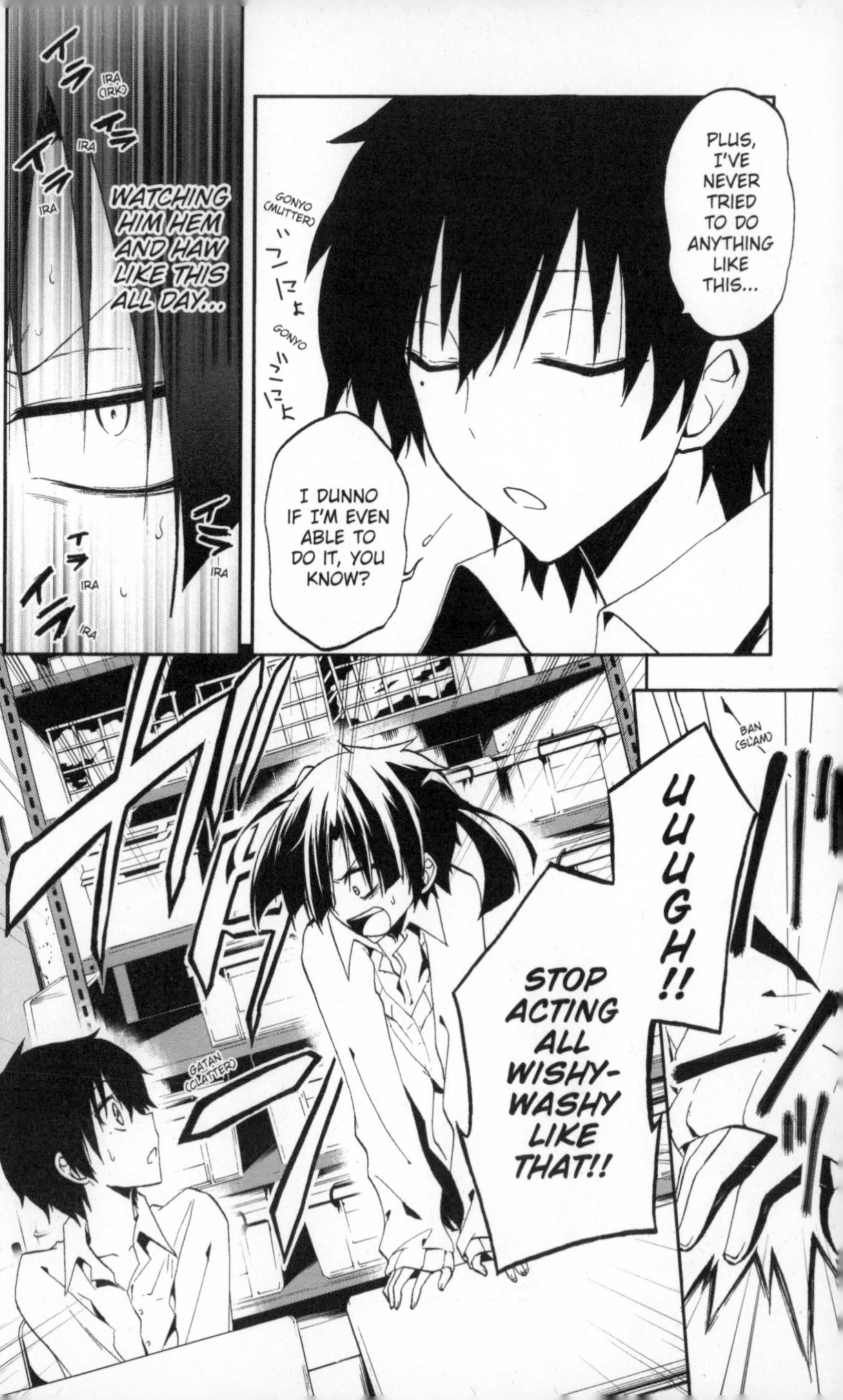
PLUS, I'VE NEVER TRIED TO DO ANYTHING LIKE THIS...
GONYO (MUTTER)
GONYO
I DUNNO IF I'M EVEN ABLE TO DO IT, YOU KNOW?
IRA (IRK)
IRA
IRA
WATCHING HIM HEM AND HAW LIKE THIS ALL DAY...
IRA
IRA
IRA
BAN (SLAM)
UUUGH!!
STOP ACTING ALL WISHY-WASHY LIKE THAT!!
GATAN (CLATTER)

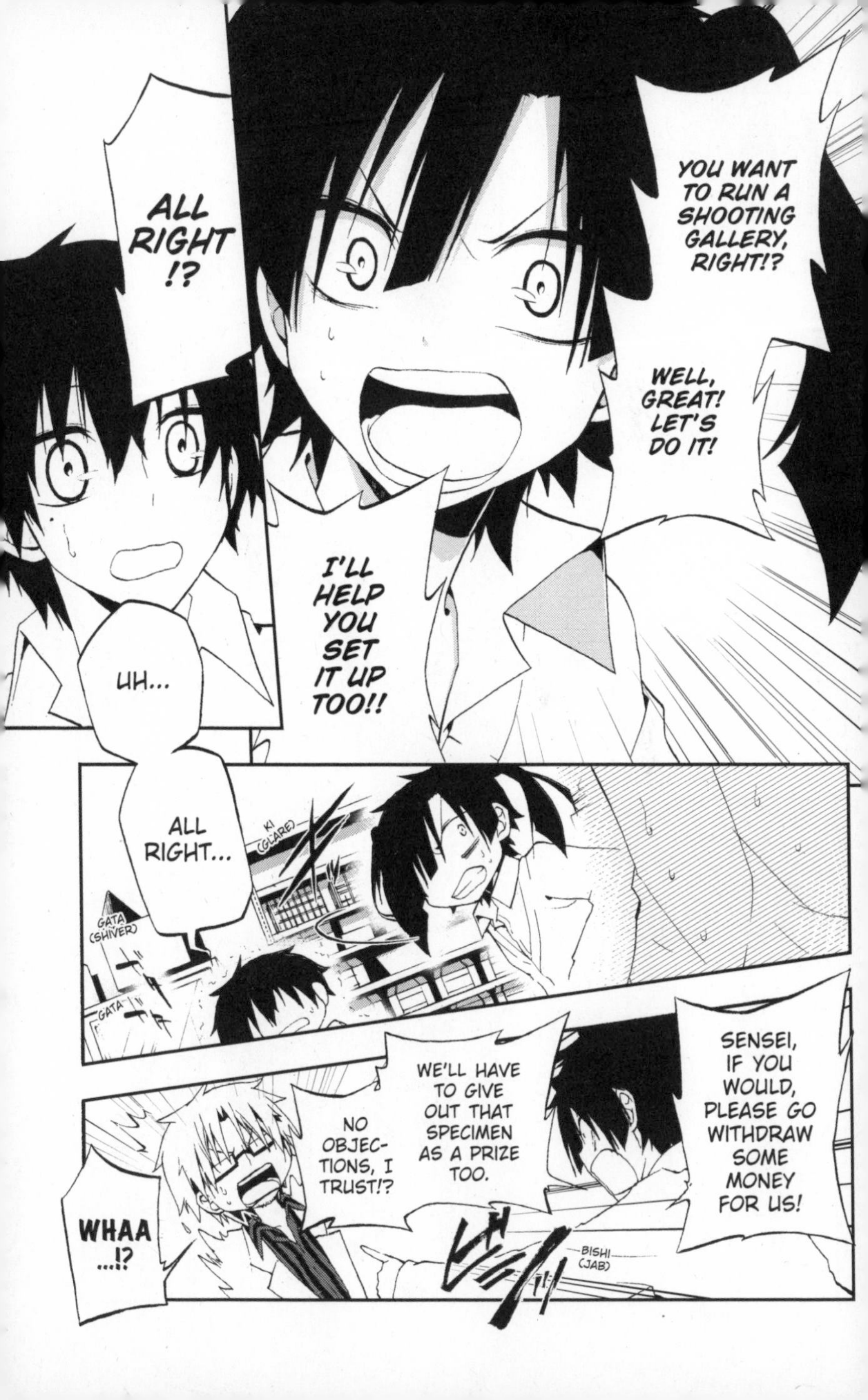
YOU WANT TO RUN A SHOOTING GALLERY, RIGHT!?
WELL, GREAT! LET'S DO IT!
I'LL HELP YOU SET IT UP TOO!!
ALL RIGHT !?
UH...
ALL RIGHT...
KI (GLARE)
GATA (SHIVER)
GATA
SENSEI, IF YOU WOULD, PLEASE GO WITHDRAW SOME MONEY FOR US!
WE'LL HAVE TO GIVE OUT THAT SPECIMEN AS A PRIZE TOO.
NO OBJECTIONS, I TRUST!?
BISHI (JAB)
WHAA ...!?

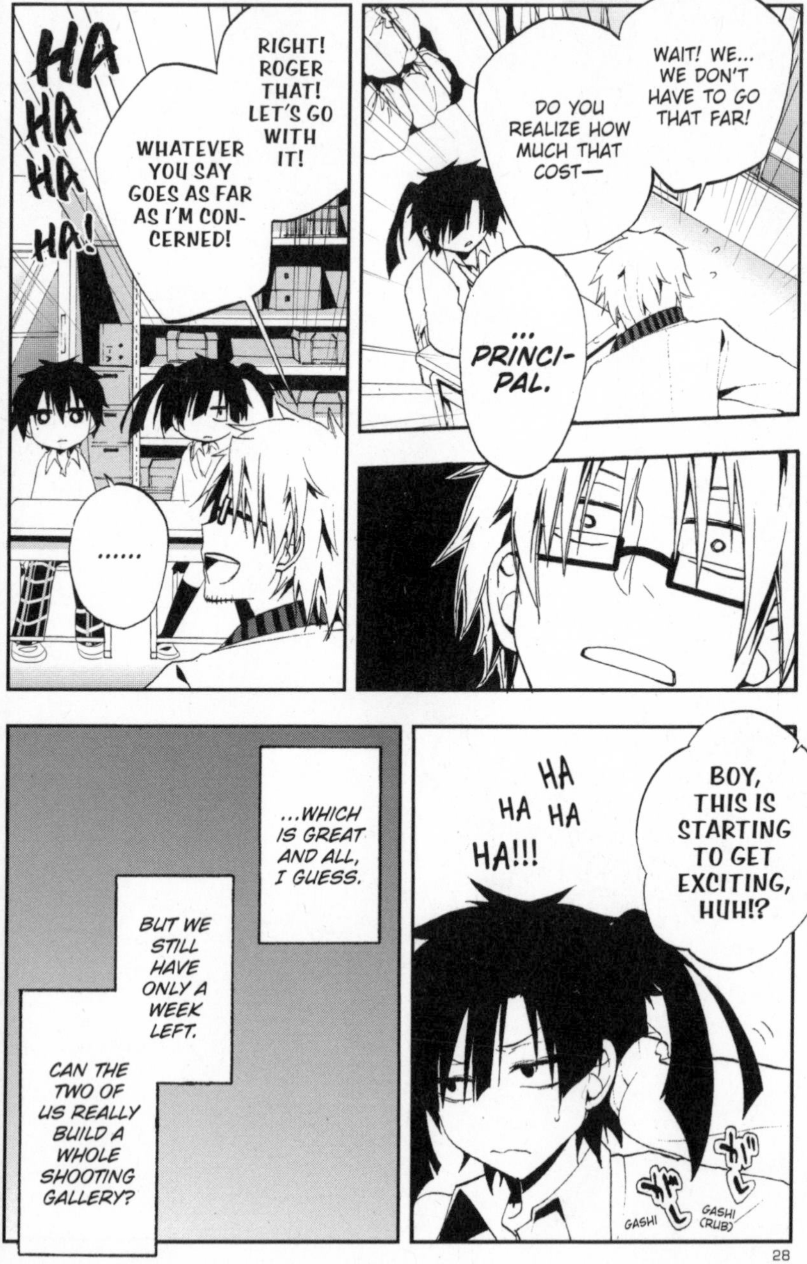
WAIT! WE... WE DON'T HAVE TO GO THAT FAR!
DO YOU REALIZE HOW MUCH THAT COST—
...PRINCIPAL.
RIGHT! ROGER THAT! LET'S GO WITH IT!
WHATEVER YOU SAY GOES AS FAR AS I'M CONCERNED!
HA HA HA HA HA!
......
BOY, THIS IS STARTING TO GET EXCITING, HUH!?
HA HA HA HA!!!
GASHI (RUB)
GASHI
...WHICH IS GREAT AND ALL, I GUESS.
BUT WE STILL HAVE ONLY A WEEK LEFT.
CAN THE TWO OF US REALLY BUILD A WHOLE SHOOTING GALLERY?

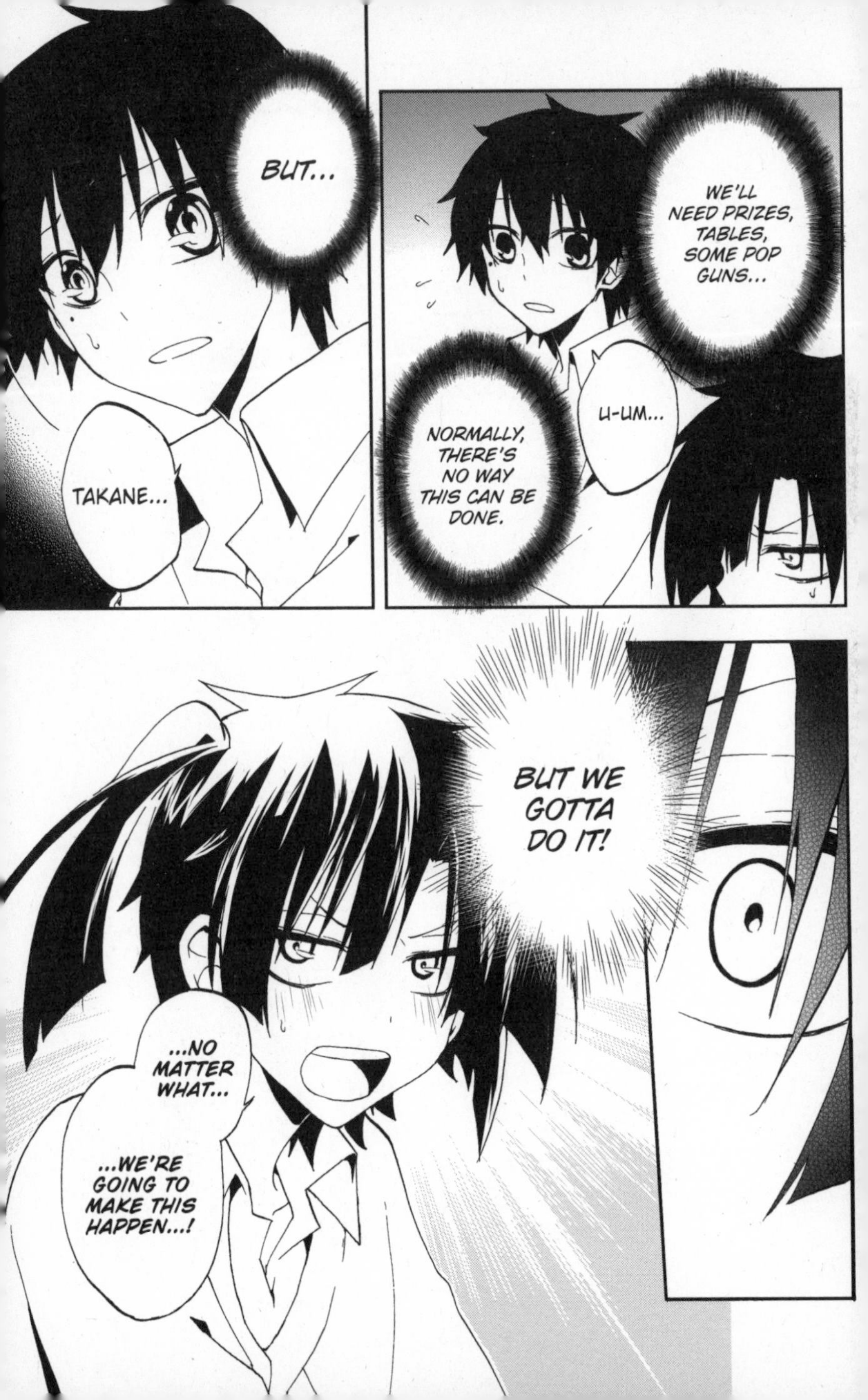
WE'LL NEED PRIZES, TABLES, SOME POP GUNS...
U-UM...
NORMALLY, THERE'S NO WAY THIS CAN BE DONE.
BUT...
TAKANE...
BUT WE GOTTA DO IT!
...NO MATTER WHAT...
...WE'RE GOING TO MAKE THIS HAPPEN...!

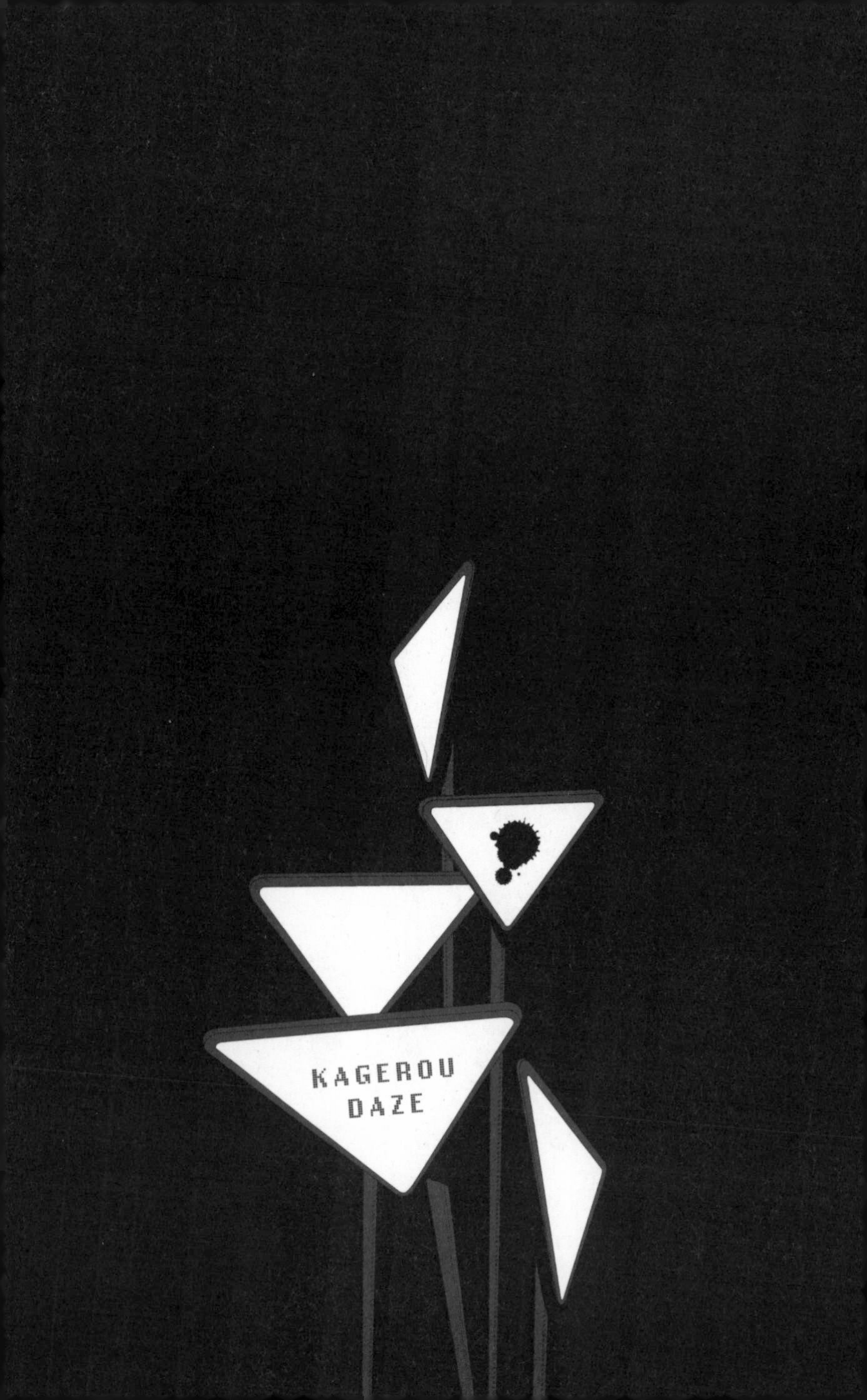
KAGEROU
DAZE

11 >> YUUKEI YESTERDAY II

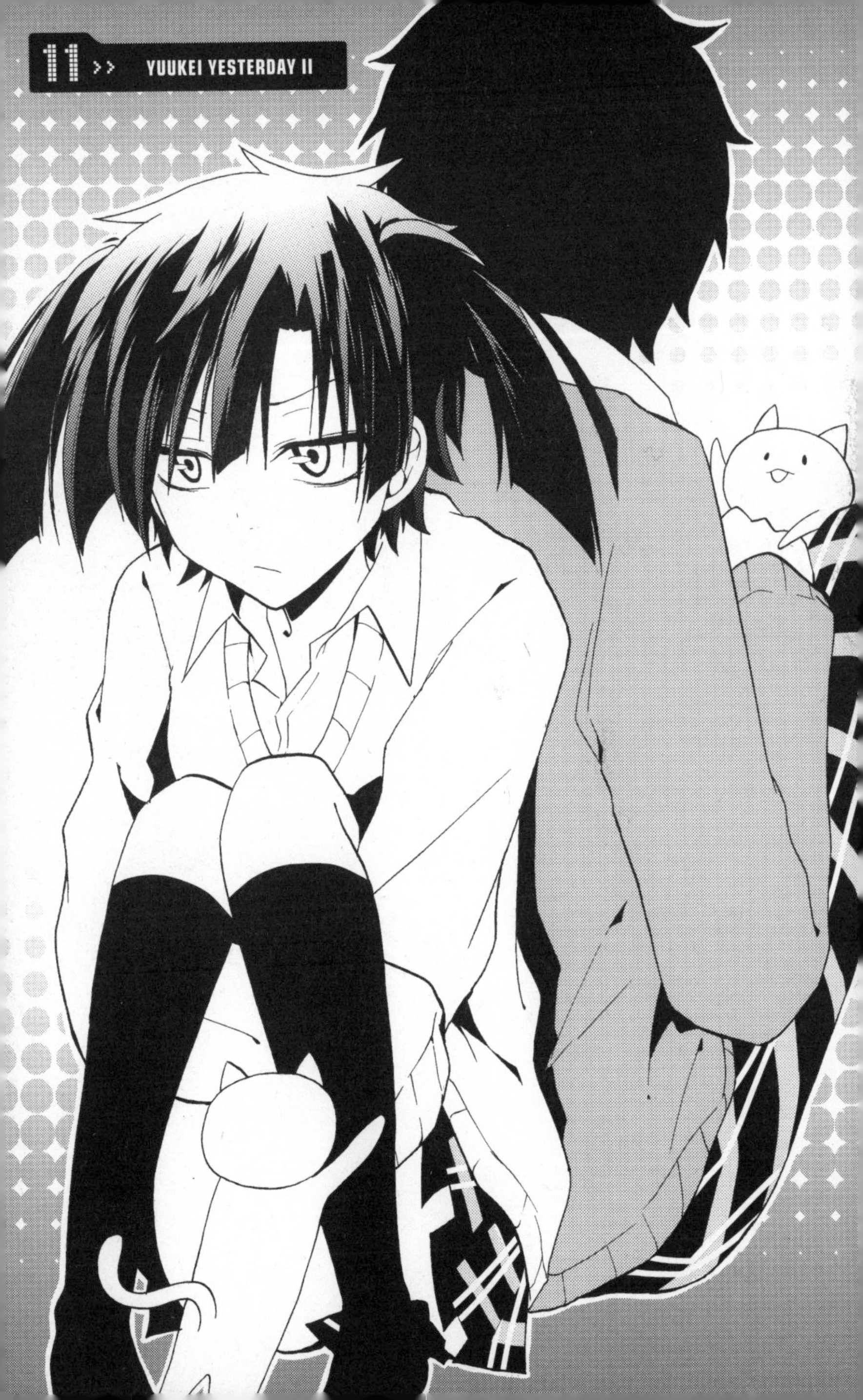

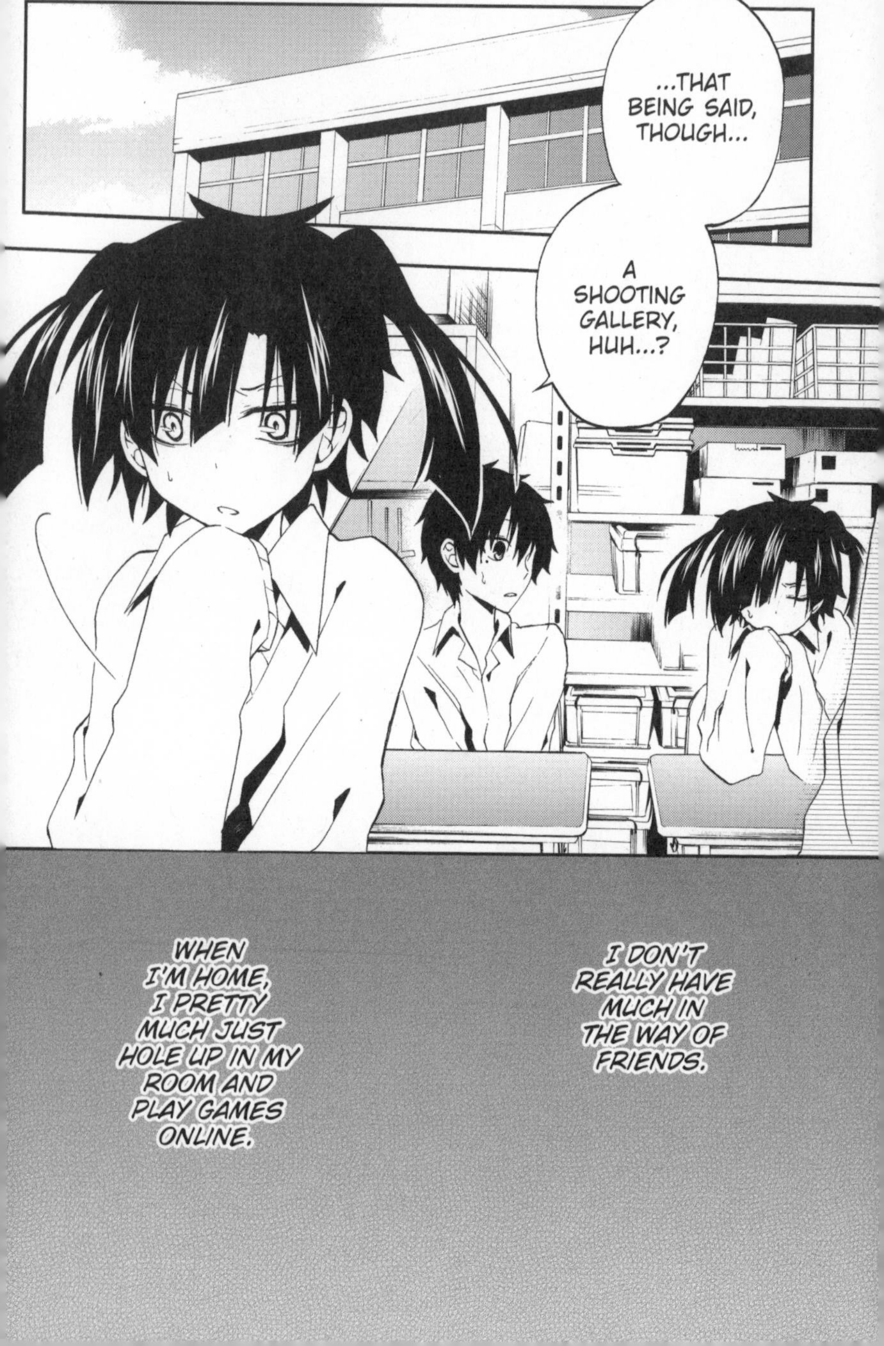
...THAT BEING SAID, THOUGH...
A SHOOTING GALLERY, HUH...?
I DON'T REALLY HAVE MUCH IN THE WAY OF FRIENDS.
WHEN I'M HOME, I PRETTY MUCH JUST HOLE UP IN MY ROOM AND PLAY GAMES ONLINE.

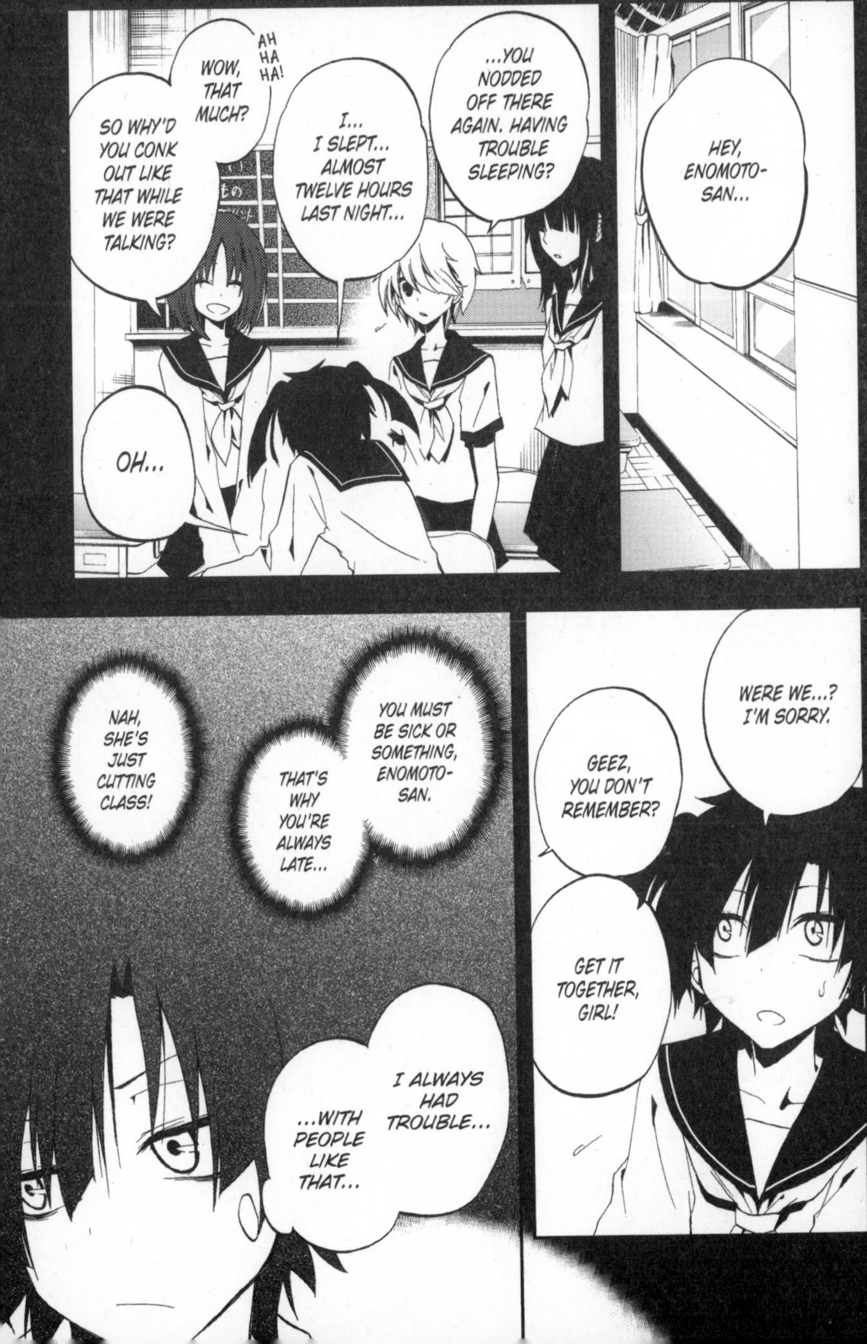
HEY, ENOMOTO-SAN...
...YOU NODDED OFF THERE AGAIN. HAVING TROUBLE SLEEPING?
I... I SLEPT... ALMOST TWELVE HOURS LAST NIGHT...
AH HA HA!
WOW, THAT MUCH?
SO WHY'D YOU CONK OUT LIKE THAT WHILE WE WERE TALKING?
OH...
WERE WE...? I'M SORRY.
GEEZ, YOU DON'T REMEMBER?
GET IT TOGETHER, GIRL!
YOU MUST BE SICK OR SOMETHING, ENOMOTO-SAN.
THAT'S WHY YOU'RE ALWAYS LATE...
NAH, SHE'S JUST CUTTING CLASS!
I ALWAYS HAD TROUBLE...
...WITH PEOPLE LIKE THAT...

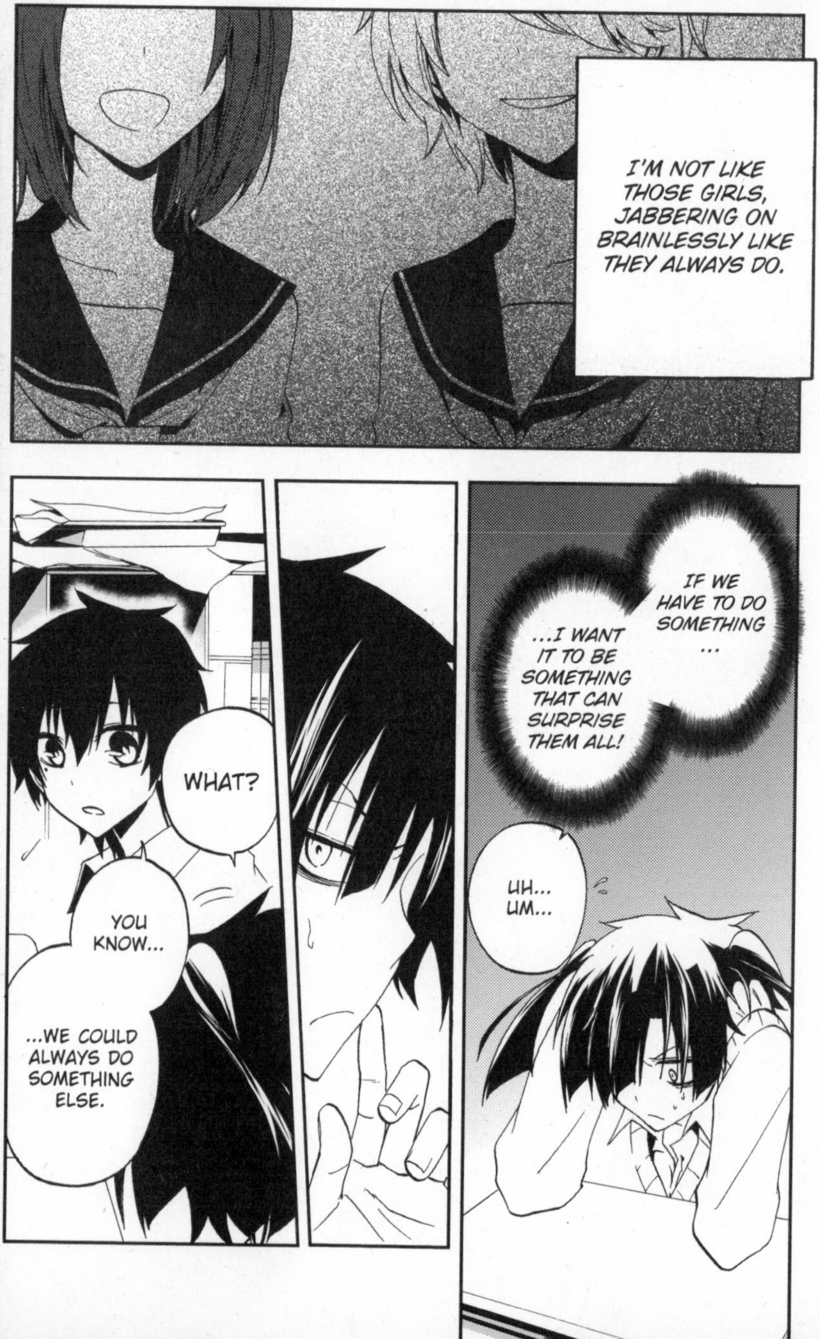
I'M NOT LIKE THOSE GIRLS, JABBERING ON BRAINLESSLY LIKE THEY ALWAYS DO.
IF WE HAVE TO DO SOMETHING ...
...I WANT IT TO BE SOMETHING THAT CAN SURPRISE THEM ALL!
UH... UM...
WHAT?
YOU KNOW...
...WE COULD ALWAYS DO SOMETHING ELSE.

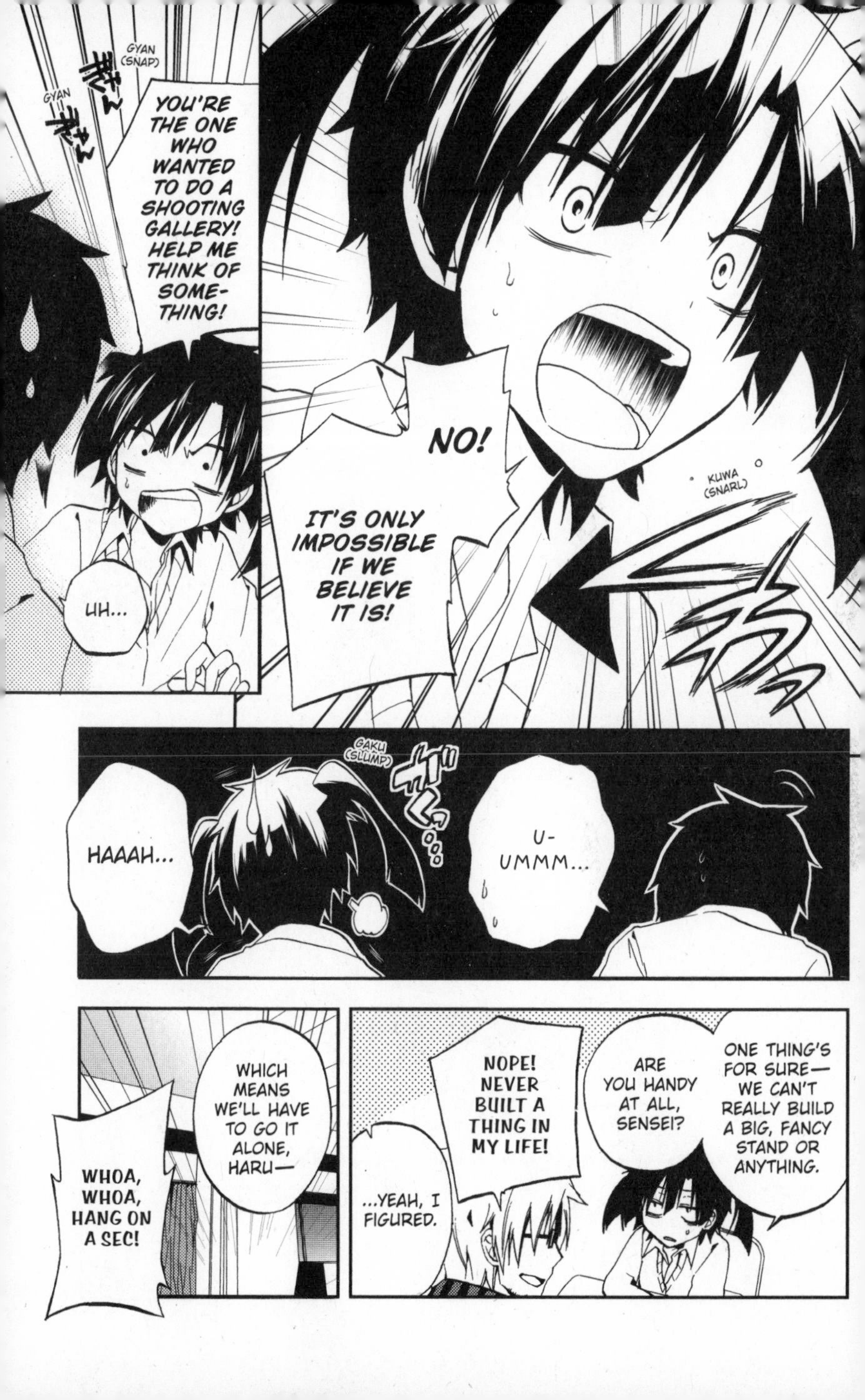
NO!
IT'S ONLY IMPOSSIBLE IF WE BELIEVE IT IS!
KUWA (SNARL)
GYAN (SNAP)
GYAN
YOU'RE THE ONE WHO WANTED TO DO A SHOOTING GALLERY! HELP ME THINK OF SOME-THING!
UH...
U-UMMM...
GAKU (SLUMP)
HAAAH...
ONE THING'S FOR SURE— WE CAN'T REALLY BUILD A BIG, FANCY STAND OR ANYTHING.
ARE YOU HANDY AT ALL, SENSEI?
NOPE! NEVER BUILT A THING IN MY LIFE!
...YEAH, I FIGURED.
WHICH MEANS WE'LL HAVE TO GO IT ALONE, HARU—
WHOA, WHOA, HANG ON A SEC!

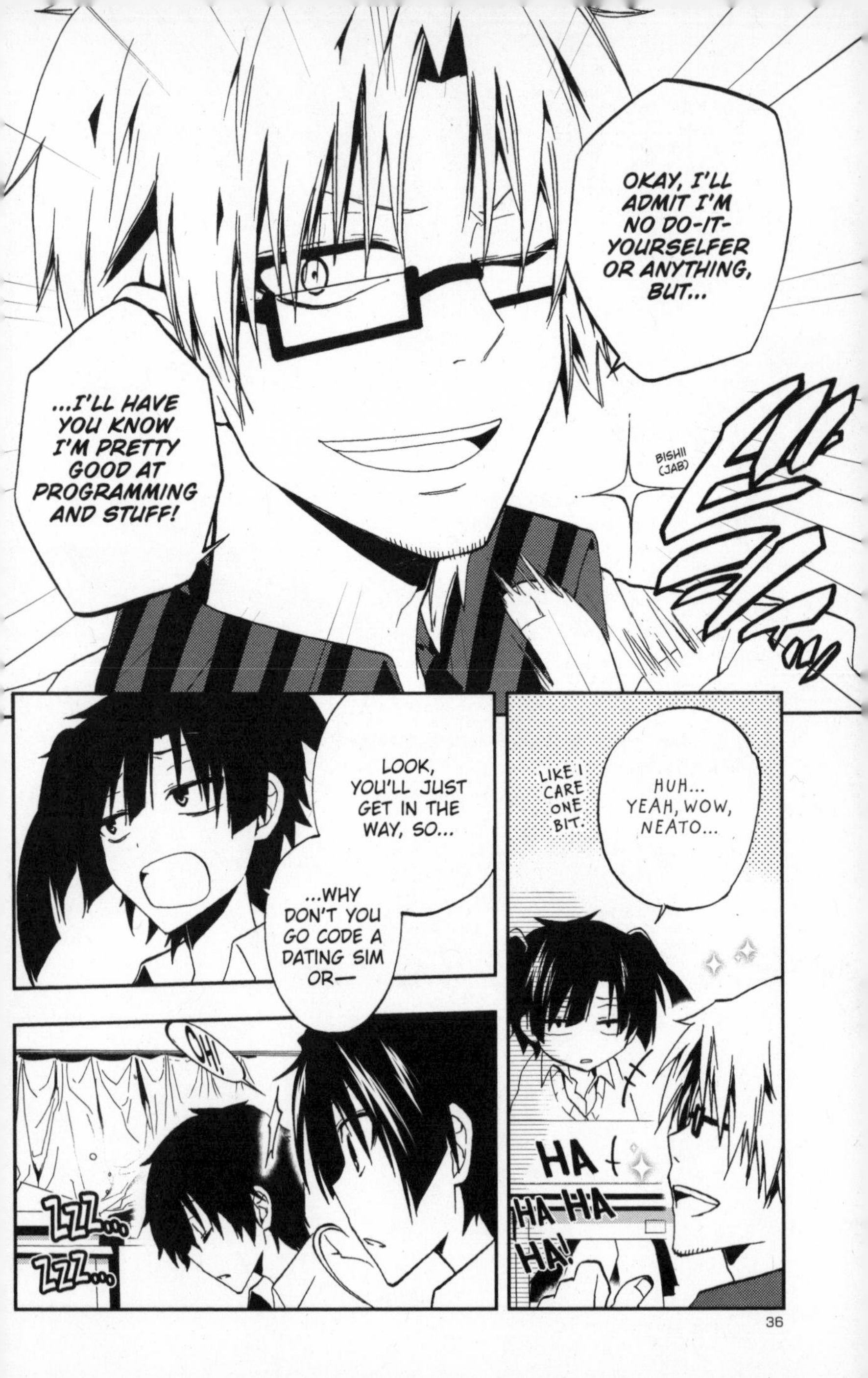
OKAY, I'LL ADMIT I'M NO DO-IT-YOURSELFER OR ANYTHING, BUT...
...I'LL HAVE YOU KNOW I'M PRETTY GOOD AT PROGRAMMING AND STUFF!
BISHII (JAB)
HUH... YEAH, WOW, NEATO...
LIKE I CARE ONE BIT.
HA HA HA HA!
LOOK, YOU'LL JUST GET IN THE WAY, SO...
...WHY DON'T YOU GO CODE A DATING SIM OR—
OH!
ZZZ...
ZZZ...

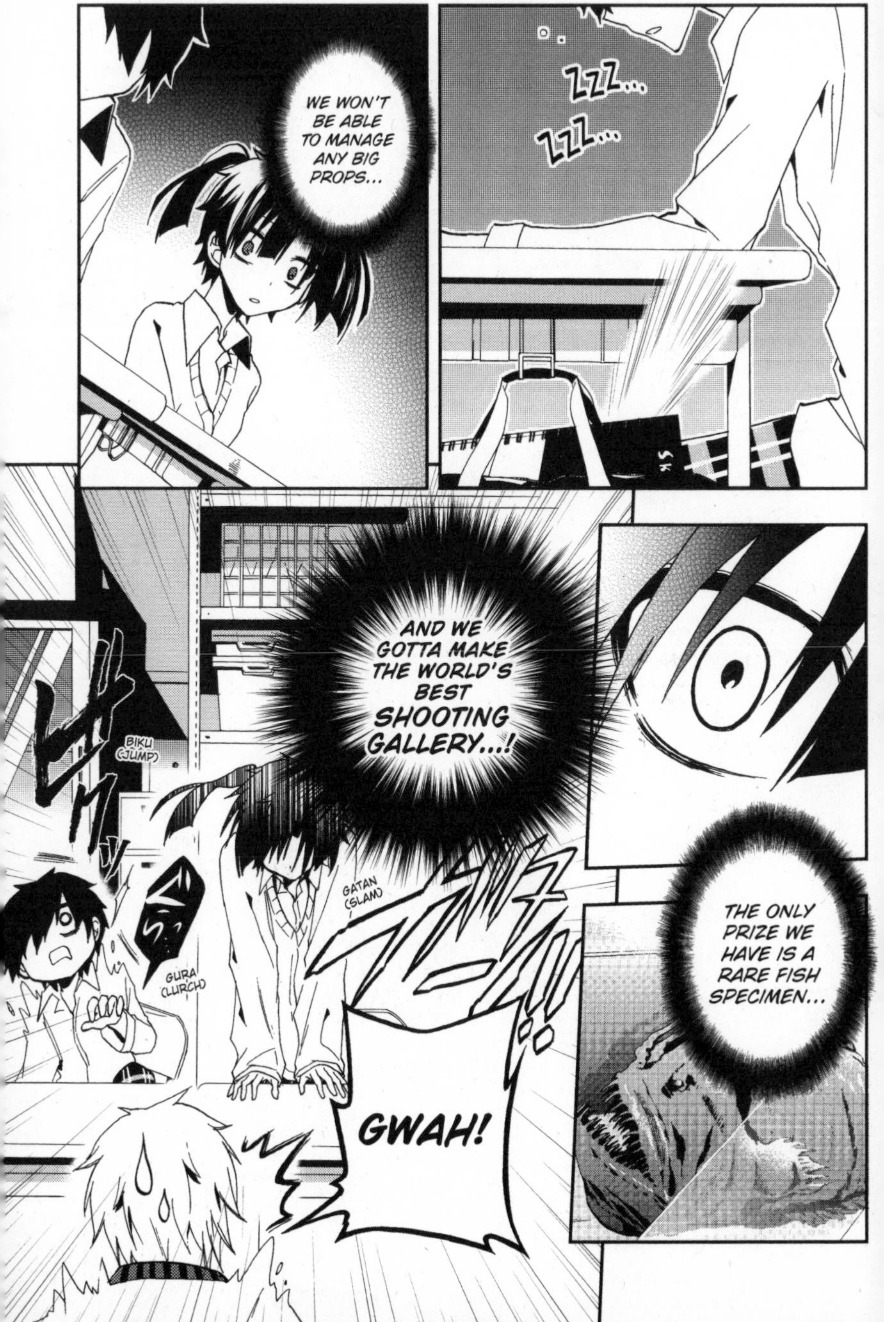
ZZZ...
ZZZ...
WE WON'T BE ABLE TO MANAGE ANY BIG PROPS...
THE ONLY PRIZE WE HAVE IS A RARE FISH SPECIMEN...
AND WE GOTTA MAKE THE WORLD'S BEST SHOOTING GALLERY...!
BIKU (JUMP)
GATAN (SLAM)
GURA (LURCH)
GWAH!

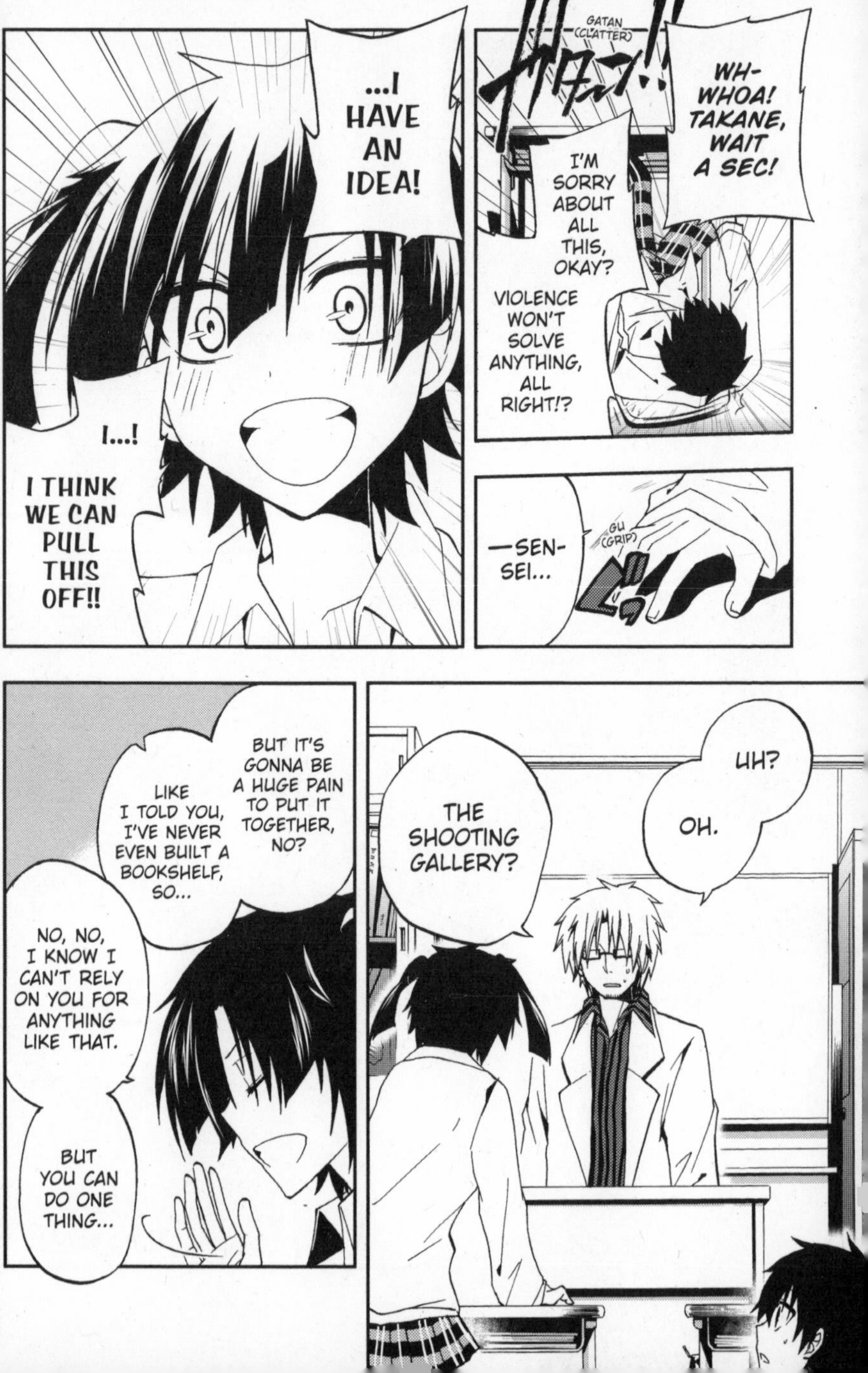
GATAN (CLATTER)
WH-WHOA! TAKANE, WAIT A SEC!
I'M SORRY ABOUT ALL THIS, OKAY?
VIOLENCE WON'T SOLVE ANYTHING, ALL RIGHT!?
GU (GRIP)
—SEN-SEI...
...I HAVE AN IDEA!
I...!
I THINK WE CAN PULL THIS OFF!!
UH?
OH.
THE SHOOTING GALLERY?
BUT IT'S GONNA BE A HUGE PAIN TO PUT IT TOGETHER, NO?
LIKE I TOLD YOU, I'VE NEVER EVEN BUILT A BOOKSHELF, SO...
NO, NO, I KNOW I CAN'T RELY ON YOU FOR ANYTHING LIKE THAT.
BUT YOU CAN DO ONE THING...

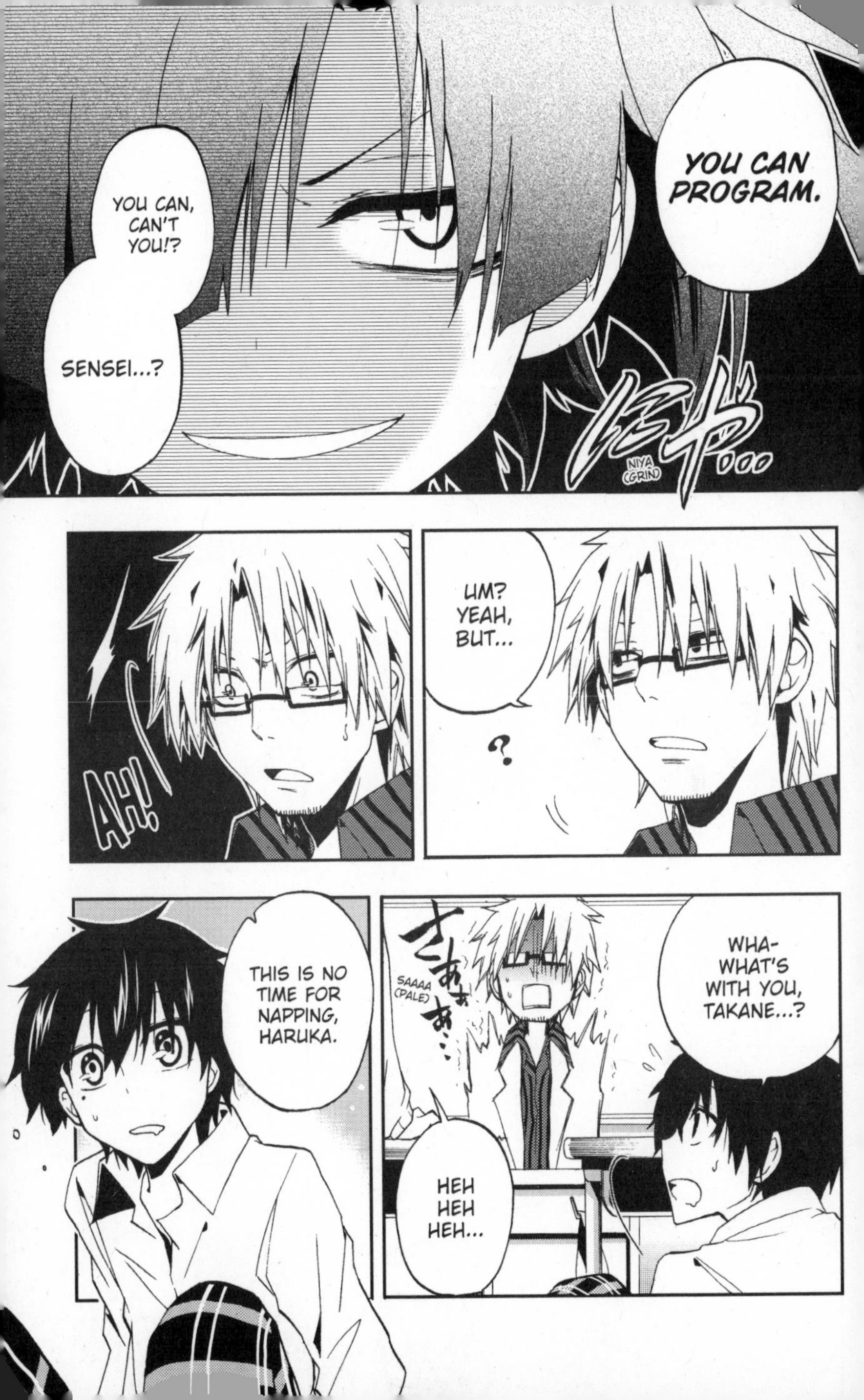
YOU CAN PROGRAM.
YOU CAN, CAN'T YOU!?
SENSEI...?
NIYA (GRIN)
UM? YEAH, BUT...
?
AH!
WHA- WHAT'S WITH YOU, TAKANE...?
SAAAA (PALE)
HEH HEH HEH...
THIS IS NO TIME FOR NAPPING, HARUKA.

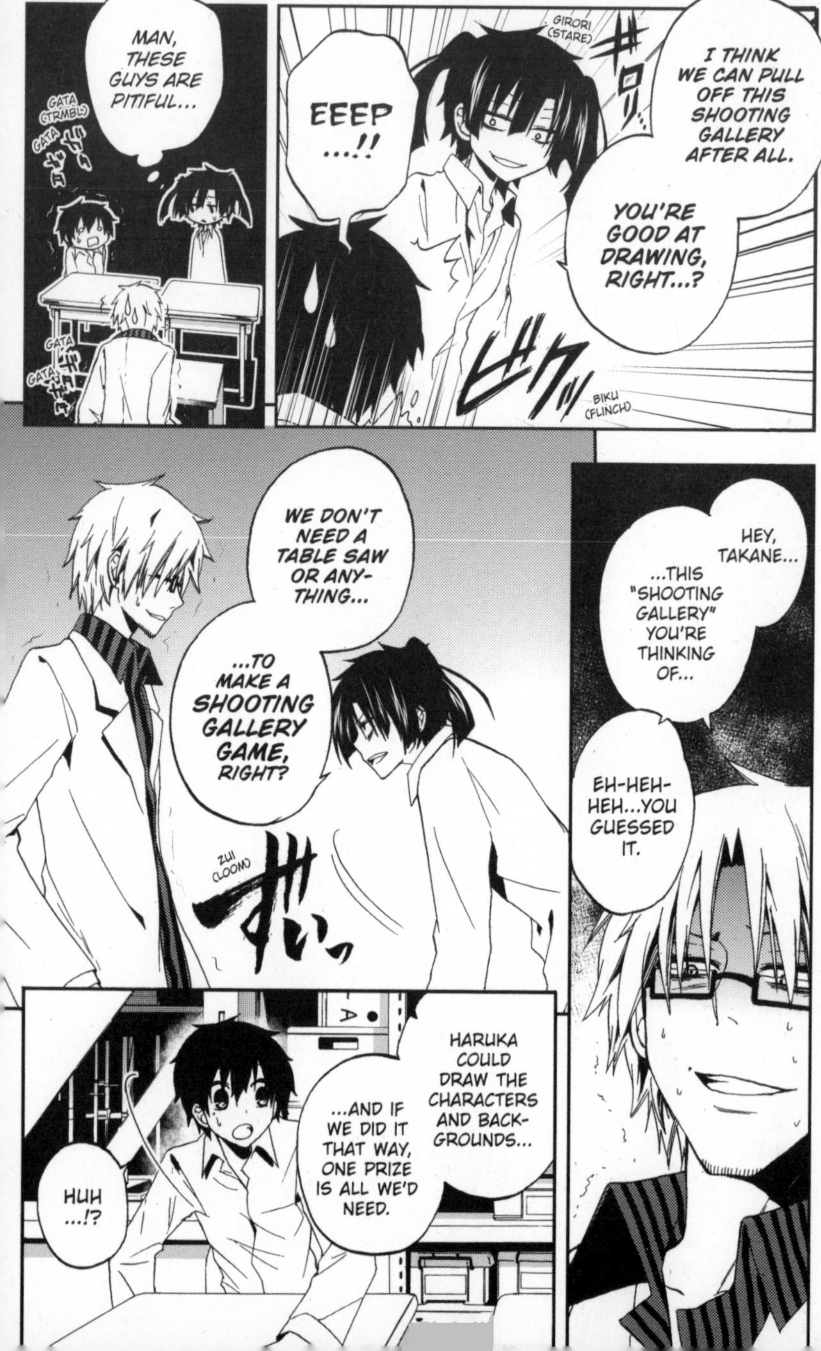
GIRORI (STARE)
I THINK WE CAN PULL OFF THIS SHOOTING GALLERY AFTER ALL.
YOU'RE GOOD AT DRAWING, RIGHT...?
EEEP ...!!
BIKU (FLINCH)
MAN, THESE GUYS ARE PITIFUL...
GATA (TRMBL) GATA
GATA GATA
HEY, TAKANE...
...THIS "SHOOTING GALLERY" YOU'RE THINKING OF...
EH-HEH-HEH...YOU GUESSED IT.
WE DON'T NEED A TABLE SAW OR ANY-THING...
...TO MAKE A SHOOTING GALLERY GAME, RIGHT?
ZUI (LOOM)
HARUKA COULD DRAW THE CHARACTERS AND BACK-GROUNDS...
...AND IF WE DID IT THAT WAY, ONE PRIZE IS ALL WE'D NEED.
HUH ...!?

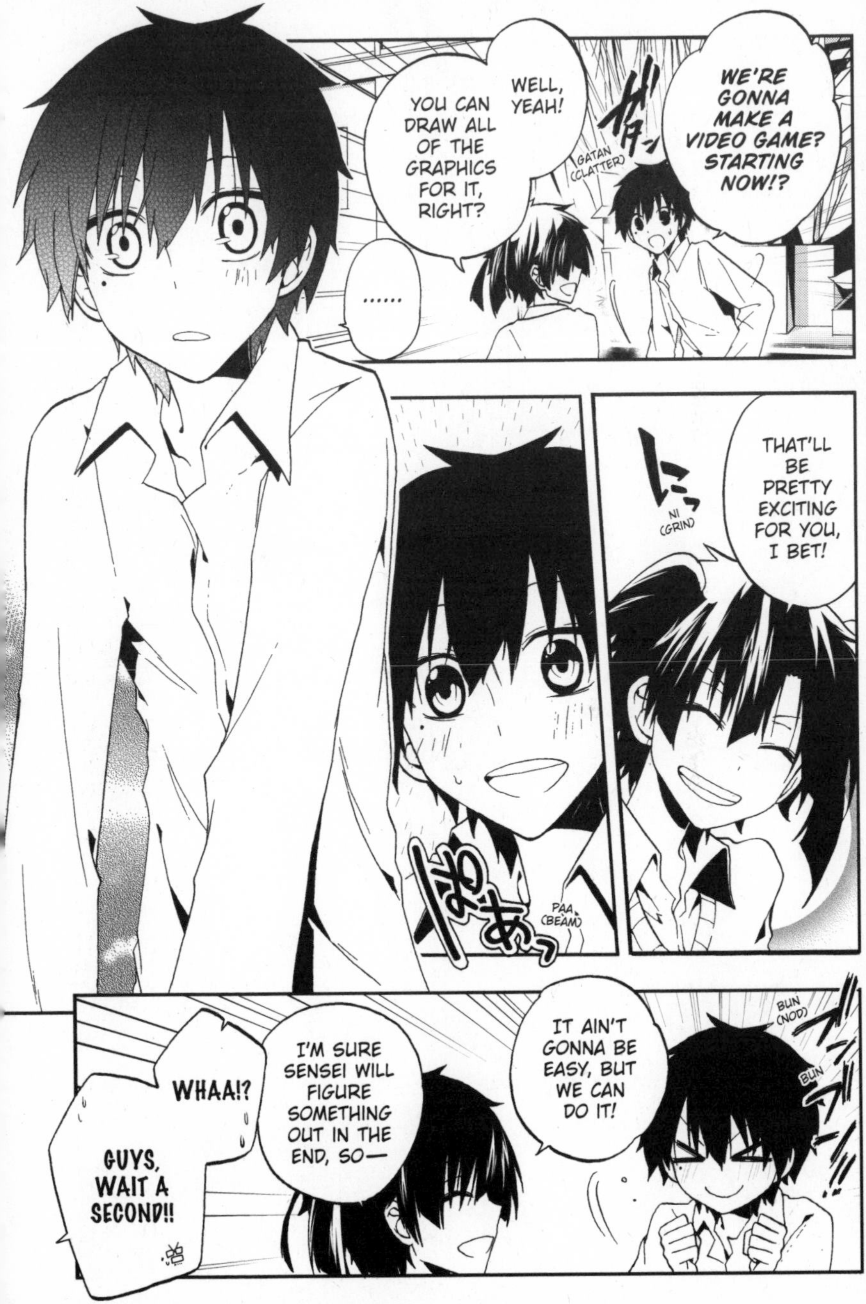
WE'RE GONNA MAKE A VIDEO GAME? STARTING NOW!?
GATAN (CLATTER)
WELL, YEAH!
YOU CAN DRAW ALL OF THE GRAPHICS FOR IT, RIGHT?
......
THAT'LL BE PRETTY EXCITING FOR YOU, I BET!
NI (GRIN)
PAA (BEAM)
BUN (NOD)
BUN
IT AIN'T GONNA BE EASY, BUT WE CAN DO IT!
I'M SURE SENSEI WILL FIGURE SOMETHING OUT IN THE END, SO—
WHAA!?
GUYS, WAIT A SECOND!!

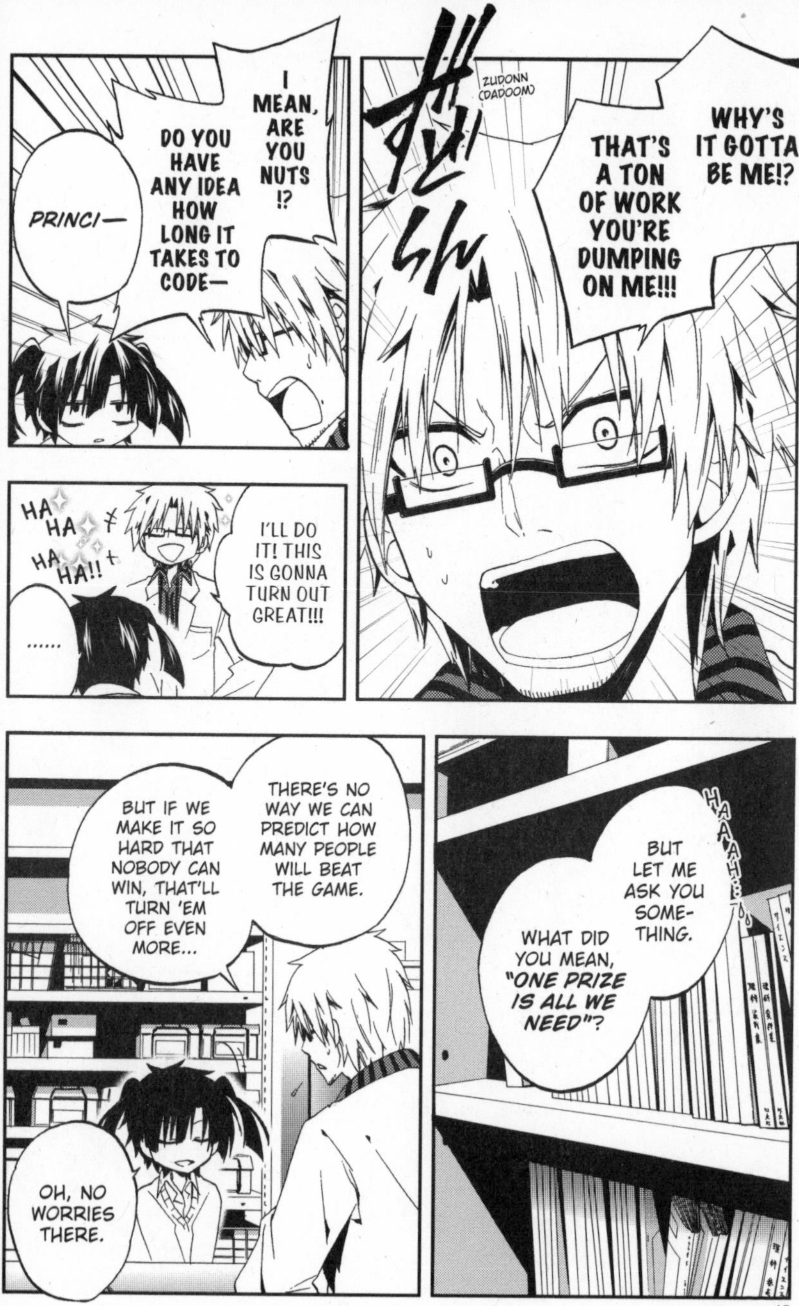
WHY'S IT GOTTA BE ME!?
THAT'S A TON OF WORK YOU'RE DUMPING ON ME!!!
ZUDONN (DADOOM)
I MEAN, ARE YOU NUTS !?
DO YOU HAVE ANY IDEA HOW LONG IT TAKES TO CODE—
PRINCI—
I'LL DO IT! THIS IS GONNA TURN OUT GREAT!!!
HA HA HA HA!!
......
HAAAAH...
BUT LET ME ASK YOU SOME-THING.
WHAT DID YOU MEAN, "ONE PRIZE IS ALL WE NEED"?
THERE'S NO WAY WE CAN PREDICT HOW MANY PEOPLE WILL BEAT THE GAME.
BUT IF WE MAKE IT SO HARD THAT NOBODY CAN WIN, THAT'LL TURN 'EM OFF EVEN MORE...
OH, NO WORRIES THERE.

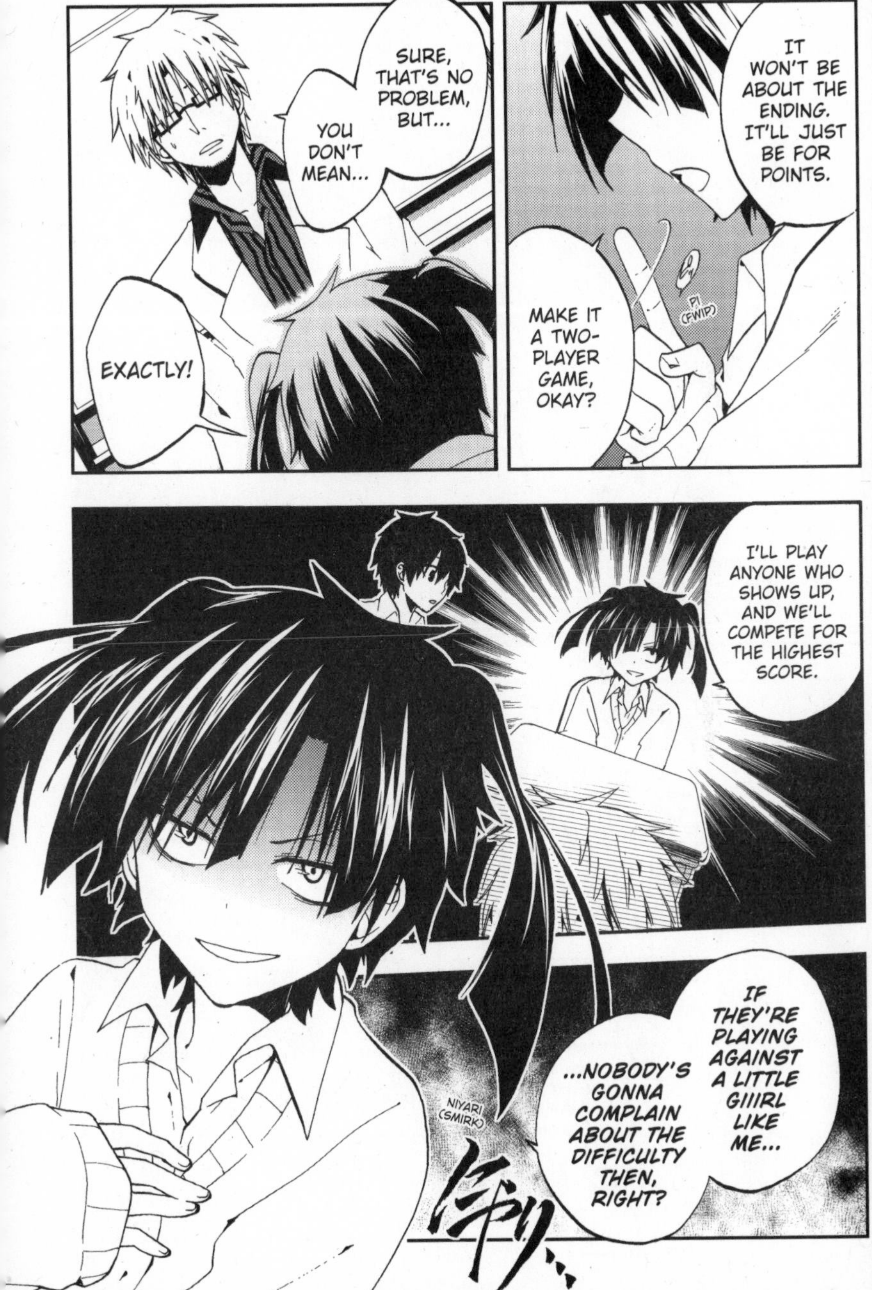
IT WON'T BE ABOUT THE ENDING. IT'LL JUST BE FOR POINTS.
PI (FWIP)
MAKE IT A TWO-PLAYER GAME, OKAY?
SURE, THAT'S NO PROBLEM, BUT...
YOU DON'T MEAN...
EXACTLY!
I'LL PLAY ANYONE WHO SHOWS UP, AND WE'LL COMPETE FOR THE HIGHEST SCORE.
IF THEY'RE PLAYING AGAINST A LITTLE GIIIRL LIKE ME...
...NOBODY'S GONNA COMPLAIN ABOUT THE DIFFICULTY THEN, RIGHT?
NIYARI (SMIRK)

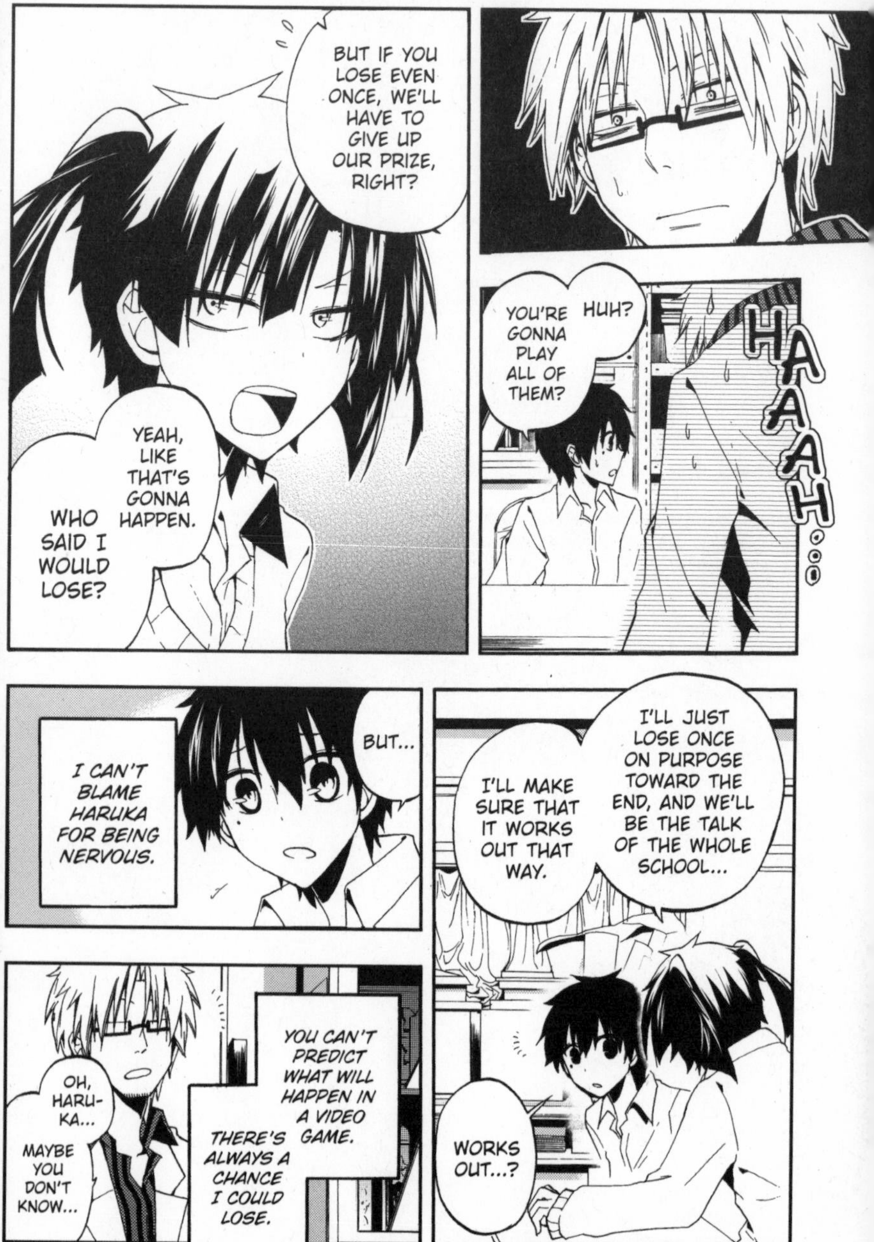
HAAAH...
HUH?
YOU'RE GONNA PLAY ALL OF THEM?
BUT IF YOU LOSE EVEN ONCE, WE'LL HAVE TO GIVE UP OUR PRIZE, RIGHT?
YEAH, LIKE THAT'S GONNA HAPPEN.
WHO SAID I WOULD LOSE?
I'LL JUST LOSE ONCE ON PURPOSE TOWARD THE END, AND WE'LL BE THE TALK OF THE WHOLE SCHOOL...
I'LL MAKE SURE THAT IT WORKS OUT THAT WAY.
WORKS OUT...?
BUT...
I CAN'T BLAME HARUKA FOR BEING NERVOUS.
YOU CAN'T PREDICT WHAT WILL HAPPEN IN A VIDEO GAME.
THERE'S ALWAYS A CHANCE I COULD LOSE.
OH, HARUKA...
MAYBE YOU DON'T KNOW...

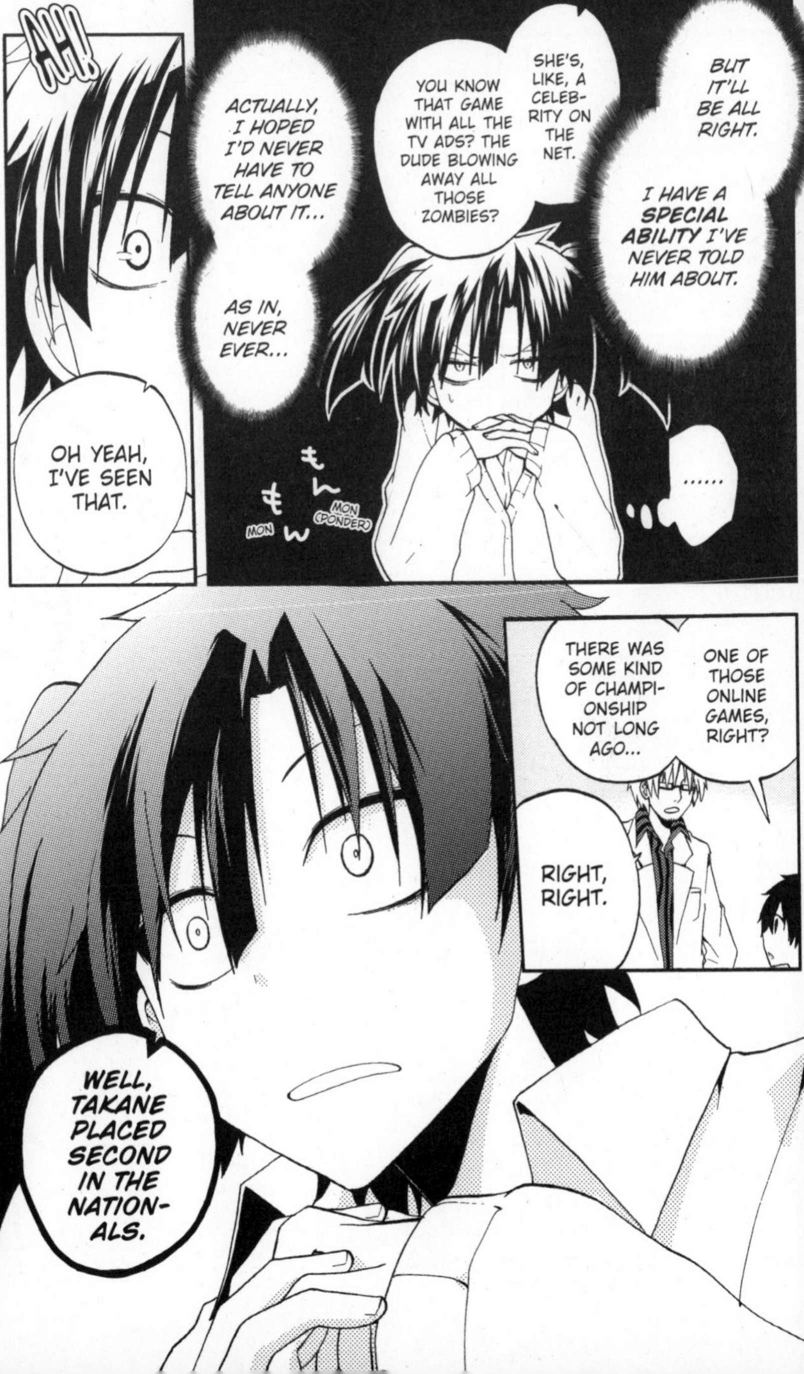
BUT IT'LL BE ALL RIGHT.
I HAVE A SPECIAL ABILITY I'VE NEVER TOLD HIM ABOUT.
SHE'S, LIKE, A CELEBRITY ON THE NET.
YOU KNOW THAT GAME WITH ALL THE TV ADS? THE DUDE BLOWING AWAY ALL THOSE ZOMBIES?
ACTUALLY, I HOPED I'D NEVER HAVE TO TELL ANYONE ABOUT IT...
AS IN, NEVER EVER...
......
もん MON (PONDER)
もん MON
AH!
OH YEAH, I'VE SEEN THAT.
ONE OF THOSE ONLINE GAMES, RIGHT?
THERE WAS SOME KIND OF CHAMPIONSHIP NOT LONG AGO...
RIGHT, RIGHT.
WELL, TAKANE PLACED SECOND IN THE NATIONALS.

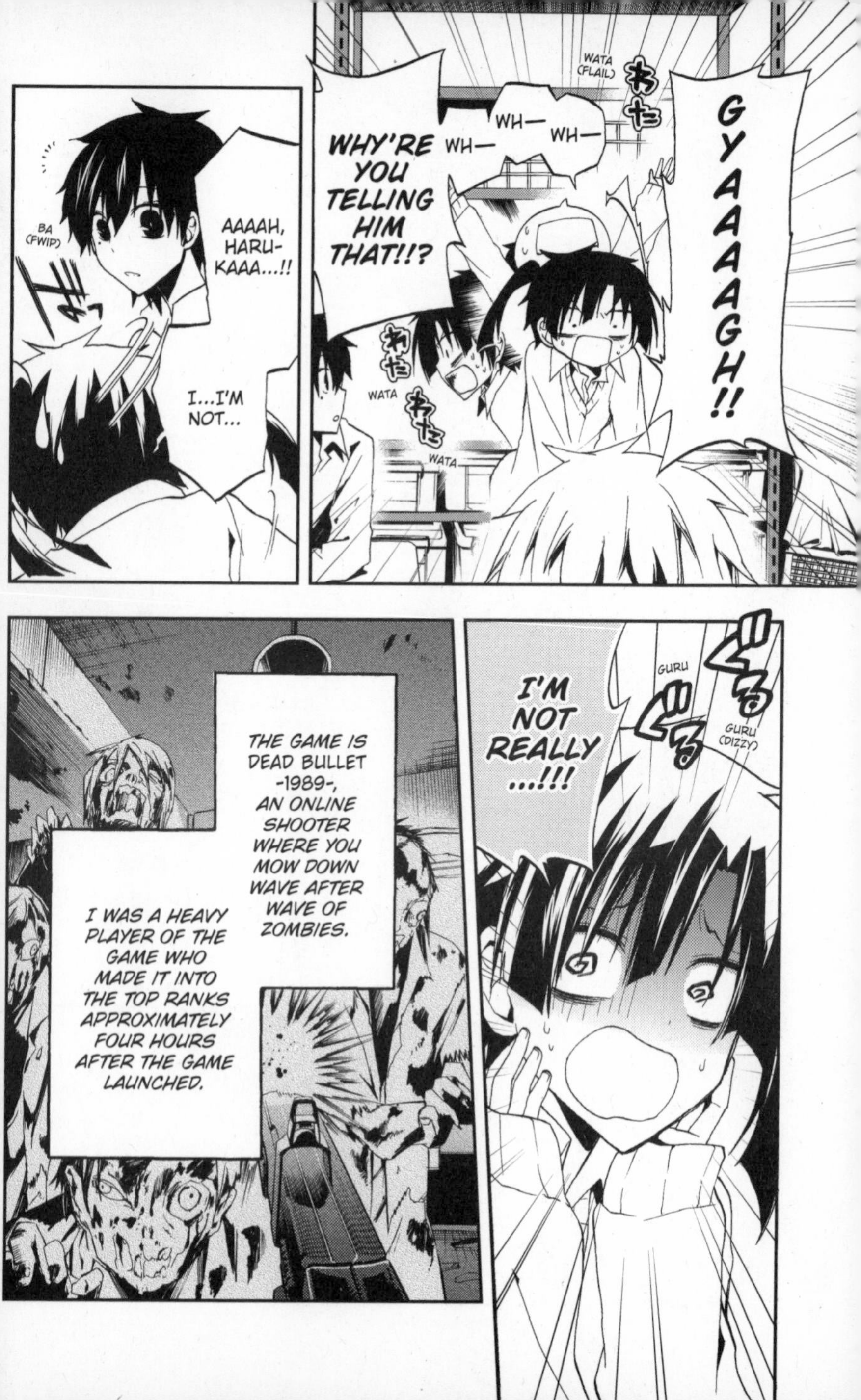
GYAAAAAGH!!
WATA (FLAIL)
WH— WH— WH—
WHY'RE YOU TELLING HIM THAT!!?
WATA
WATA
AAAAH, HARU-KAAA...!!
BA (FWIP)
I...I'M NOT...
GURU
GURU (DIZZY)
I'M NOT REALLY ...!!!
THE GAME IS DEAD BULLET -1989-, AN ONLINE SHOOTER WHERE YOU MOW DOWN WAVE AFTER WAVE OF ZOMBIES.
I WAS A HEAVY PLAYER OF THE GAME WHO MADE IT INTO THE TOP RANKS APPROXIMATELY FOUR HOURS AFTER THE GAME LAUNCHED.

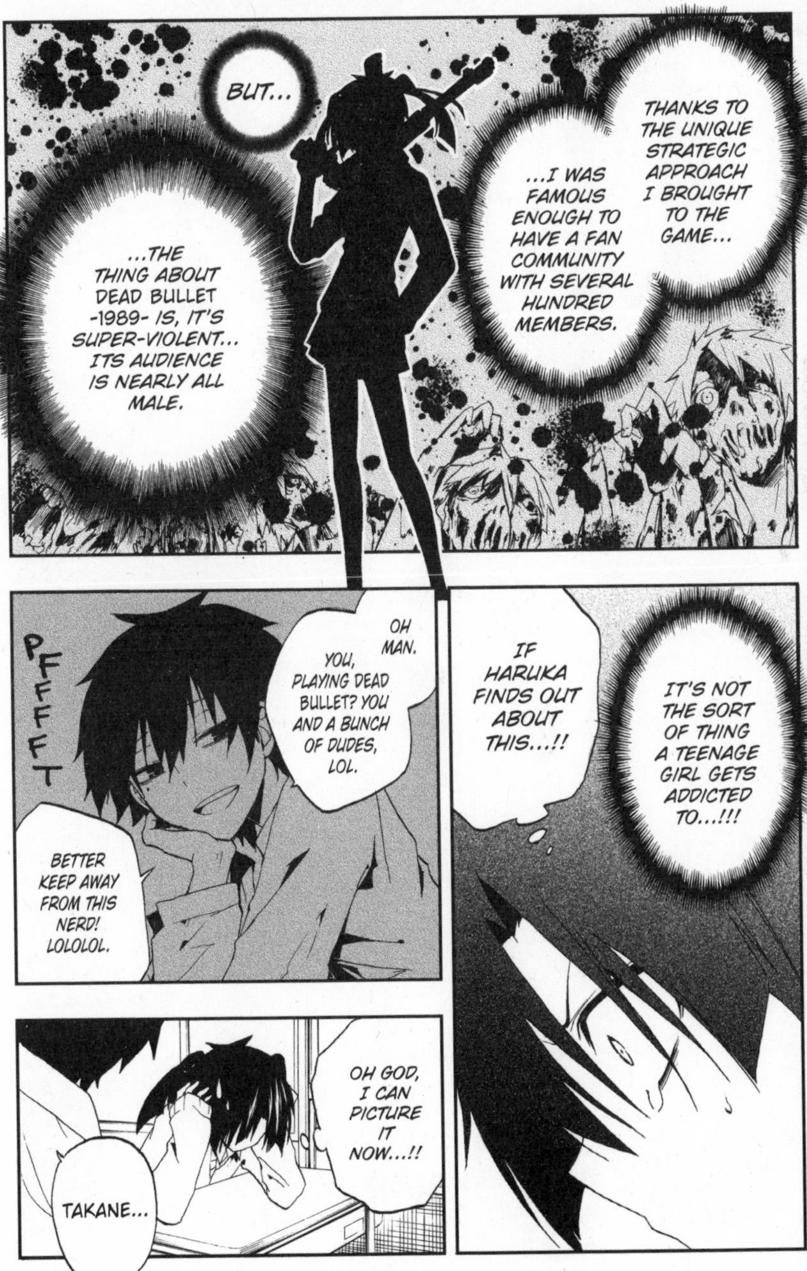
THANKS TO THE UNIQUE STRATEGIC APPROACH I BROUGHT TO THE GAME...
...I WAS FAMOUS ENOUGH TO HAVE A FAN COMMUNITY WITH SEVERAL HUNDRED MEMBERS.
BUT...
...THE THING ABOUT DEAD BULLET -1989- IS, IT'S SUPER-VIOLENT... ITS AUDIENCE IS NEARLY ALL MALE.
IT'S NOT THE SORT OF THING A TEENAGE GIRL GETS ADDICTED TO...!!!
IF HARUKA FINDS OUT ABOUT THIS...!!
OH MAN. YOU, PLAYING DEAD BULLET? YOU AND A BUNCH OF DUDES, LOL.
PFFFFT
BETTER KEEP AWAY FROM THIS NERD! LOLOLOL.
OH GOD, I CAN PICTURE IT NOW...!!
TAKANE...

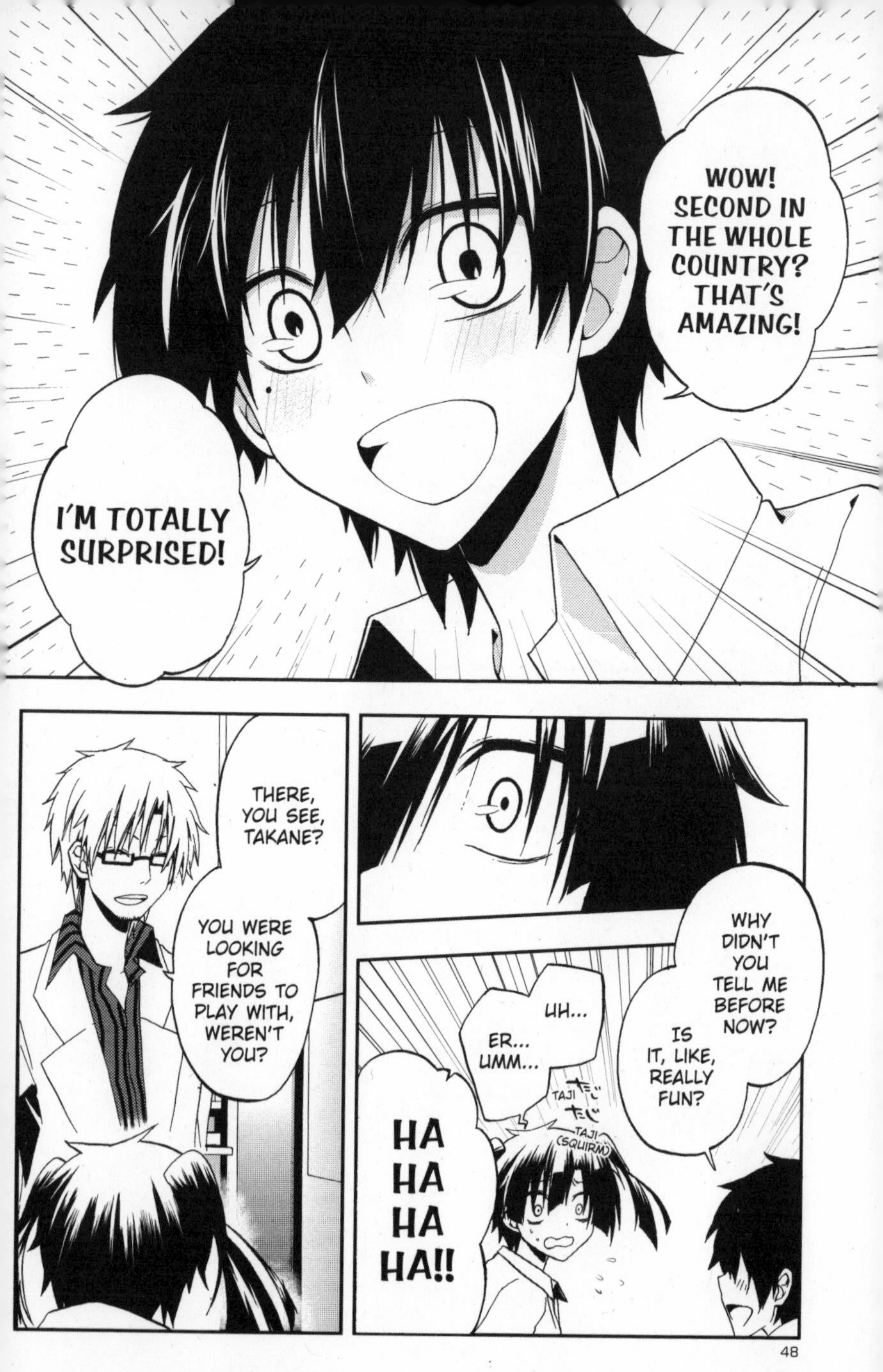
WOW! SECOND IN THE WHOLE COUNTRY? THAT'S AMAZING!
I'M TOTALLY SURPRISED!
WHY DIDN'T YOU TELL ME BEFORE NOW?
IS IT, LIKE, REALLY FUN?
UH...
ER... UMM...
TAJI TAJI (SQUIRM)
HA HA HA HA!!
THERE, YOU SEE, TAKANE?
YOU WERE LOOKING FOR FRIENDS TO PLAY WITH, WEREN'T YOU?

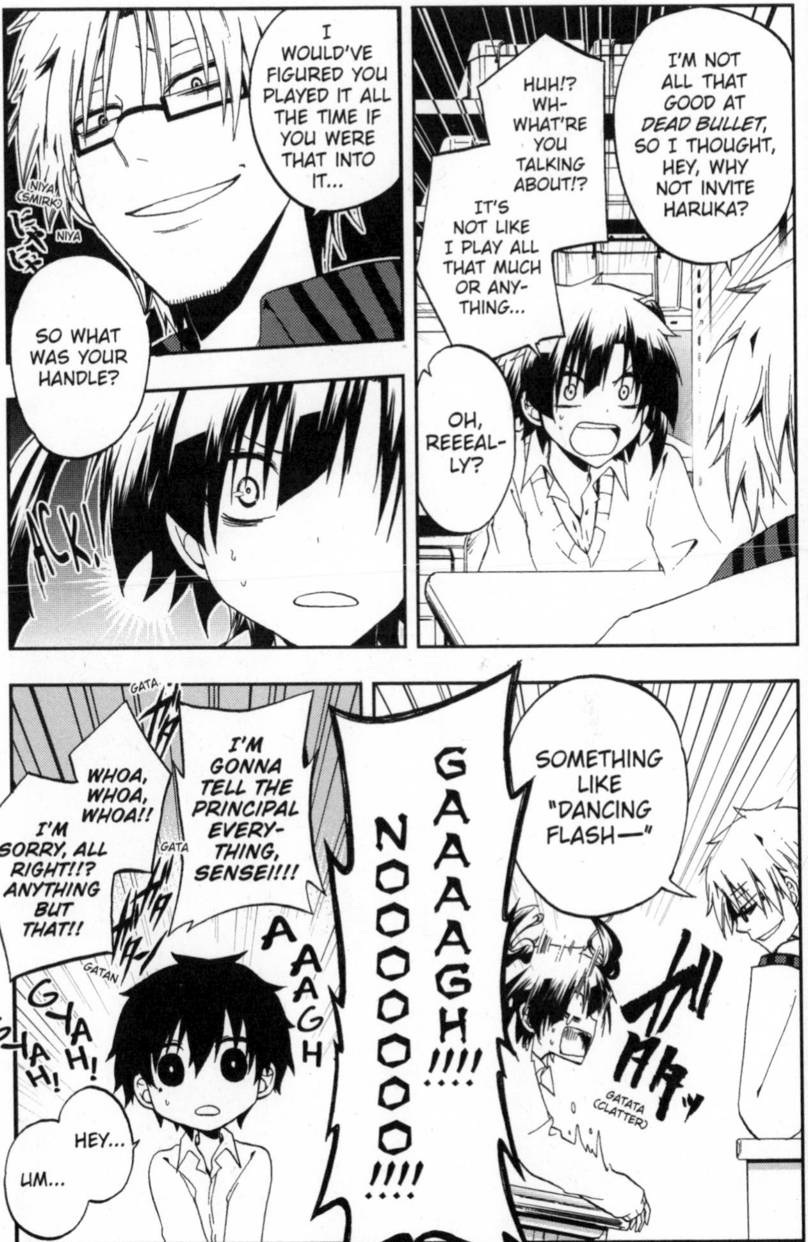
I'M NOT ALL THAT GOOD AT *DEAD BULLET*, SO I THOUGHT, HEY, WHY NOT INVITE HARUKA?
HUH!? WH-WHAT'RE YOU TALKING ABOUT!?
IT'S NOT LIKE I PLAY ALL THAT MUCH OR ANYTHING...
OH, REEEALLY?
I WOULD'VE FIGURED YOU PLAYED IT ALL THE TIME IF YOU WERE THAT INTO IT...
NIYA (SMIRK)
NIYA
SO WHAT WAS YOUR HANDLE?
ACK!
SOMETHING LIKE "DANCING FLASH—"
GATATA (CLATTER)
GAAAAAGH!!!!
NOOOOOOOOO!!!!
I'M GONNA TELL THE PRINCIPAL EVERYTHING, SENSEI!!!!
GATA
WHOA, WHOA, WHOA!!
I'M SORRY, ALL RIGHT!!? ANYTHING BUT THAT!!
GATA
GATAN
AAAGH
GYAH!
GYAH!
HEY...
UM...

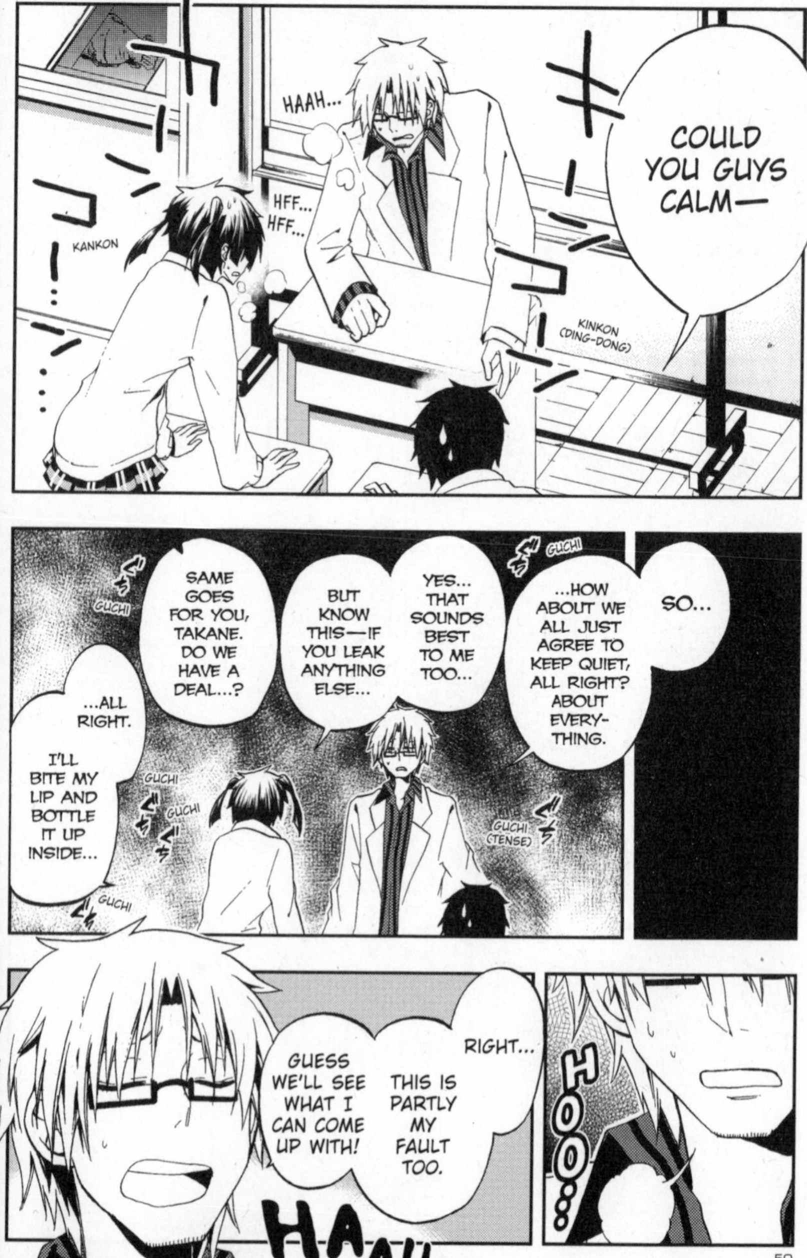
COULD YOU GUYS CALM—
KINKON (DING-DONG)
HAAH...
HFF... HFF...
KANKON
SO...
...HOW ABOUT WE ALL JUST AGREE TO KEEP QUIET, ALL RIGHT? ABOUT EVERY-THING.
GUCHI
YES... THAT SOUNDS BEST TO ME TOO...
BUT KNOW THIS—IF YOU LEAK ANYTHING ELSE...
SAME GOES FOR YOU, TAKANE. DO WE HAVE A DEAL...?
GUCHI
GUCHI (TENSE)
...ALL RIGHT.
I'LL BITE MY LIP AND BOTTLE IT UP INSIDE...
GUCHI
GUCHI
GUCHI
HOO...
RIGHT...
THIS IS PARTLY MY FAULT TOO.
GUESS WE'LL SEE WHAT I CAN COME UP WITH!
HAAH...

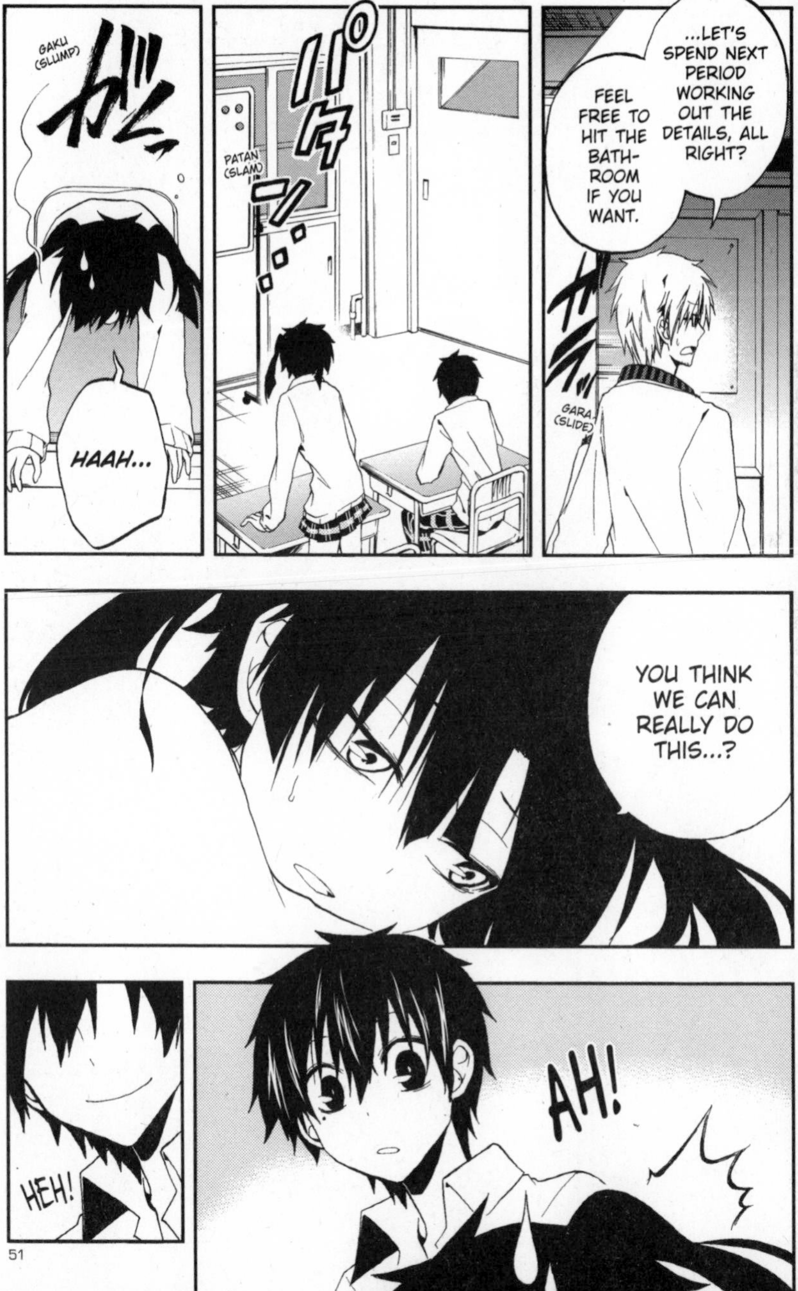
...LET'S SPEND NEXT PERIOD WORKING OUT THE DETAILS, ALL RIGHT?
FEEL FREE TO HIT THE BATH-ROOM IF YOU WANT.
GARA (SLIDE)
PATAN (SLAM)
GAKU (SLUMP)
HAAH...
YOU THINK WE CAN REALLY DO THIS...?
AH!
HEH!

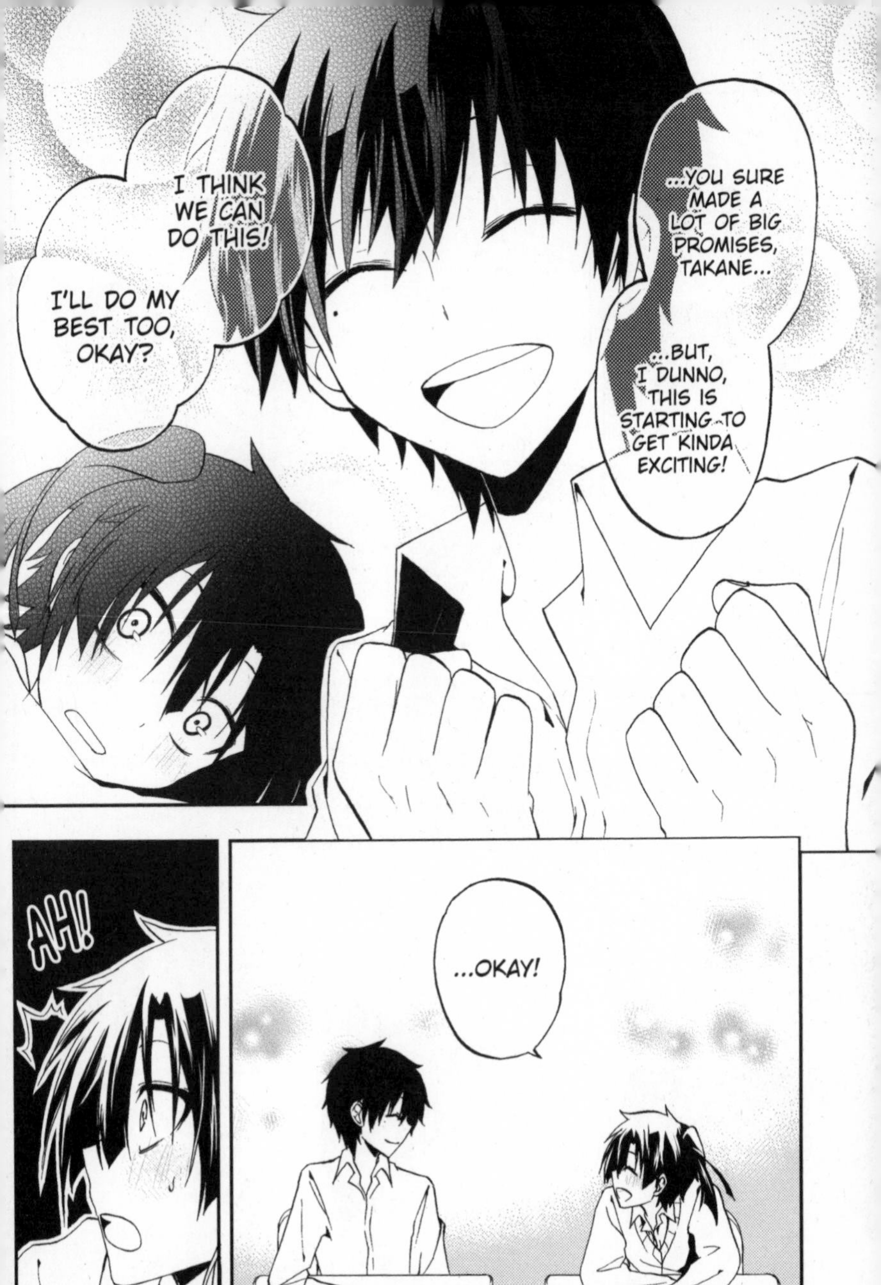
...YOU SURE MADE A LOT OF BIG PROMISES, TAKANE...
...BUT, I DUNNO, THIS IS STARTING TO GET KINDA EXCITING!
I THINK WE CAN DO THIS!
I'LL DO MY BEST TOO, OKAY?
...OKAY!
AH!

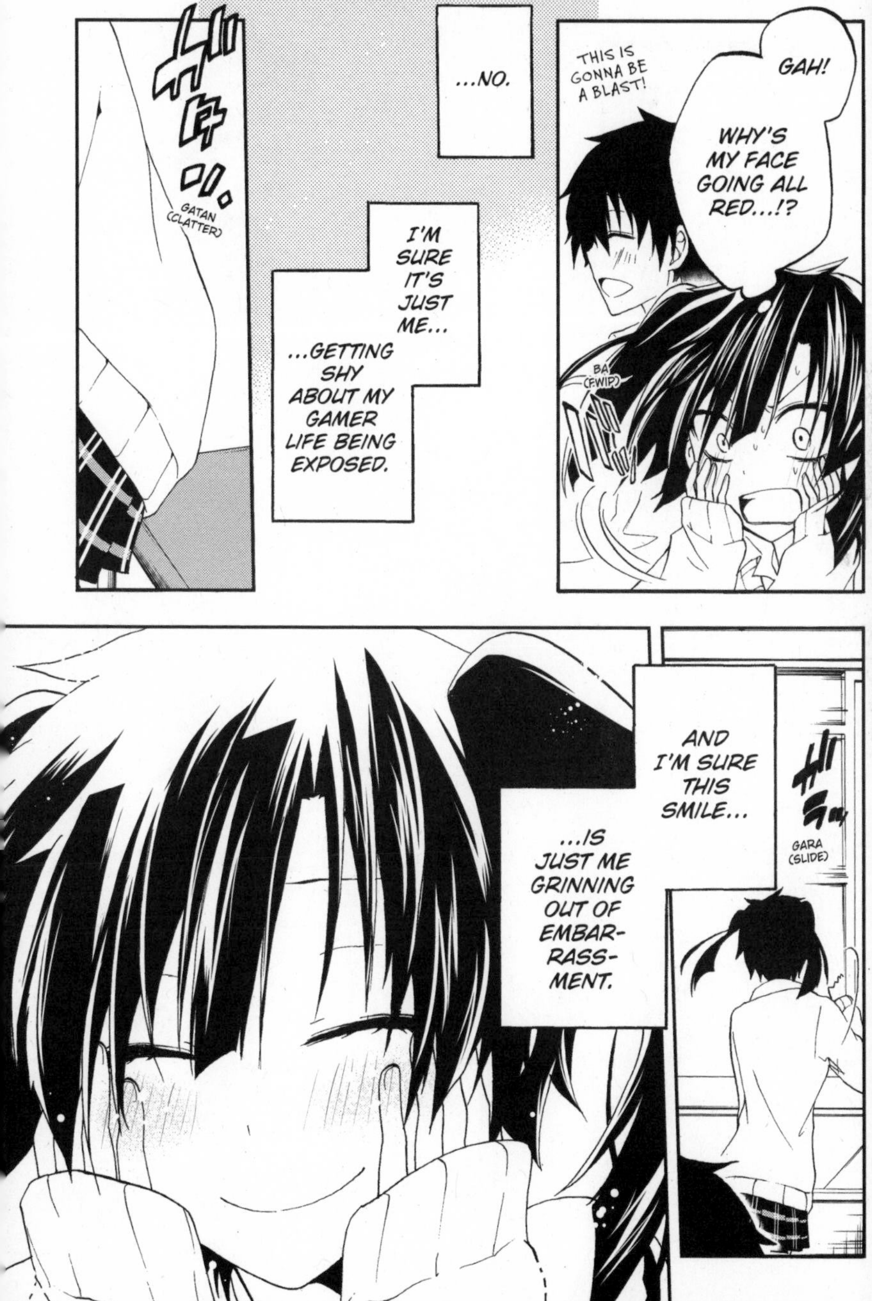
GAH!
WHY'S MY FACE GOING ALL RED...!?
THIS IS GONNA BE A BLAST!
BA (F.WIP)
...NO.
I'M SURE IT'S JUST ME...
...GETTING SHY ABOUT MY GAMER LIFE BEING EXPOSED.
GATAN (CLATTER)
GARA (SLIDE)
AND I'M SURE THIS SMILE...
...IS JUST ME GRINNING OUT OF EMBARRASSMENT.

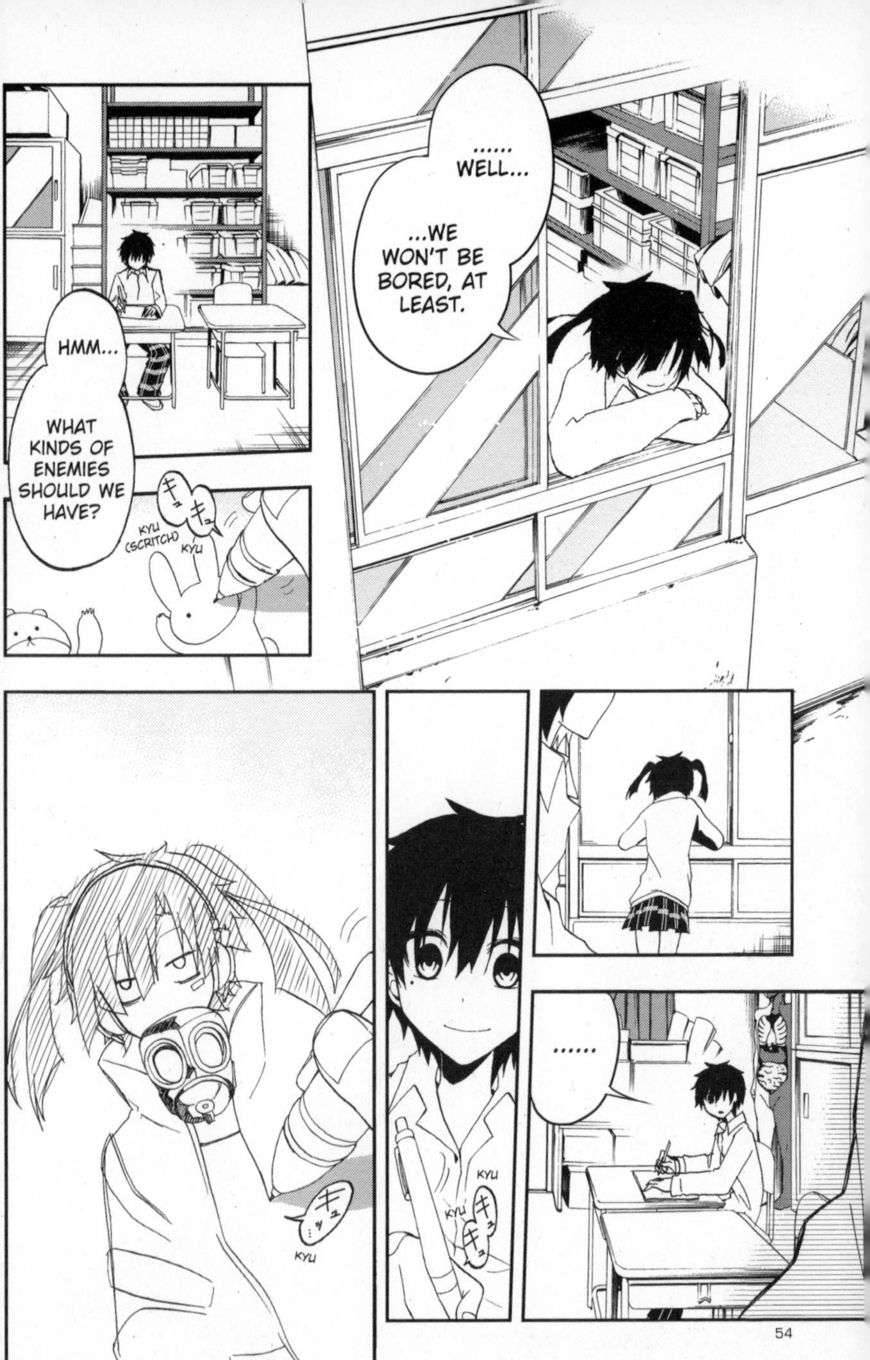

......
WELL...
...WE WON'T BE BORED, AT LEAST.
HMM...
WHAT KINDS OF ENEMIES SHOULD WE HAVE?
キュ キュ
KYU (SCRITCH) KYU
......
KYU
KYU
キュ キュ
KYU
キュッ

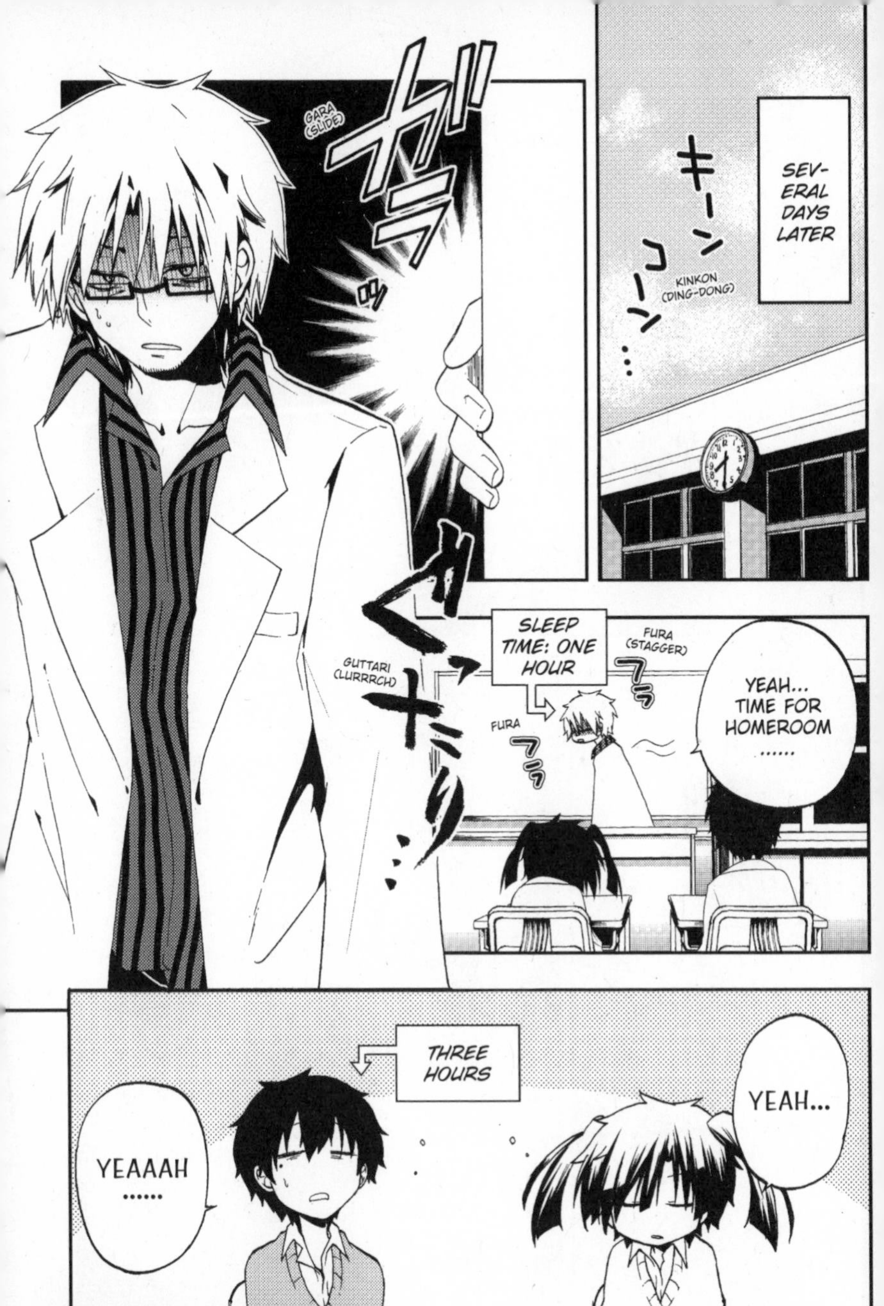
SEV-ERAL DAYS LATER
KINKON (DING-DONG)
YEAH... TIME FOR HOMEROOM ......
FURA (STAGGER)
SLEEP TIME: ONE HOUR
FURA
GARA (SLIDE)
GUTTARI (LURRRCH)
YEAH...
THREE HOURS
YEAAAH ......

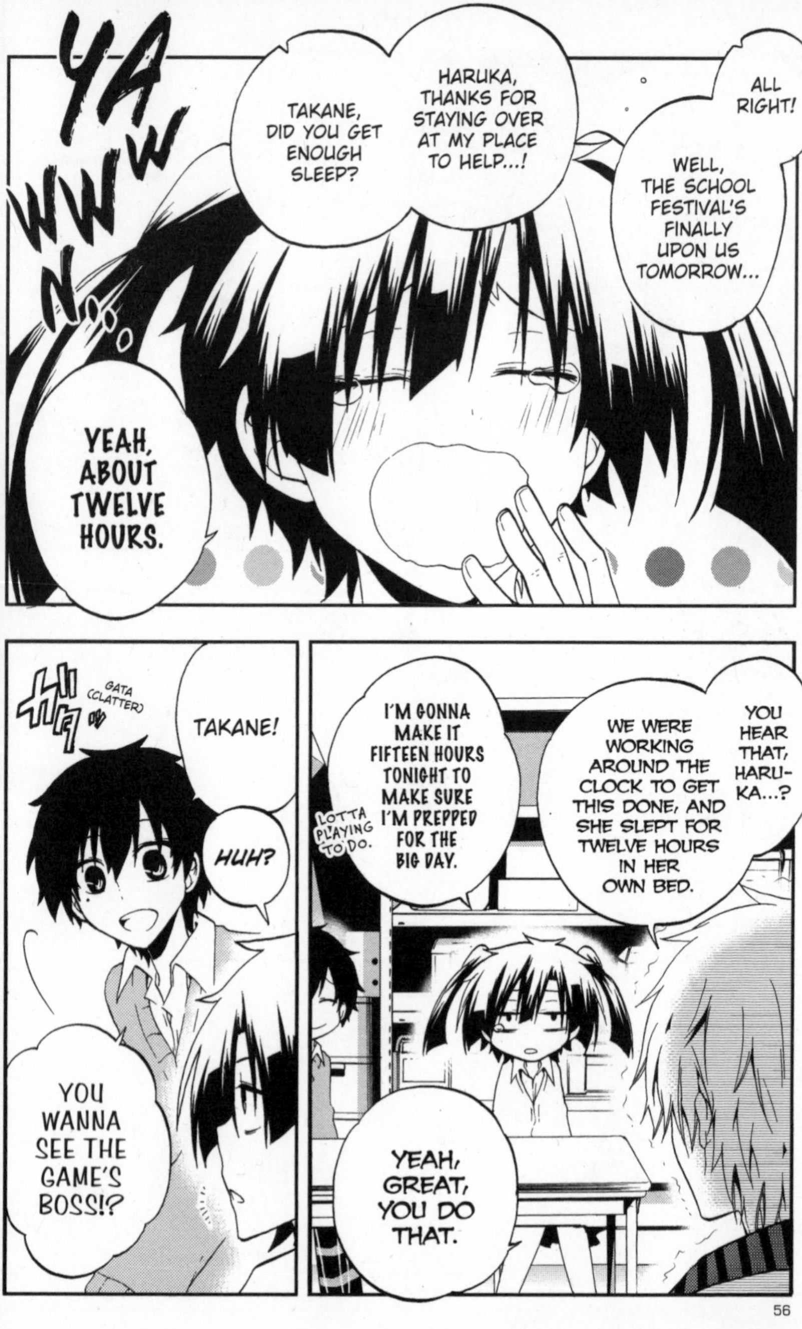
ALL RIGHT!
WELL, THE SCHOOL FESTIVAL'S FINALLY UPON US TOMORROW...
HARUKA, THANKS FOR STAYING OVER AT MY PLACE TO HELP...!
TAKANE, DID YOU GET ENOUGH SLEEP?
YAWWWN...
YEAH, ABOUT TWELVE HOURS.
YOU HEAR THAT, HARUKA...?
WE WERE WORKING AROUND THE CLOCK TO GET THIS DONE, AND SHE SLEPT FOR TWELVE HOURS IN HER OWN BED.
I'M GONNA MAKE IT FIFTEEN HOURS TONIGHT TO MAKE SURE I'M PREPPED FOR THE BIG DAY.
LOTTA PLAYING TO DO.
YEAH, GREAT, YOU DO THAT.
GATA (CLATTER)
TAKANE!
HUH?
YOU WANNA SEE THE GAME'S BOSS!?

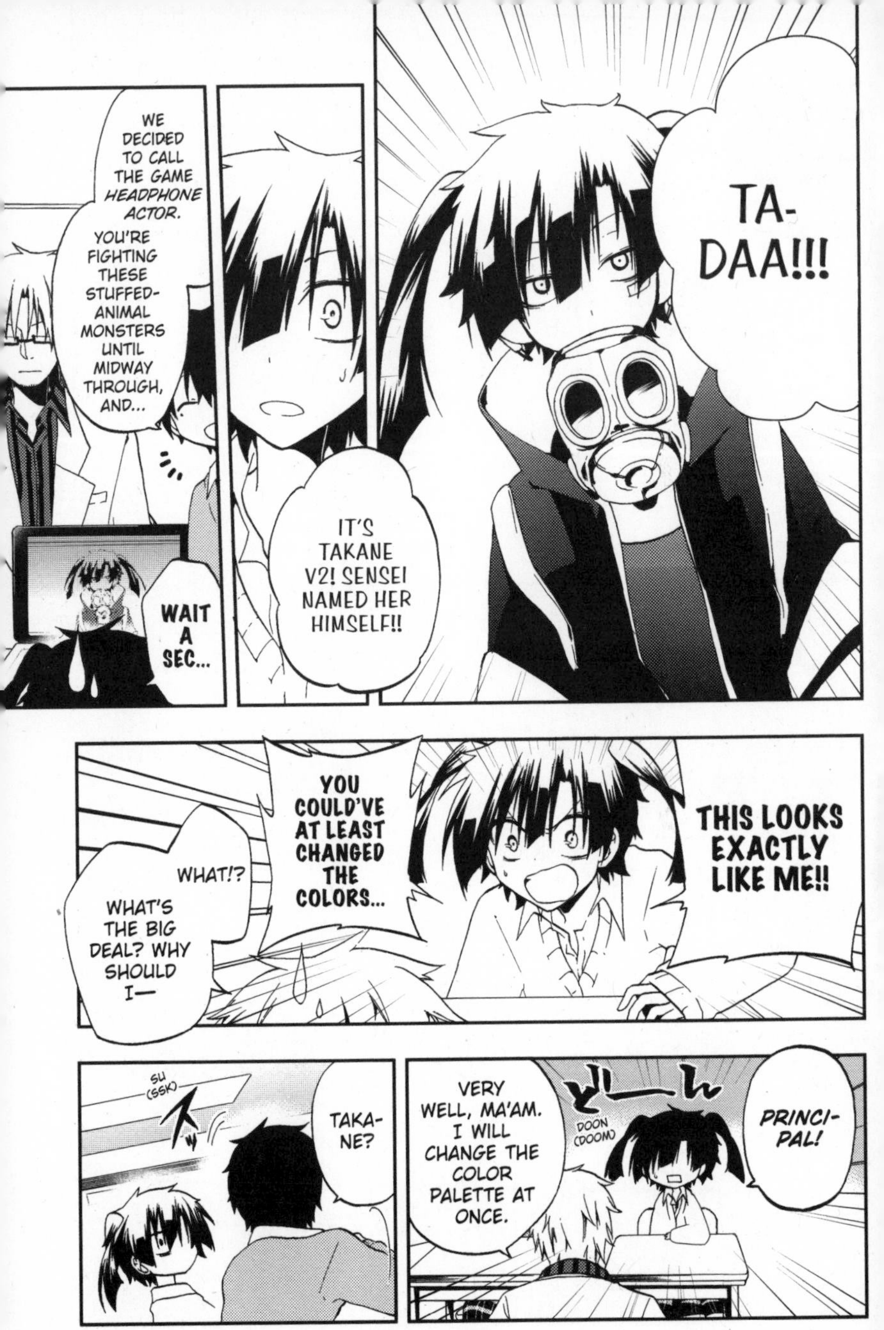
TA-DAA!!!
IT'S TAKANE V2! SENSEI NAMED HER HIMSELF!!
WE DECIDED TO CALL THE GAME *HEADPHONE ACTOR*.
YOU'RE FIGHTING THESE STUFFED-ANIMAL MONSTERS UNTIL MIDWAY THROUGH, AND...
WAIT A SEC...
THIS LOOKS EXACTLY LIKE ME!!
YOU COULD'VE AT LEAST CHANGED THE COLORS...
WHAT!?
WHAT'S THE BIG DEAL? WHY SHOULD I—
PRINCI-PAL!
どーん
DOON (DOOM)
VERY WELL, MA'AM. I WILL CHANGE THE COLOR PALETTE AT ONCE.
TAKA-NE?
ス
SU (SSK)

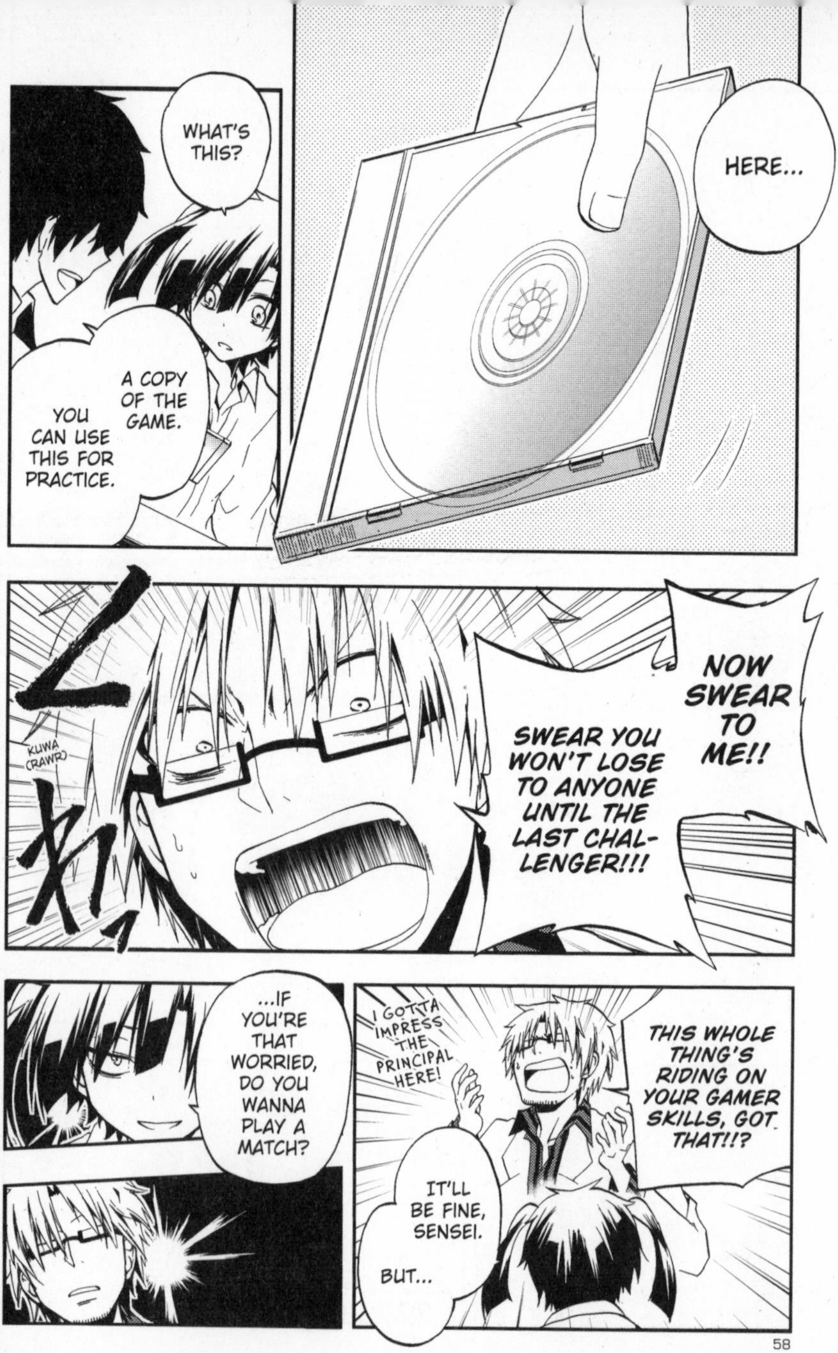
HERE...
WHAT'S THIS?
A COPY OF THE GAME.
YOU CAN USE THIS FOR PRACTICE.
NOW SWEAR TO ME!!
SWEAR YOU WON'T LOSE TO ANYONE UNTIL THE LAST CHAL-LENGER!!!
KUWA (CRAWR)
THIS WHOLE THING'S RIDING ON YOUR GAMER SKILLS, GOT THAT!!?
I GOTTA IMPRESS THE PRINCIPAL HERE!
IT'LL BE FINE, SENSEI.
BUT...
...IF YOU'RE THAT WORRIED, DO YOU WANNA PLAY A MATCH?

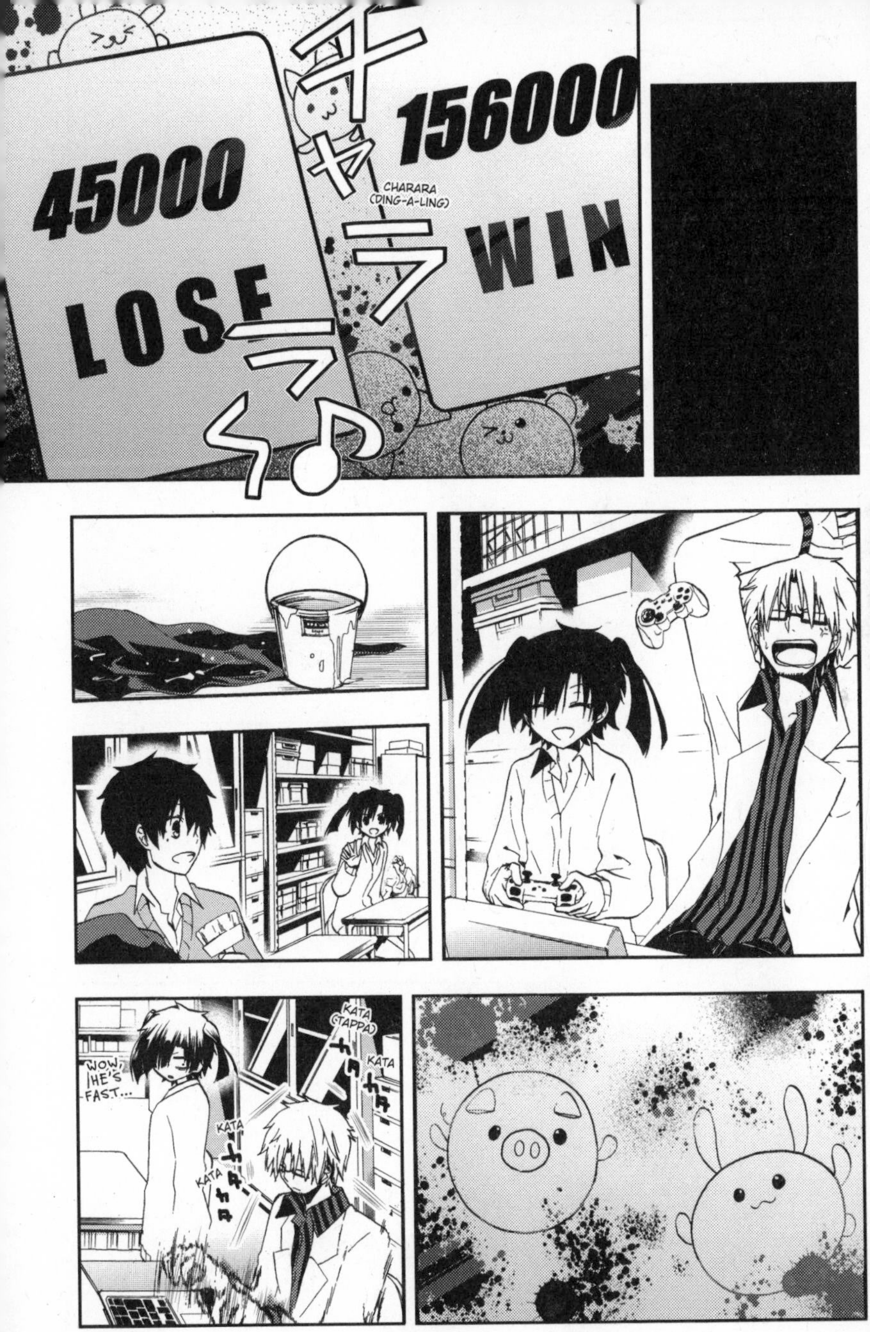
45000
LOSE
156000
WIN
チャラララ〜♪
CHARARA (DING-A-LING)
KATA (TAPPA)
KATA
WOW, HE'S FAST...
KATA
KATA

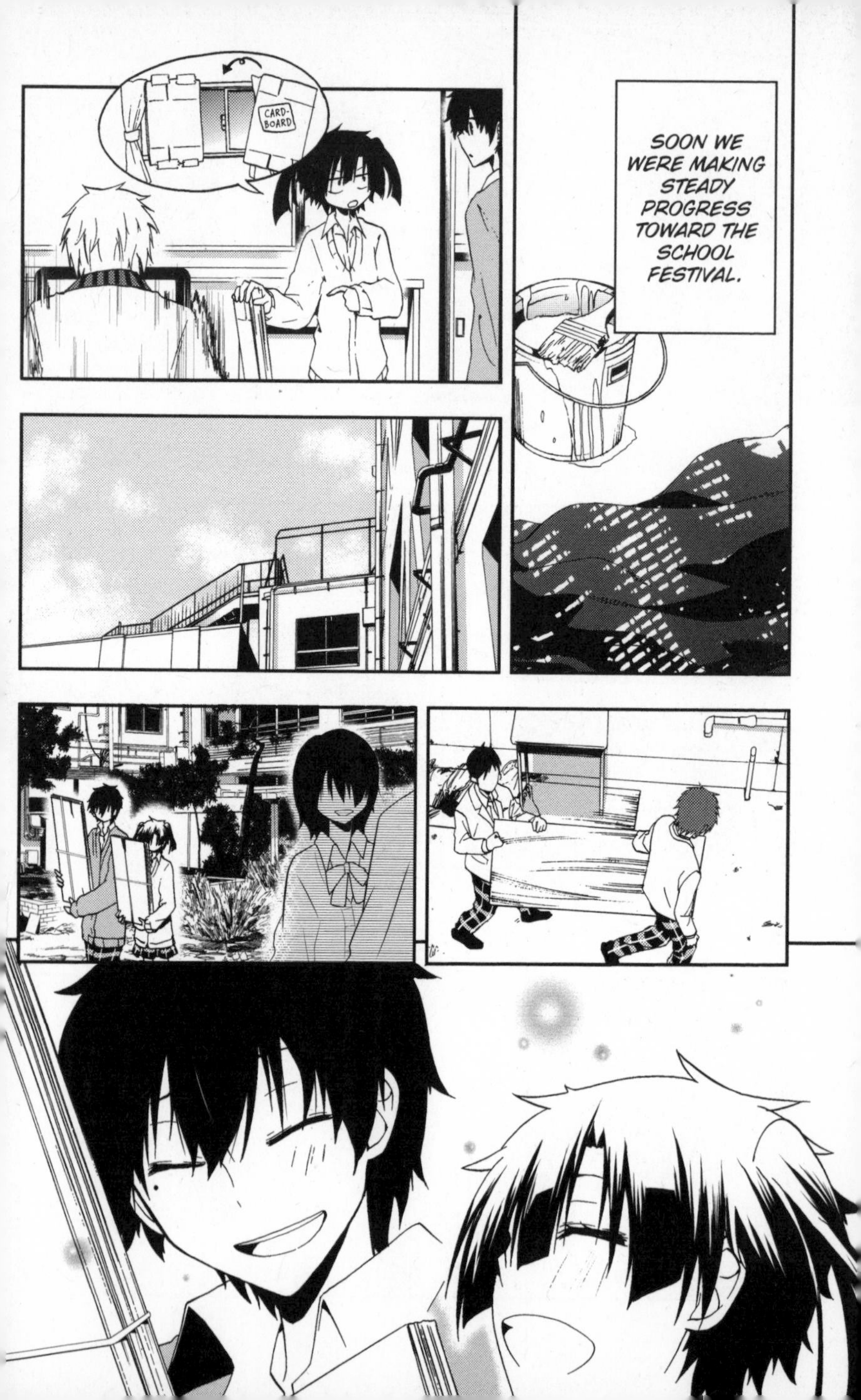
SOON WE WERE MAKING STEADY PROGRESS TOWARD THE SCHOOL FESTIVAL.
CARD-BOARD

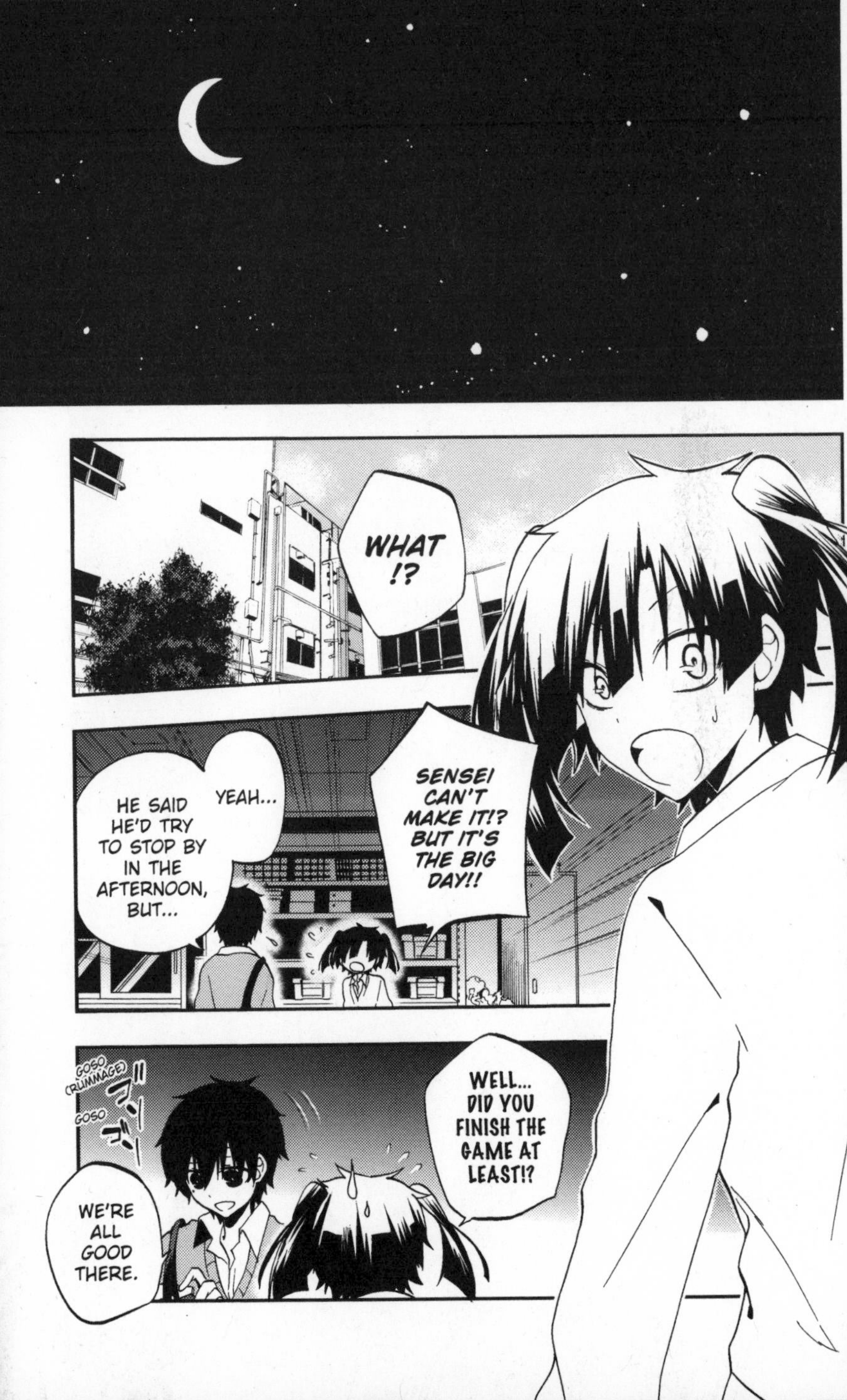
WHAT!?
SENSEI CAN'T MAKE IT!? BUT IT'S THE BIG DAY!!
YEAH...
HE SAID HE'D TRY TO STOP BY IN THE AFTERNOON, BUT...
WELL... DID YOU FINISH THE GAME AT LEAST!?
GOSO (RUMMAGE) GOSO
WE'RE ALL GOOD THERE.

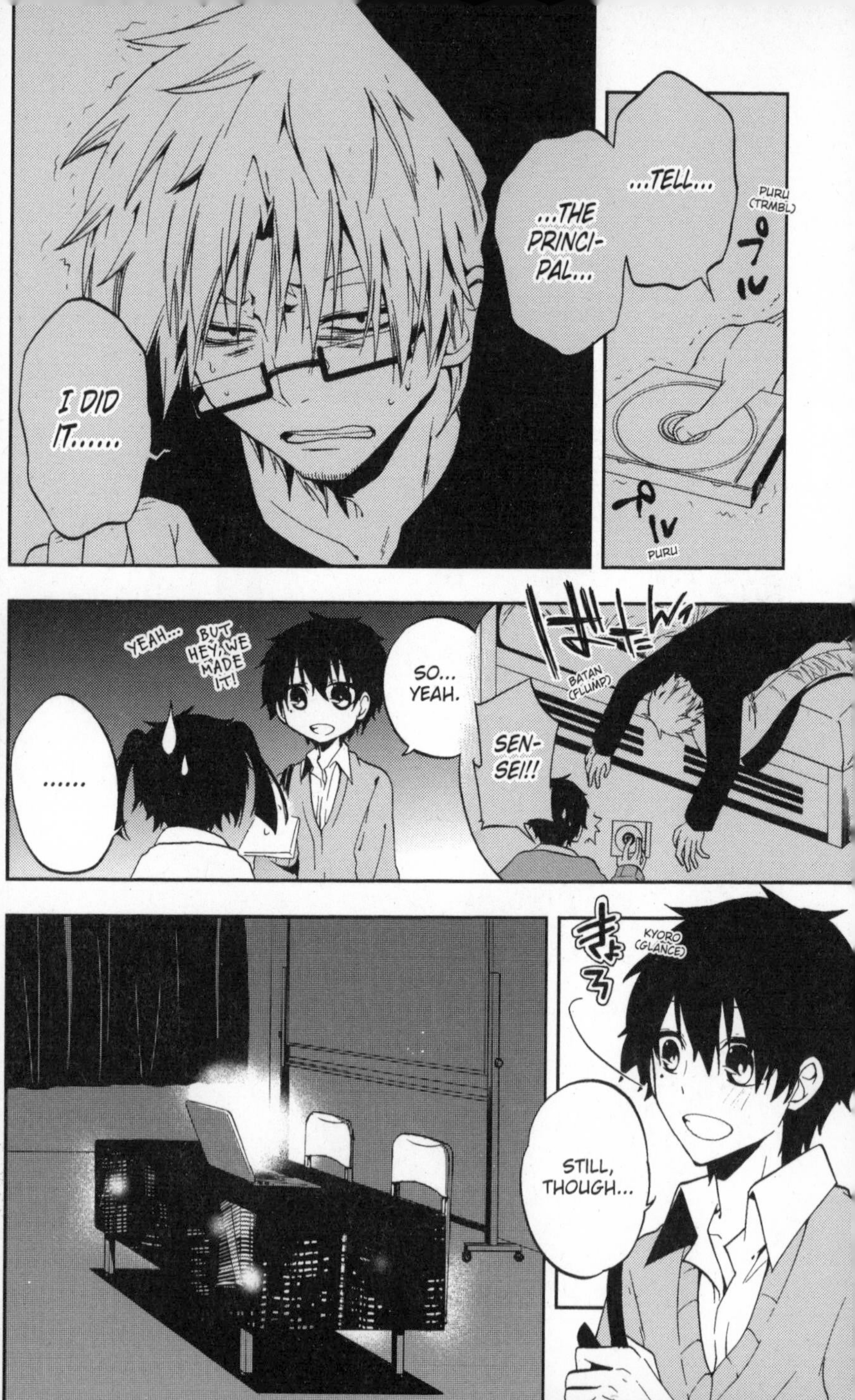
...TELL...
...THE PRINCI-PAL...
PURU (TRMBL)
PURU
I DID IT......
BATAN (FLUMP)
SEN-SEI!!
SO... YEAH.
YEAH... BUT HEY, WE MADE IT!
......
KYORO (GLANCE)
STILL, THOUGH...

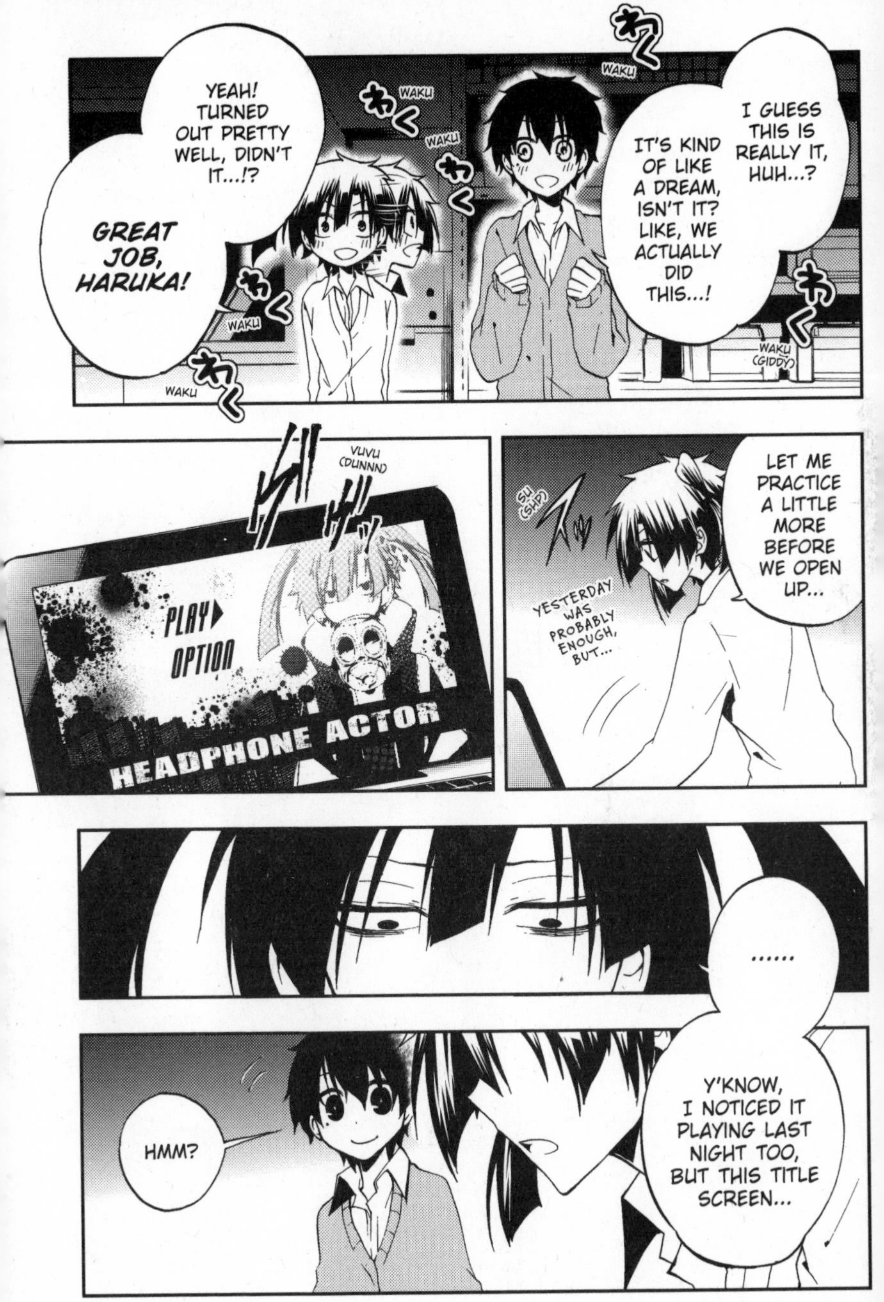
わく
WAKU
I GUESS THIS IS REALLY IT, HUH...?
IT'S KIND OF LIKE A DREAM, ISN'T IT? LIKE, WE ACTUALLY DID THIS...!
わく
WAKU (GIDDY)
わく
WAKU
わく
WAKU
YEAH! TURNED OUT PRETTY WELL, DIDN'T IT...!?
GREAT JOB, HARUKA!
わく
WAKU
わく
WAKU
LET ME PRACTICE A LITTLE MORE BEFORE WE OPEN UP...
SU (SHP)
YESTERDAY WAS PROBABLY ENOUGH, BUT...
VUVU (DUNNN)
PLAY▶
OPTION
HEADPHONE ACTOR
......
Y'KNOW, I NOTICED IT PLAYING LAST NIGHT TOO, BUT THIS TITLE SCREEN...
HMM?

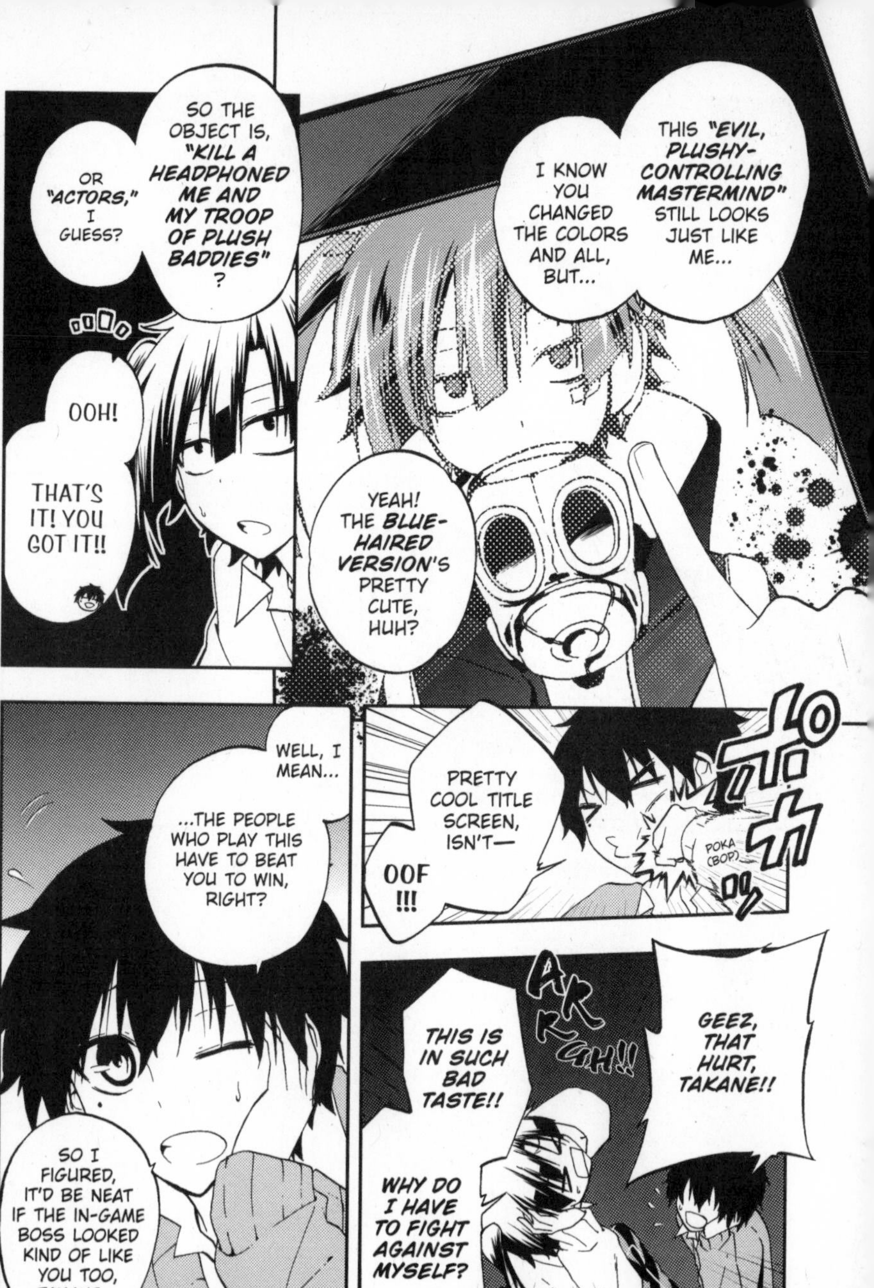
THIS "EVIL, PLUSHY-CONTROLLING MASTERMIND" STILL LOOKS JUST LIKE ME...
I KNOW YOU CHANGED THE COLORS AND ALL, BUT...
YEAH! THE BLUE-HAIRED VERSION'S PRETTY CUTE, HUH?
SO THE OBJECT IS, "KILL A HEADPHONED ME AND MY TROOP OF PLUSH BADDIES"?
OR "ACTORS," I GUESS?
OOH!
THAT'S IT! YOU GOT IT!!
PRETTY COOL TITLE SCREEN, ISN'T—
OOF!!!
POKA (BOP)
GEEZ, THAT HURT, TAKANE!!
ARKGH!!
THIS IS IN SUCH BAD TASTE!!
WHY DO I HAVE TO FIGHT AGAINST MYSELF?
WELL, I MEAN...
...THE PEOPLE WHO PLAY THIS HAVE TO BEAT YOU TO WIN, RIGHT?
SO I FIGURED, IT'D BE NEAT IF THE IN-GAME BOSS LOOKED KIND OF LIKE YOU TOO, TAKANE...

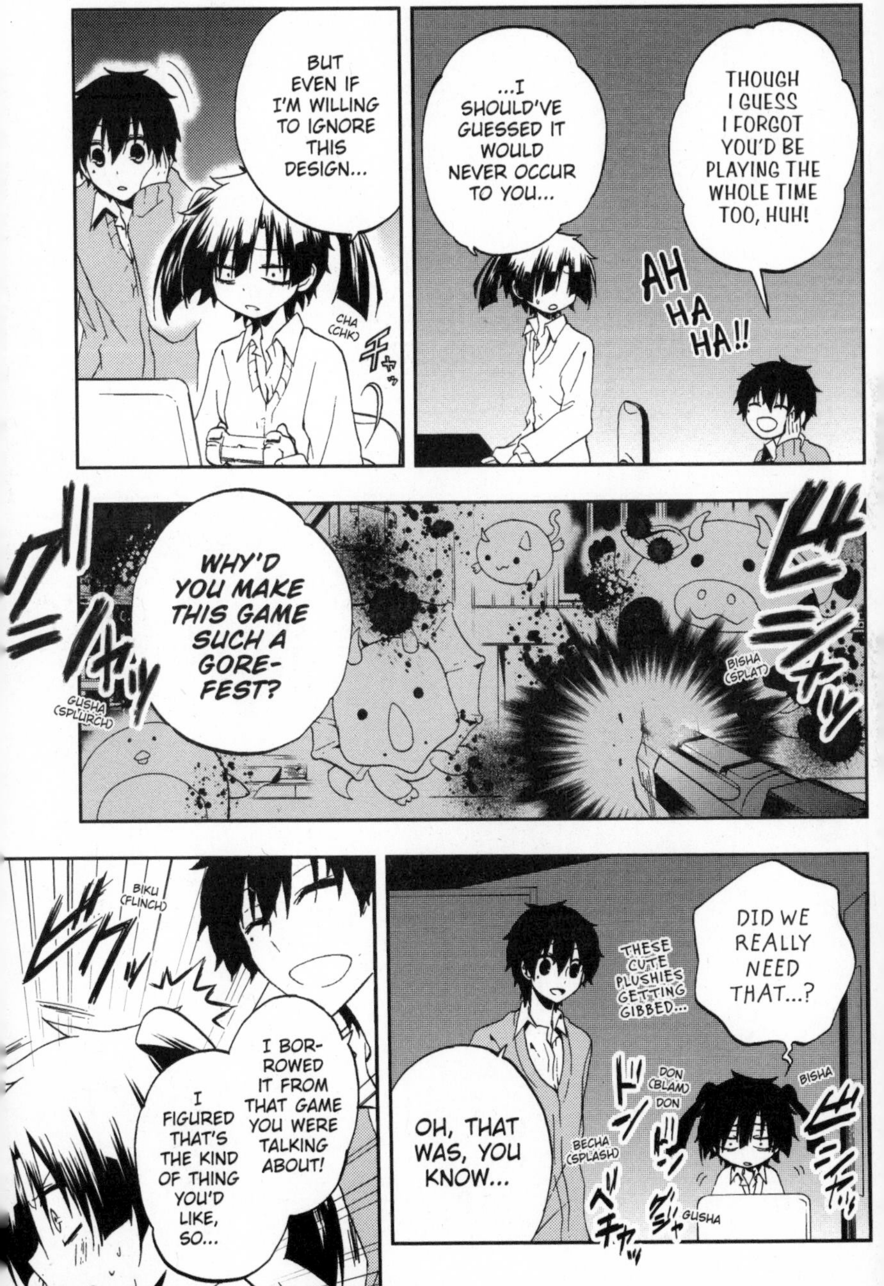
THOUGH I GUESS I FORGOT YOU'D BE PLAYING THE WHOLE TIME TOO, HUH!
...I SHOULD'VE GUESSED IT WOULD NEVER OCCUR TO YOU...
AH HA HA!!
BUT EVEN IF I'M WILLING TO IGNORE THIS DESIGN...
CHA (CHK)
BISHA (SPLAT)
WHY'D YOU MAKE THIS GAME SUCH A GORE-FEST?
GUSHA (SPLURCH)
DID WE REALLY NEED THAT...?
THESE CUTE PLUSHIES GETTING GIBBED...
BISHA
DON (BLAM) DON
OH, THAT WAS, YOU KNOW...
BECHA (SPLASH)
GUSHA
BIKU (FLINCH)
I BOR-ROWED IT FROM THAT GAME YOU WERE TALKING ABOUT!
I FIGURED THAT'S THE KIND OF THING YOU'D LIKE, SO...

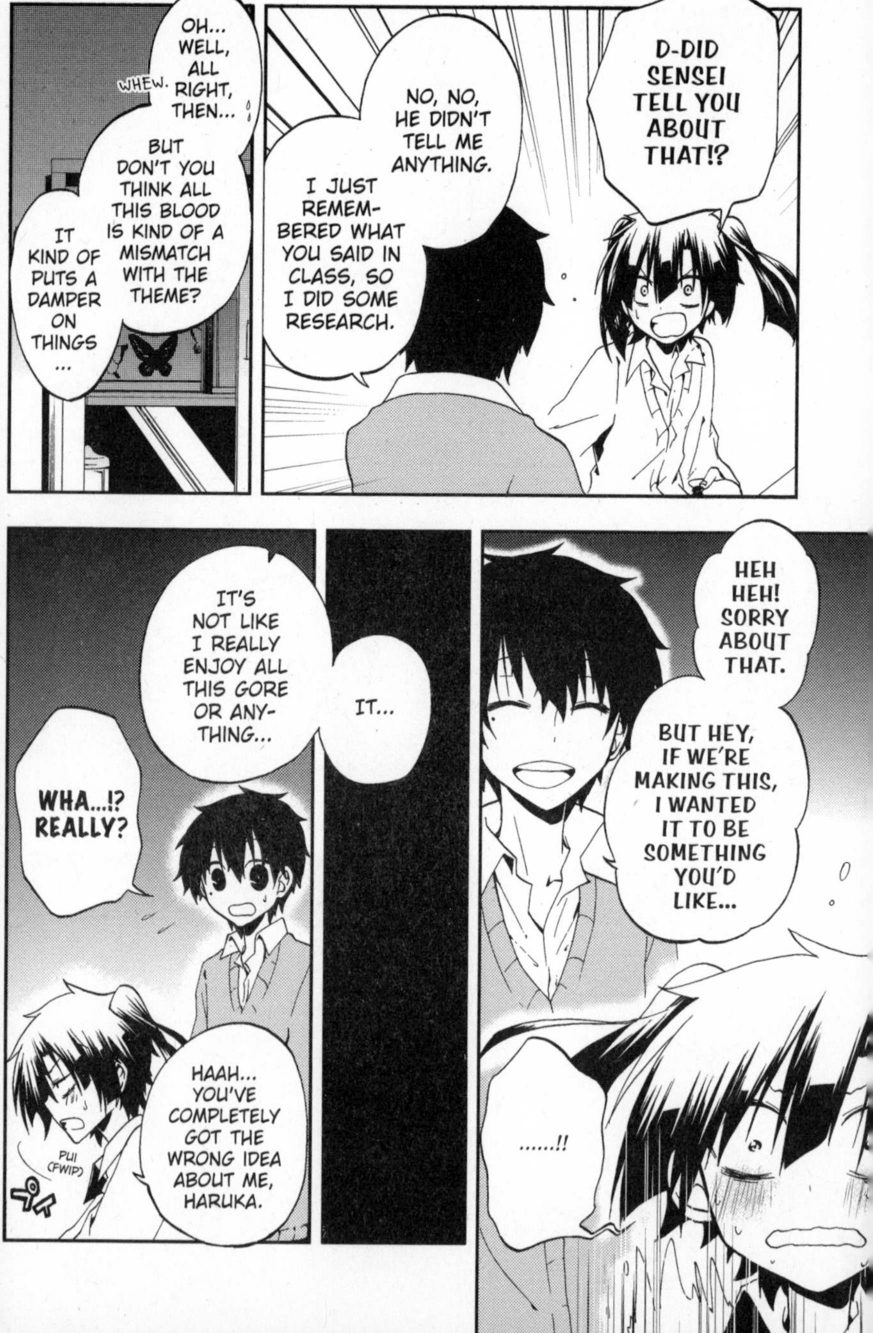
D-DID SENSEI TELL YOU ABOUT THAT!?
NO, NO, HE DIDN'T TELL ME ANYTHING.
I JUST REMEMBERED WHAT YOU SAID IN CLASS, SO I DID SOME RESEARCH.
OH... WELL, ALL RIGHT, THEN...
WHEW.
BUT DON'T YOU THINK ALL THIS BLOOD IS KIND OF A MISMATCH WITH THE THEME?
IT KIND OF PUTS A DAMPER ON THINGS...
HEH HEH! SORRY ABOUT THAT.
BUT HEY, IF WE'RE MAKING THIS, I WANTED IT TO BE SOMETHING YOU'D LIKE...
......!!
IT...
IT'S NOT LIKE I REALLY ENJOY ALL THIS GORE OR ANYTHING...
WHA...!? REALLY?
HAAH... YOU'VE COMPLETELY GOT THE WRONG IDEA ABOUT ME, HARUKA.
PUI (FWIP)

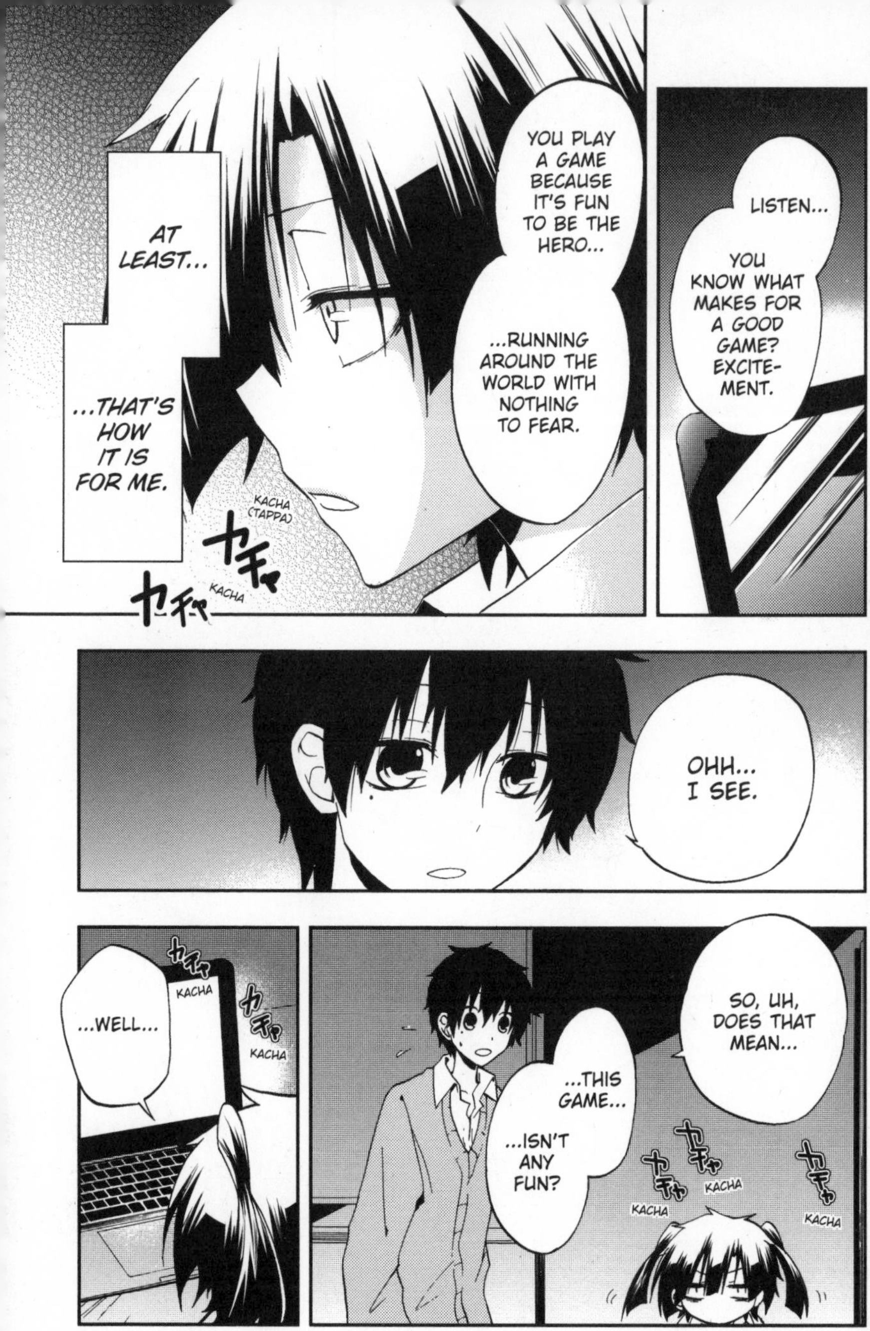
LISTEN...
YOU KNOW WHAT MAKES FOR A GOOD GAME? EXCITE-MENT.
YOU PLAY A GAME BECAUSE IT'S FUN TO BE THE HERO...
...RUNNING AROUND THE WORLD WITH NOTHING TO FEAR.
AT LEAST...
...THAT'S HOW IT IS FOR ME.
KACHA (TAPPA)
KACHA
OHH... I SEE.
SO, UH, DOES THAT MEAN...
...THIS GAME...
...ISN'T ANY FUN?
KACHA
KACHA
KACHA
...WELL...
KACHA
KACHA

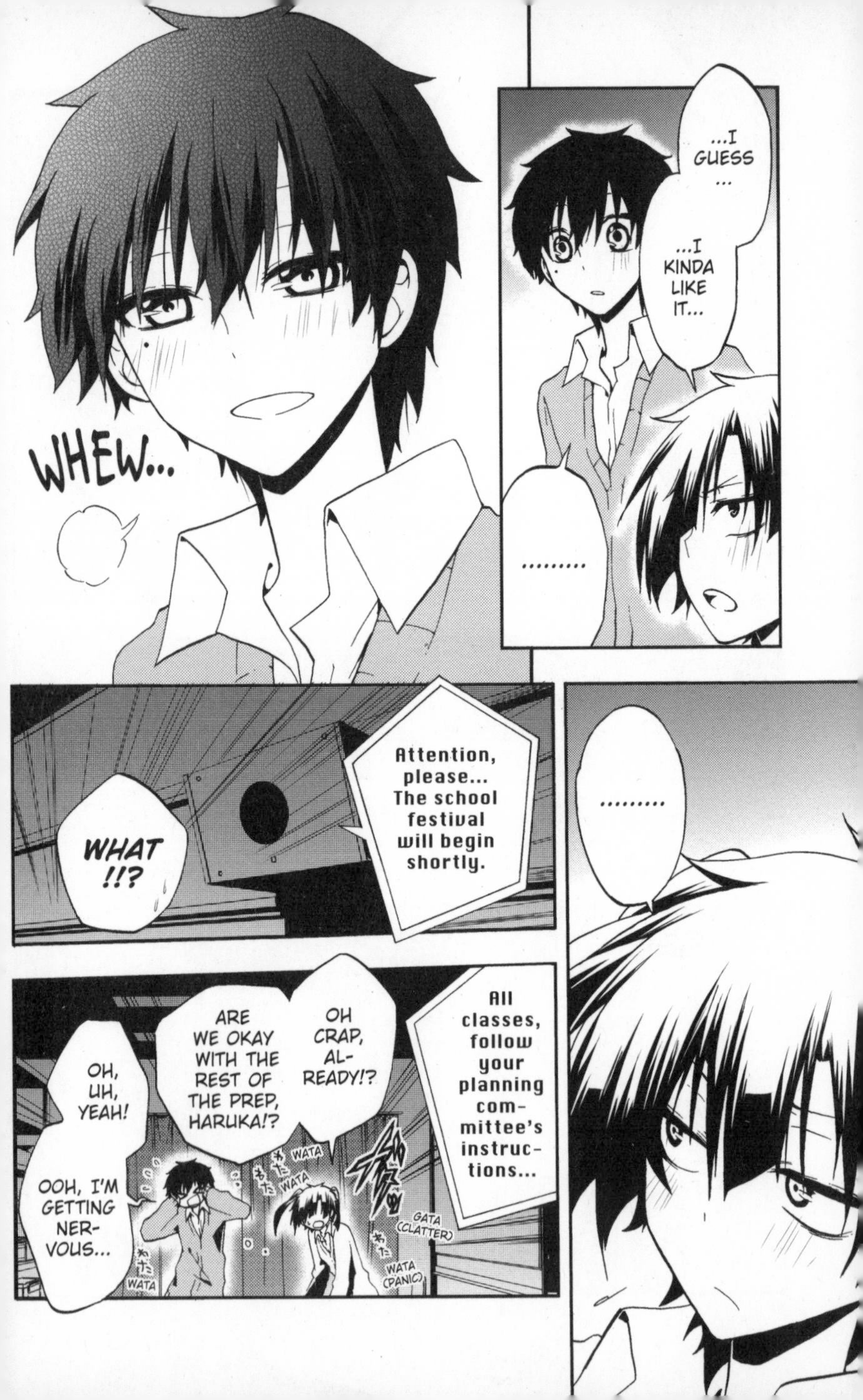
...I GUESS ...
...I KINDA LIKE IT...
....
WHEW...
....
Attention, please... The school festival will begin shortly.
WHAT !!?
All classes, follow your planning com-mittee's instruc-tions...
OH CRAP, AL-READY!?
ARE WE OKAY WITH THE REST OF THE PREP, HARUKA!?
OH, UH, YEAH!
OOH, I'M GETTING NER-VOUS...
WATA WATA
GATA (CLATTER)
WATA (PANIC)
WATA

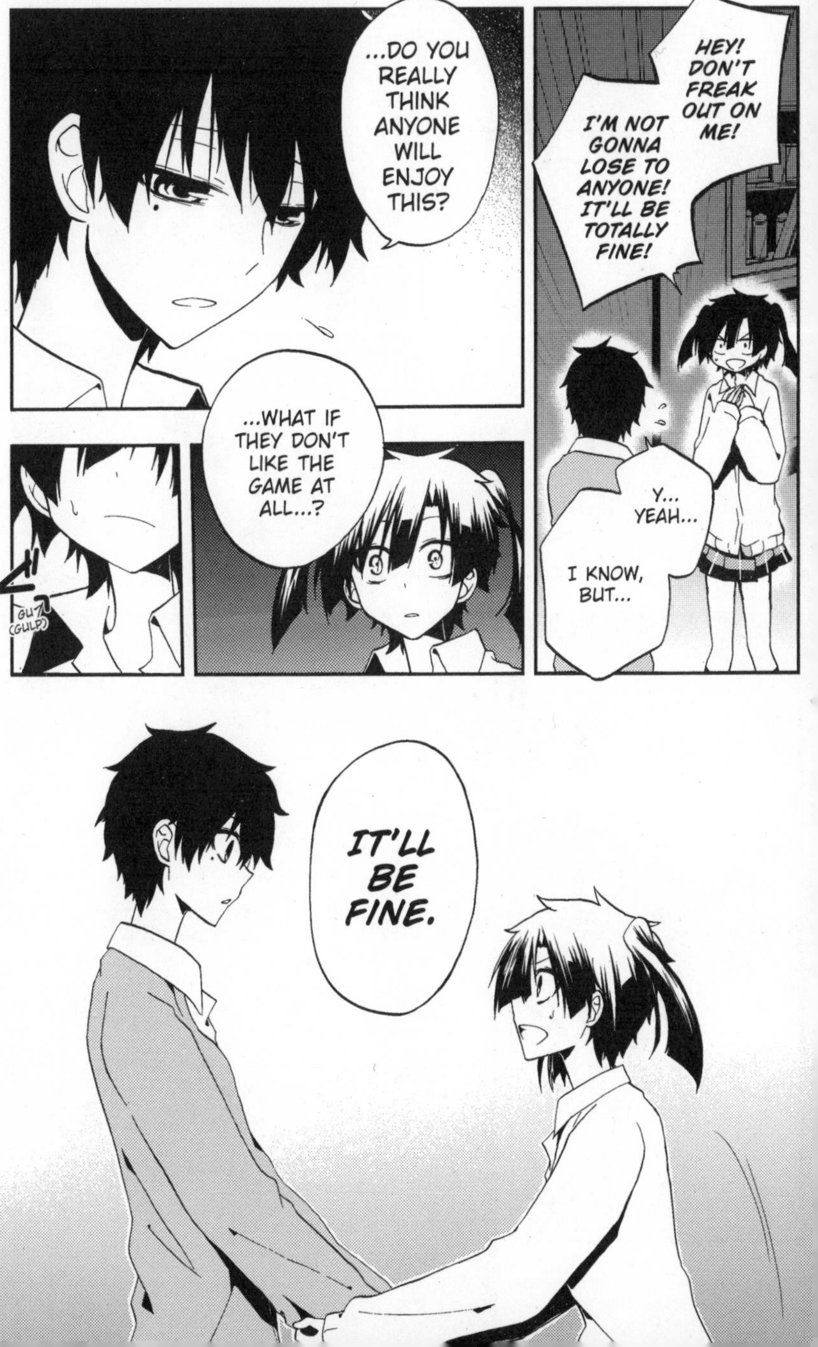
HEY! DON'T FREAK OUT ON ME!
I'M NOT GONNA LOSE TO ANYONE! IT'LL BE TOTALLY FINE!
Y... YEAH...
I KNOW, BUT...
...DO YOU REALLY THINK ANYONE WILL ENJOY THIS?
...WHAT IF THEY DON'T LIKE THE GAME AT ALL...?
(GULP)
IT'LL BE FINE.

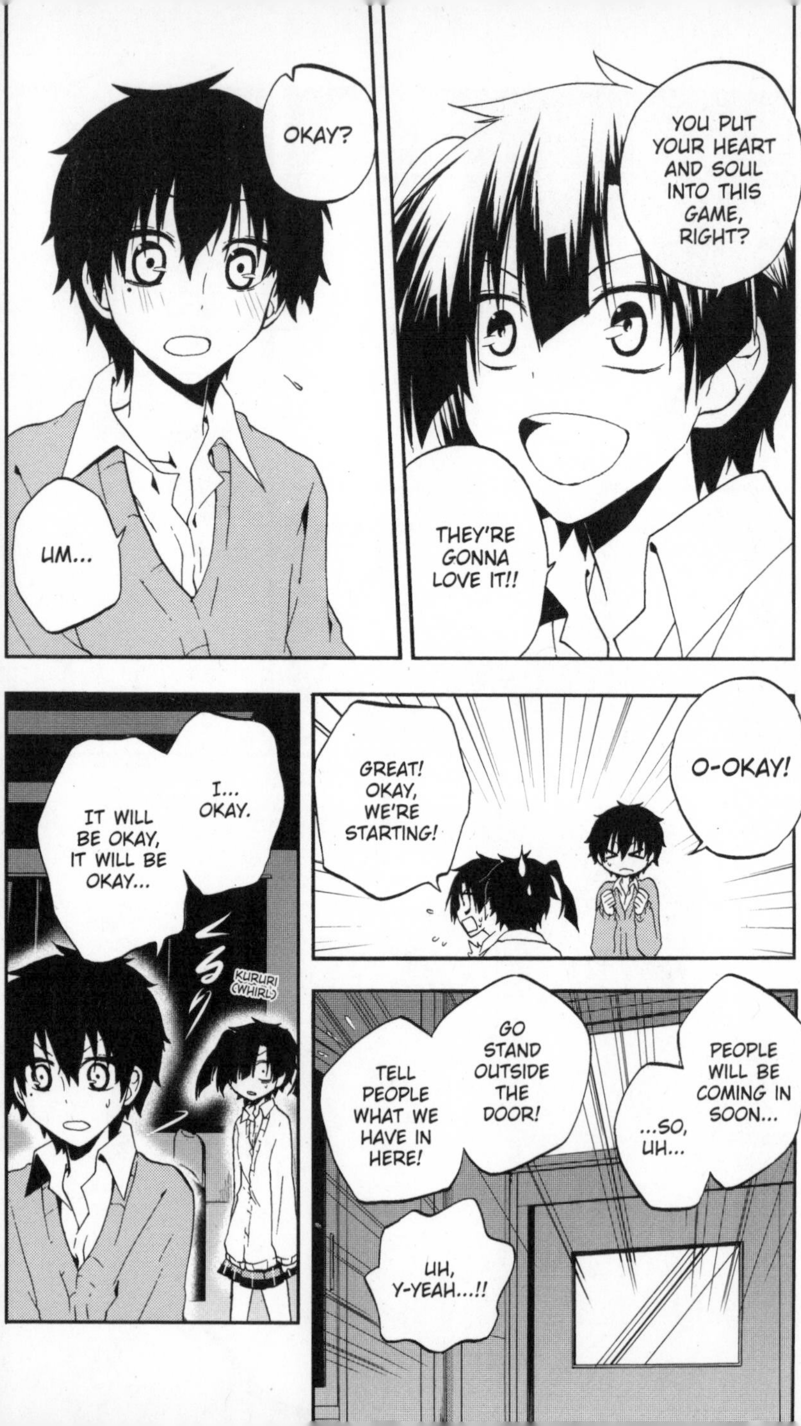
YOU PUT YOUR HEART AND SOUL INTO THIS GAME, RIGHT?
THEY'RE GONNA LOVE IT!!
OKAY?
UM...
O-OKAY!
GREAT! OKAY, WE'RE STARTING!
PEOPLE WILL BE COMING IN SOON...
...SO, UH...
GO STAND OUTSIDE THE DOOR!
TELL PEOPLE WHAT WE HAVE IN HERE!
UH, Y-YEAH...!!
I... OKAY.
IT WILL BE OKAY, IT WILL BE OKAY...
KURURI (WHIRL)

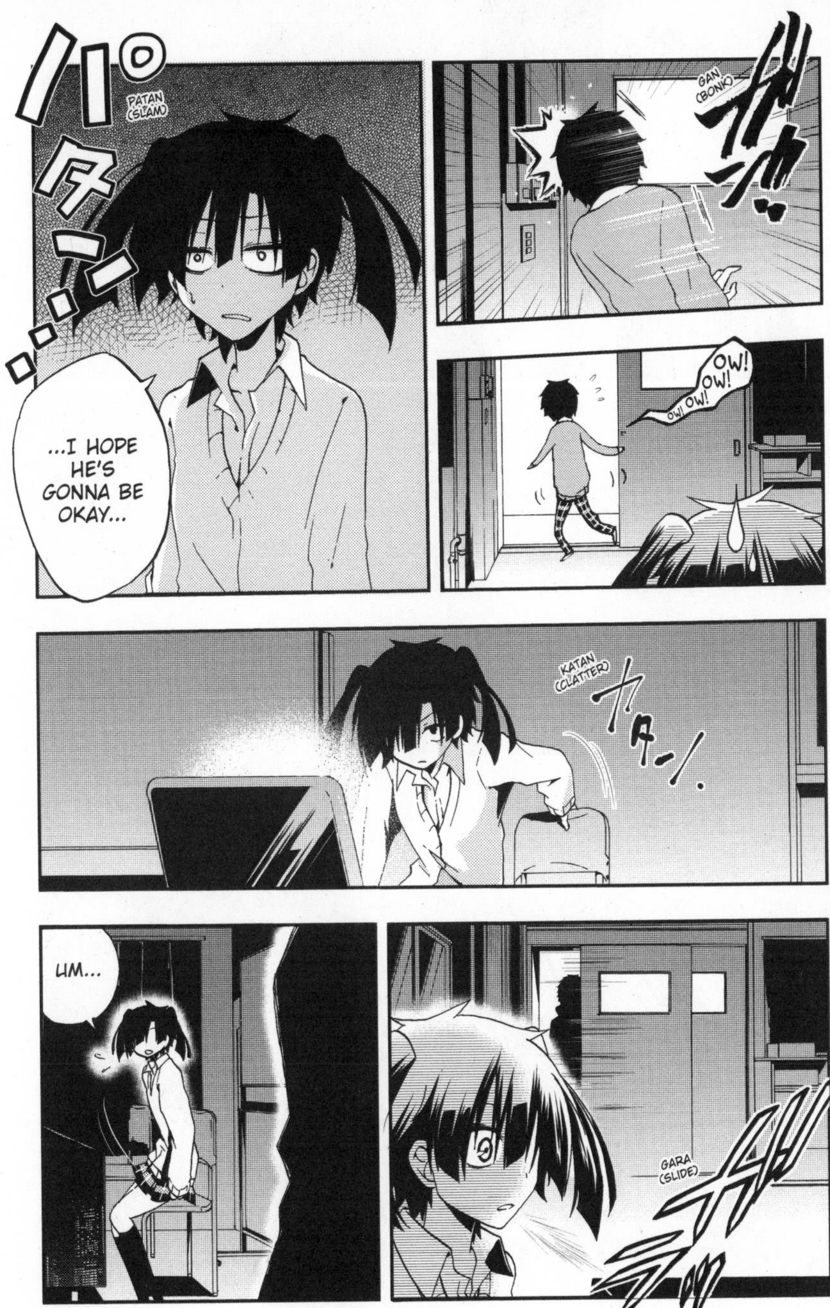
GAN (BONK)
OW! OW! OW! OW!
PATAN (SLAM)
...I HOPE HE'S GONNA BE OKAY...
KATAN (CLATTER)
GARA (SLIDE)
UM...

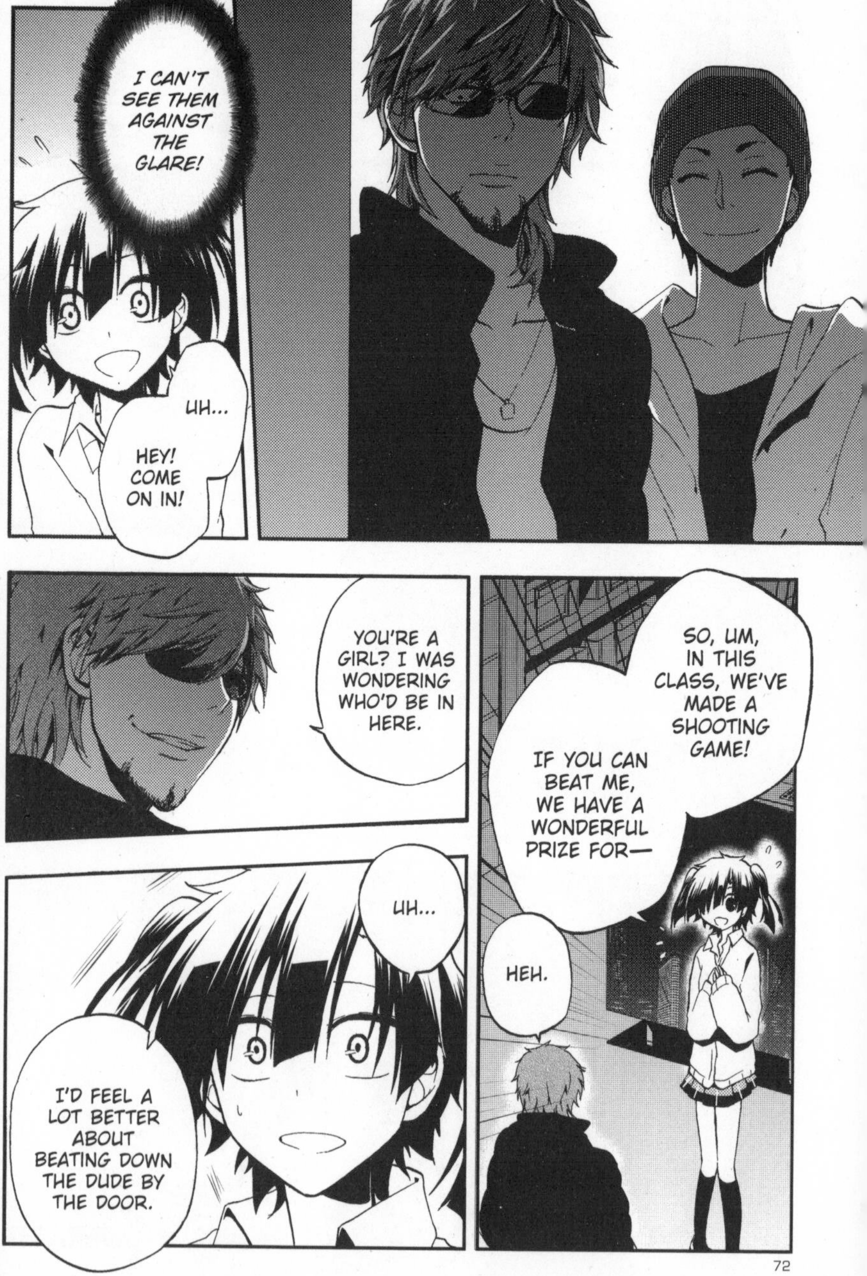
I CAN'T SEE THEM AGAINST THE GLARE!
UH...
HEY! COME ON IN!
SO, UM, IN THIS CLASS, WE'VE MADE A SHOOTING GAME!
IF YOU CAN BEAT ME, WE HAVE A WONDERFUL PRIZE FOR—
HEH.
YOU'RE A GIRL? I WAS WONDERING WHO'D BE IN HERE.
UH...
I'D FEEL A LOT BETTER ABOUT BEATING DOWN THE DUDE BY THE DOOR.

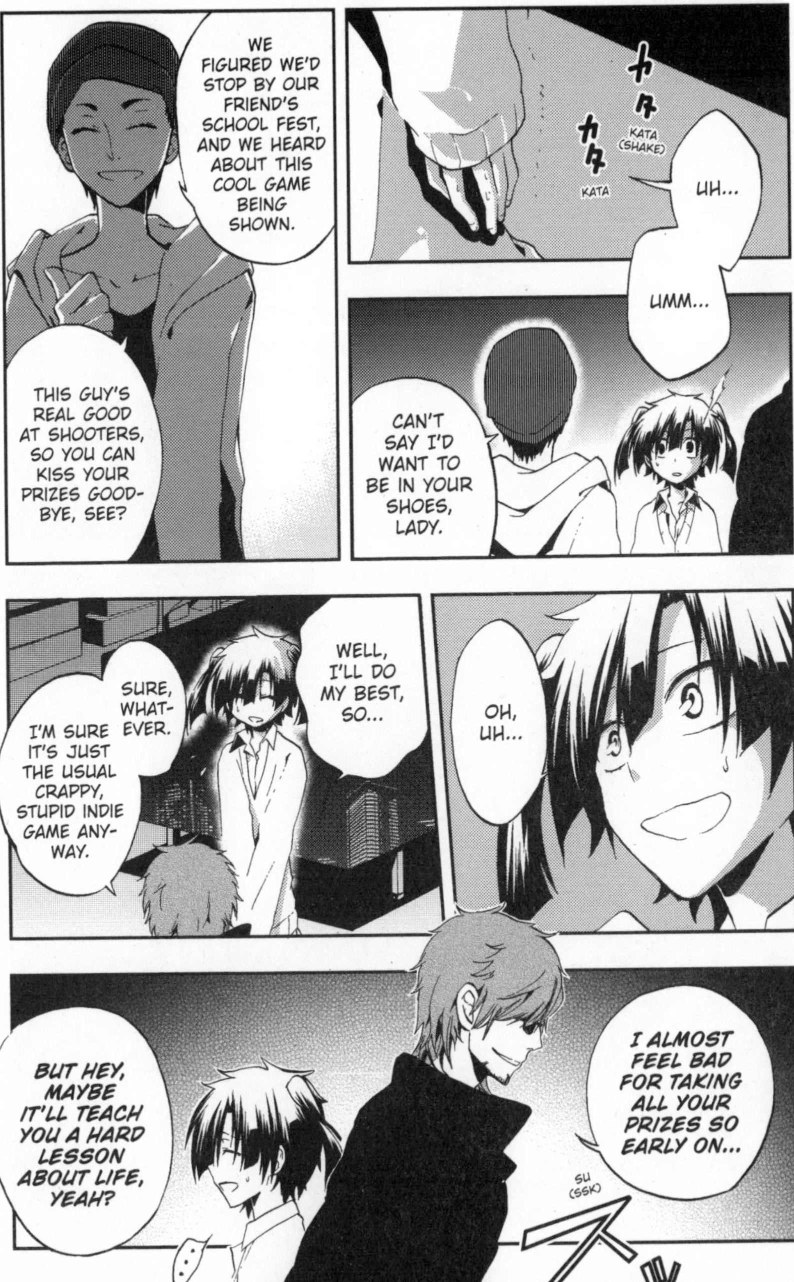
KATA (SHAKE)
KATA
UH...
UMM...
CAN'T SAY I'D WANT TO BE IN YOUR SHOES, LADY.
WE FIGURED WE'D STOP BY OUR FRIEND'S SCHOOL FEST, AND WE HEARD ABOUT THIS COOL GAME BEING SHOWN.
THIS GUY'S REAL GOOD AT SHOOTERS, SO YOU CAN KISS YOUR PRIZES GOOD-BYE, SEE?
OH, UH...
WELL, I'LL DO MY BEST, SO...
SURE, WHAT-EVER.
I'M SURE IT'S JUST THE USUAL CRAPPY, STUPID INDIE GAME ANY-WAY.
I ALMOST FEEL BAD FOR TAKING ALL YOUR PRIZES SO EARLY ON...
SU (SSK)
BUT HEY, MAYBE IT'LL TEACH YOU A HARD LESSON ABOUT LIFE, YEAH?
...

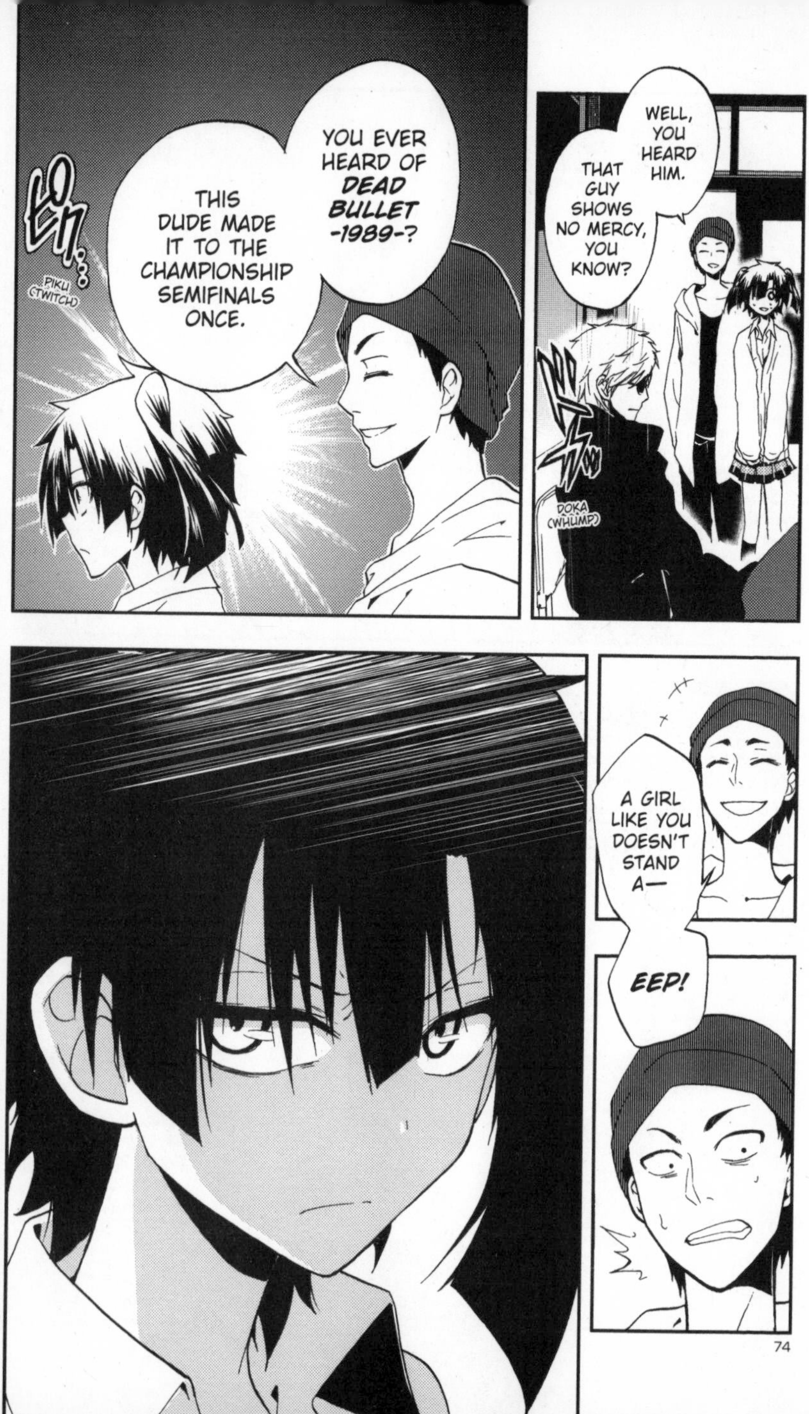
WELL, YOU HEARD HIM.
THAT GUY SHOWS NO MERCY, YOU KNOW?
DOKA (WHUMP)
YOU EVER HEARD OF ***DEAD BULLET -1989-***?
THIS DUDE MADE IT TO THE CHAMPIONSHIP SEMIFINALS ONCE.
PIKU (TWITCH)
A GIRL LIKE YOU DOESN'T STAND A—
EEP!

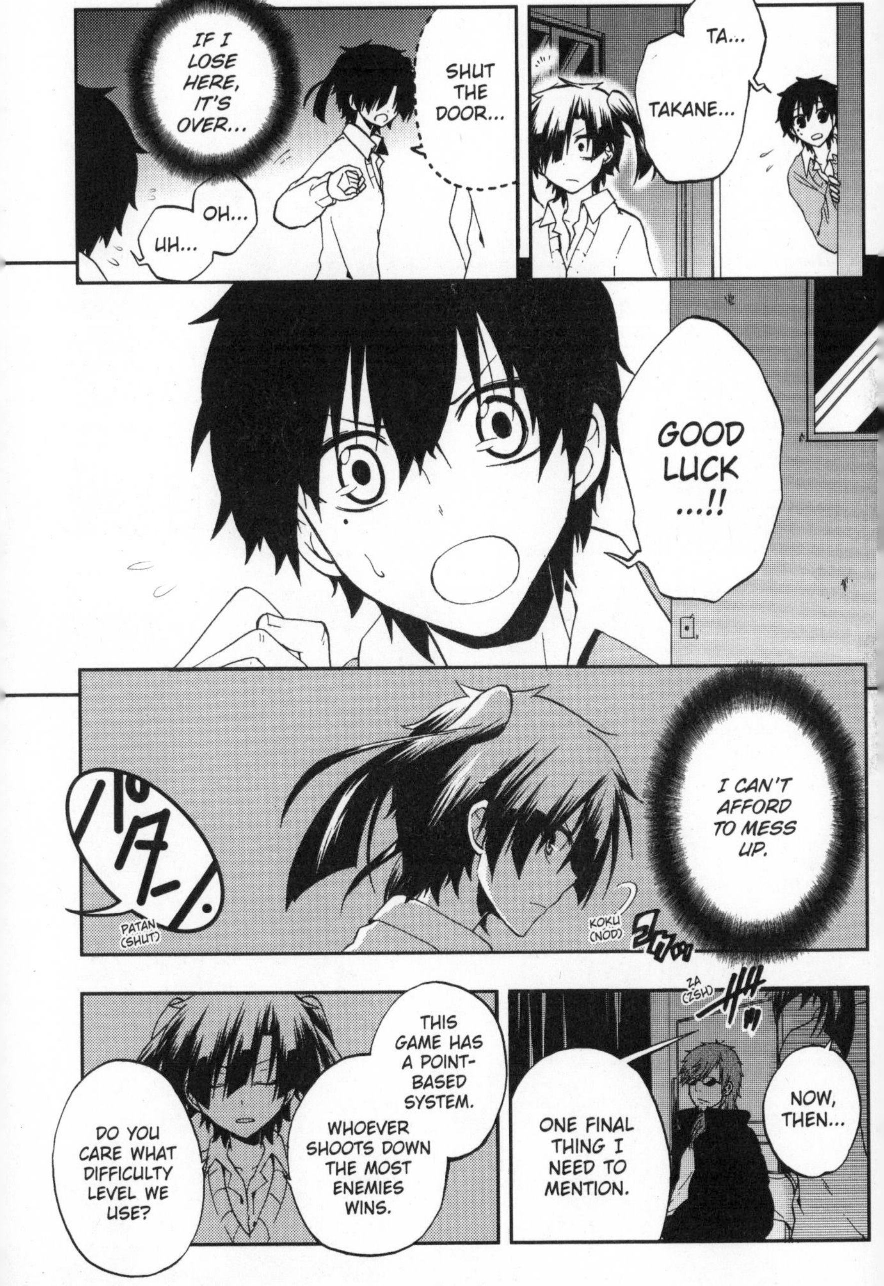

TA...
TAKANE...
SHUT THE DOOR...
IF I LOSE HERE, IT'S OVER...
OH...
UH...
GOOD LUCK ...!!
I CAN'T AFFORD TO MESS UP.
KOKU (NOD)
PATAN (SHUT)
ZA (ZSH)
NOW, THEN...
ONE FINAL THING I NEED TO MENTION.
THIS GAME HAS A POINT-BASED SYSTEM.
WHOEVER SHOOTS DOWN THE MOST ENEMIES WINS.
DO YOU CARE WHAT DIFFICULTY LEVEL WE USE?

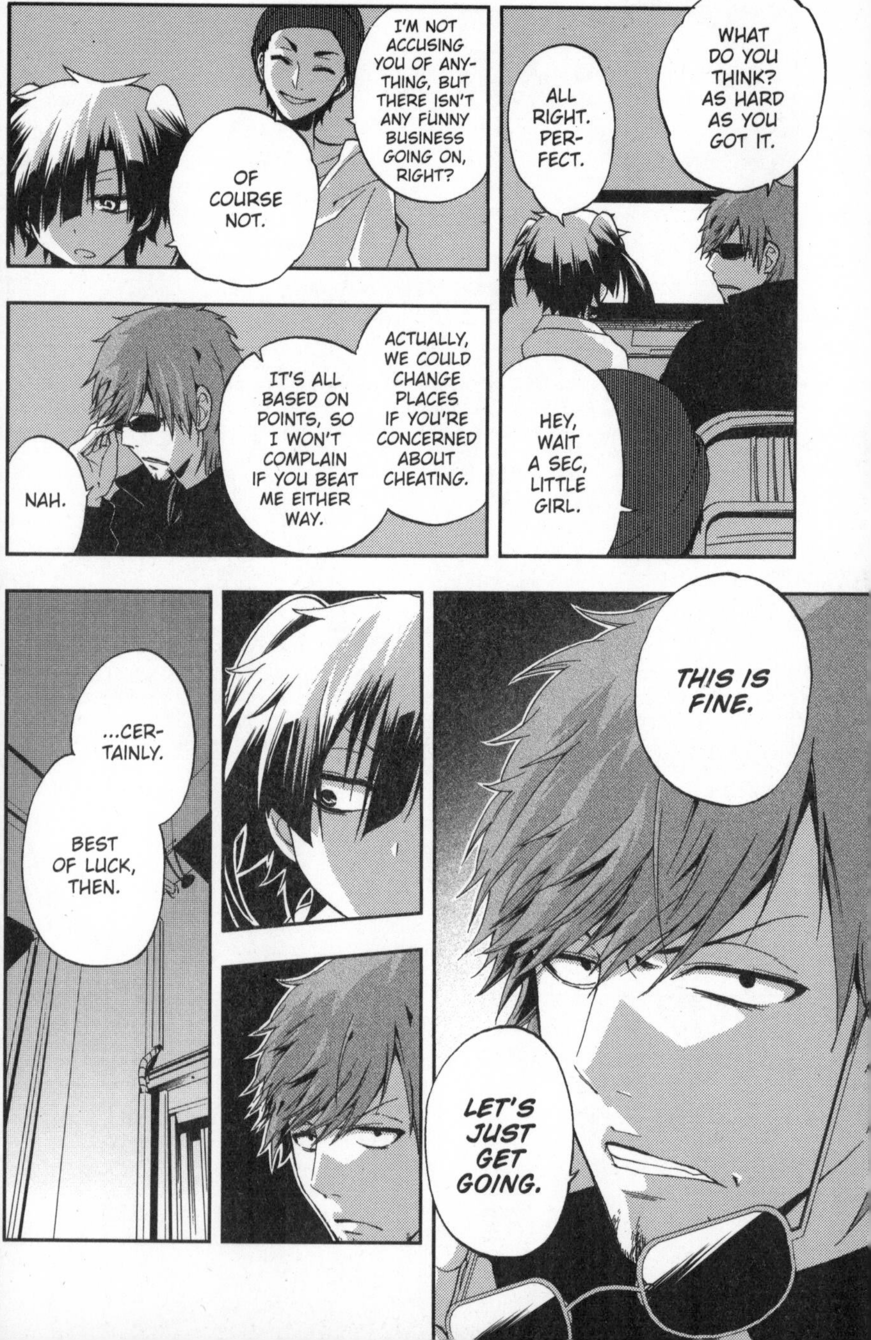
WHAT DO YOU THINK? AS HARD AS YOU GOT IT.
ALL RIGHT. PERFECT.
HEY, WAIT A SEC, LITTLE GIRL.
I'M NOT ACCUSING YOU OF ANYTHING, BUT THERE ISN'T ANY FUNNY BUSINESS GOING ON, RIGHT?
OF COURSE NOT.
ACTUALLY, WE COULD CHANGE PLACES IF YOU'RE CONCERNED ABOUT CHEATING.
IT'S ALL BASED ON POINTS, SO I WON'T COMPLAIN IF YOU BEAT ME EITHER WAY.
NAH.
THIS IS FINE.
LET'S JUST GET GOING.
...CERTAINLY.
BEST OF LUCK, THEN.

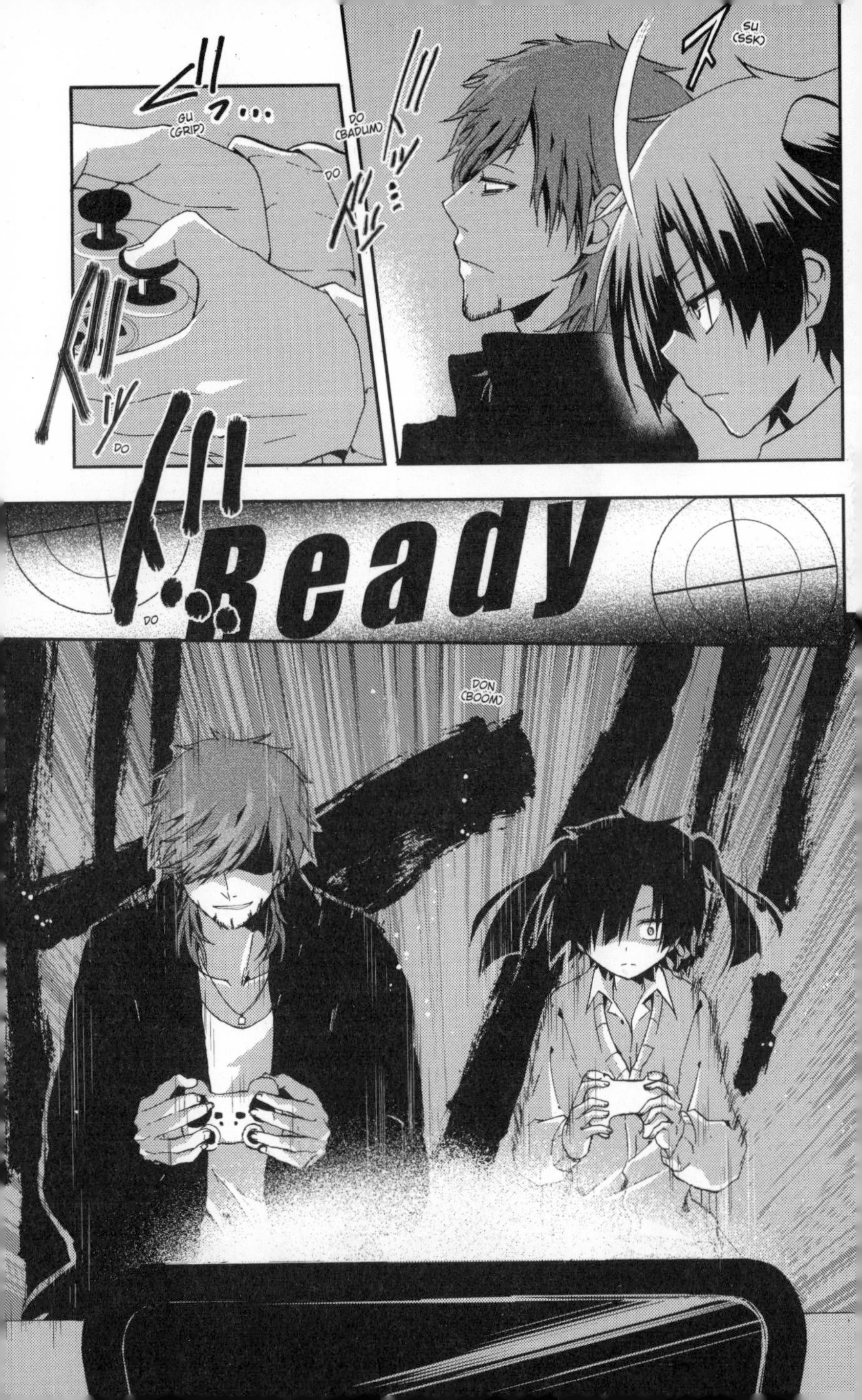
SU (SSK)
DO (BADUM)
DO
GU (GRIP)
DO
Ready
DO
DON (BOOM)

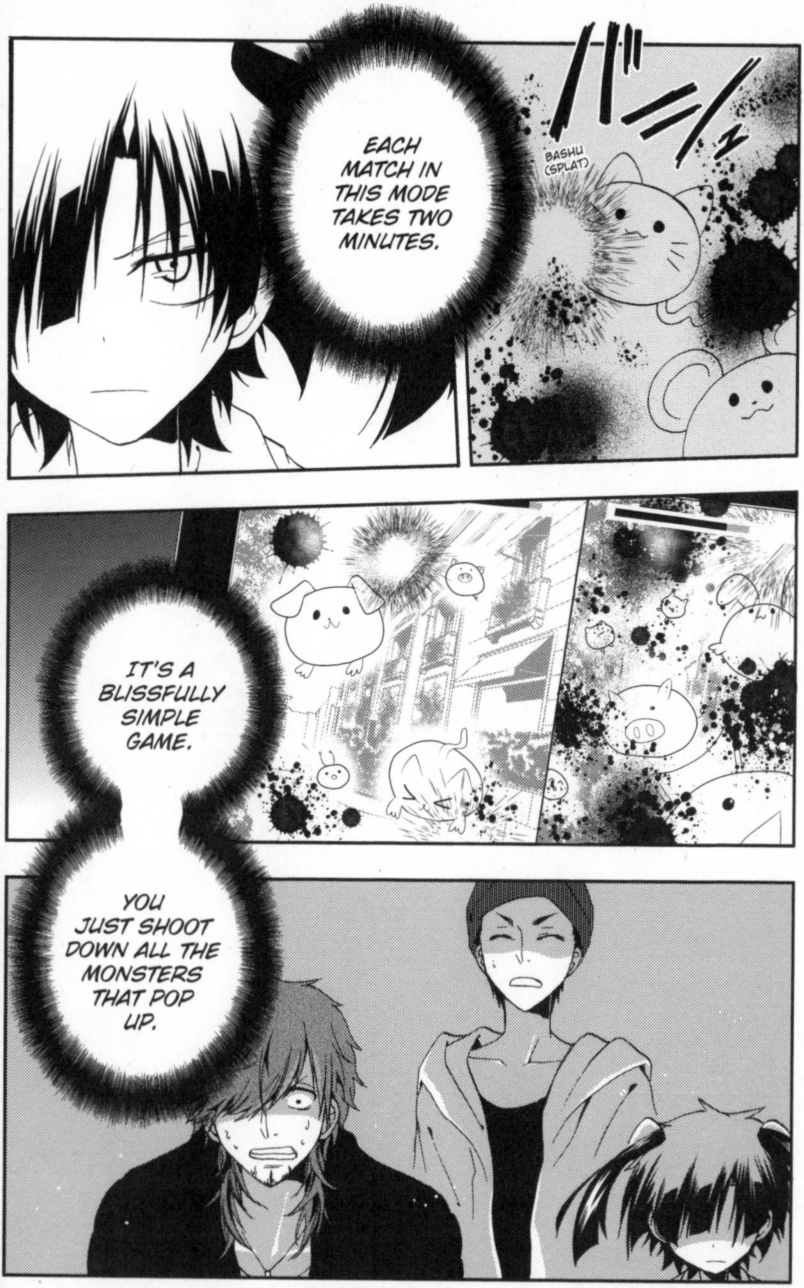
BASHU (SPLAT)
EACH MATCH IN THIS MODE TAKES TWO MINUTES.
IT'S A BLISSFULLY SIMPLE GAME.
YOU JUST SHOOT DOWN ALL THE MONSTERS THAT POP UP.

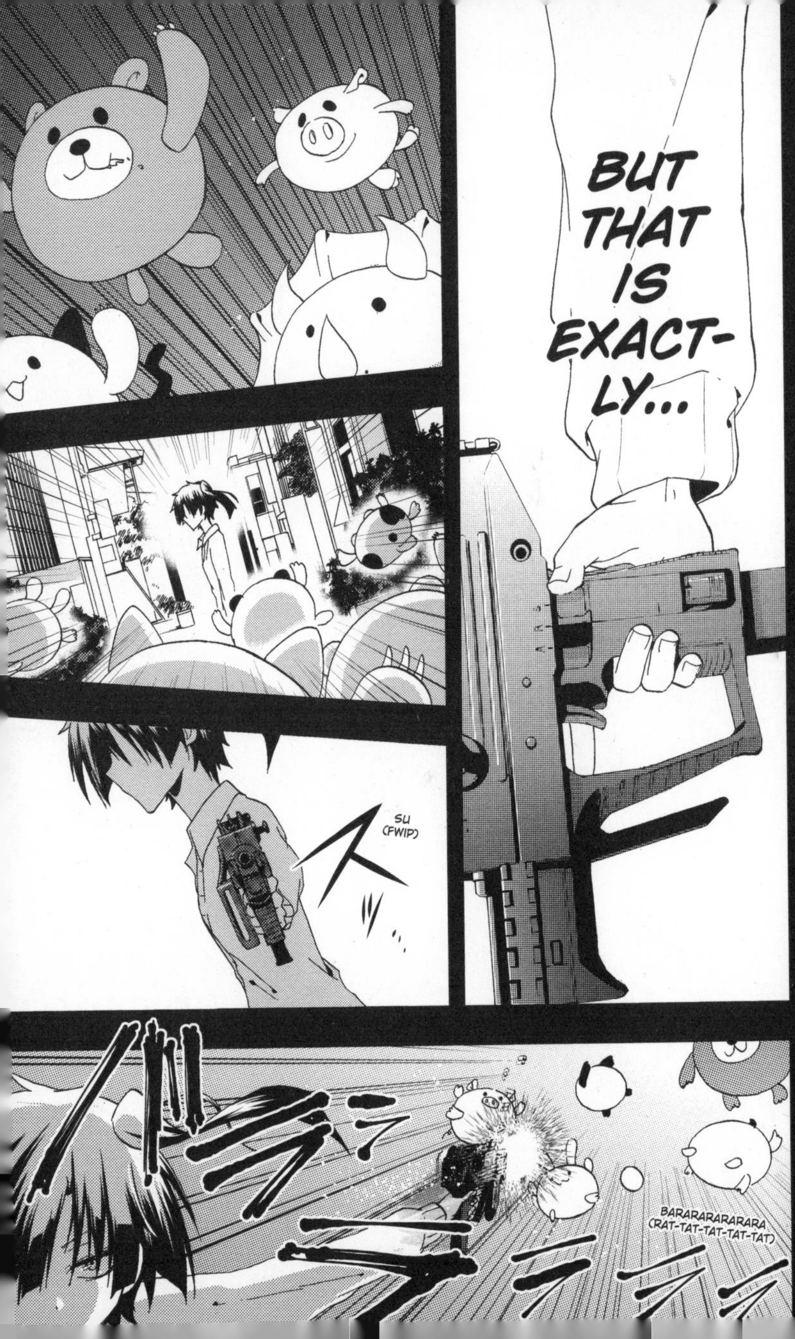
BUT THAT IS EXACT-LY...
SU (FWIP)
BARARARARARARA (RAT-TAT-TAT-TAT-TAT)

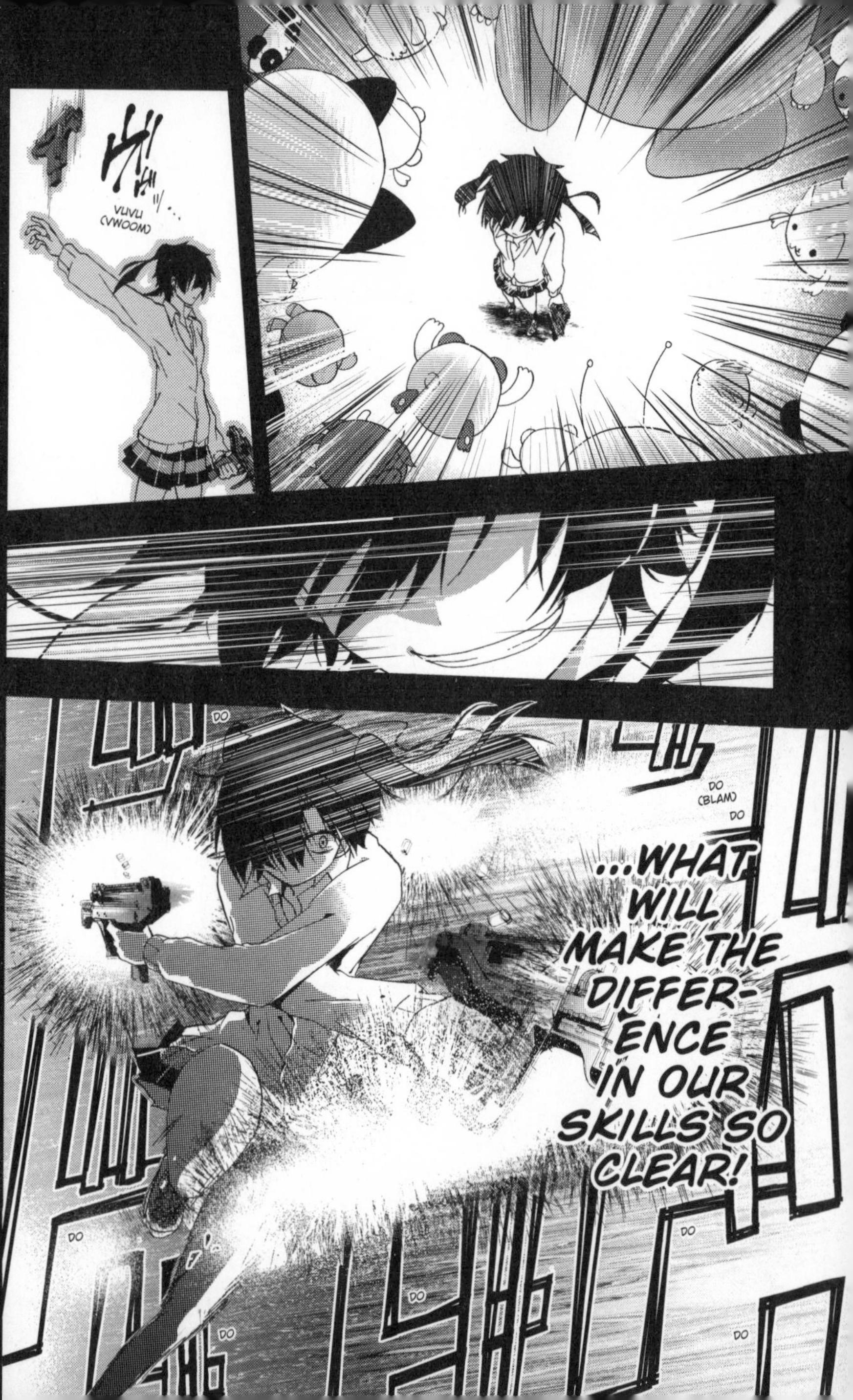
VUVU (VWOOM)
DO (BLAM) DO
...WHAT WILL MAKE THE DIFFER-ENCE IN OUR SKILLS SO CLEAR!
DO
DO
DO
DO
DO

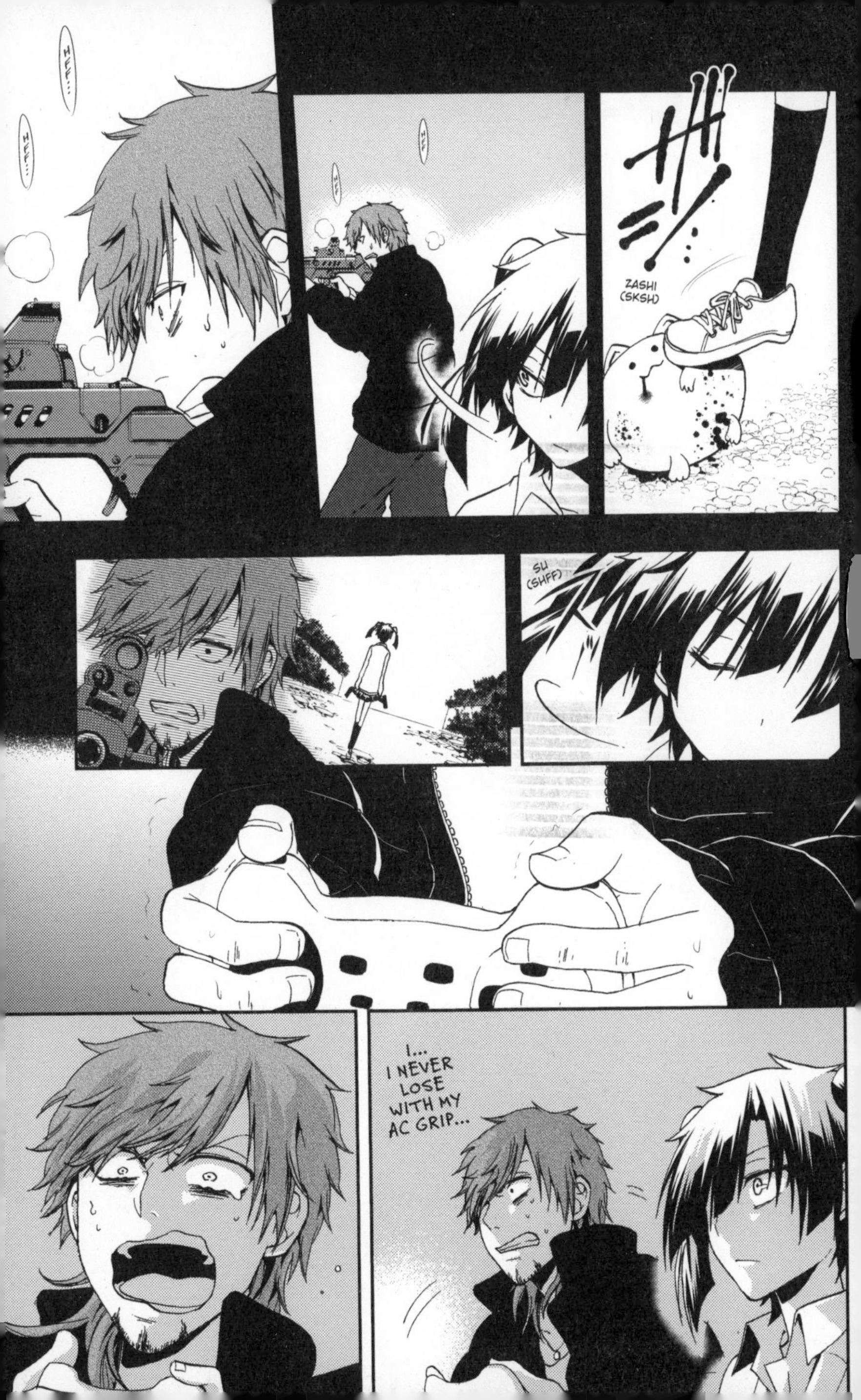
ZASHI
(SKSH)
HEF
HEF
HEF...
HEF...
SU
(SHFF)
I...
I NEVER
LOSE
WITH MY
AC GRIP...

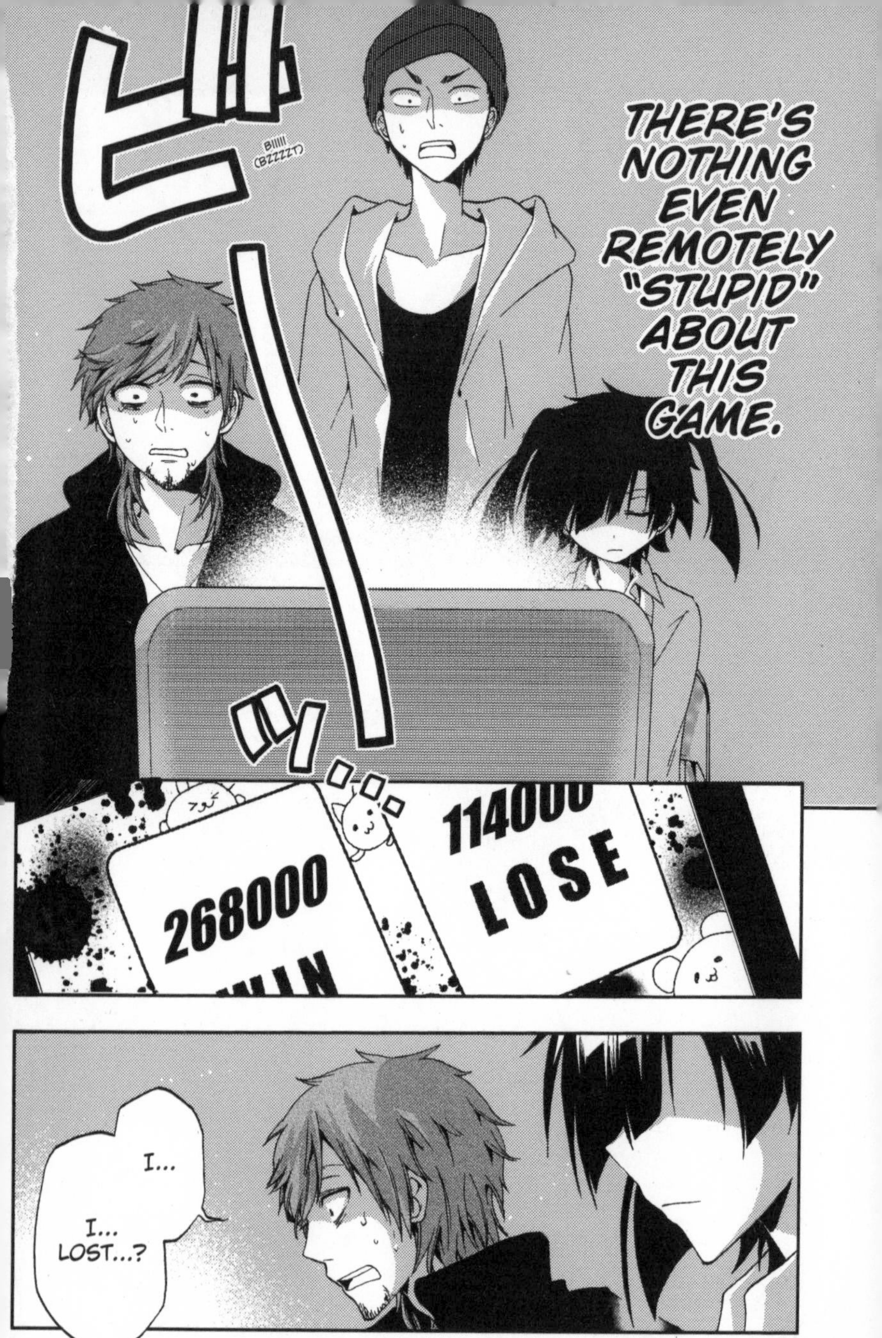
THERE'S NOTHING EVEN REMOTELY "STUPID" ABOUT THIS GAME.
BIIIII (BZZZZT)
114000
LOSE
268000
I...
I... LOST...?

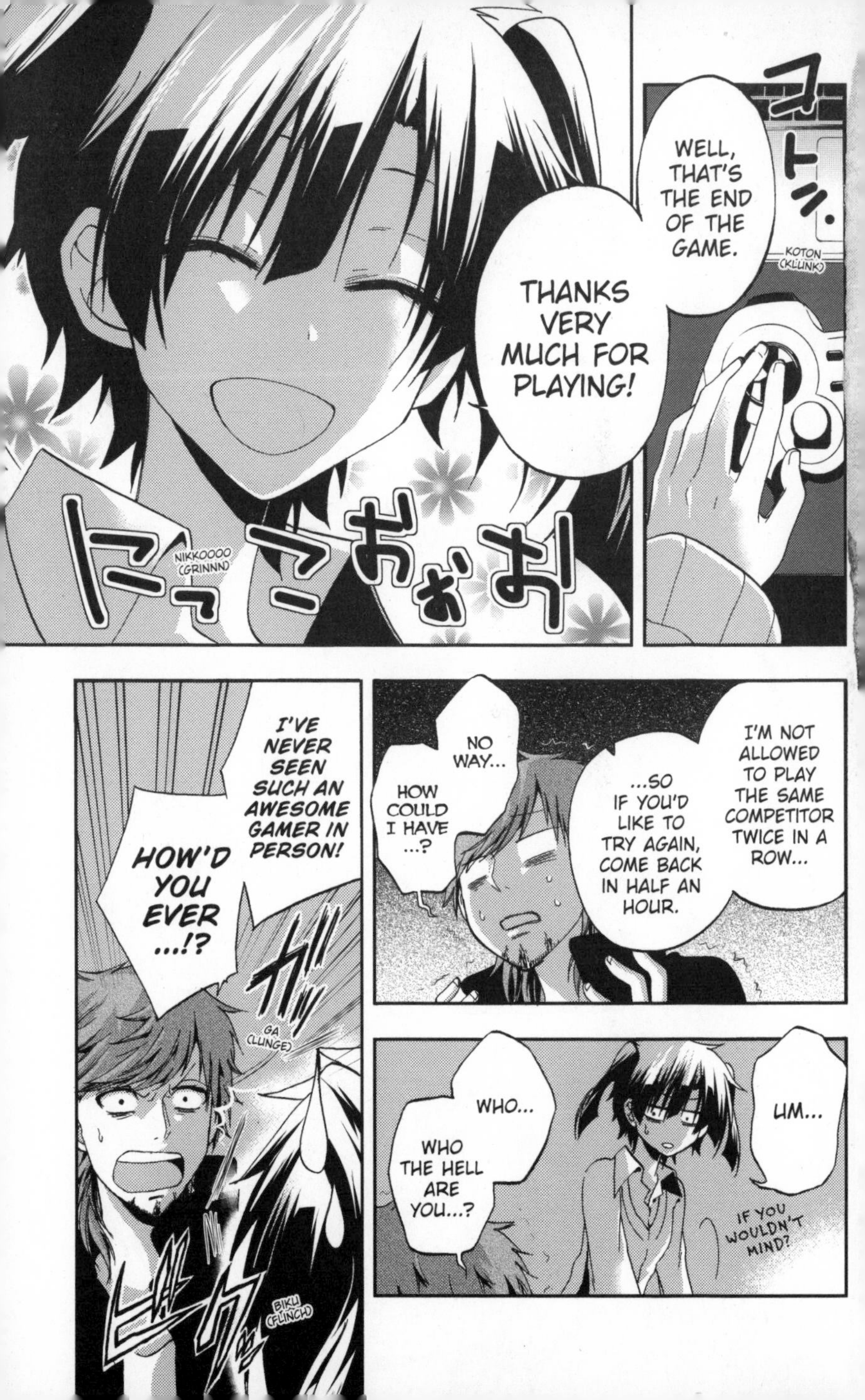
WELL, THAT'S THE END OF THE GAME.
KOTON (KLUNK)
THANKS VERY MUCH FOR PLAYING!
NIKKOOOO (GRINNN)
I'M NOT ALLOWED TO PLAY THE SAME COMPETITOR TWICE IN A ROW...
...SO IF YOU'D LIKE TO TRY AGAIN, COME BACK IN HALF AN HOUR.
NO WAY...
HOW COULD I HAVE ...?
UM...
IF YOU WOULDN'T MIND?
WHO...
WHO THE HELL ARE YOU...?
I'VE NEVER SEEN SUCH AN AWESOME GAMER IN PERSON!
HOW'D YOU EVER ...!?
GA (LUNGE)
BIKU (FLINCH)

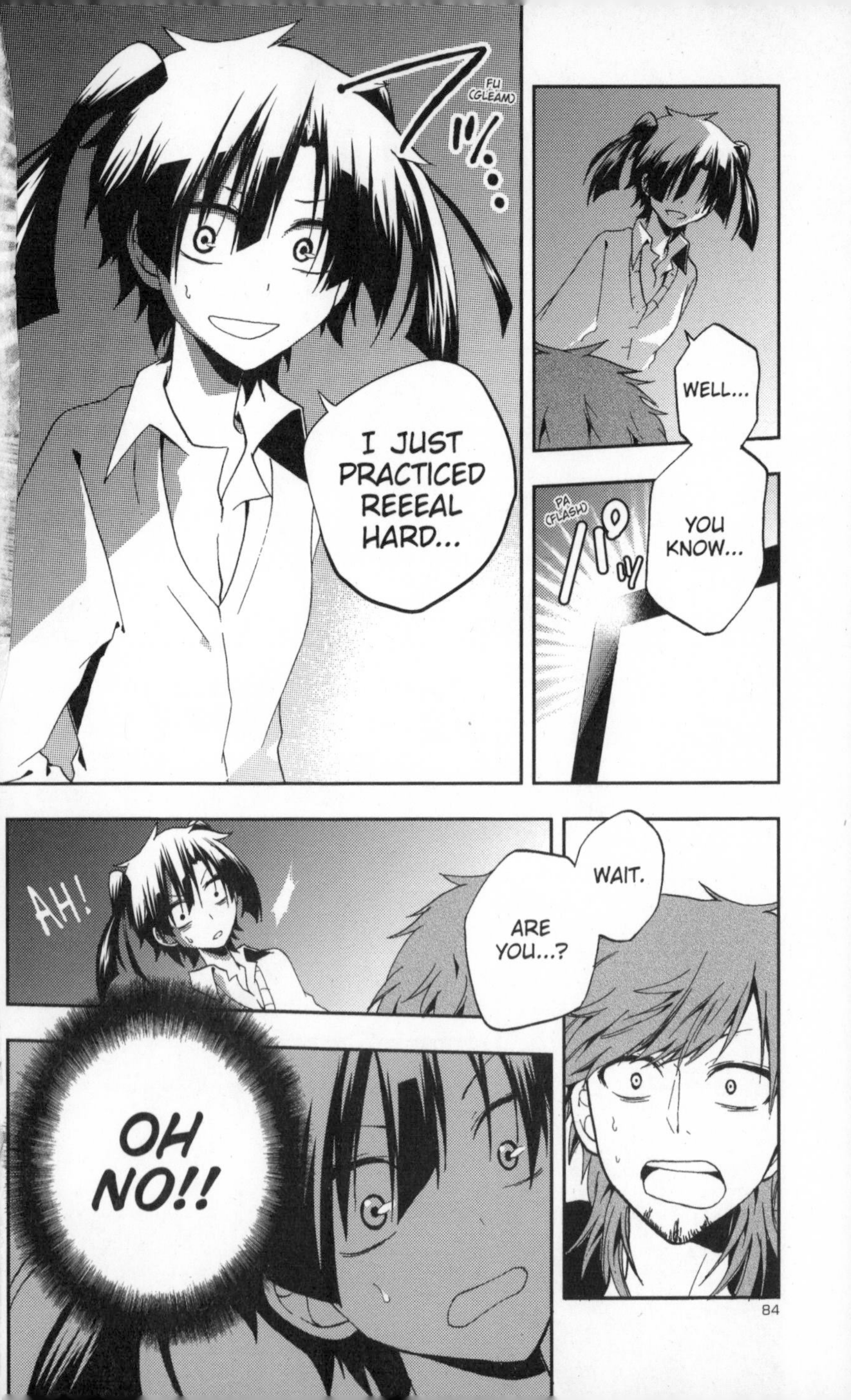
WELL...
YOU KNOW...
PA (FLASH)
FU (GLEAM)
I JUST PRACTICED REEEAL HARD...
WAIT.
ARE YOU...?
AH!
OH NO!!

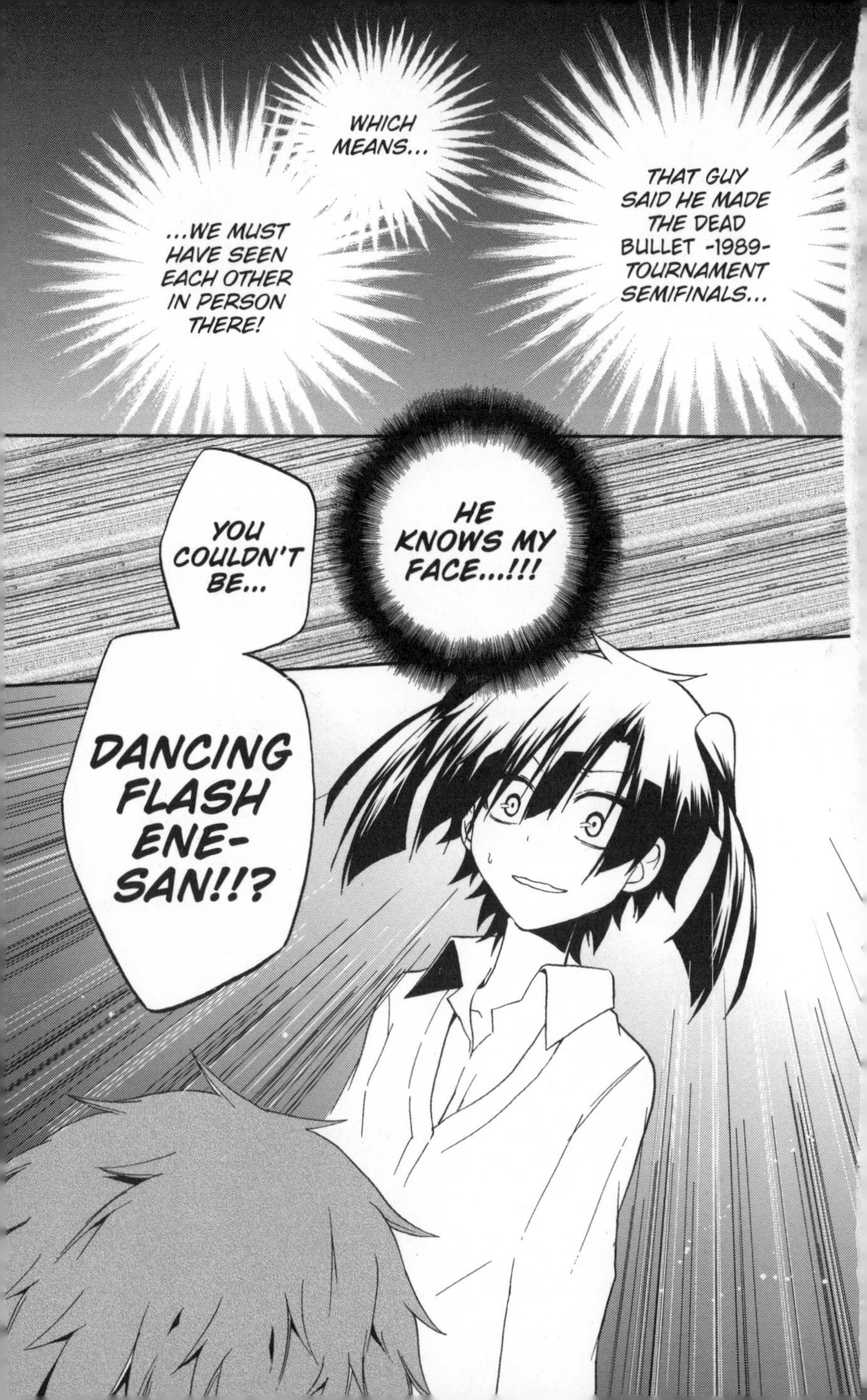
THAT GUY SAID HE MADE THE DEAD BULLET -1989- TOURNAMENT SEMIFINALS...
WHICH MEANS...
...WE MUST HAVE SEEN EACH OTHER IN PERSON THERE!
HE KNOWS MY FACE...!!!
YOU COULDN'T BE...
DANCING FLASH ENE-SAN!!?

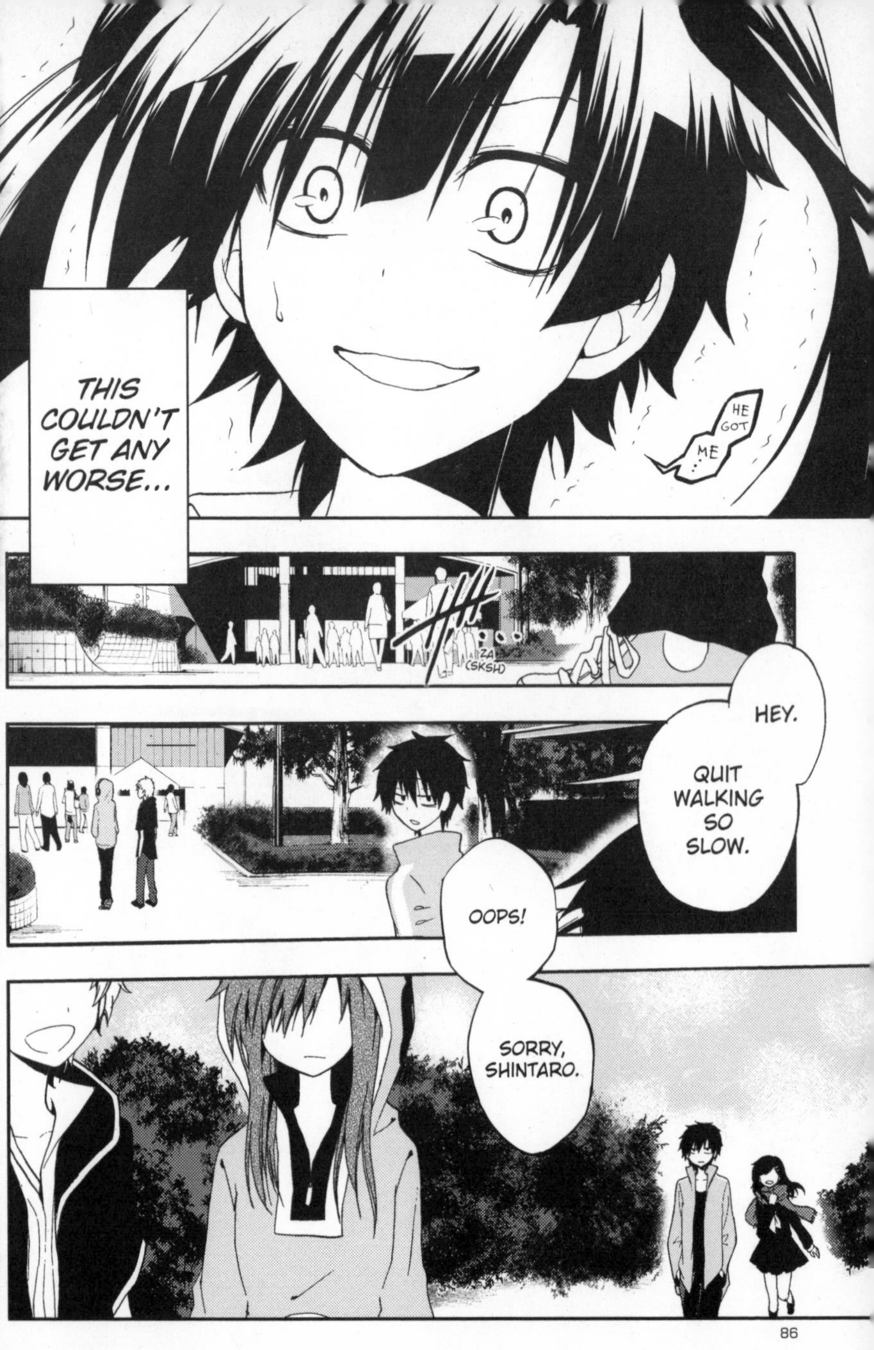
HE GOT ME...
THIS COULDN'T GET ANY WORSE...
ZA (SKSH)
HEY.
QUIT WALKING SO SLOW.
OOPS!
SORRY, SHINTARO.

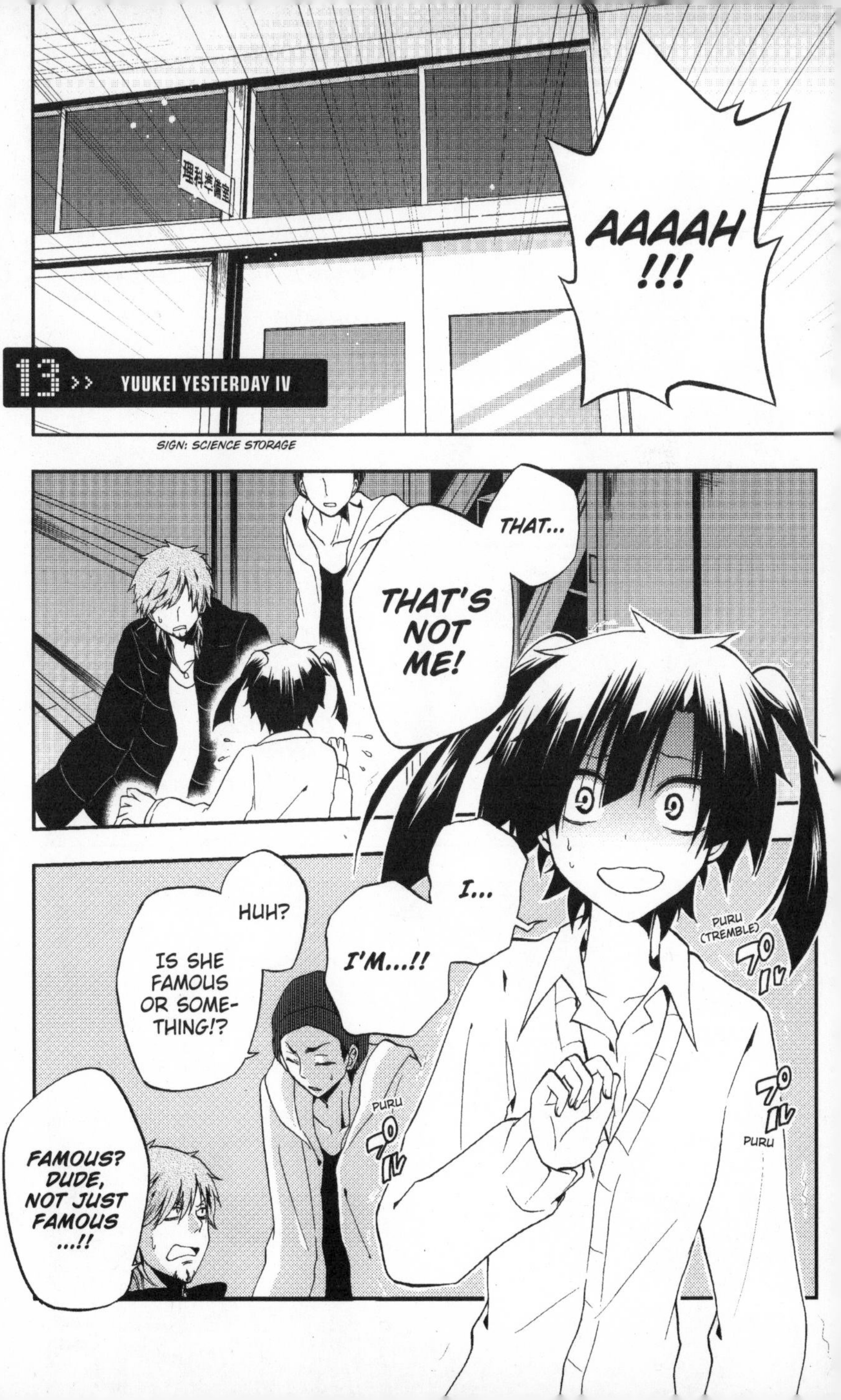
AAAAH!!!
理科準備室
13 >> YUUKEI YESTERDAY IV
SIGN: SCIENCE STORAGE
THAT...
THAT'S NOT ME!
I...
I'M...!!
PURU (TREMBLE)
プル
プル
PURU
HUH?
IS SHE FAMOUS OR SOME-THING!?
PURU
プル
FAMOUS? DUDE, NOT JUST FAMOUS...!!

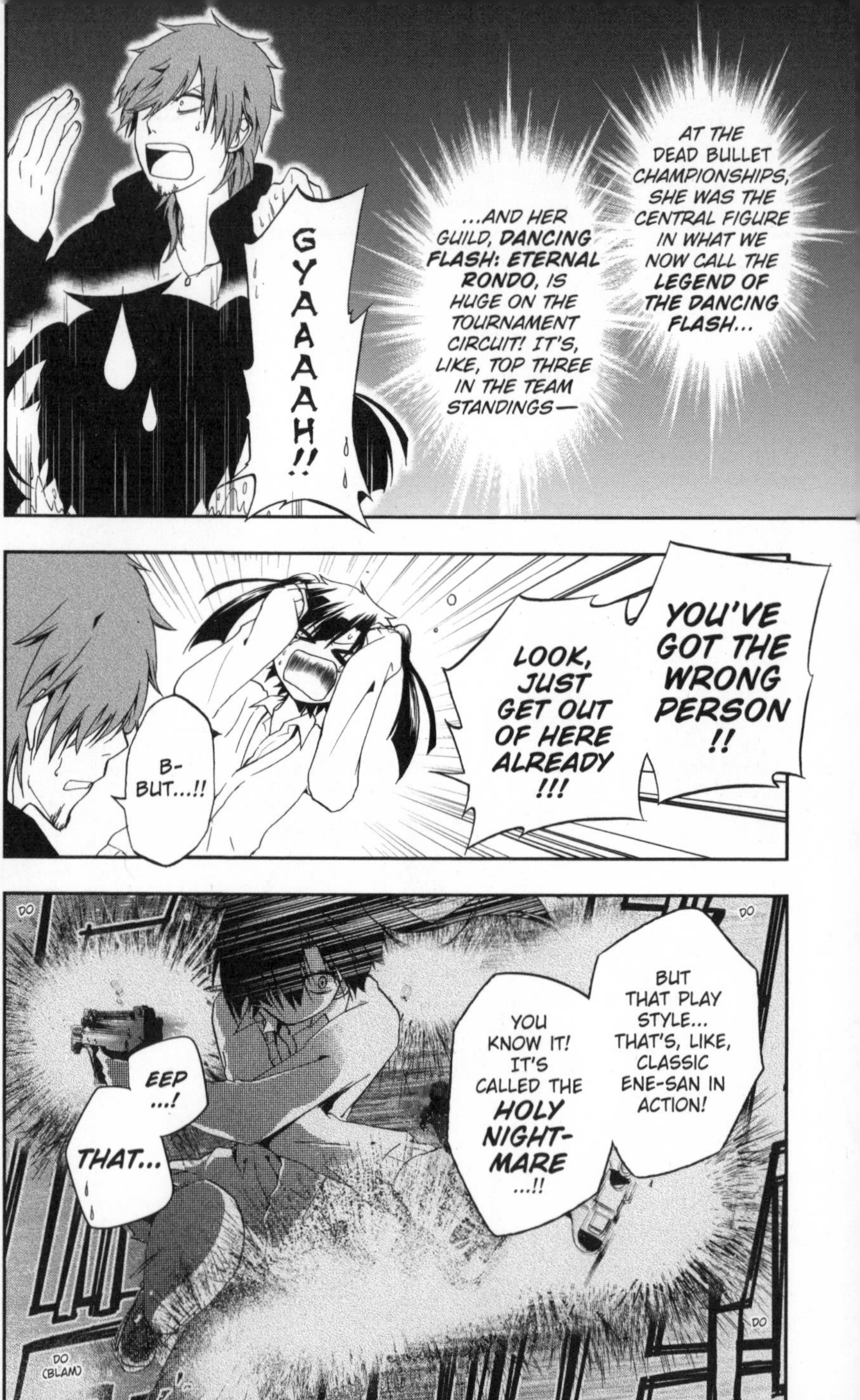
AT THE DEAD BULLET CHAMPIONSHIPS, SHE WAS THE CENTRAL FIGURE IN WHAT WE NOW CALL THE LEGEND OF THE DANCING FLASH...
...AND HER GUILD, DANCING FLASH: ETERNAL RONDO, IS HUGE ON THE TOURNAMENT CIRCUIT! IT'S, LIKE, TOP THREE IN THE TEAM STANDINGS—
GYAAAAAH!!
YOU'VE GOT THE WRONG PERSON!!
LOOK, JUST GET OUT OF HERE ALREADY!!!
B-BUT...!!
DO
BUT THAT PLAY STYLE... THAT'S, LIKE, CLASSIC ENE-SAN IN ACTION!
YOU KNOW IT! IT'S CALLED THE HOLY NIGHTMARE...!!
DO
EEP...!
THAT...
DO
DO (BLAM)

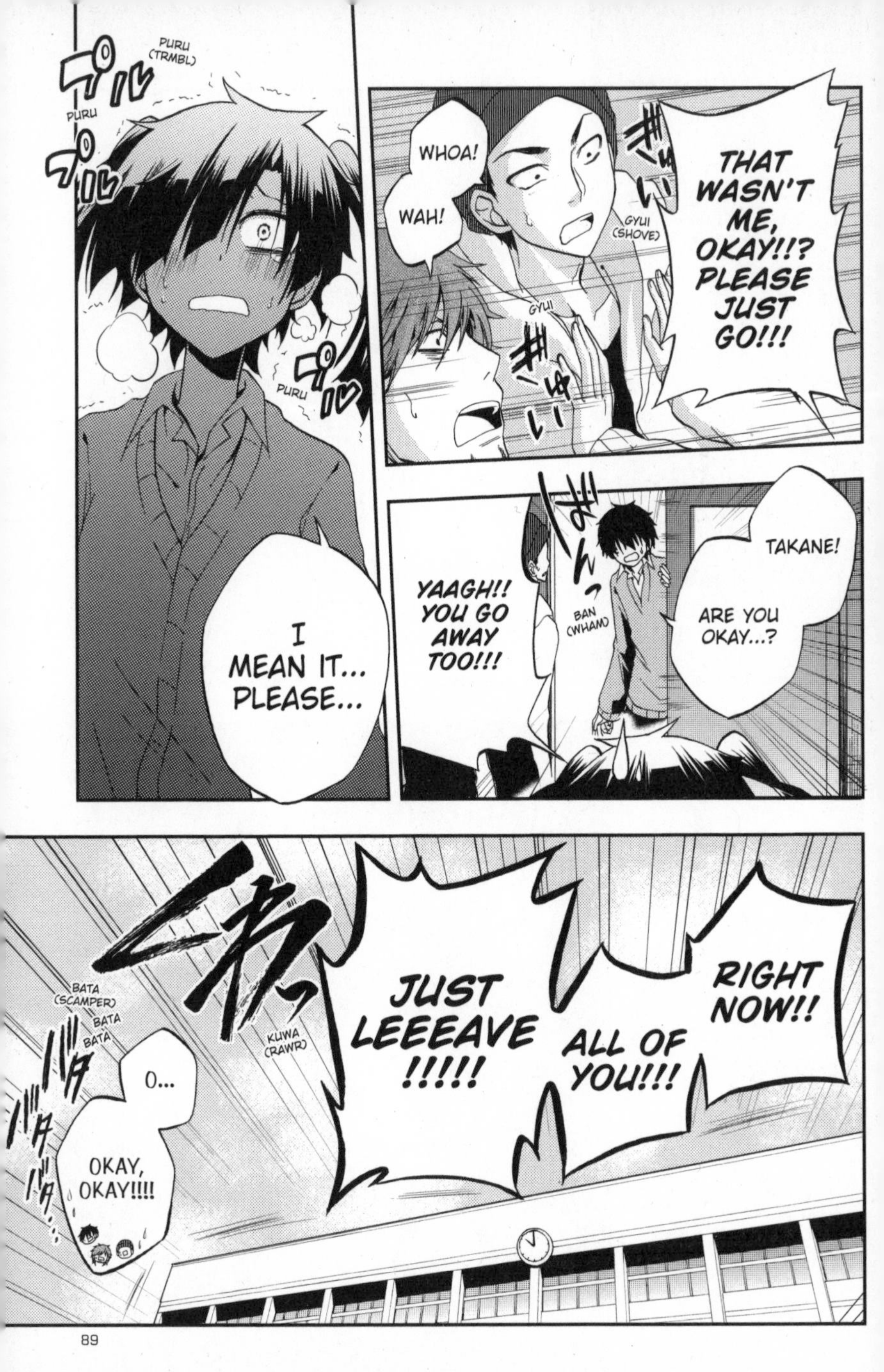
THAT WASN'T ME, OKAY!!? PLEASE JUST GO!!!
GYUI (SHOVE)
WHOA!
WAH!
GYUI
TAKANE!
ARE YOU OKAY...?
BAN (WHAM)
YAAGH!! YOU GO AWAY TOO!!!
PURU (TRMBL)
PURU
PURU
I MEAN IT... PLEASE...
RIGHT NOW!!
ALL OF YOU!!!
JUST LEEEAVE !!!!!
KUWA (RAWR)
BATA (SCAMPER) BATA BATA
O...
OKAY, OKAY!!!!

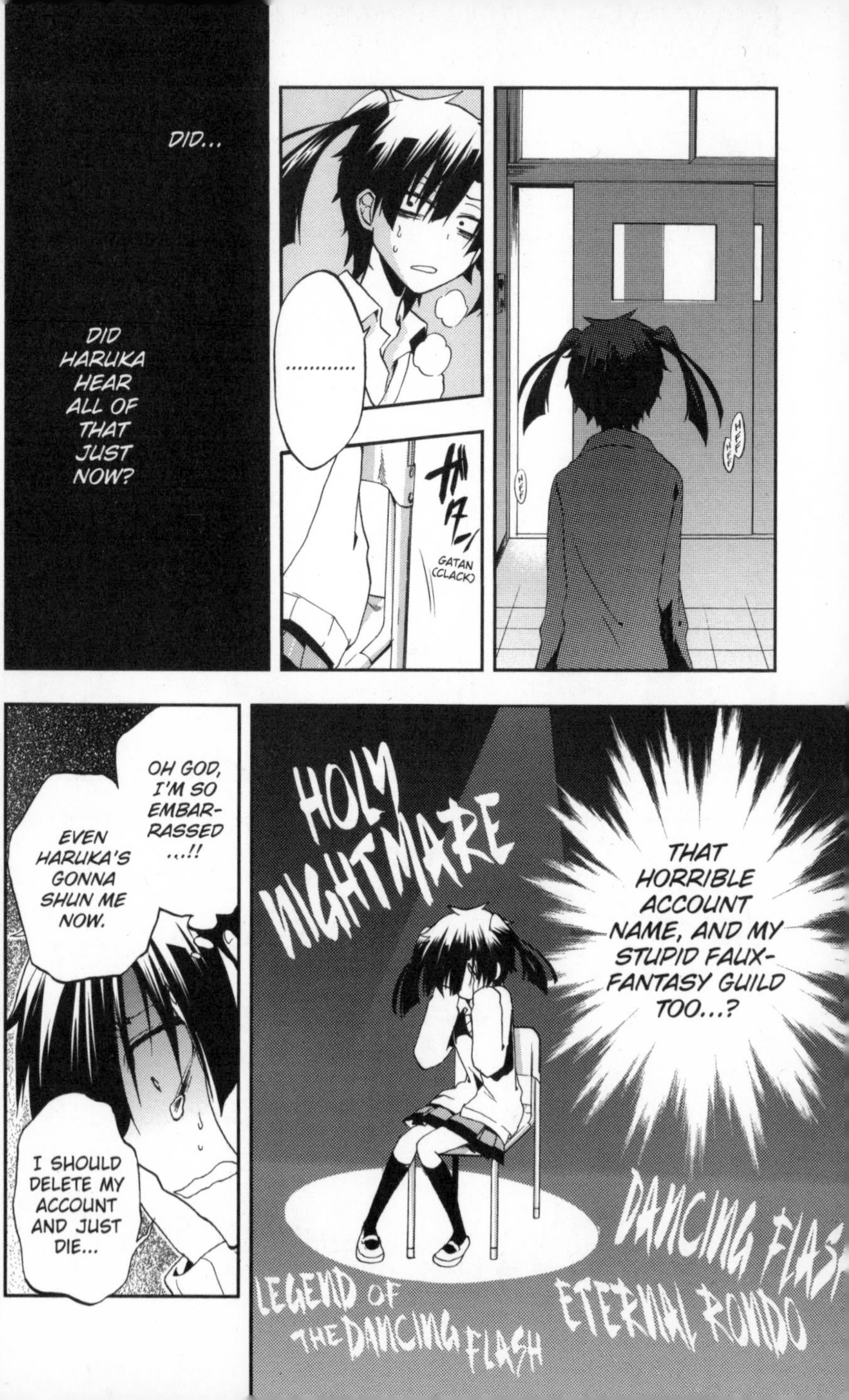
HFF HFF
HFF
....
GATAN (CLACK)
DID...
DID HARUKA HEAR ALL OF THAT JUST NOW?
THAT HORRIBLE ACCOUNT NAME, AND MY STUPID FAUX-FANTASY GUILD TOO...?
HOLY NIGHTMARE
DANCING FLASH ETERNAL RONDO
LEGEND OF THE DANCING FLASH
OH GOD, I'M SO EMBAR-RASSED ...!!
EVEN HARUKA'S GONNA SHUN ME NOW.
I SHOULD DELETE MY ACCOUNT AND JUST DIE...

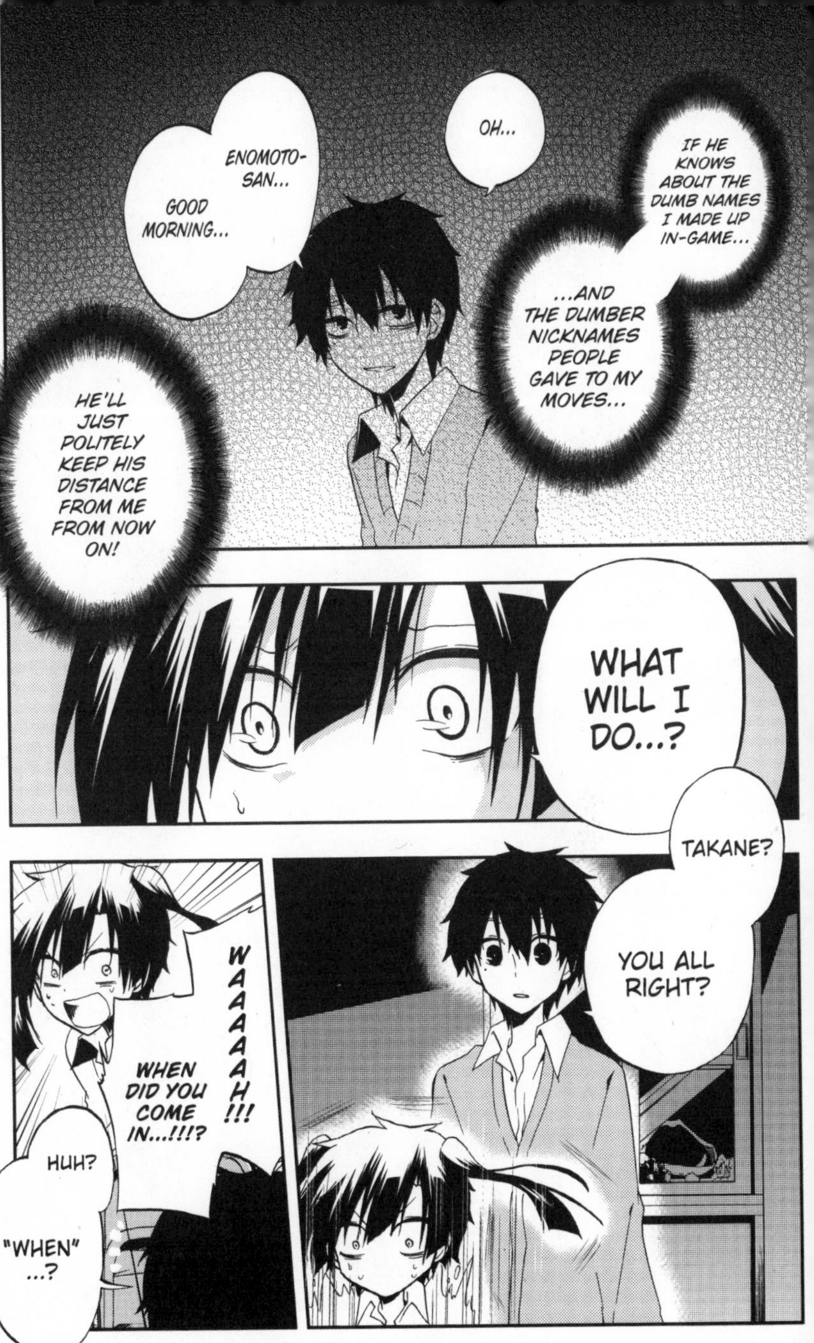
ENOMOTO-SAN... GOOD MORNING...
OH...
IF HE KNOWS ABOUT THE DUMB NAMES I MADE UP IN-GAME...
...AND THE DUMBER NICKNAMES PEOPLE GAVE TO MY MOVES...
HE'LL JUST POLITELY KEEP HIS DISTANCE FROM ME FROM NOW ON!
WHAT WILL I DO...?
TAKANE?
YOU ALL RIGHT?
WAAAAAAAH!!!
WHEN DID YOU COME IN...!!!?
HUH?
"WHEN" ...?

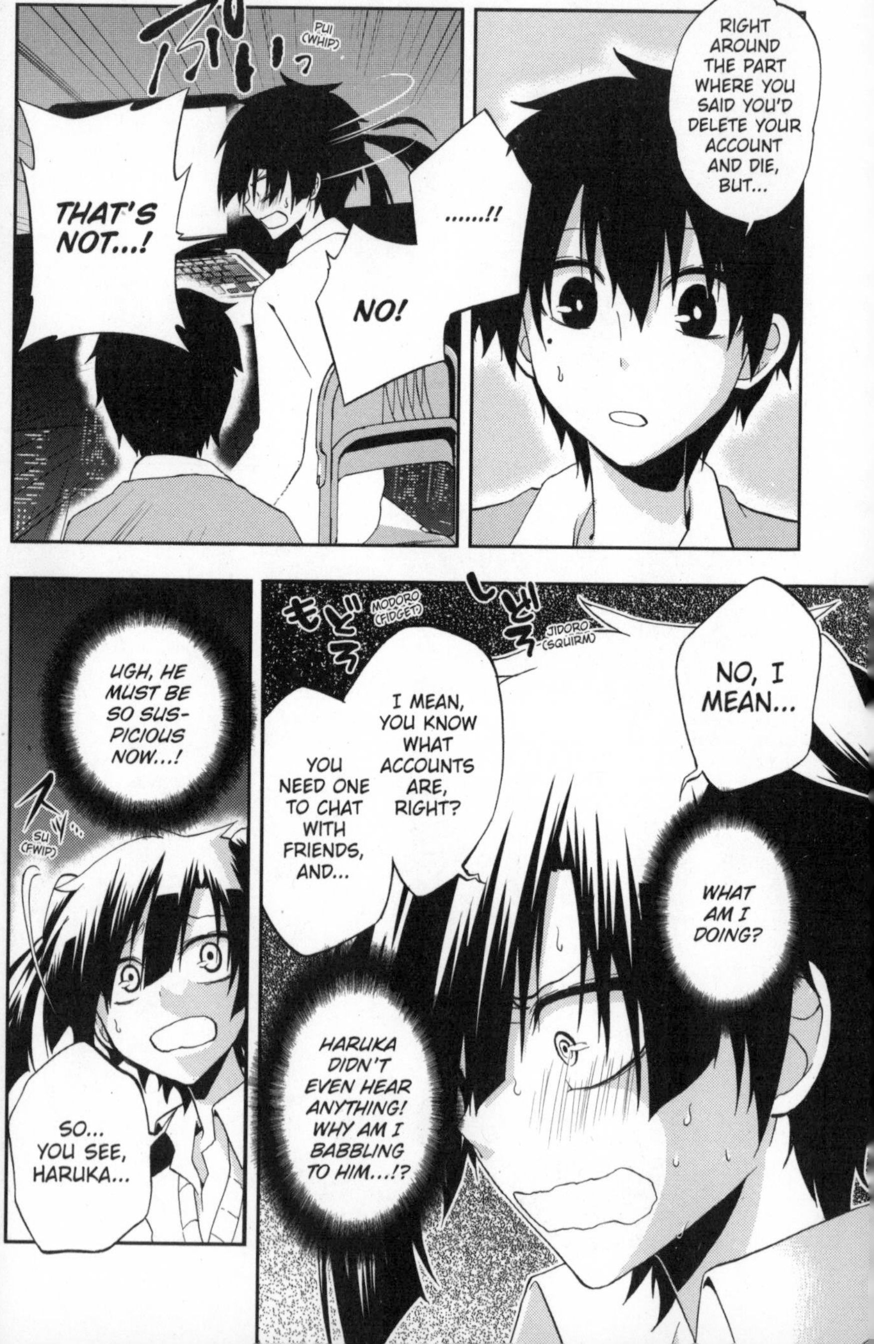
RIGHT AROUND THE PART WHERE YOU SAID YOU'D DELETE YOUR ACCOUNT AND DIE, BUT...
PUI (WHIP)
......!!
THAT'S NOT...!
NO!
JIDORO (SQUIRM)
NO, I MEAN...
MODORO (FIDGET)
I MEAN, YOU KNOW WHAT ACCOUNTS ARE, RIGHT?
YOU NEED ONE TO CHAT WITH FRIENDS, AND...
WHAT AM I DOING?
HARUKA DIDN'T EVEN HEAR ANYTHING! WHY AM I BABBLING TO HIM...!?
UGH, HE MUST BE SO SUS-PICIOUS NOW...!
SU (FWIP)
SO... YOU SEE, HARUKA...

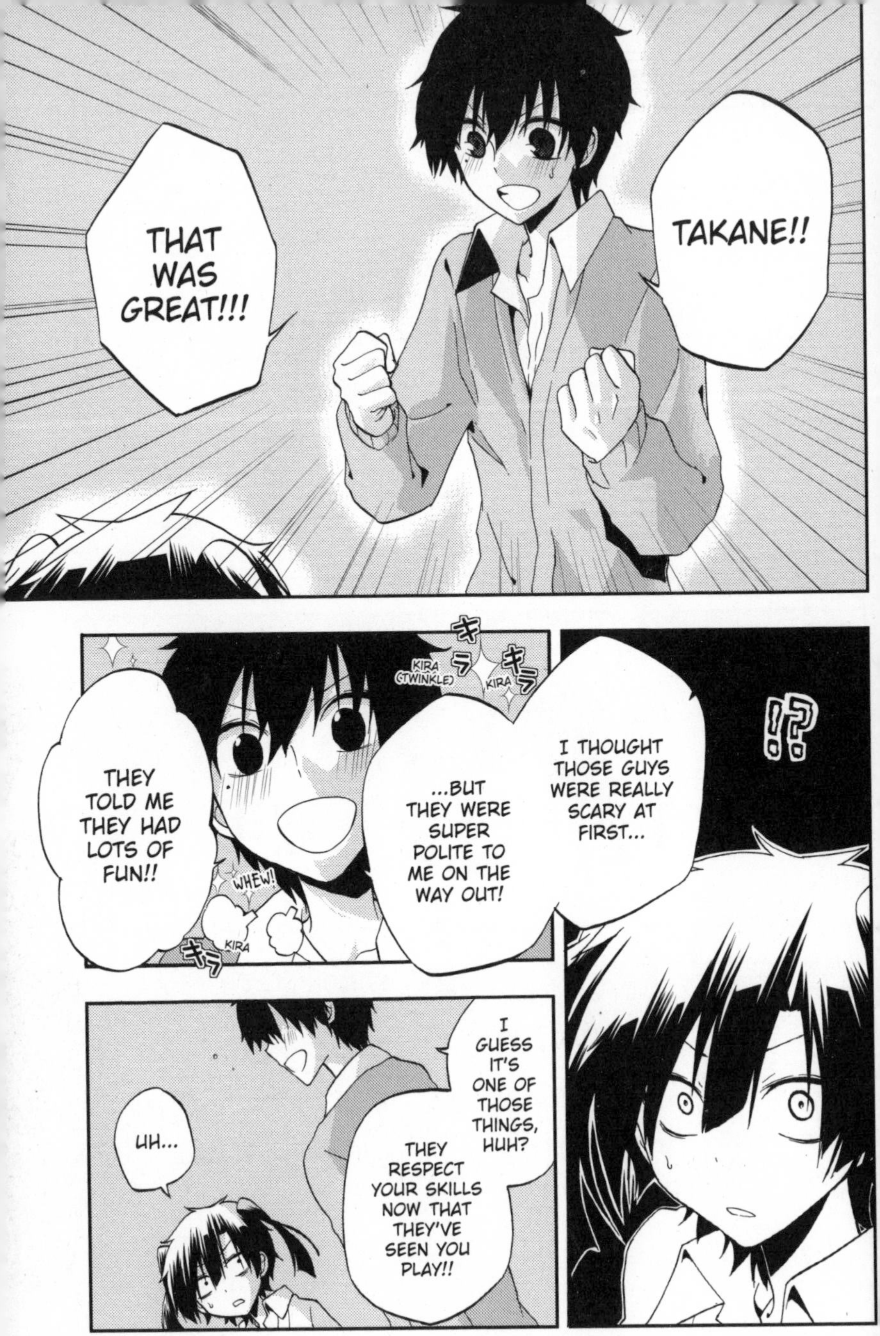
TAKANE!!
THAT WAS GREAT!!!
!?
I THOUGHT THOSE GUYS WERE REALLY SCARY AT FIRST...
...BUT THEY WERE SUPER POLITE TO ME ON THE WAY OUT!
KIRA (TWINKLE) KIRA
THEY TOLD ME THEY HAD LOTS OF FUN!!
WHEW!
KIRA
I GUESS IT'S ONE OF THOSE THINGS, HUH?
THEY RESPECT YOUR SKILLS NOW THAT THEY'VE SEEN YOU PLAY!!
UH...

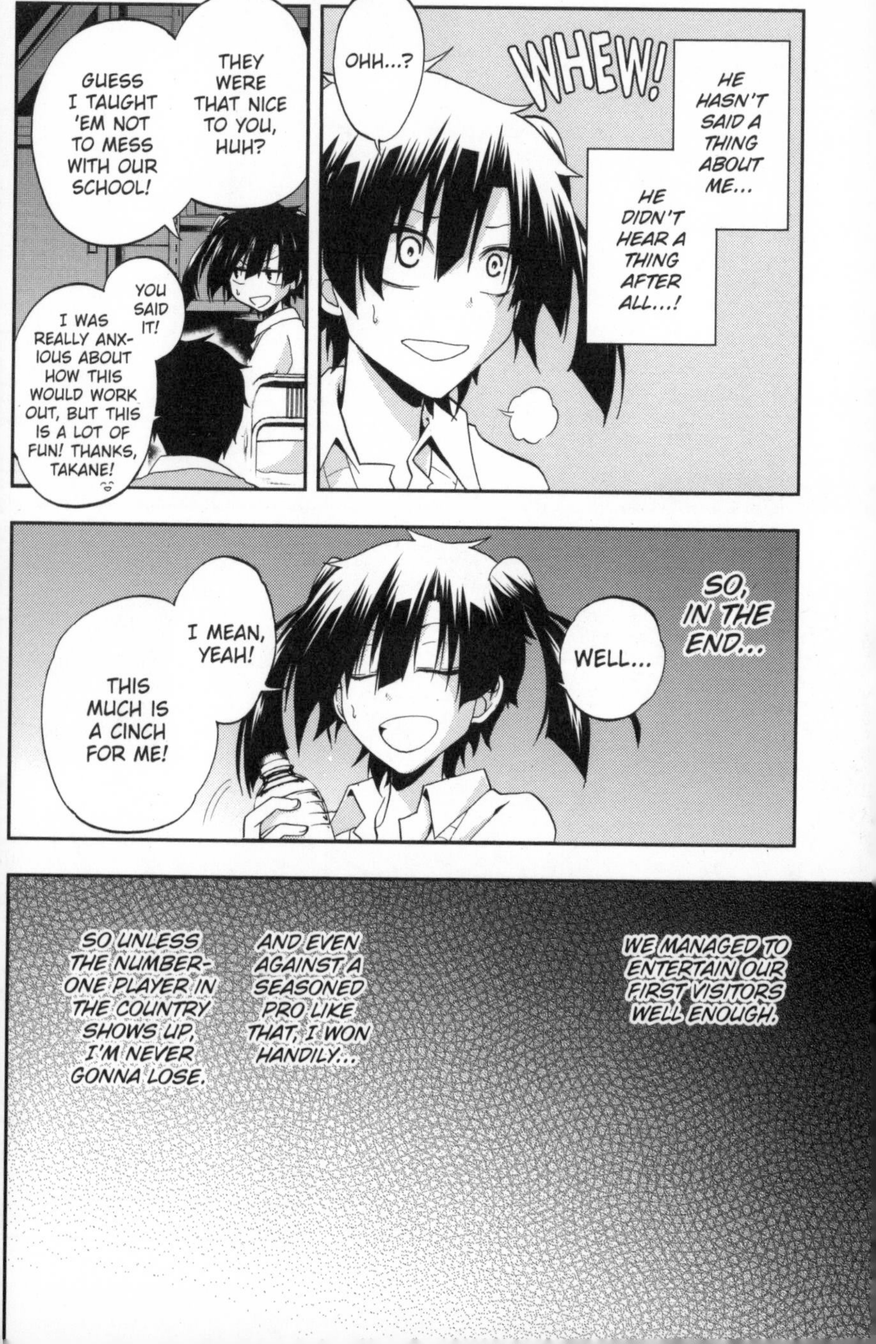
OHH...?
WHEW!
HE HASN'T SAID A THING ABOUT ME...
HE DIDN'T HEAR A THING AFTER ALL...!
THEY WERE THAT NICE TO YOU, HUH?
GUESS I TAUGHT 'EM NOT TO MESS WITH OUR SCHOOL!
YOU SAID IT!
I WAS REALLY ANX-IOUS ABOUT HOW THIS WOULD WORK OUT, BUT THIS IS A LOT OF FUN! THANKS, TAKANE!
SO, IN THE END...
WELL...
I MEAN, YEAH!
THIS MUCH IS A CINCH FOR ME!
WE MANAGED TO ENTERTAIN OUR FIRST VISITORS WELL ENOUGH.
AND EVEN AGAINST A SEASONED PRO LIKE THAT, I WON HANDILY...
SO UNLESS THE NUMBER-ONE PLAYER IN THE COUNTRY SHOWS UP, I'M NEVER GONNA LOSE.

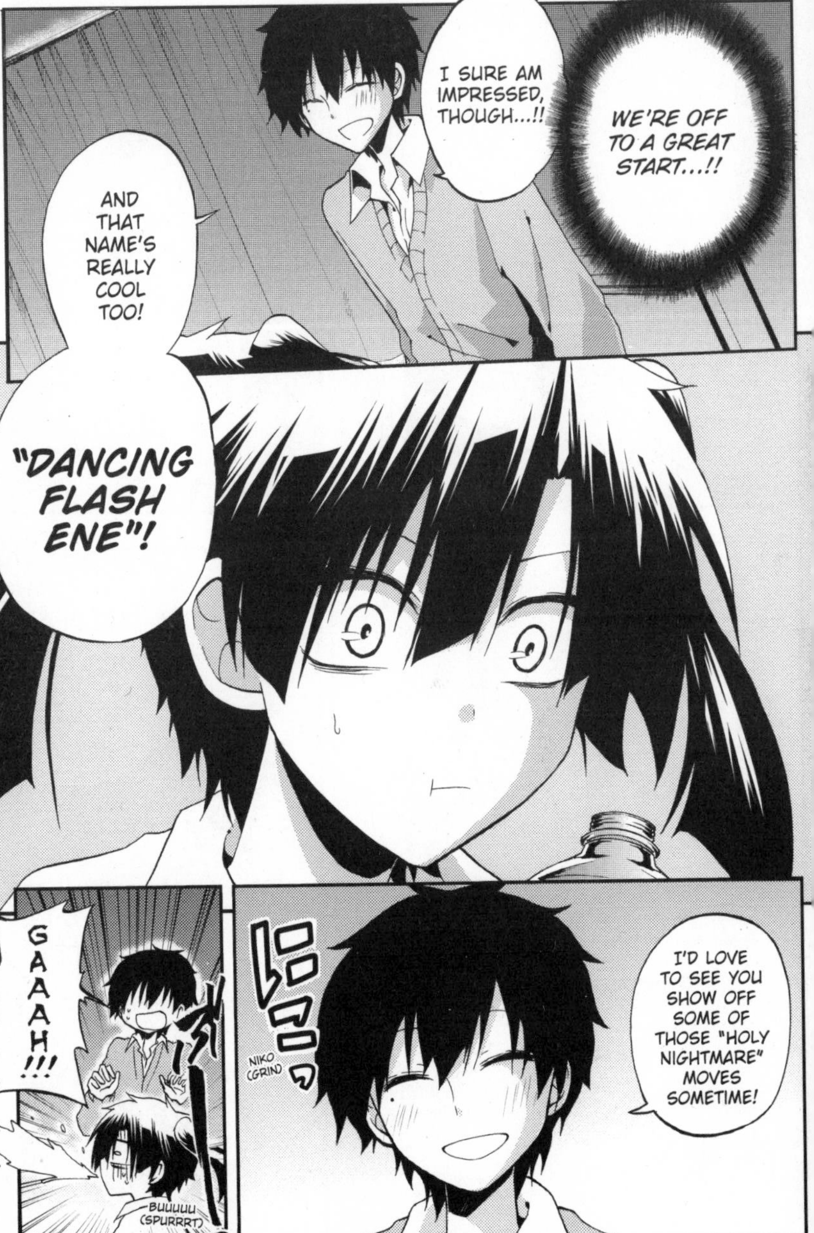
WE'RE OFF TO A GREAT START...!!
I SURE AM IMPRESSED, THOUGH...!!
AND THAT NAME'S REALLY COOL TOO!
"DANCING FLASH ENE"!
I'D LOVE TO SEE YOU SHOW OFF SOME OF THOSE "HOLY NIGHTMARE" MOVES SOMETIME!
NIKO (GRIN)
GAAAH!!!
BUUUUU (SPURRRT)

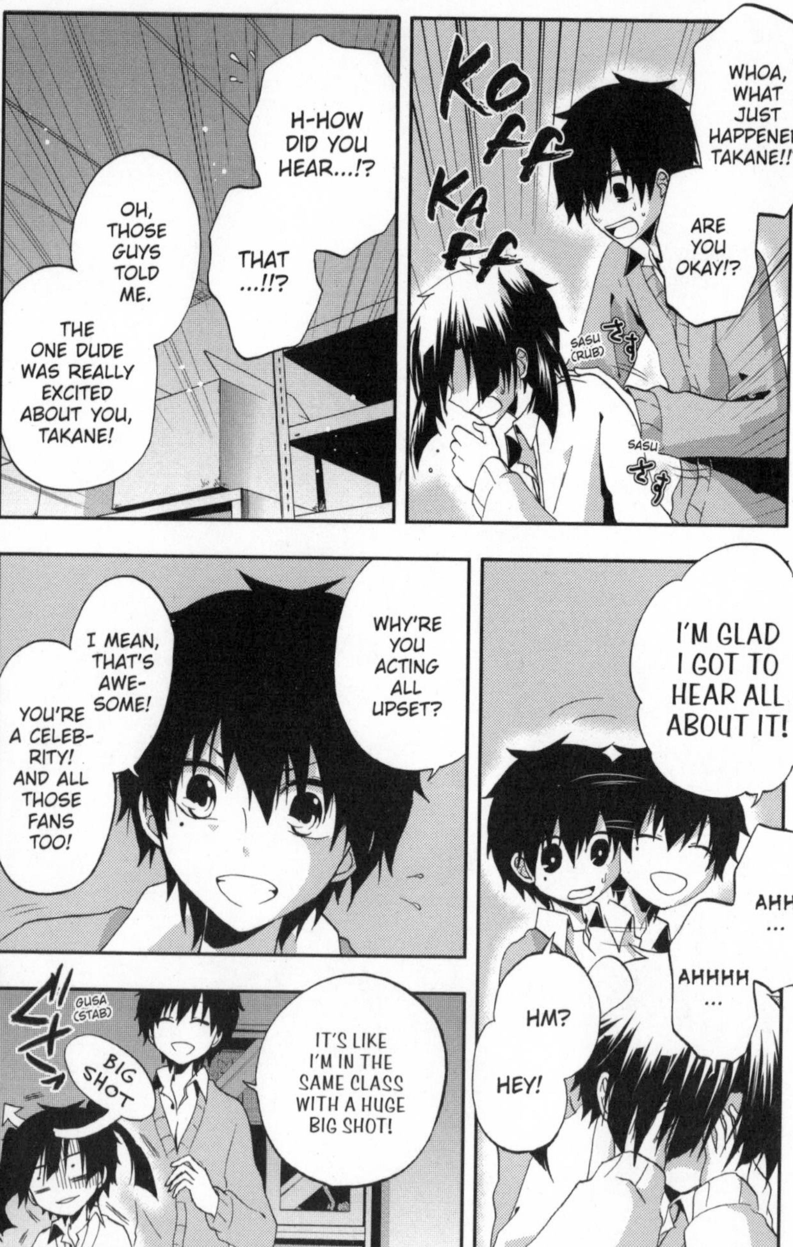
KOFF
KAFF
WHOA, WHAT JUST HAPPENED, TAKANE!!?
ARE YOU OKAY!?
SASU (RUB) さす
SASU さす
H-HOW DID YOU HEAR...!?
THAT ...!!?
OH, THOSE GUYS TOLD ME.
THE ONE DUDE WAS REALLY EXCITED ABOUT YOU, TAKANE!
I'M GLAD I GOT TO HEAR ALL ABOUT IT!
AHH ...
AHHHH ...
HM?
HEY!
WHY'RE YOU ACTING ALL UPSET?
I MEAN, THAT'S AWE-SOME!
YOU'RE A CELEB-RITY! AND ALL THOSE FANS TOO!
IT'S LIKE I'M IN THE SAME CLASS WITH A HUGE BIG SHOT!
GUSA (STAB)
BIG SHOT

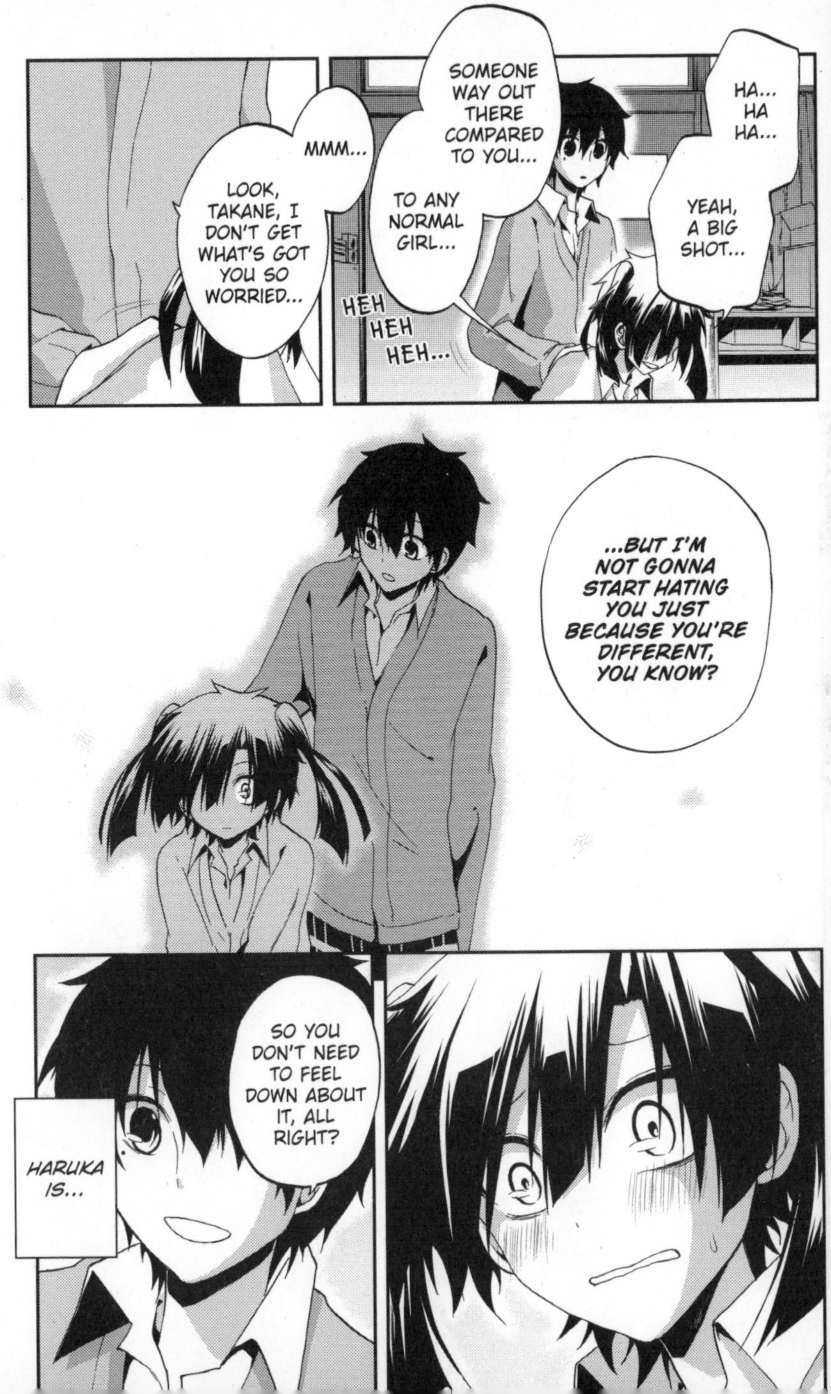
HA... HA HA...
YEAH, A BIG SHOT...
SOMEONE WAY OUT THERE COMPARED TO YOU...
TO ANY NORMAL GIRL...
HEH HEH HEH...
MMM...
LOOK, TAKANE, I DON'T GET WHAT'S GOT YOU SO WORRIED...
...BUT I'M NOT GONNA START HATING YOU JUST BECAUSE YOU'RE DIFFERENT, YOU KNOW?
SO YOU DON'T NEED TO FEEL DOWN ABOUT IT, ALL RIGHT?
HARUKA IS...

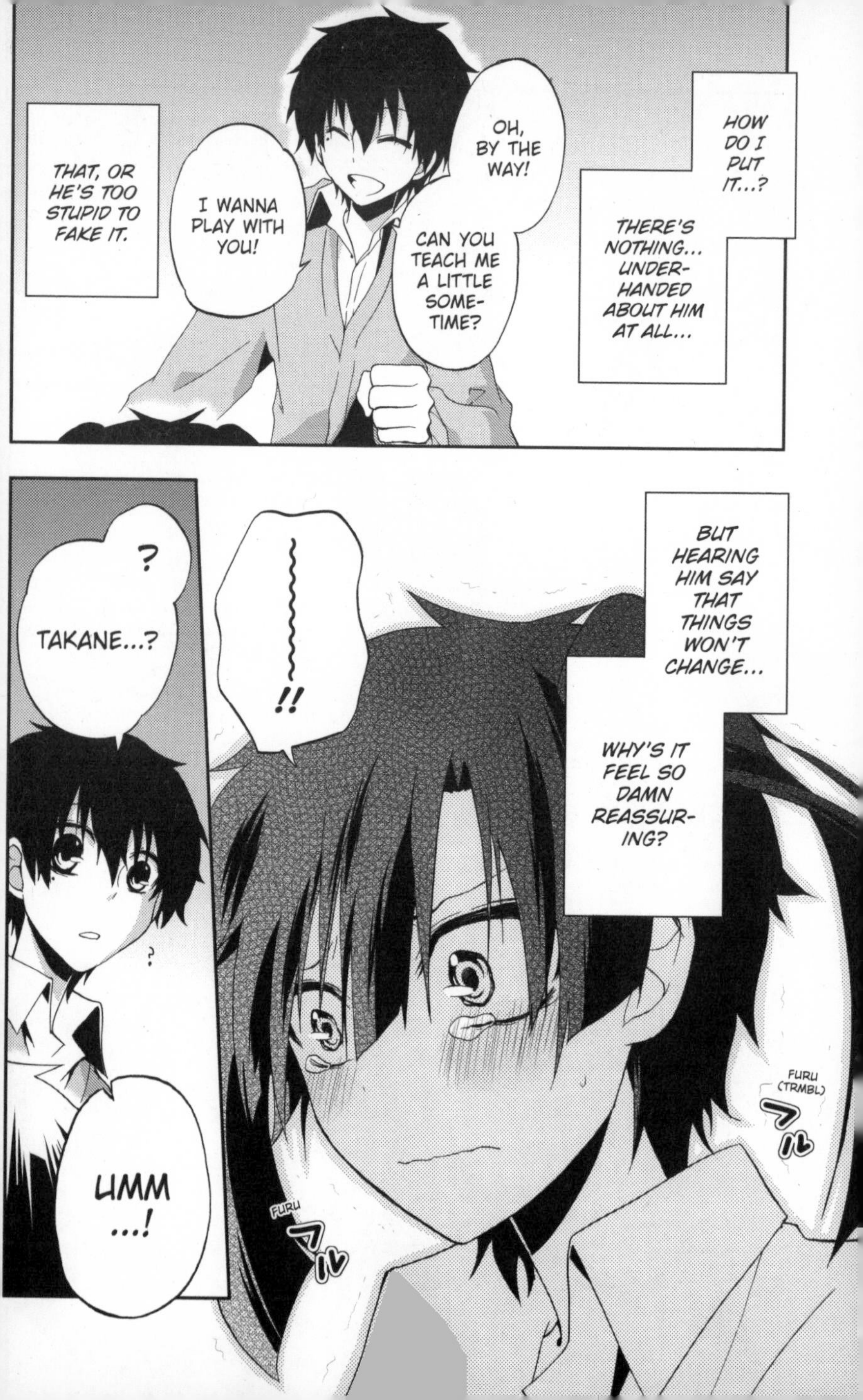

HOW DO I PUT IT...?
THERE'S NOTHING... UNDER-HANDED ABOUT HIM AT ALL...
OH, BY THE WAY!
CAN YOU TEACH ME A LITTLE SOME-TIME?
I WANNA PLAY WITH YOU!
THAT, OR HE'S TOO STUPID TO FAKE IT.
BUT HEARING HIM SAY THAT THINGS WON'T CHANGE...
WHY'S IT FEEL SO DAMN REASSUR-ING?
~~~!!
?
TAKANE...?
FURU (TRMBL)
UMM ...!
FURU
~~~

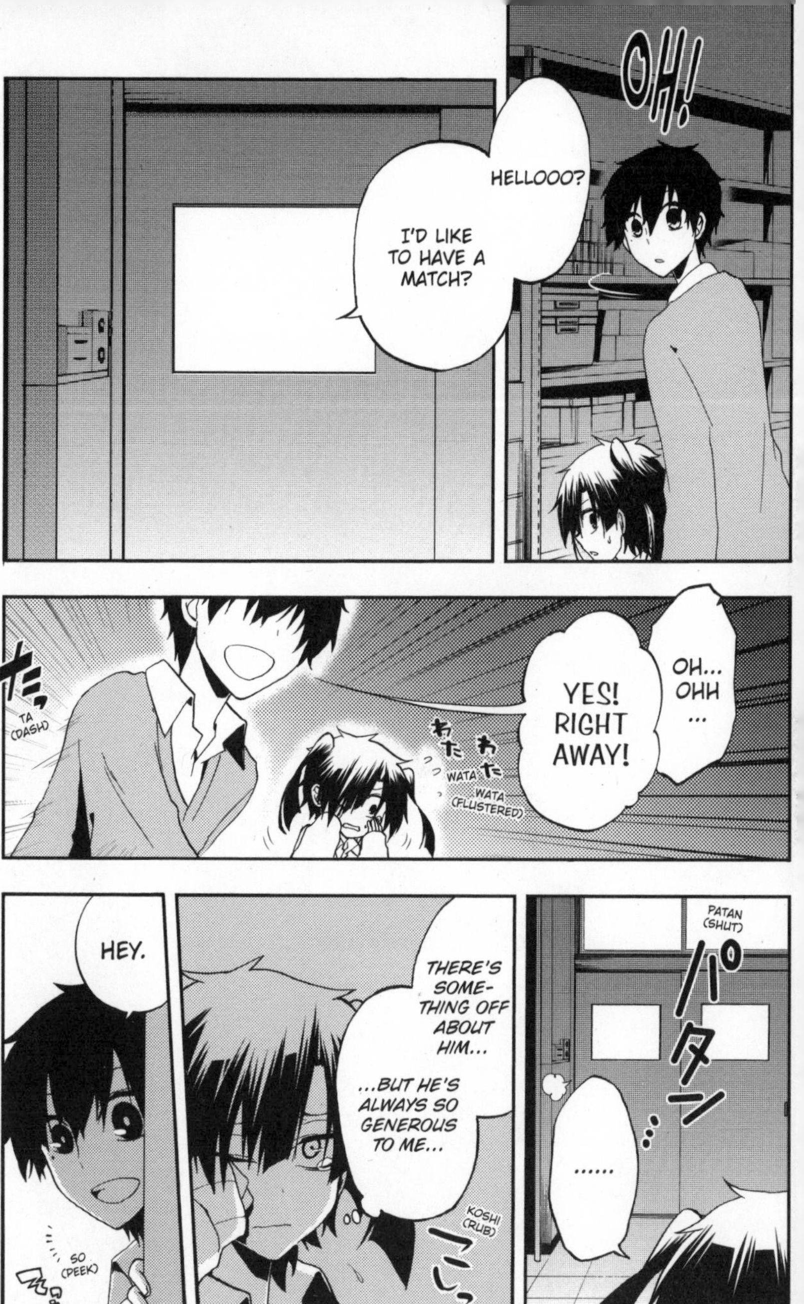
OH!
HELLOOO?
I'D LIKE TO HAVE A MATCH?
OH... OHH...
YES! RIGHT AWAY!
WATA WATA (FLUSTERED)
TA (DASH)
PATAN (SHUT)
......
THERE'S SOMETHING OFF ABOUT HIM...
...BUT HE'S ALWAYS SO GENEROUS TO ME...
KOSHI (RUB)
HEY.
SO (PEEK)

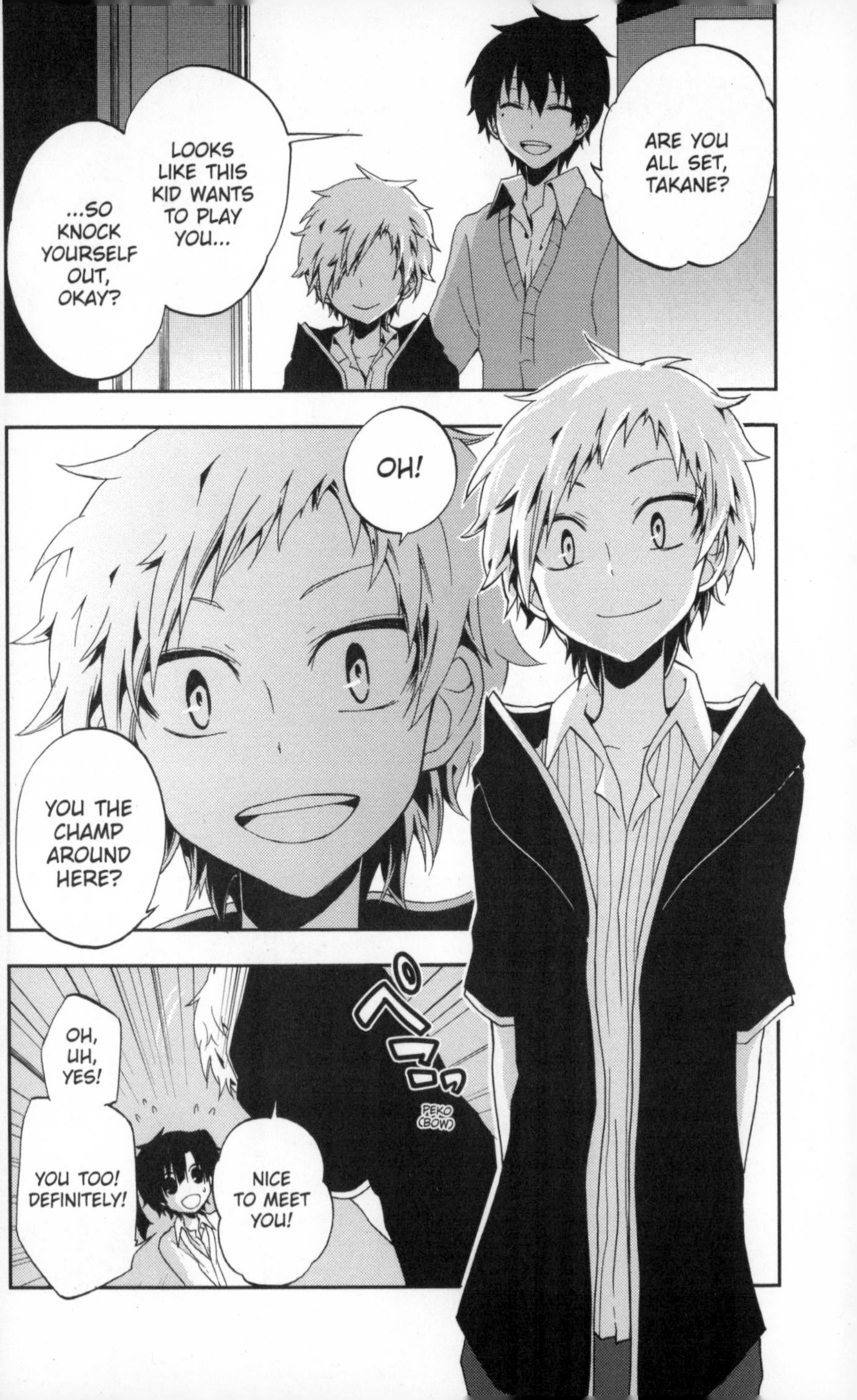
ARE YOU ALL SET, TAKANE?
LOOKS LIKE THIS KID WANTS TO PLAY YOU...
...SO KNOCK YOURSELF OUT, OKAY?
OH!
YOU THE CHAMP AROUND HERE?
PEKO (BOW)
NICE TO MEET YOU!
OH, UH, YES!
YOU TOO! DEFINITELY!

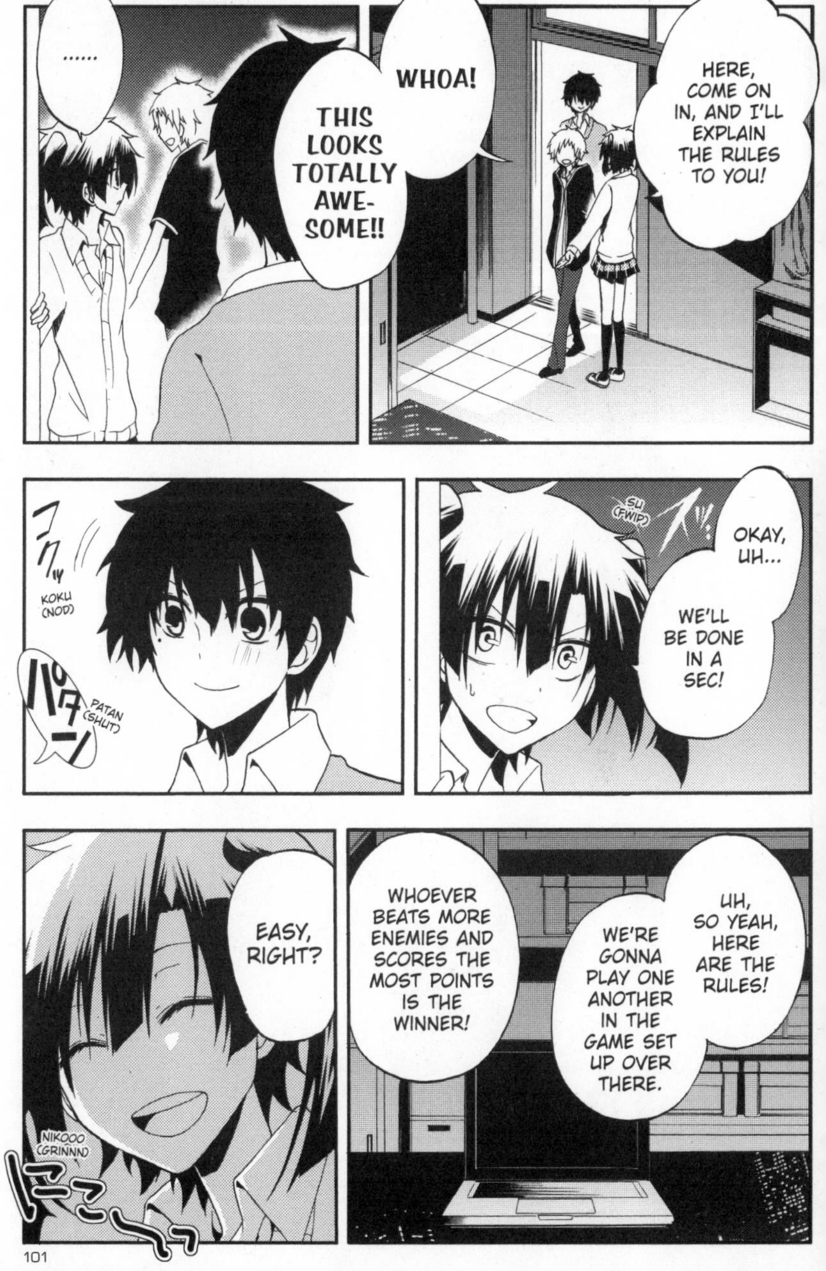
HERE, COME ON IN, AND I'LL EXPLAIN THE RULES TO YOU!
WHOA!
THIS LOOKS TOTALLY AWE-SOME!!
......
SU (FWIP)
OKAY, UH...
WE'LL BE DONE IN A SEC!
KOKU (NOD)
PATAN (SHUT)
UH, SO YEAH, HERE ARE THE RULES!
WE'RE GONNA PLAY ONE ANOTHER IN THE GAME SET UP OVER THERE.
WHOEVER BEATS MORE ENEMIES AND SCORES THE MOST POINTS IS THE WINNER!
EASY, RIGHT?
NIKOOO (GRINNN)

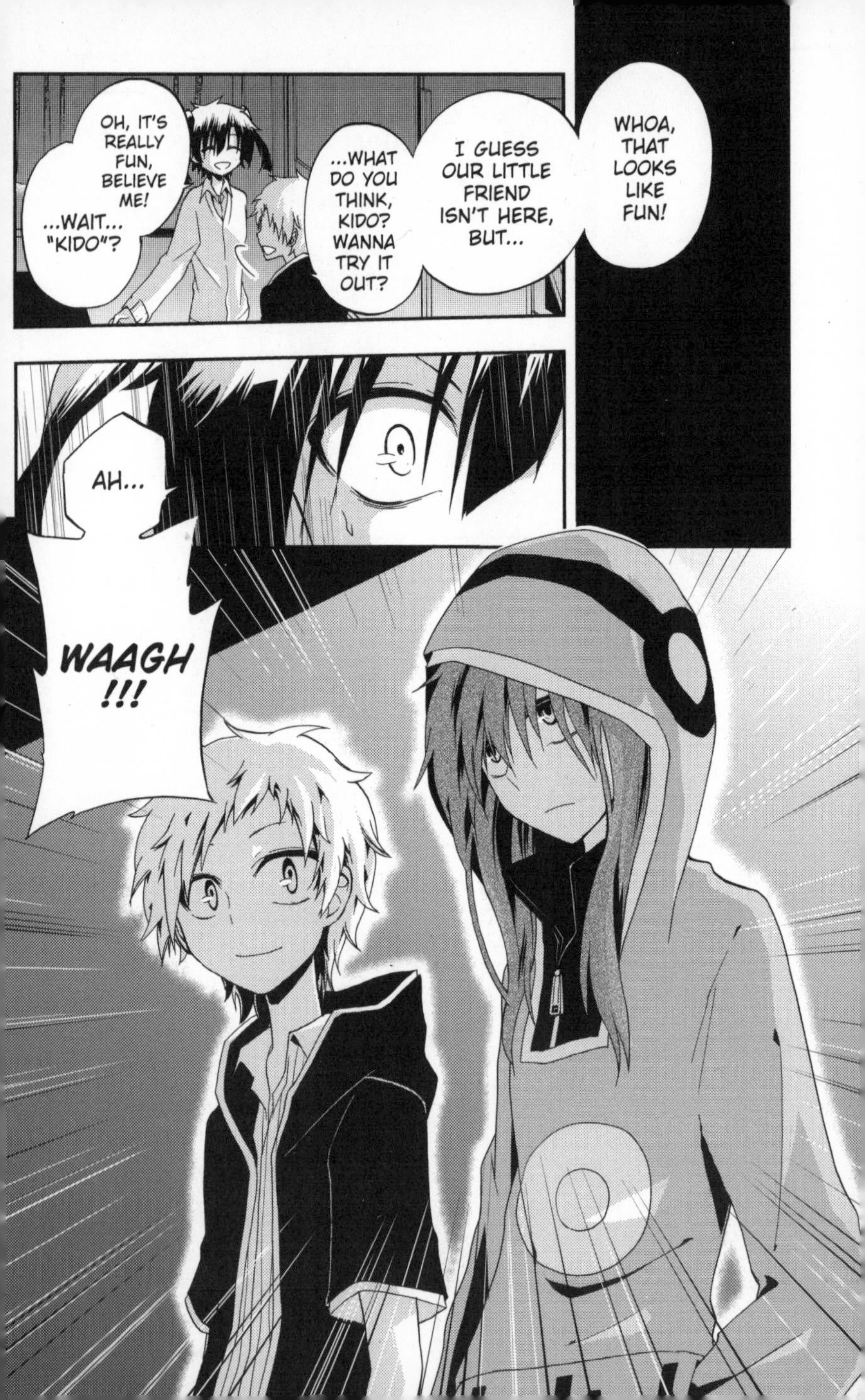
WHOA, THAT LOOKS LIKE FUN!
I GUESS OUR LITTLE FRIEND ISN'T HERE, BUT...
...WHAT DO YOU THINK, KIDO? WANNA TRY IT OUT?
OH, IT'S REALLY FUN, BELIEVE ME!
...WAIT... "KIDO"?
AH...
WAAGH!!!

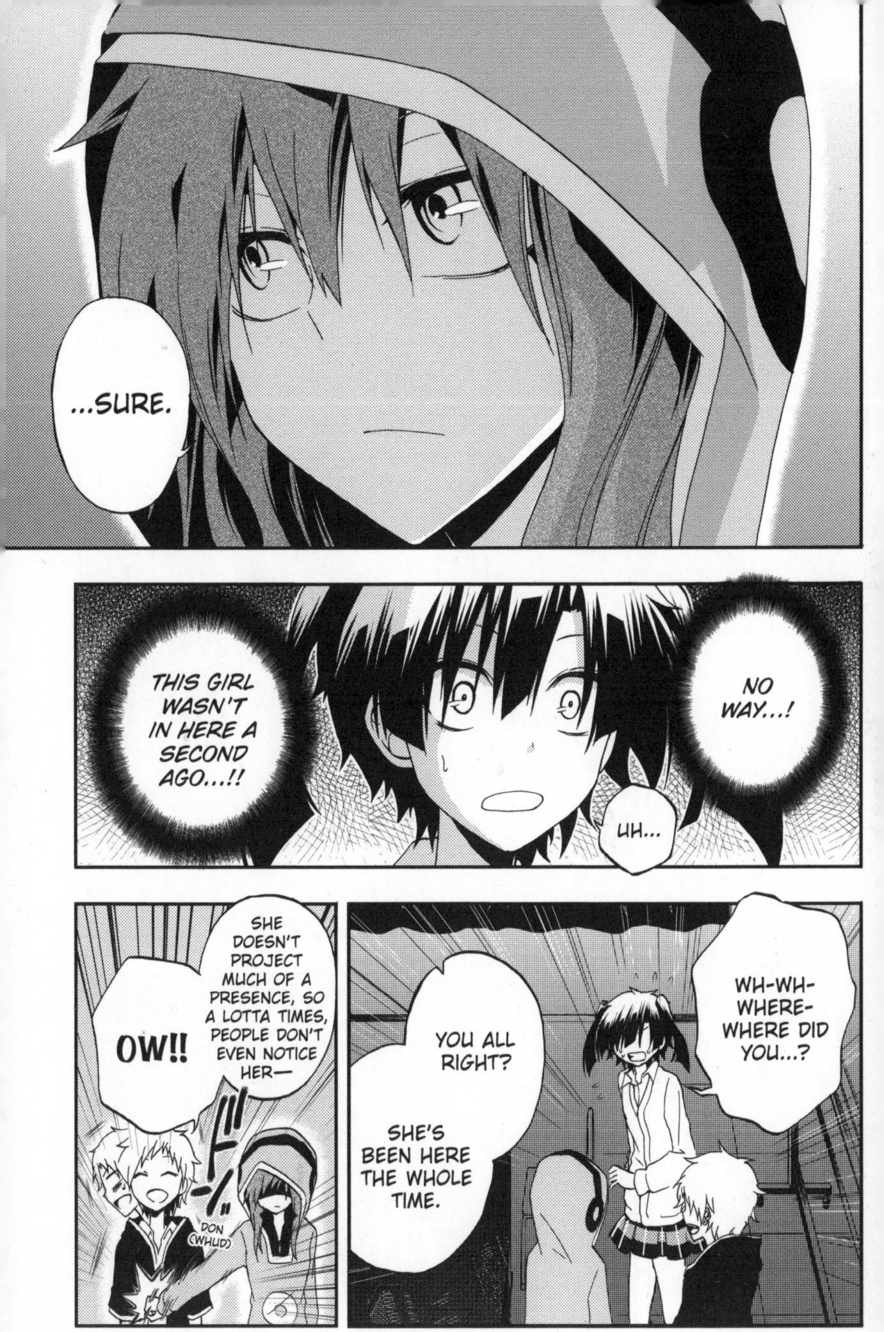
...SURE.
NO WAY...!
THIS GIRL WASN'T IN HERE A SECOND AGO...!!
UH...
WH-WH-WHERE-WHERE DID YOU...?
YOU ALL RIGHT?
SHE'S BEEN HERE THE WHOLE TIME.
SHE DOESN'T PROJECT MUCH OF A PRESENCE, SO A LOTTA TIMES, PEOPLE DON'T EVEN NOTICE HER—
OW!!
DON (WHUD)

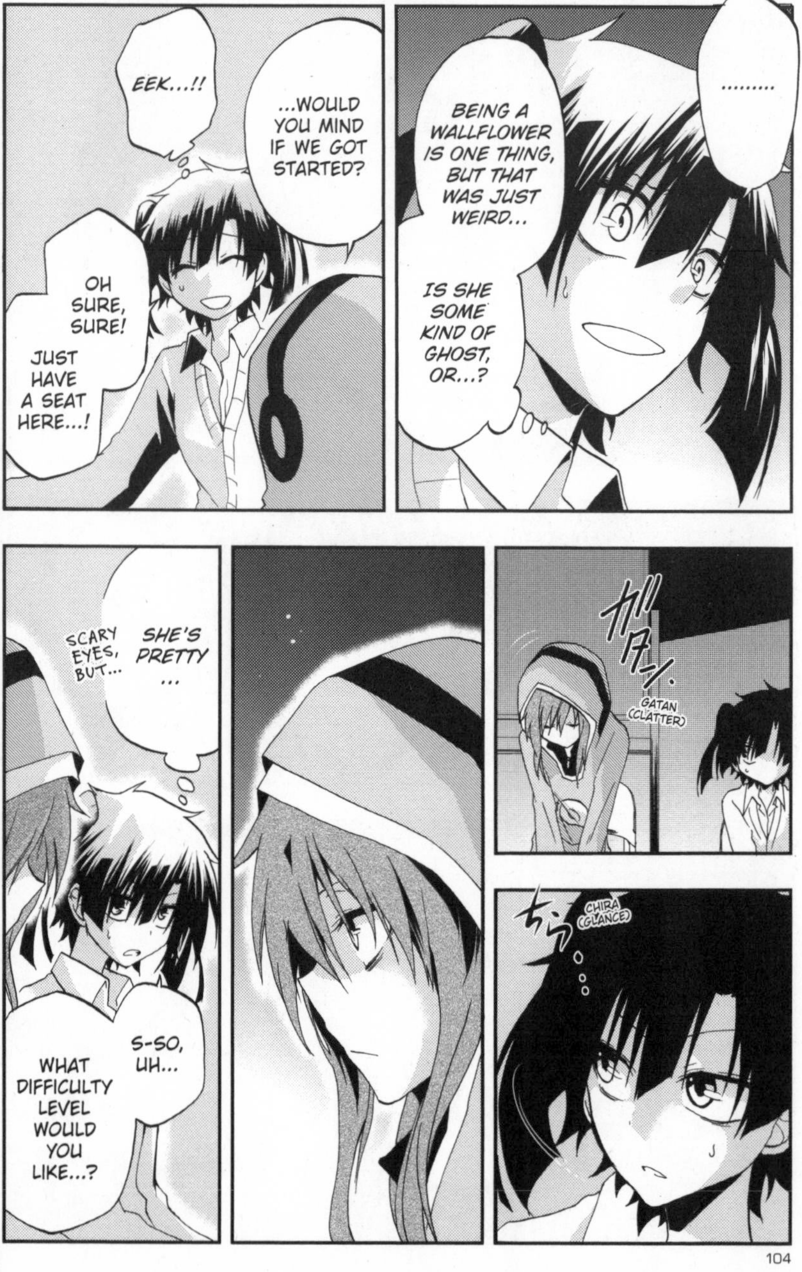
....
BEING A WALLFLOWER IS ONE THING, BUT THAT WAS JUST WEIRD...
IS SHE SOME KIND OF GHOST, OR...?
...WOULD YOU MIND IF WE GOT STARTED?
EEK...!!
OH SURE, SURE!
JUST HAVE A SEAT HERE...!
GATAN (CLATTER)
CHIRA (GLANCE)
SHE'S PRETTY ...
SCARY EYES, BUT...
S-SO, UH...
WHAT DIFFICULTY LEVEL WOULD YOU LIKE...?

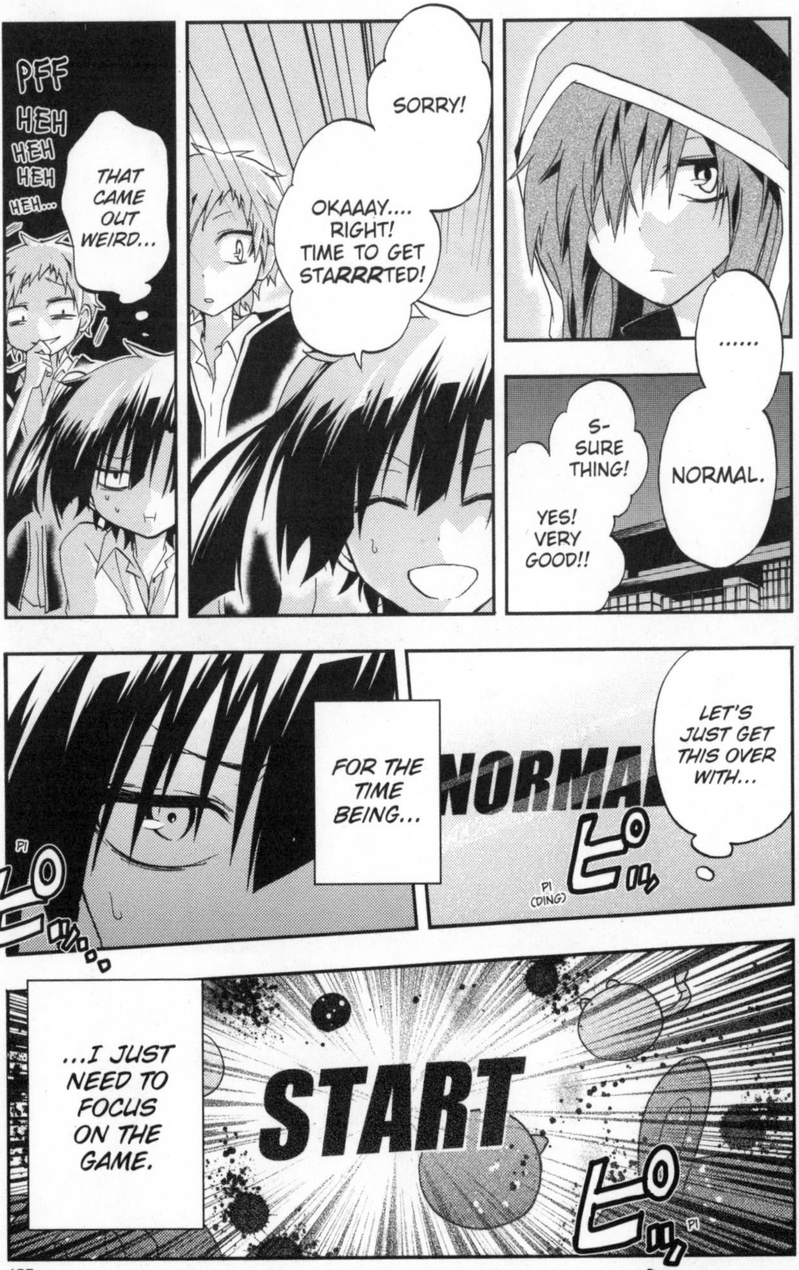
......
NORMAL.
S- SURE THING!
YES! VERY GOOD!!
SORRY!
OKAAAY.... RIGHT! TIME TO GET STARRRTED!
PFF HEH HEH HEH HEH...
THAT CAME OUT WEIRD...
LET'S JUST GET THIS OVER WITH...
NORMAL
PI (DING)
FOR THE TIME BEING...
PI
START
PI
...I JUST NEED TO FOCUS ON THE GAME.

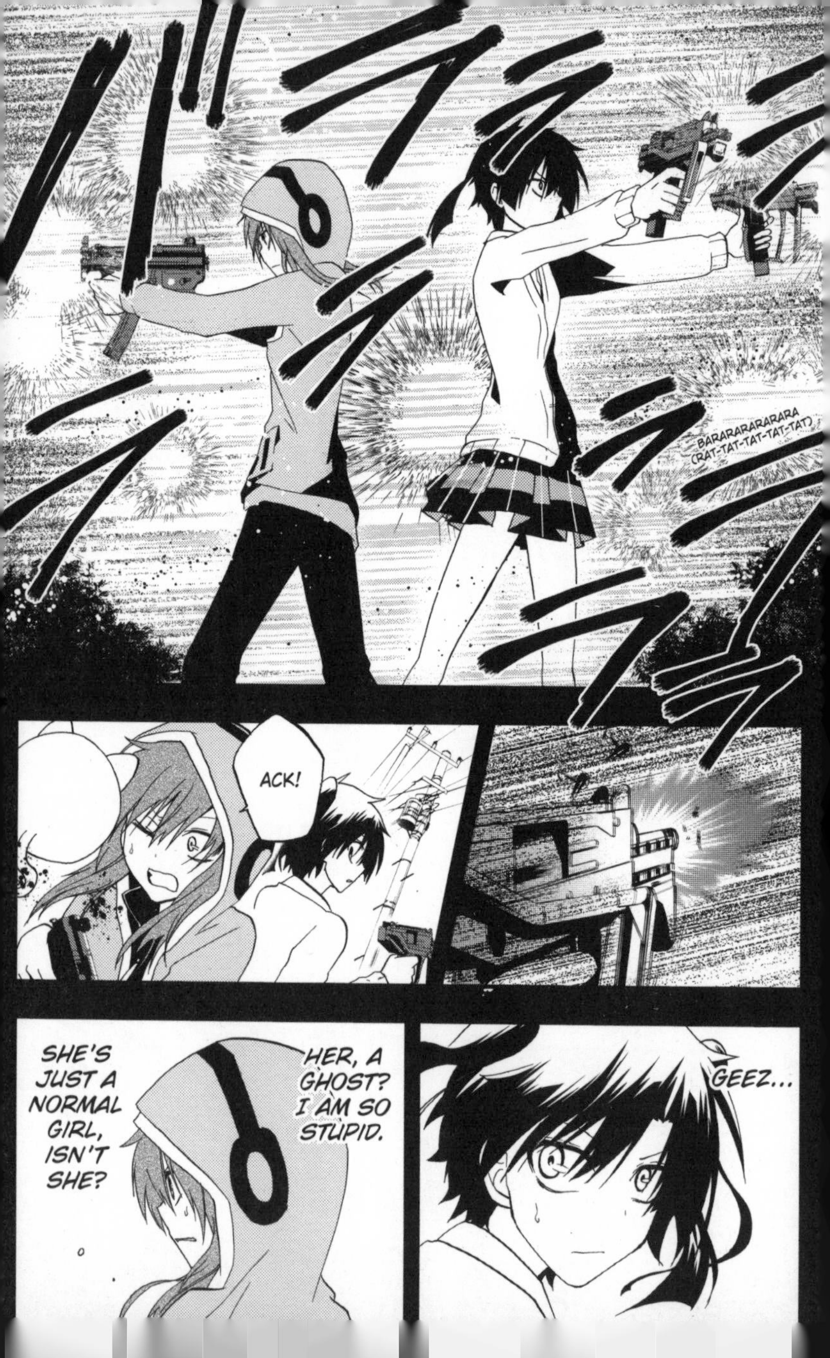
BARARARARARARA
(RAT-TAT-TAT-TAT-TAT)
ACK!
GEEZ...
HER, A GHOST? I AM SO STUPID.
SHE'S JUST A NORMAL GIRL, ISN'T SHE?

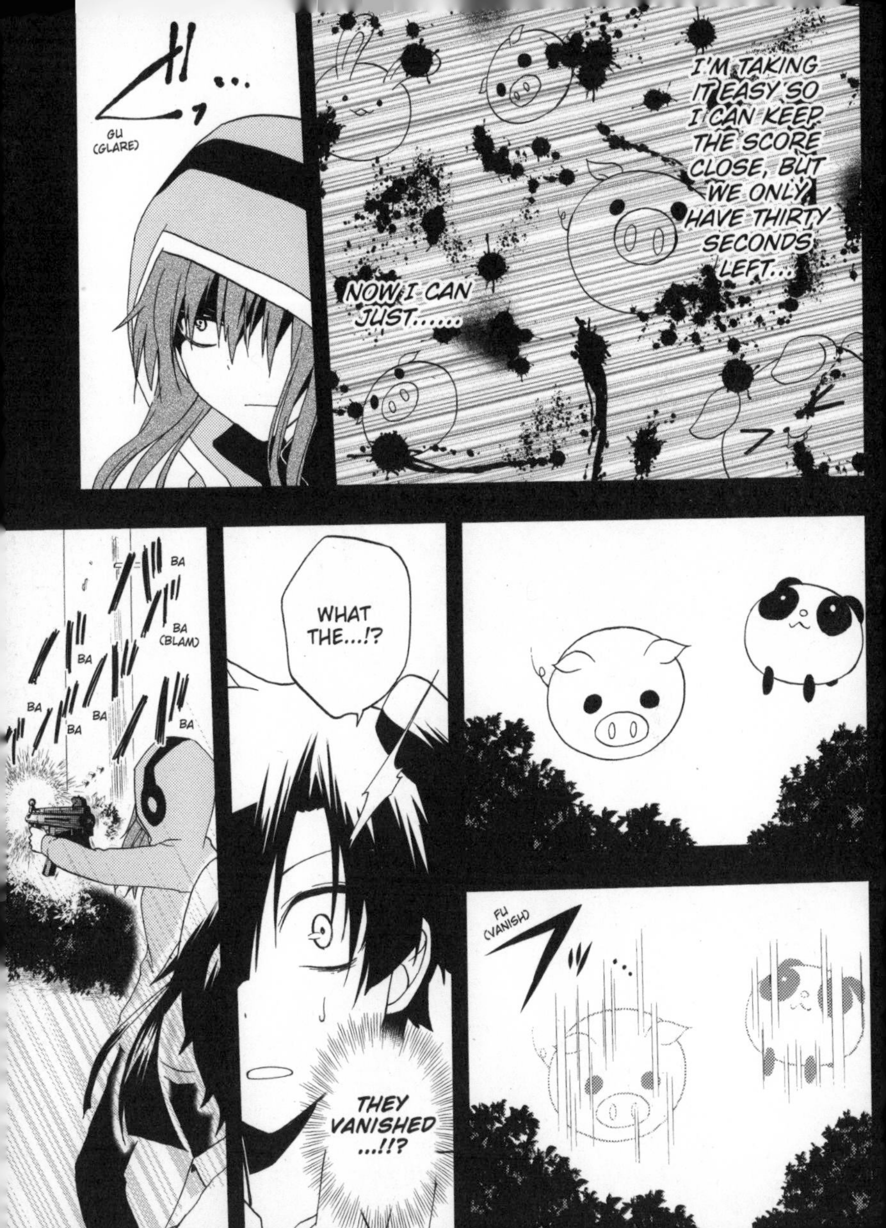
I'M TAKING IT EASY SO I CAN KEEP THE SCORE CLOSE, BUT WE ONLY HAVE THIRTY SECONDS LEFT...
NOW I CAN JUST......
GU (GLARE)
FU (VANISH)
WHAT THE...!?
THEY VANISHED ...!!?
BA
BA (BLAM)
BA
BA
BA
BA
BA

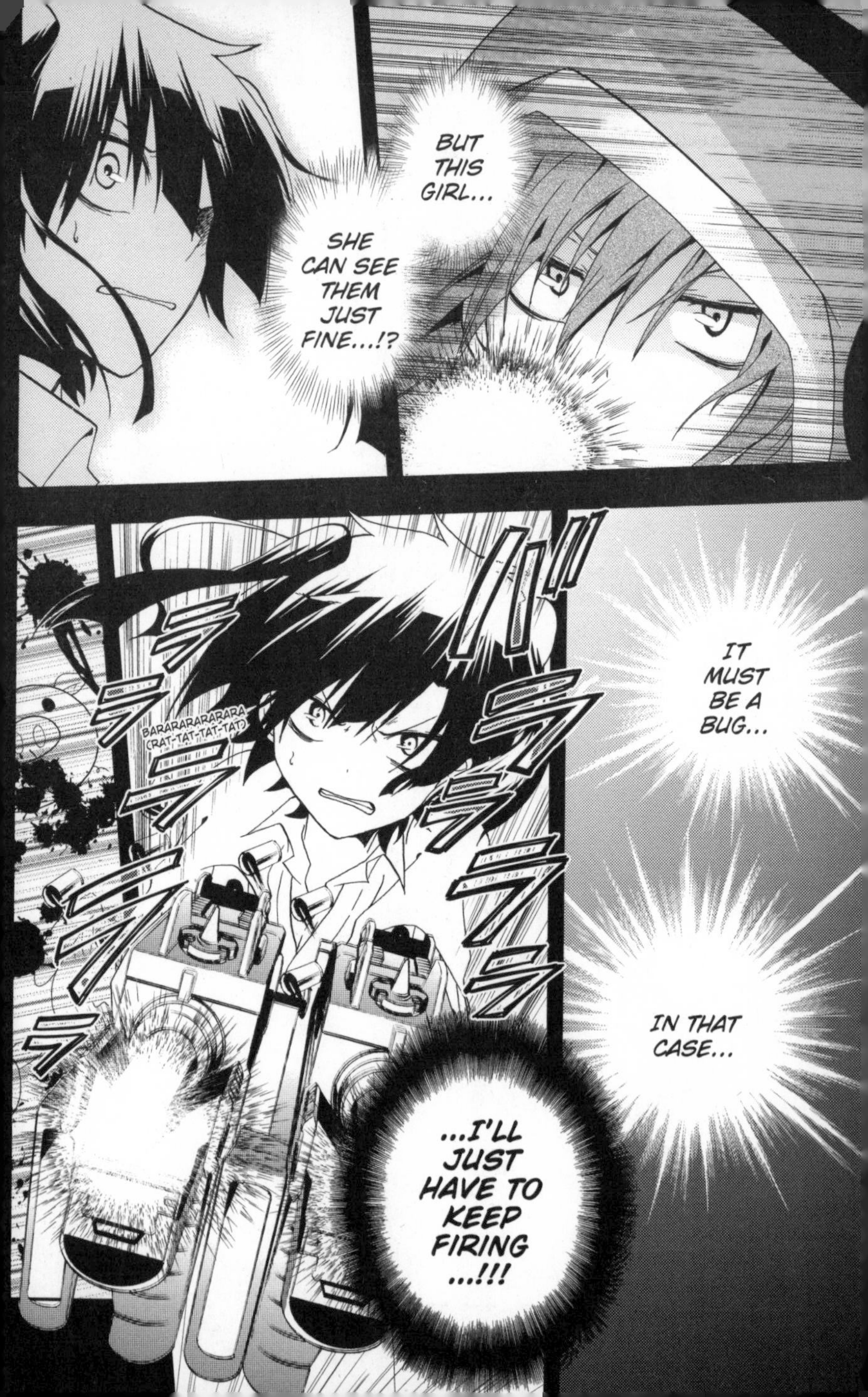
BUT THIS GIRL...
SHE CAN SEE THEM JUST FINE...!?
IT MUST BE A BUG...
IN THAT CASE...
...I'LL JUST HAVE TO KEEP FIRING...!!!
BARARARARARARA (RAT-TAT-TAT-TAT)

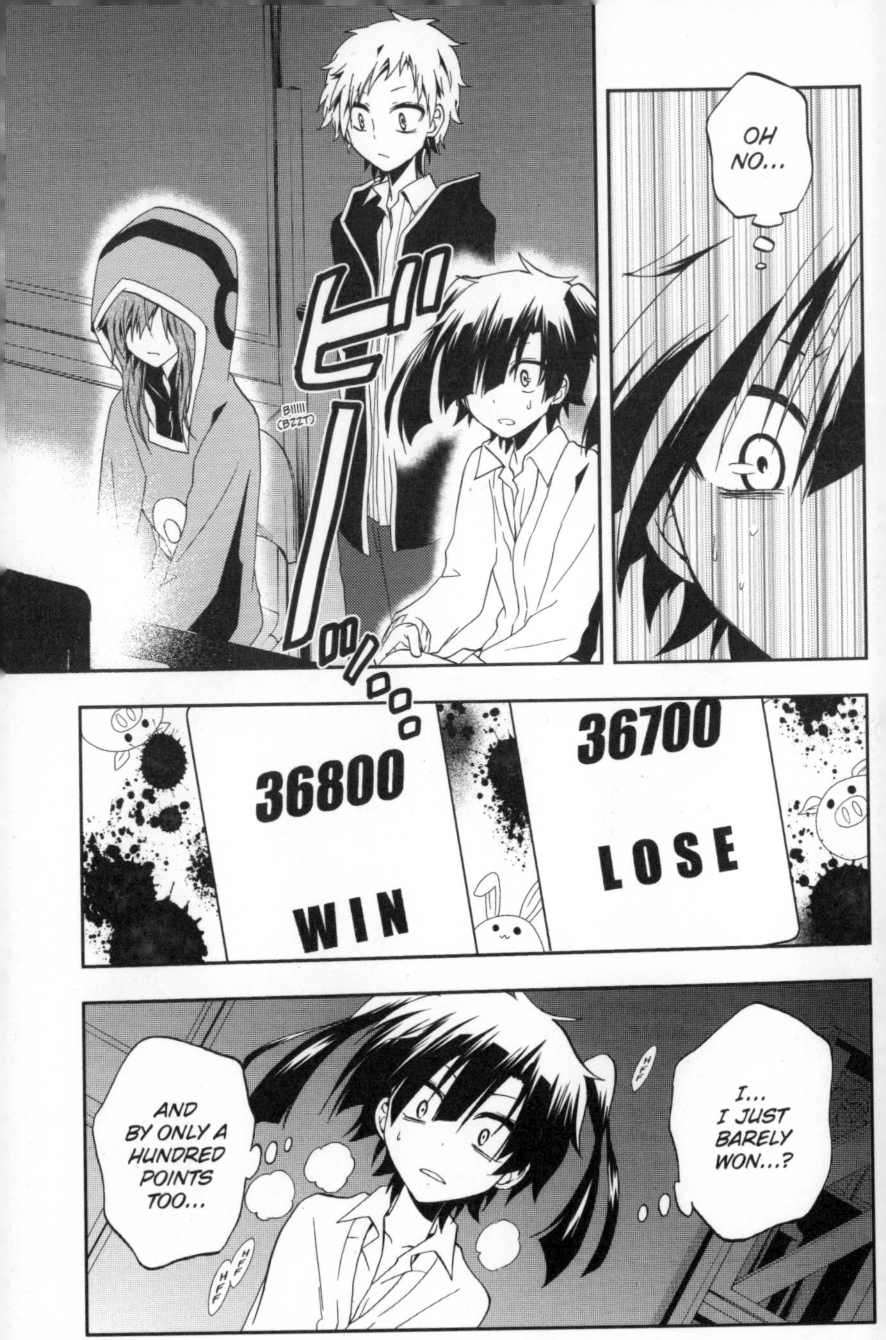
OH NO...
BIIIII (BZZT)
36700
LOSE
36800
WIN
HFF
I... I JUST BARELY WON...?
AND BY ONLY A HUNDRED POINTS TOO...
HFF HFF

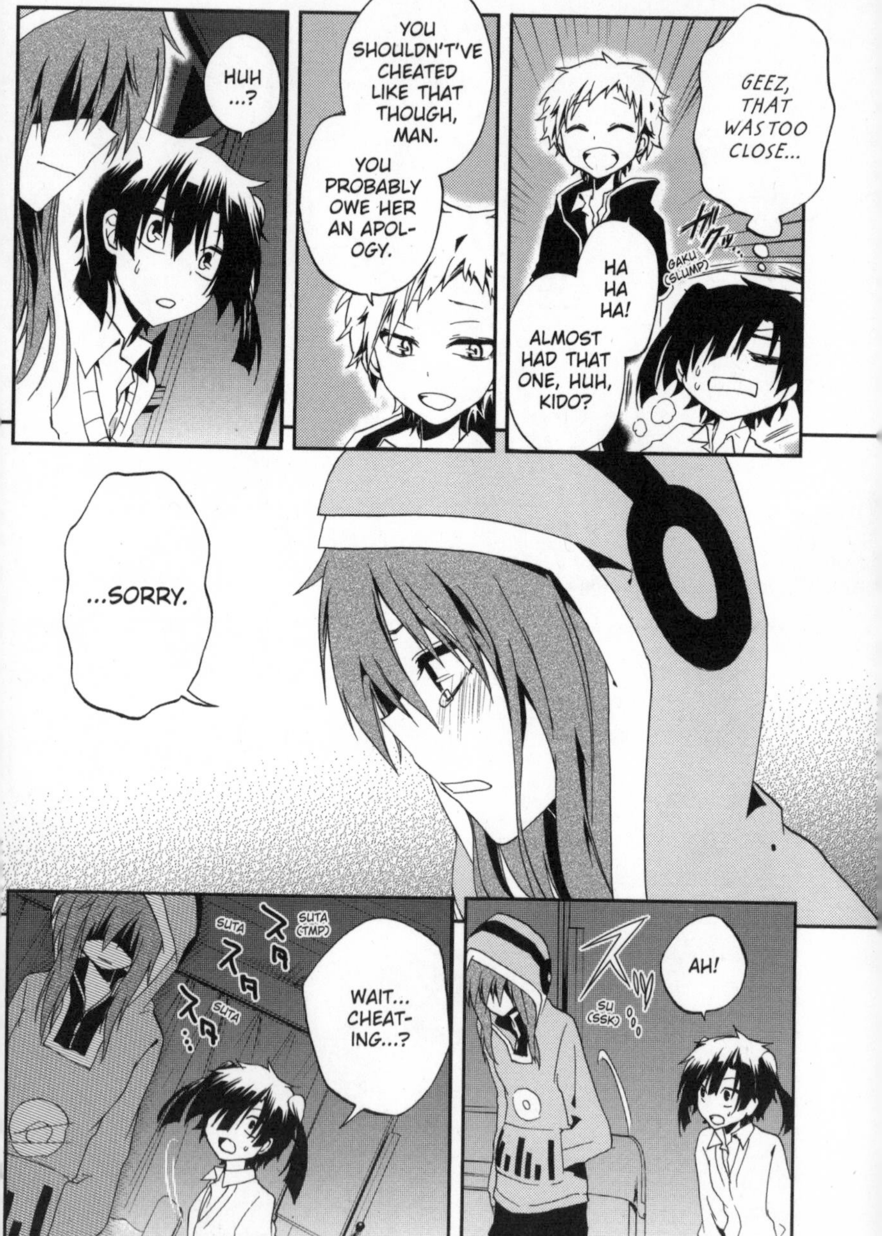
GEEZ, THAT WAS TOO CLOSE...
GAKU (SLUMP)
HA HA HA! ALMOST HAD THAT ONE, HUH, KIDO?
YOU SHOULDN'T'VE CHEATED LIKE THAT THOUGH, MAN.
YOU PROBABLY OWE HER AN APOLOGY.
HUH ...?
...SORRY.
SU (SSK)
AH!
SUTA (TMP)
SUTA
SUTA
WAIT... CHEAT-ING...?

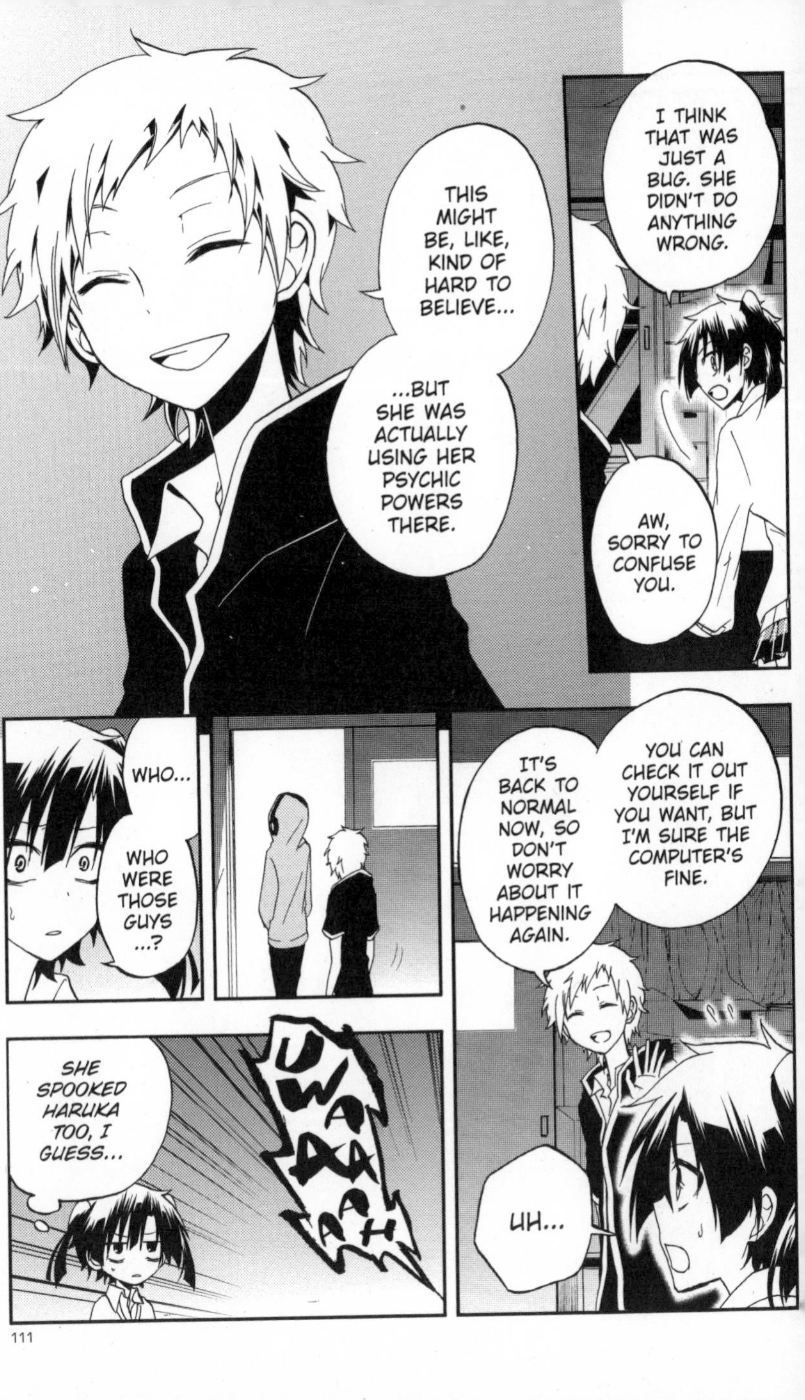
I THINK THAT WAS JUST A BUG. SHE DIDN'T DO ANYTHING WRONG.
AW, SORRY TO CONFUSE YOU.
THIS MIGHT BE, LIKE, KIND OF HARD TO BELIEVE...
...BUT SHE WAS ACTUALLY USING HER PSYCHIC POWERS THERE.
YOU CAN CHECK IT OUT YOURSELF IF YOU WANT, BUT I'M SURE THE COMPUTER'S FINE.
IT'S BACK TO NORMAL NOW, SO DON'T WORRY ABOUT IT HAPPENING AGAIN.
UH...
WHO...
WHO WERE THOSE GUYS ...?
UWAAAAAH
SHE SPOOKED HARUKA TOO, I GUESS...

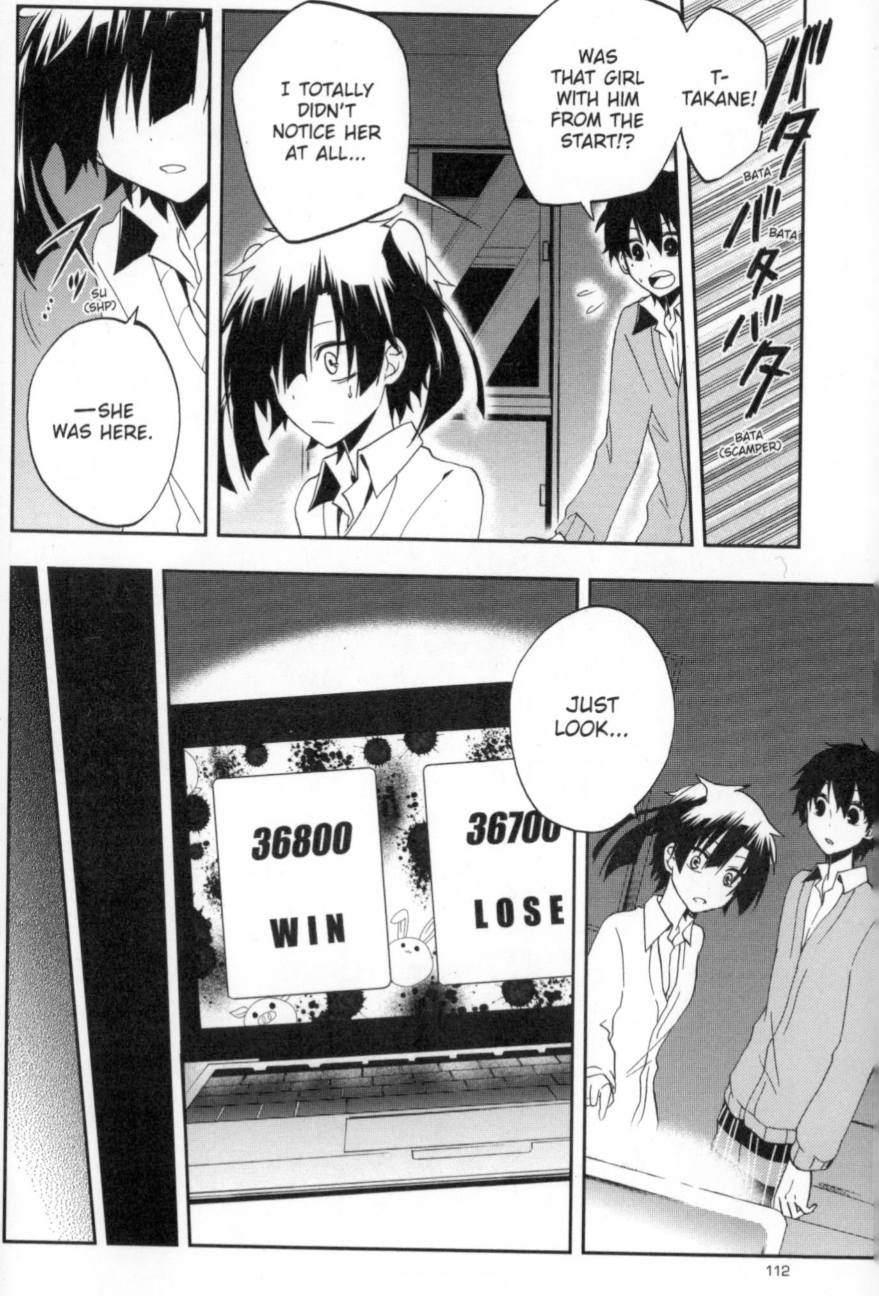

BATA
BATA
BATA (SCAMPER)
T-TAKANE!
WAS THAT GIRL WITH HIM FROM THE START!?
I TOTALLY DIDN'T NOTICE HER AT ALL...
SU (SHP)
—SHE WAS HERE.
JUST LOOK...
36800
WIN
36700
LOSE

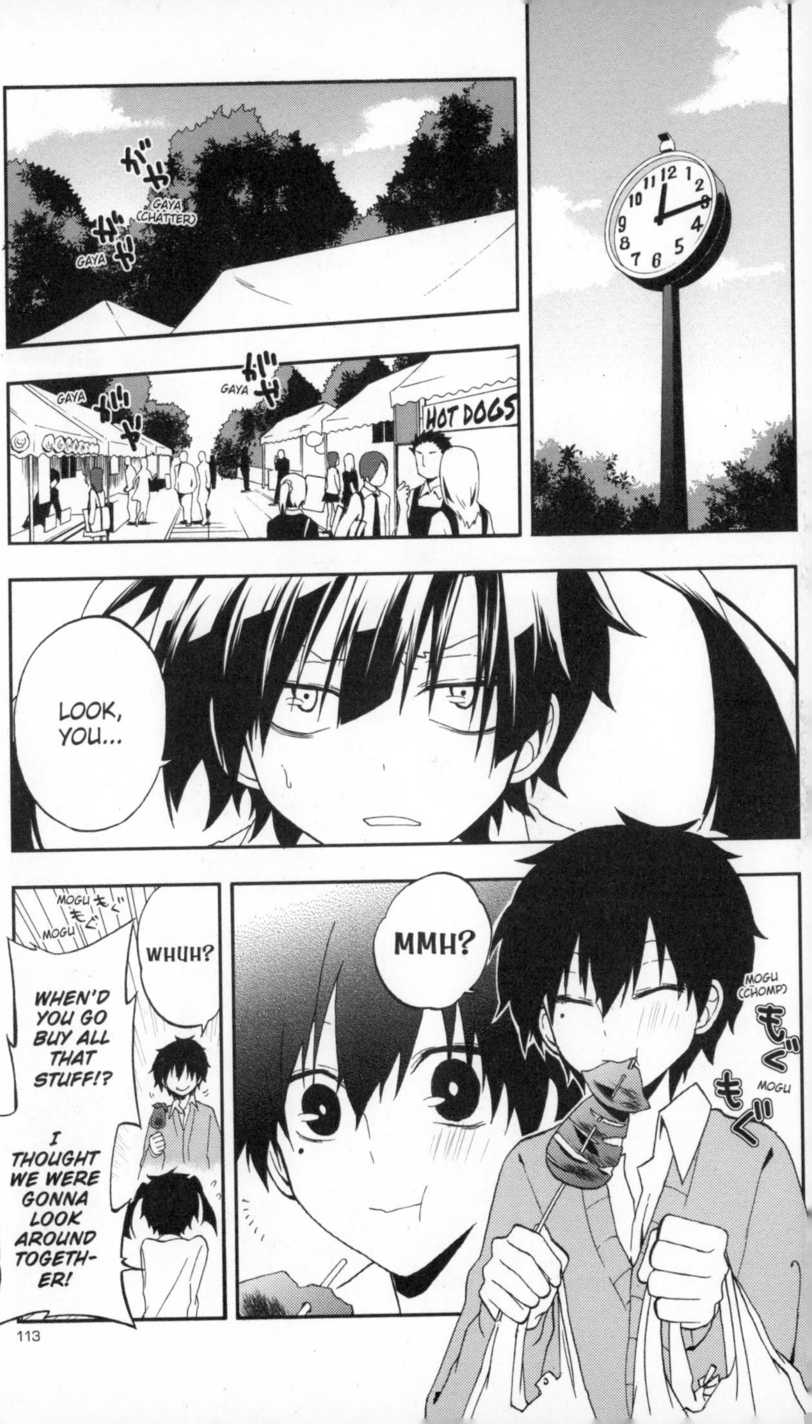
ガヤ
GAYA (CHATTER)
ガヤ
GAYA
ガヤ
GAYA
ガヤ
GAYA
HOT DOGS
LOOK, YOU...
MMH?
もぐ
MOGU (CHOMP)
もぐ
MOGU
もぐ
MOGU
もぐ
MOGU
WHUH?
WHEN'D YOU GO BUY ALL THAT STUFF!?
I THOUGHT WE WERE GONNA LOOK AROUND TOGETH-ER!

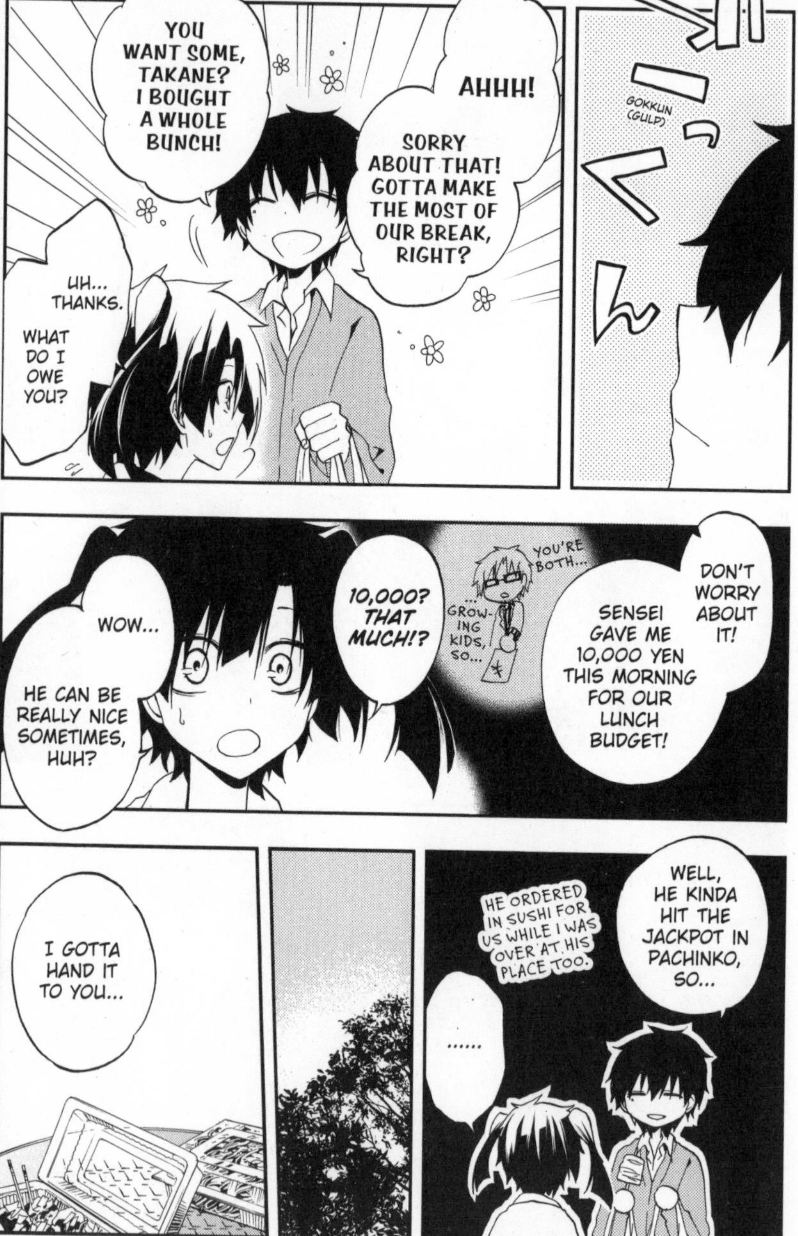
GOKKUN (GULP)
AHHH!
SORRY ABOUT THAT! GOTTA MAKE THE MOST OF OUR BREAK, RIGHT?
YOU WANT SOME, TAKANE? I BOUGHT A WHOLE BUNCH!
UH... THANKS.
WHAT DO I OWE YOU?
DON'T WORRY ABOUT IT!
SENSEI GAVE ME 10,000 YEN THIS MORNING FOR OUR LUNCH BUDGET!
YOU'RE BOTH...
...GROWING KIDS, SO...
10,000? THAT MUCH!?
WOW...
HE CAN BE REALLY NICE SOMETIMES, HUH?
WELL, HE KINDA HIT THE JACKPOT IN PACHINKO, SO...
HE ORDERED IN SUSHI FOR US WHILE I WAS OVER AT HIS PLACE TOO.
......
I GOTTA HAND IT TO YOU...

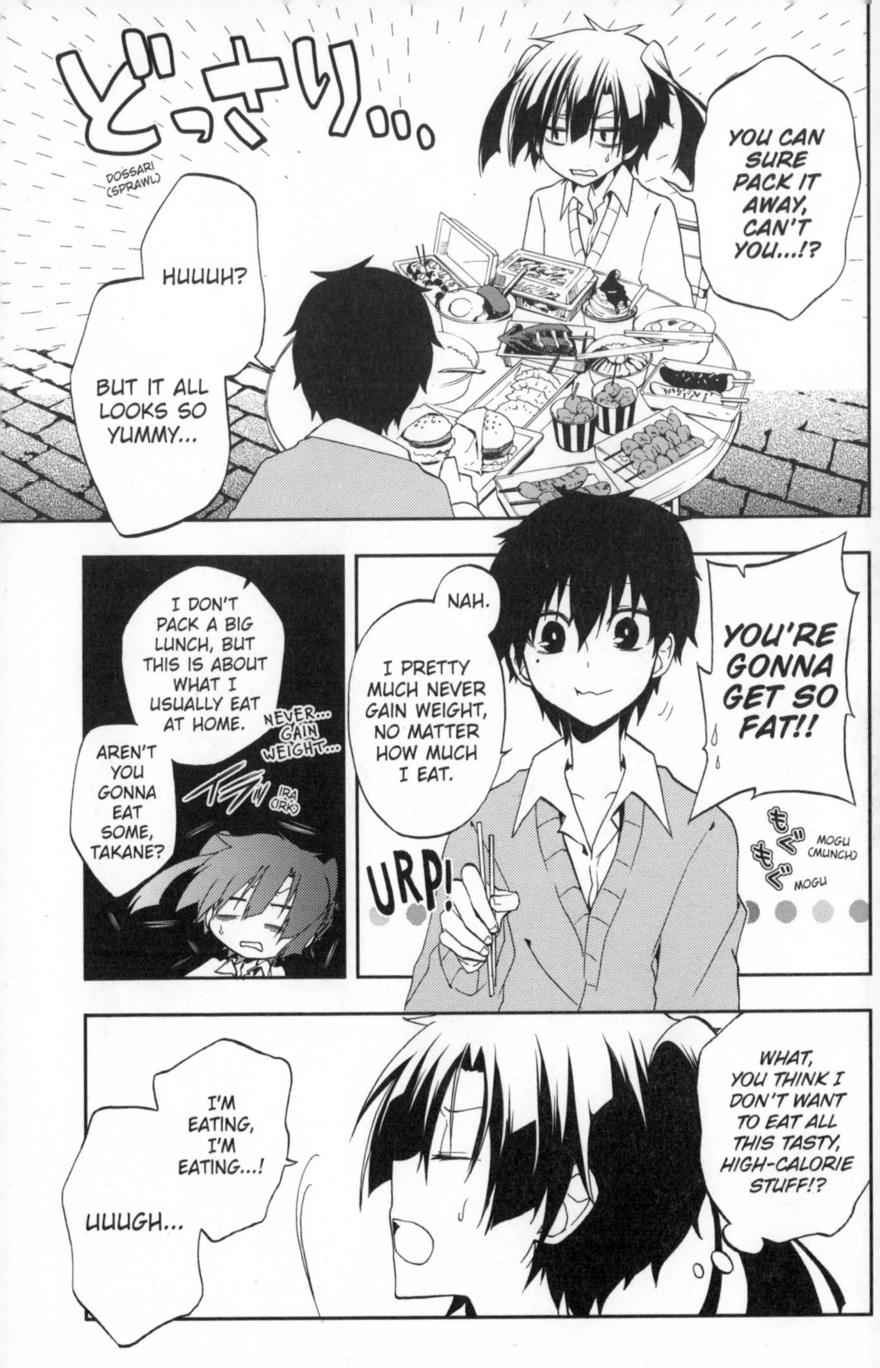
YOU CAN SURE PACK IT AWAY, CAN'T YOU...!?
どっさり...
DOSSARI (SPRAWL)
HUUUH?
BUT IT ALL LOOKS SO YUMMY...
YOU'RE GONNA GET SO FAT!!
NAH.
I PRETTY MUCH NEVER GAIN WEIGHT, NO MATTER HOW MUCH I EAT.
もぐもぐ
MOGU (MUNCH) MOGU
URP!
I DON'T PACK A BIG LUNCH, BUT THIS IS ABOUT WHAT I USUALLY EAT AT HOME.
NEVER... GAIN WEIGHT...
IRA (IRK)
AREN'T YOU GONNA EAT SOME, TAKANE?
WHAT, YOU THINK I DON'T WANT TO EAT ALL THIS TASTY, HIGH-CALORIE STUFF!?
I'M EATING, I'M EATING...!
UUUGH...

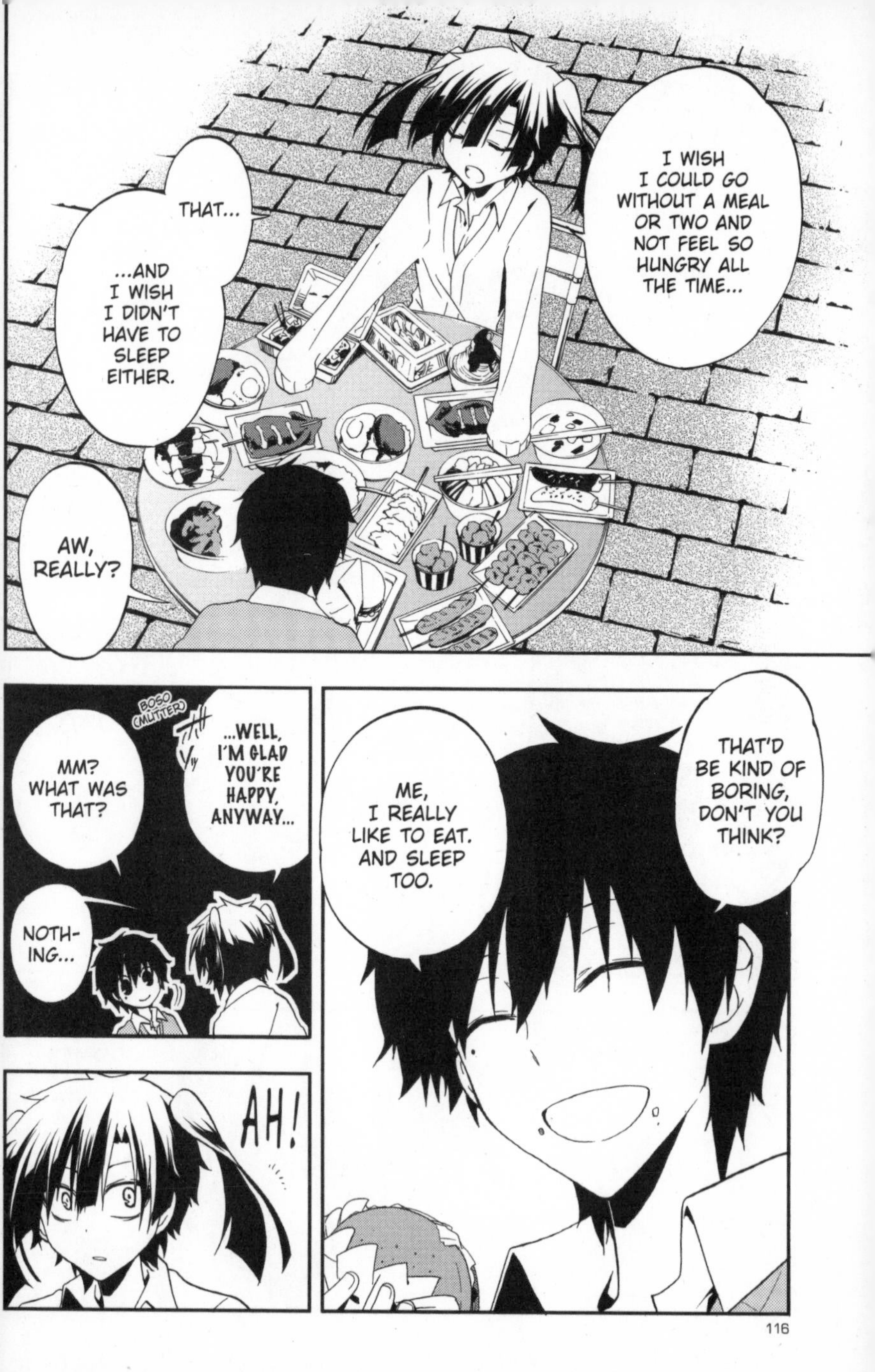
I WISH I COULD GO WITHOUT A MEAL OR TWO AND NOT FEEL SO HUNGRY ALL THE TIME...
THAT...
...AND I WISH I DIDN'T HAVE TO SLEEP EITHER.
AW, REALLY?
THAT'D BE KIND OF BORING, DON'T YOU THINK?
ME, I REALLY LIKE TO EAT. AND SLEEP TOO.
BOSO (MUTTER)
...WELL, I'M GLAD YOU'RE HAPPY, ANYWAY...
MM? WHAT WAS THAT?
NOTH-ING...
AH!

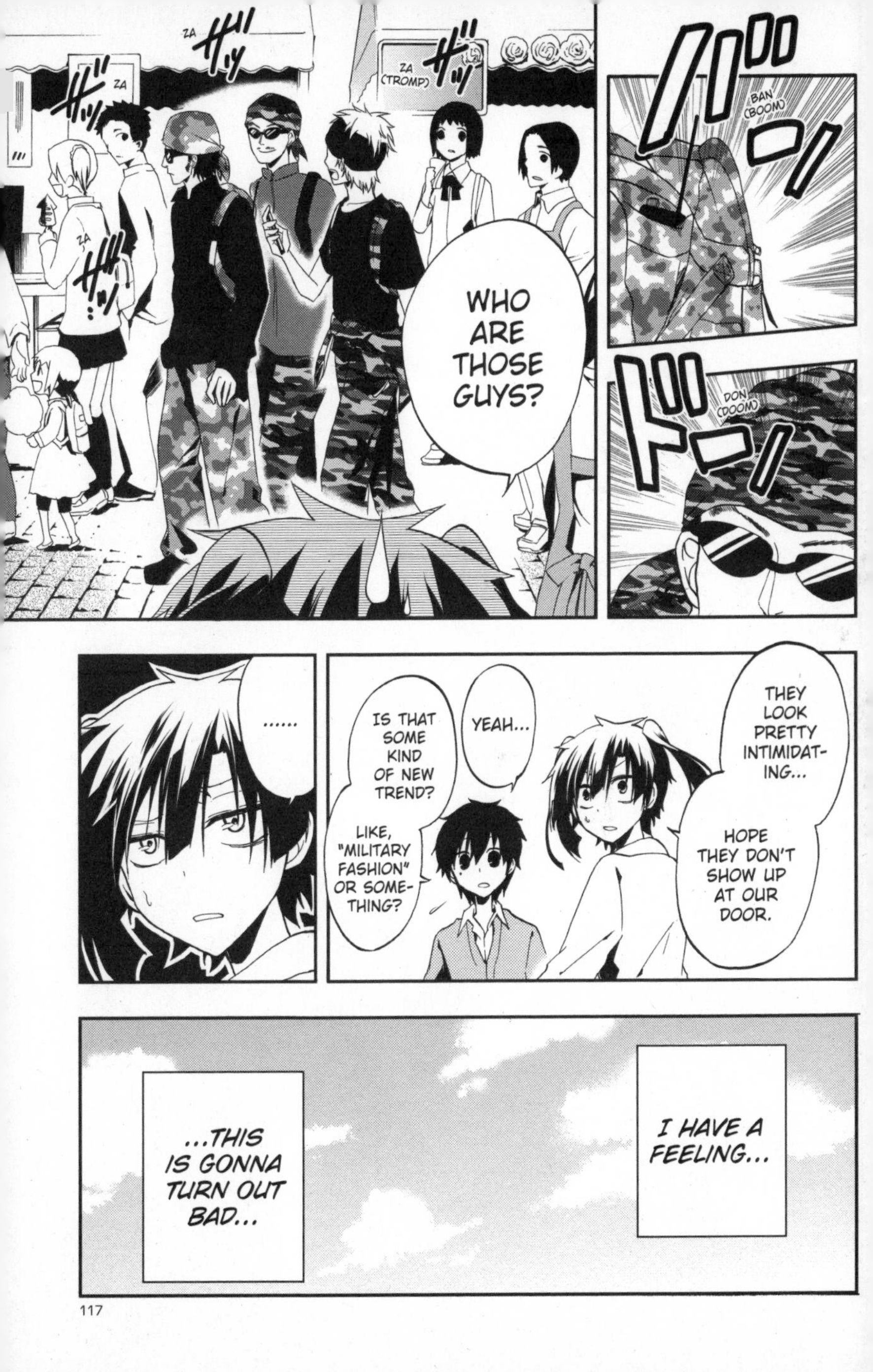
BAN (BOOM)
DON (DOOM)
ZA (TROMP)
ZA
ZA
ZA
WHO ARE THOSE GUYS?
THEY LOOK PRETTY INTIMIDAT-ING...
HOPE THEY DON'T SHOW UP AT OUR DOOR.
YEAH...
IS THAT SOME KIND OF NEW TREND?
LIKE, "MILITARY FASHION" OR SOME-THING?
......
I HAVE A FEELING...
...THIS IS GONNA TURN OUT BAD...

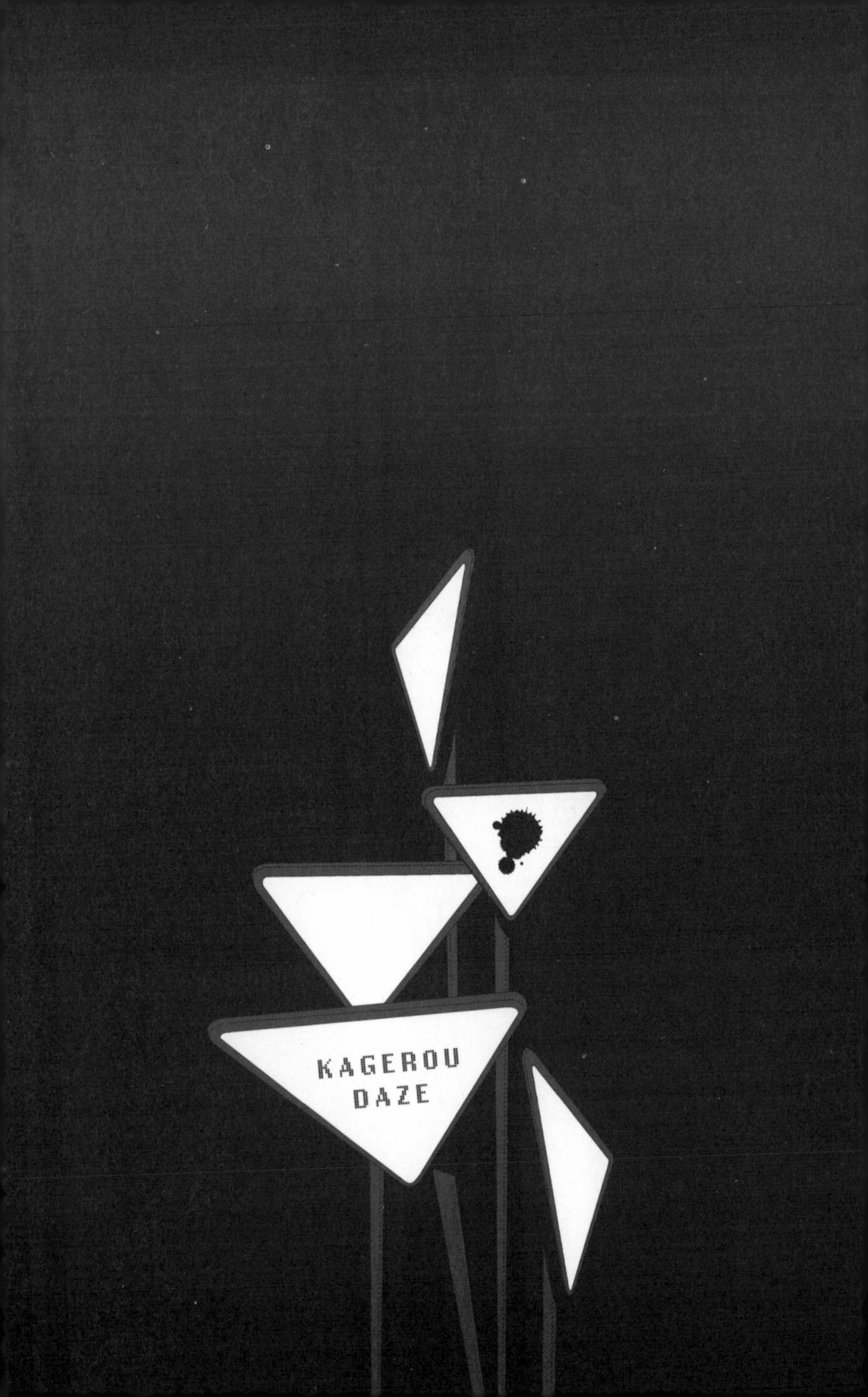
KAGEROU
DAZE

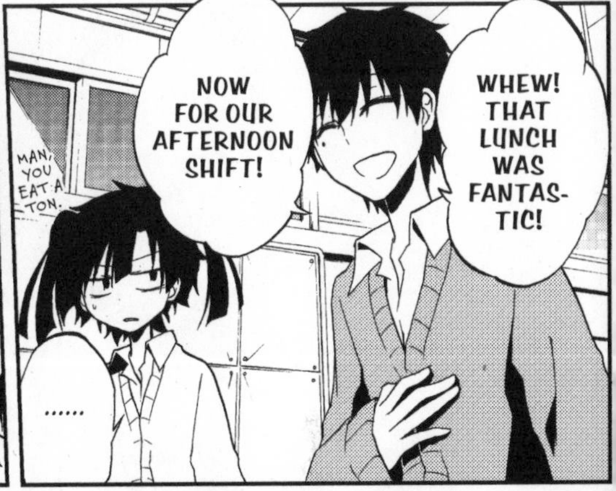
WHEW! THAT LUNCH WAS FANTAS-TIC!
NOW FOR OUR AFTERNOON SHIFT!
MAN, YOU EAT A TON.
......

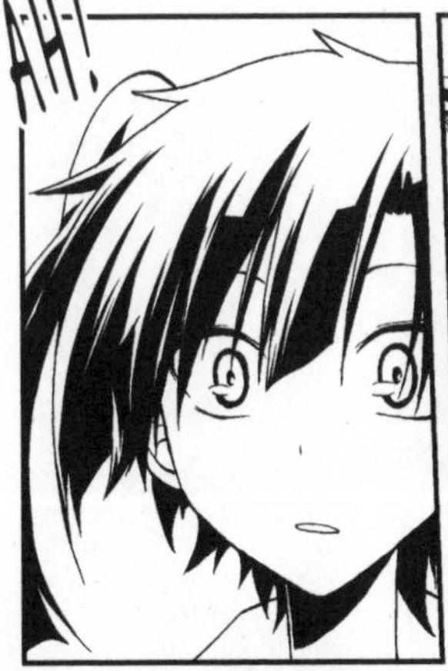
AH!

SIGN: SCIENCE STORAGE

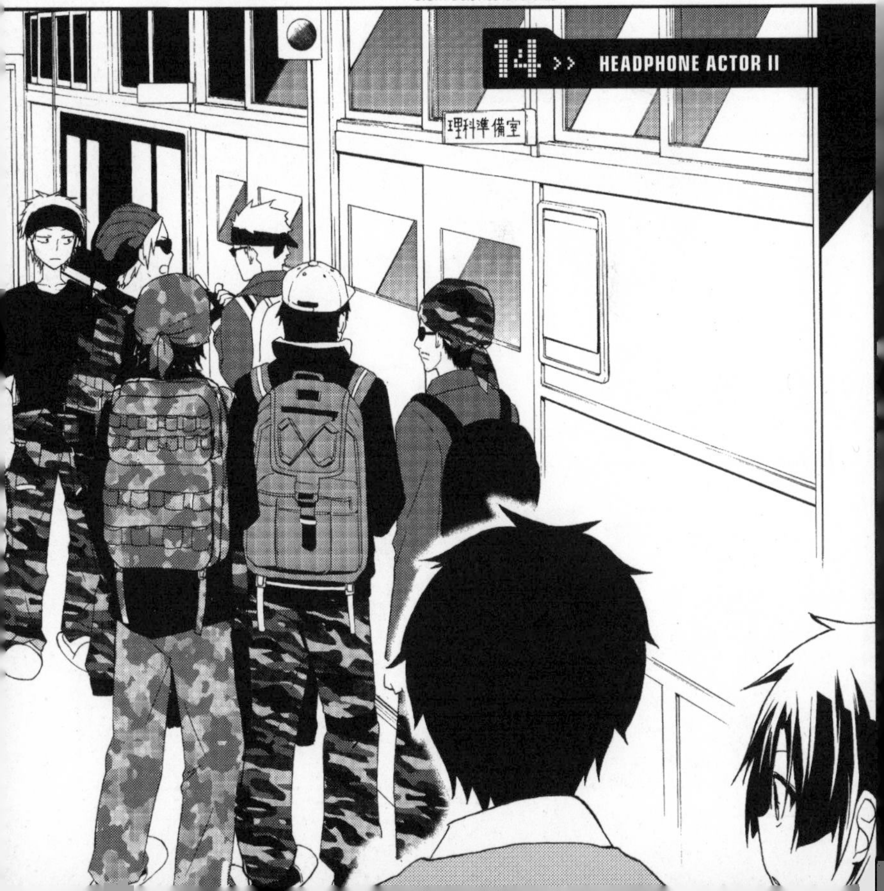
14 >> HEADPHONE ACTOR II
理科準備室

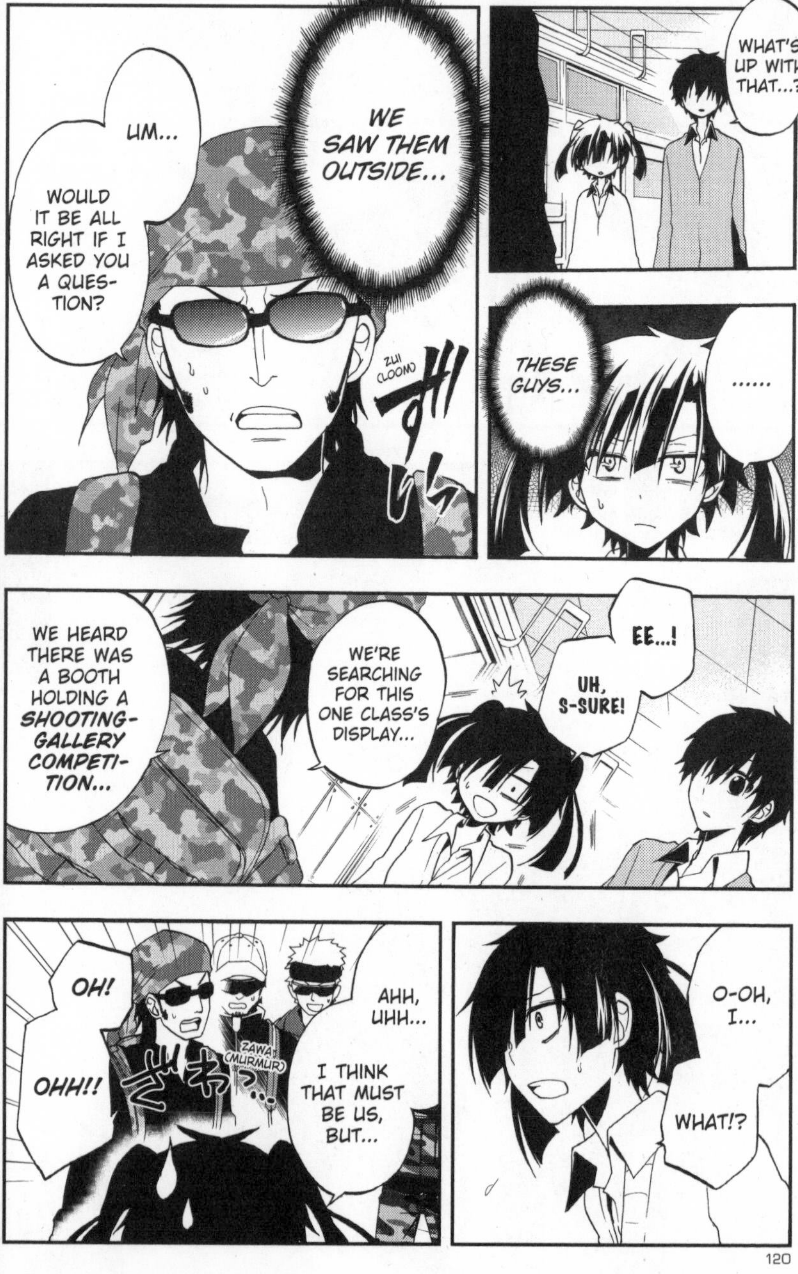
WHAT'S UP WITH THAT...?
......
THESE GUYS...
WE SAW THEM OUTSIDE...
UM...
WOULD IT BE ALL RIGHT IF I ASKED YOU A QUES-TION?
ZUI (LOOM)
EE...!
UH, S-SURE!
WE'RE SEARCHING FOR THIS ONE CLASS'S DISPLAY...
WE HEARD THERE WAS A BOOTH HOLDING A SHOOTING-GALLERY COMPETI-TION...
O-OH, I...
WHAT!?
AHH, UHH...
I THINK THAT MUST BE US, BUT...
ZAWA (MURMUR)
OH!
OHH!!

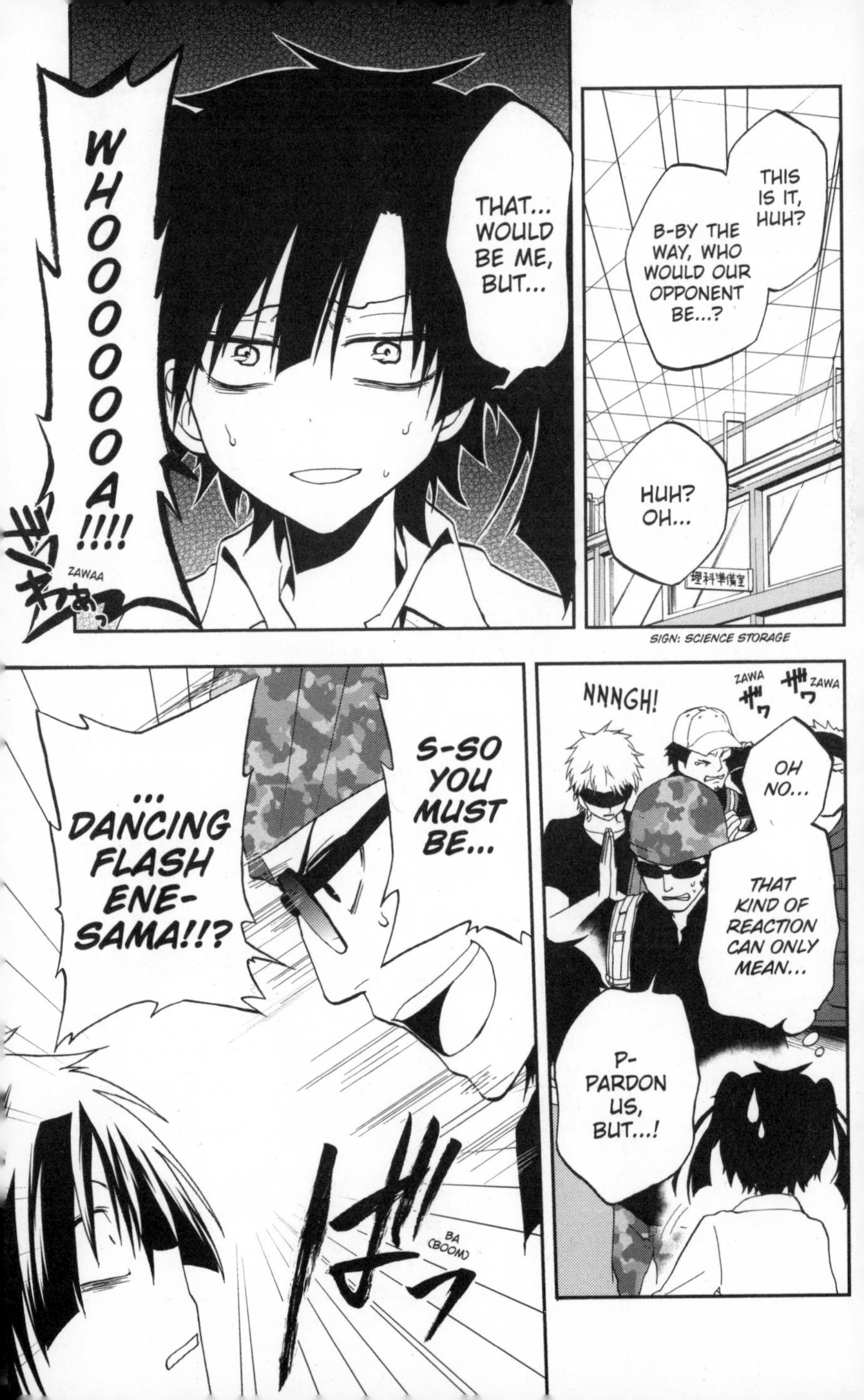
THIS IS IT, HUH?
B-BY THE WAY, WHO WOULD OUR OPPONENT BE...?
HUH? OH...
理科準備室
SIGN: SCIENCE STORAGE
THAT... WOULD BE ME, BUT...
WHOOOOOOOA!!!!
ZAWAA
NNNGH!
ZAWA
ZAWA
OH NO...
THAT KIND OF REACTION CAN ONLY MEAN...
P-PARDON US, BUT...!
S-SO YOU MUST BE...
...DANCING FLASH ENE-SAMA!!?
BA (BOOM)

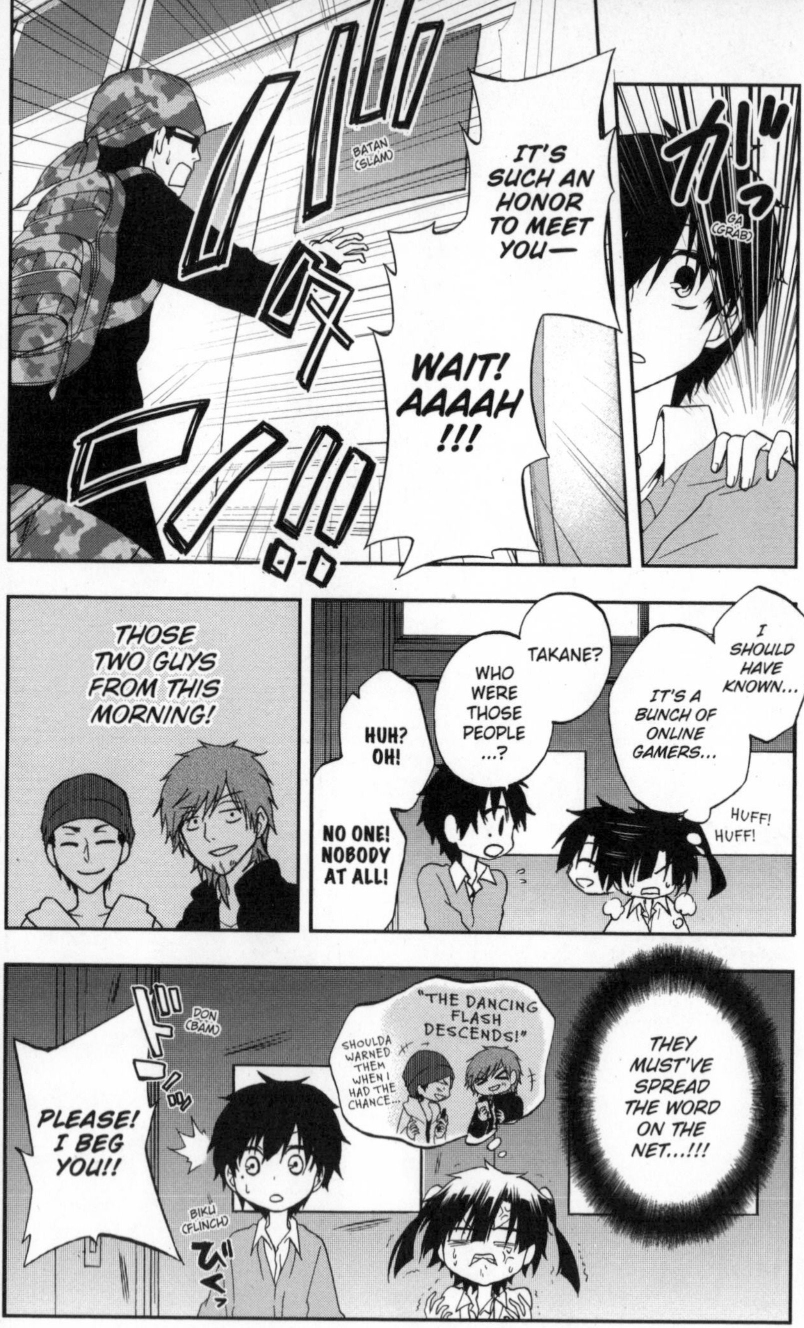
GA (GRAB)
IT'S SUCH AN HONOR TO MEET YOU—
BATAN (SLAM)
WAIT! AAAAH!!!
I SHOULD HAVE KNOWN...
IT'S A BUNCH OF ONLINE GAMERS...
TAKANE?
WHO WERE THOSE PEOPLE ...?
HUFF! HUFF!
HUH? OH!
NO ONE! NOBODY AT ALL!
THOSE TWO GUYS FROM THIS MORNING!
THEY MUST'VE SPREAD THE WORD ON THE NET...!!!
"THE DANCING FLASH DESCENDS!"
SHOULDA WARNED THEM WHEN I HAD THE CHANCE...
DON (BAM)
PLEASE! I BEG YOU!!
BIKU (FLINCH)

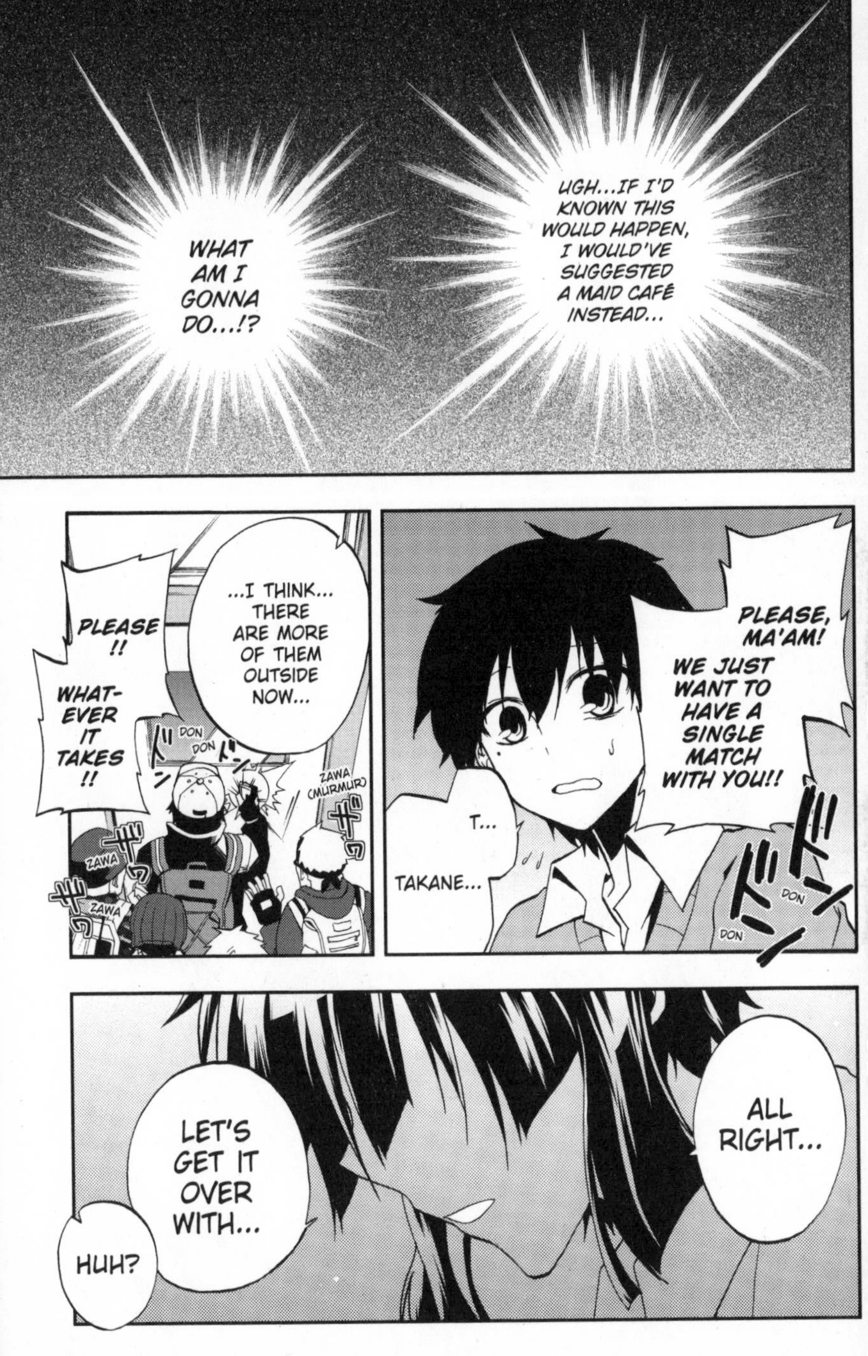
UGH...IF I'D KNOWN THIS WOULD HAPPEN, I WOULD'VE SUGGESTED A MAID CAFÉ INSTEAD...
WHAT AM I GONNA DO...!?
PLEASE, MA'AM! WE JUST WANT TO HAVE A SINGLE MATCH WITH YOU!!
DON
DON
T... TAKANE...
...I THINK... THERE ARE MORE OF THEM OUTSIDE NOW...
PLEASE!!
WHAT-EVER IT TAKES!!
DON
DON
ZAWA (MURMUR)
ZAWA
ZAWA
ALL RIGHT...
LET'S GET IT OVER WITH...
HUH?

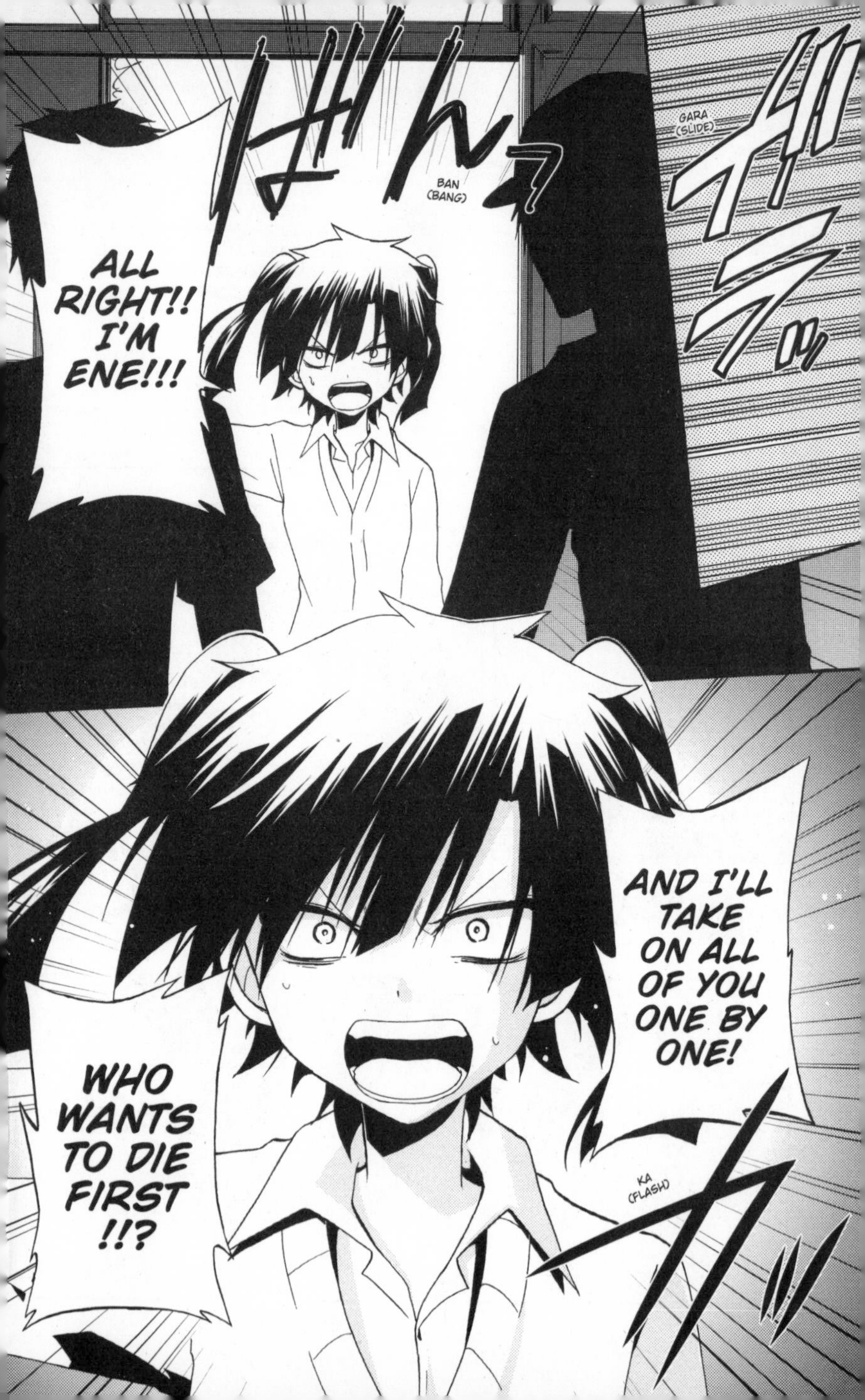
GARA (SLIDE)
BAN (BANG)
ALL RIGHT!! I'M ENE!!!
AND I'LL TAKE ON ALL OF YOU ONE BY ONE!
KA (FLASH)
WHO WANTS TO DIE FIRST !!?

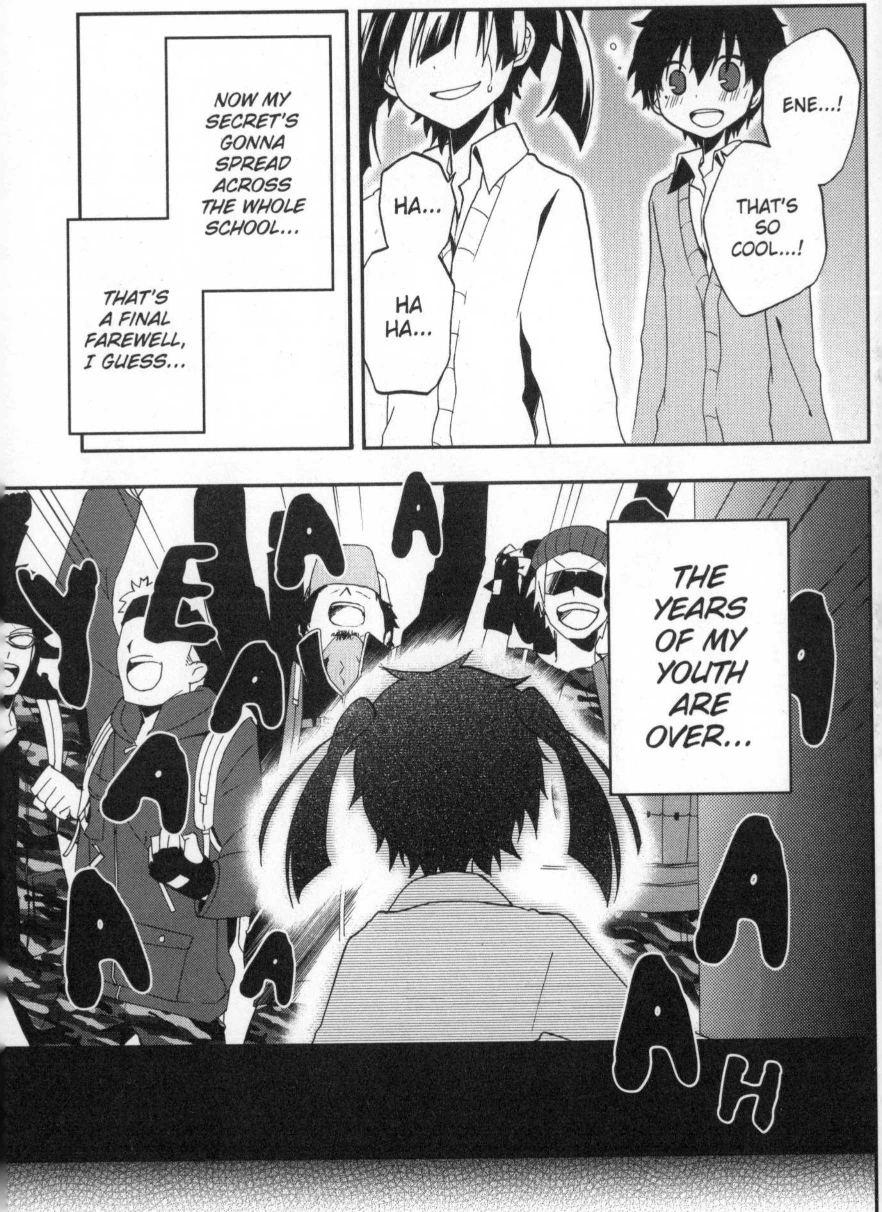
ENE...!
THAT'S SO COOL...!
HA...
HA HA...
NOW MY SECRET'S GONNA SPREAD ACROSS THE WHOLE SCHOOL...
THAT'S A FINAL FAREWELL, I GUESS...
THE YEARS OF MY YOUTH ARE OVER...
YEAAAAAAAAAH

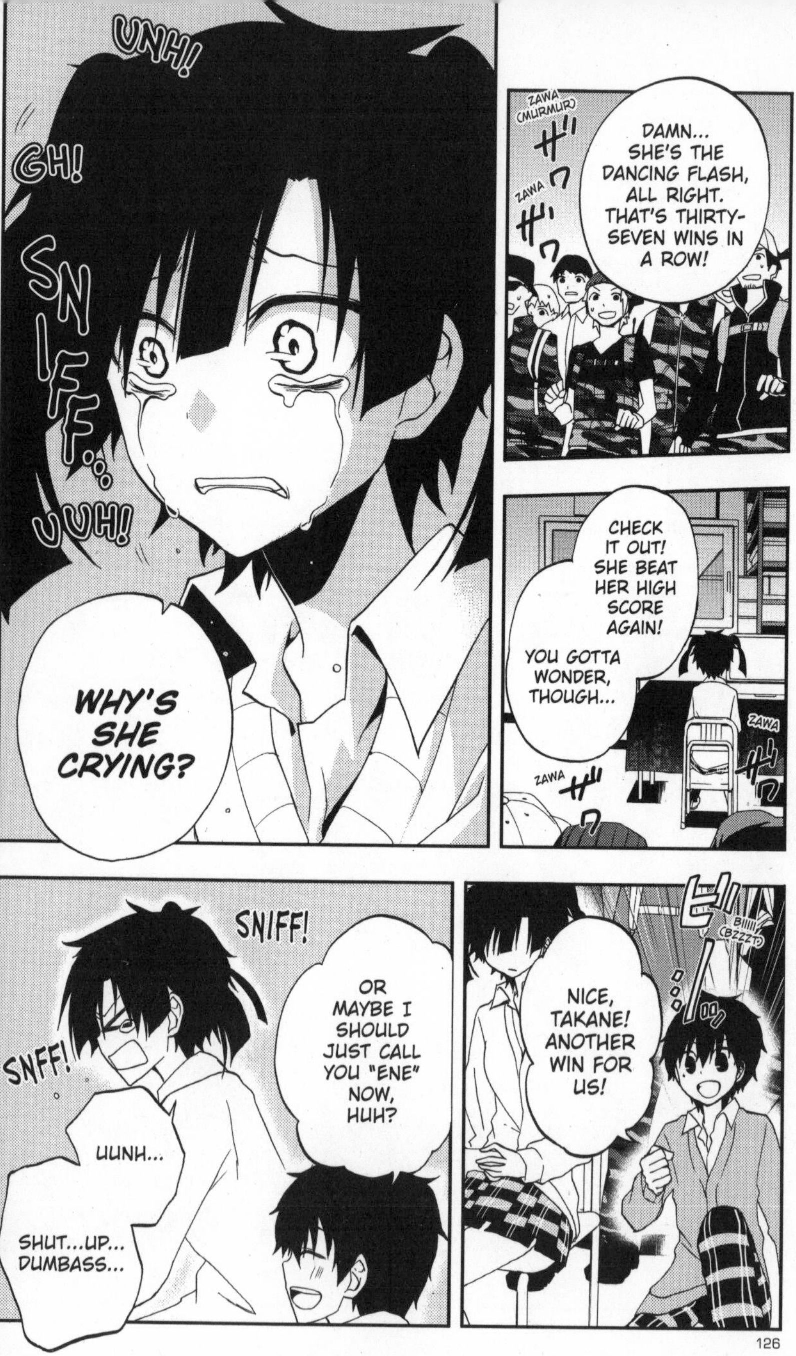

ZAWA (MURMUR)
ZAWA
DAMN... SHE'S THE DANCING FLASH, ALL RIGHT. THAT'S THIRTY-SEVEN WINS IN A ROW!
CHECK IT OUT! SHE BEAT HER HIGH SCORE AGAIN!
YOU GOTTA WONDER, THOUGH...
ZAWA
ZAWA
UNH!
GH!
SNIFF...
UUH!
WHY'S SHE CRYING?
BIIIII (BZZZT)
NICE, TAKANE! ANOTHER WIN FOR US!
SNIFF!
OR MAYBE I SHOULD JUST CALL YOU "ENE" NOW, HUH?
SNFF!
UUNH...
SHUT...UP... DUMBASS...

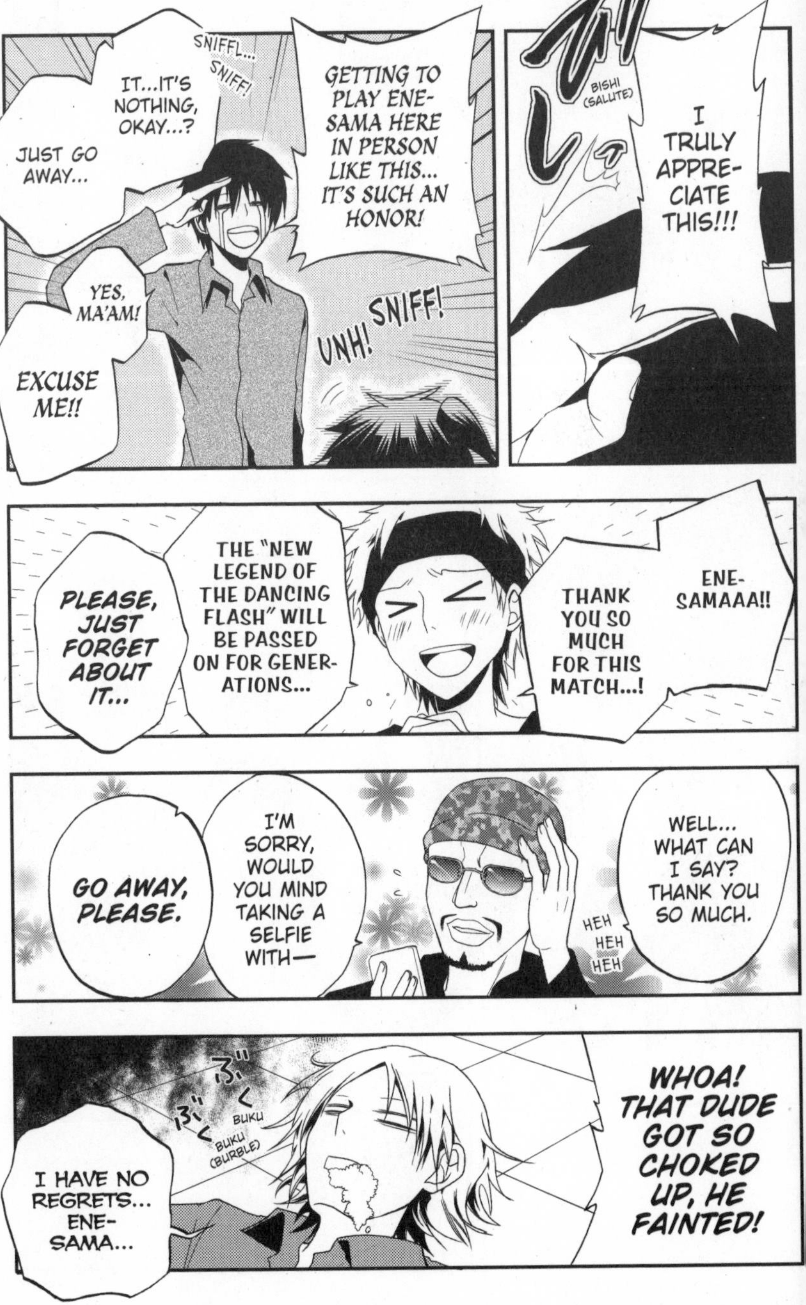
BISHI (SALUTE)
I TRULY APPRECIATE THIS!!!
GETTING TO PLAY ENE-SAMA HERE IN PERSON LIKE THIS... IT'S SUCH AN HONOR!
SNIFFL... SNIFF!
IT...IT'S NOTHING, OKAY...?
JUST GO AWAY...
UNH! SNIFF!
YES, MA'AM!
EXCUSE ME!!
ENE-SAMAAA!!
THANK YOU SO MUCH FOR THIS MATCH...!
THE "NEW LEGEND OF THE DANCING FLASH" WILL BE PASSED ON FOR GENERATIONS...
PLEASE, JUST FORGET ABOUT IT...
WELL... WHAT CAN I SAY? THANK YOU SO MUCH.
HEH HEH HEH
I'M SORRY, WOULD YOU MIND TAKING A SELFIE WITH—
GO AWAY, PLEASE.
WHOA! THAT DUDE GOT SO CHOKED UP, HE FAINTED!
ぶく ぶく
BUKU BUKU (BURBLE)
I HAVE NO REGRETS... ENE-SAMA...

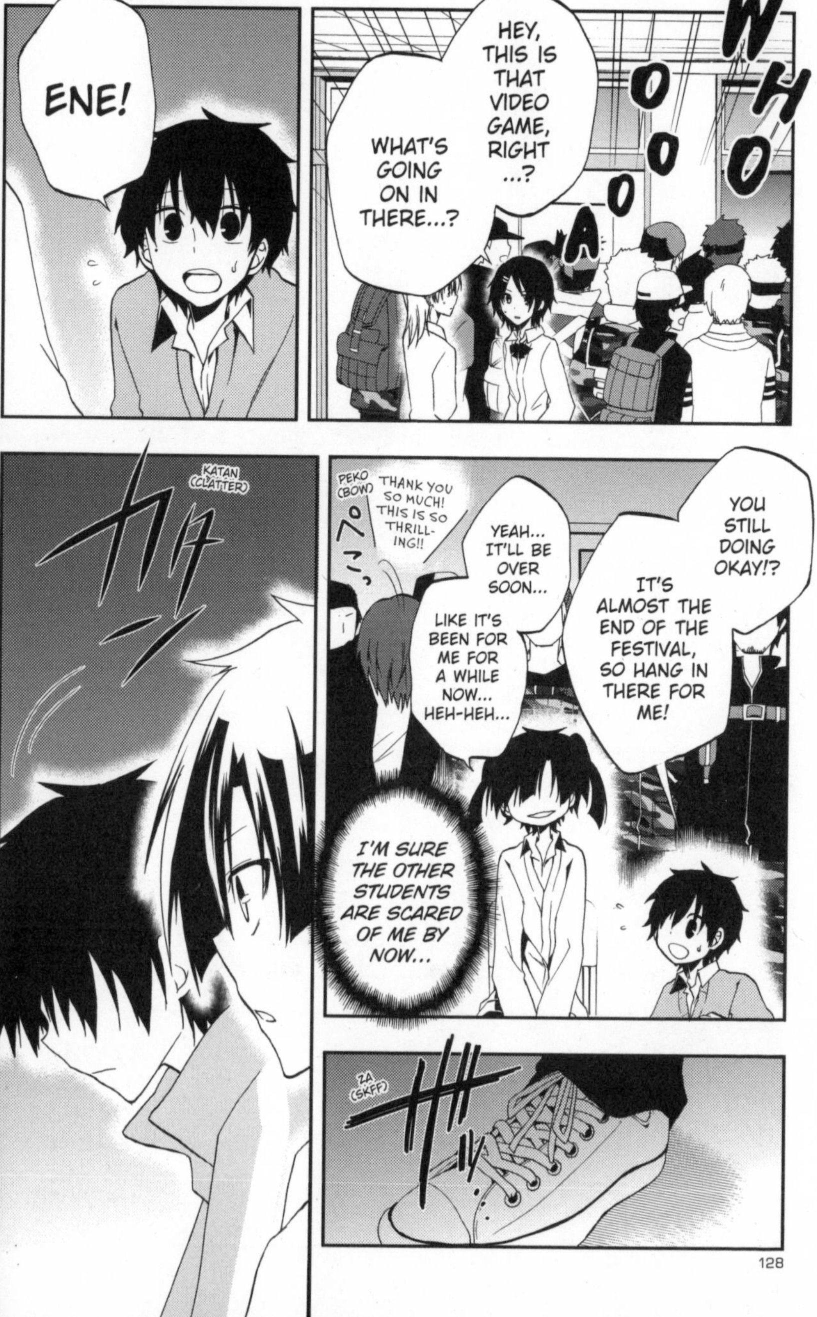
WHOOOO
HEY, THIS IS THAT VIDEO GAME, RIGHT ...?
WHAT'S GOING ON IN THERE...?
ENE!
YOU STILL DOING OKAY!?
IT'S ALMOST THE END OF THE FESTIVAL, SO HANG IN THERE FOR ME!
YEAH... IT'LL BE OVER SOON...
PEKO (BOW)
THANK YOU SO MUCH! THIS IS SO THRILL-ING!!
LIKE IT'S BEEN FOR ME FOR A WHILE NOW... HEH-HEH...
I'M SURE THE OTHER STUDENTS ARE SCARED OF ME BY NOW...
ZA (SKFF)
KATAN (CLATTER)

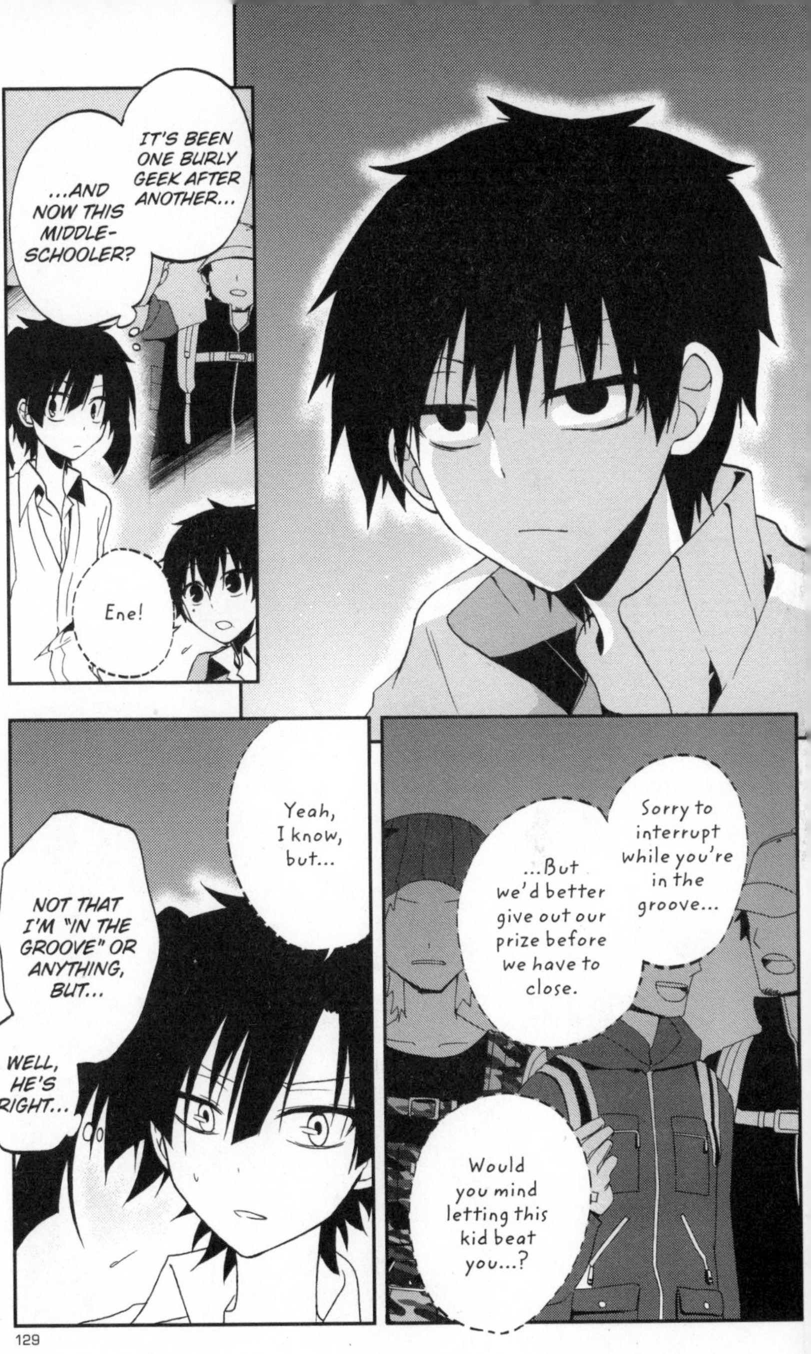
IT'S BEEN ONE BURLY GEEK AFTER ANOTHER...
...AND NOW THIS MIDDLE-SCHOOLER?
Ene!
Sorry to interrupt while you're in the groove...
...But we'd better give out our prize before we have to close.
Would you mind letting this kid beat you...?
Yeah, I know, but...
NOT THAT I'M "IN THE GROOVE" OR ANYTHING, BUT...
WELL, HE'S RIGHT...

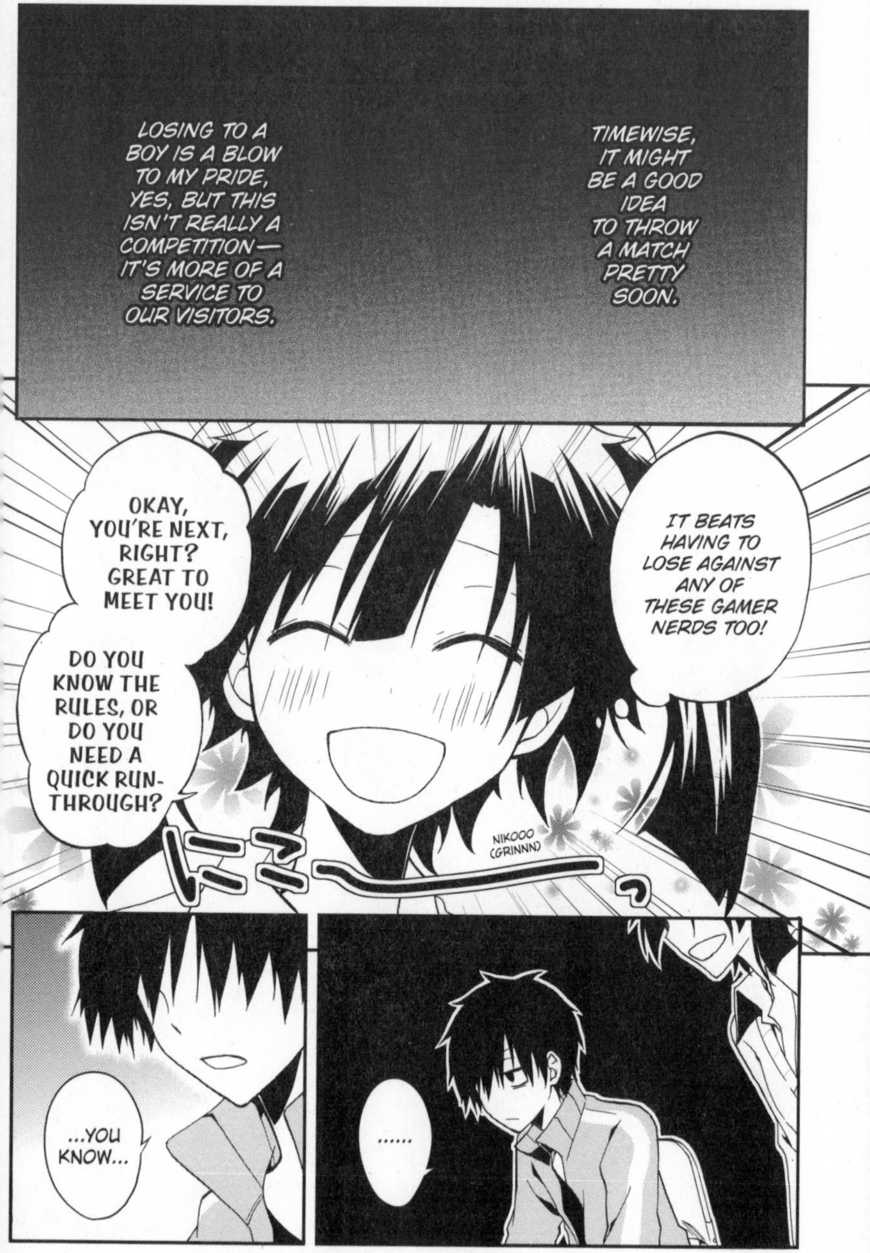
TIMEWISE, IT MIGHT BE A GOOD IDEA TO THROW A MATCH PRETTY SOON.
LOSING TO A BOY IS A BLOW TO MY PRIDE, YES, BUT THIS ISN'T REALLY A COMPETITION—IT'S MORE OF A SERVICE TO OUR VISITORS.
IT BEATS HAVING TO LOSE AGAINST ANY OF THESE GAMER NERDS TOO!
OKAY, YOU'RE NEXT, RIGHT? GREAT TO MEET YOU!
NIKOOO (GRINNN)
DO YOU KNOW THE RULES, OR DO YOU NEED A QUICK RUN-THROUGH?
......
...YOU KNOW...

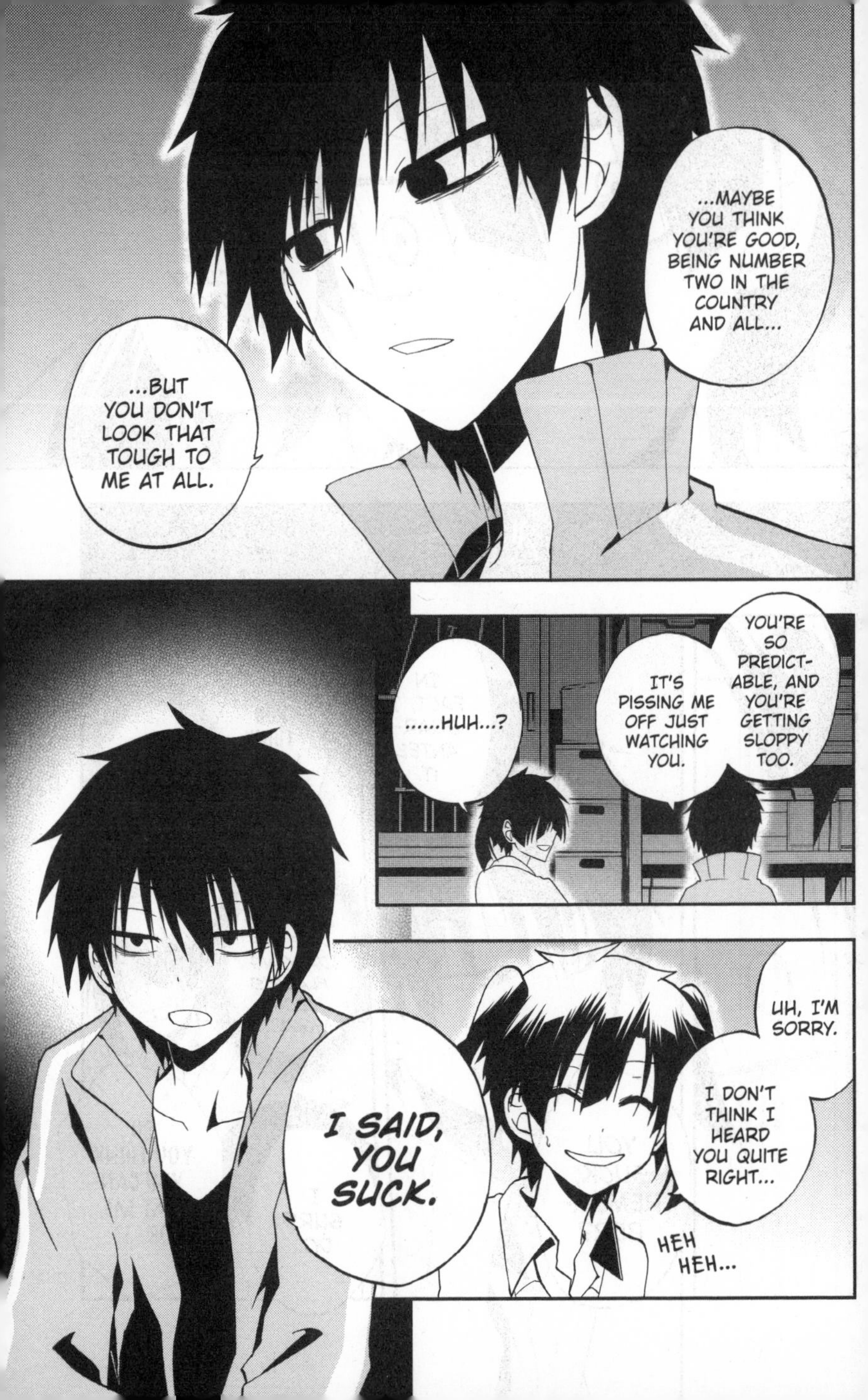
...MAYBE YOU THINK YOU'RE GOOD, BEING NUMBER TWO IN THE COUNTRY AND ALL...
...BUT YOU DON'T LOOK THAT TOUGH TO ME AT ALL.
YOU'RE SO PREDICT-ABLE, AND YOU'RE GETTING SLOPPY TOO.
IT'S PISSING ME OFF JUST WATCHING YOU.
......HUH...?
UH, I'M SORRY.
I DON'T THINK I HEARD YOU QUITE RIGHT...
HEH HEH...
I SAID, YOU SUCK.

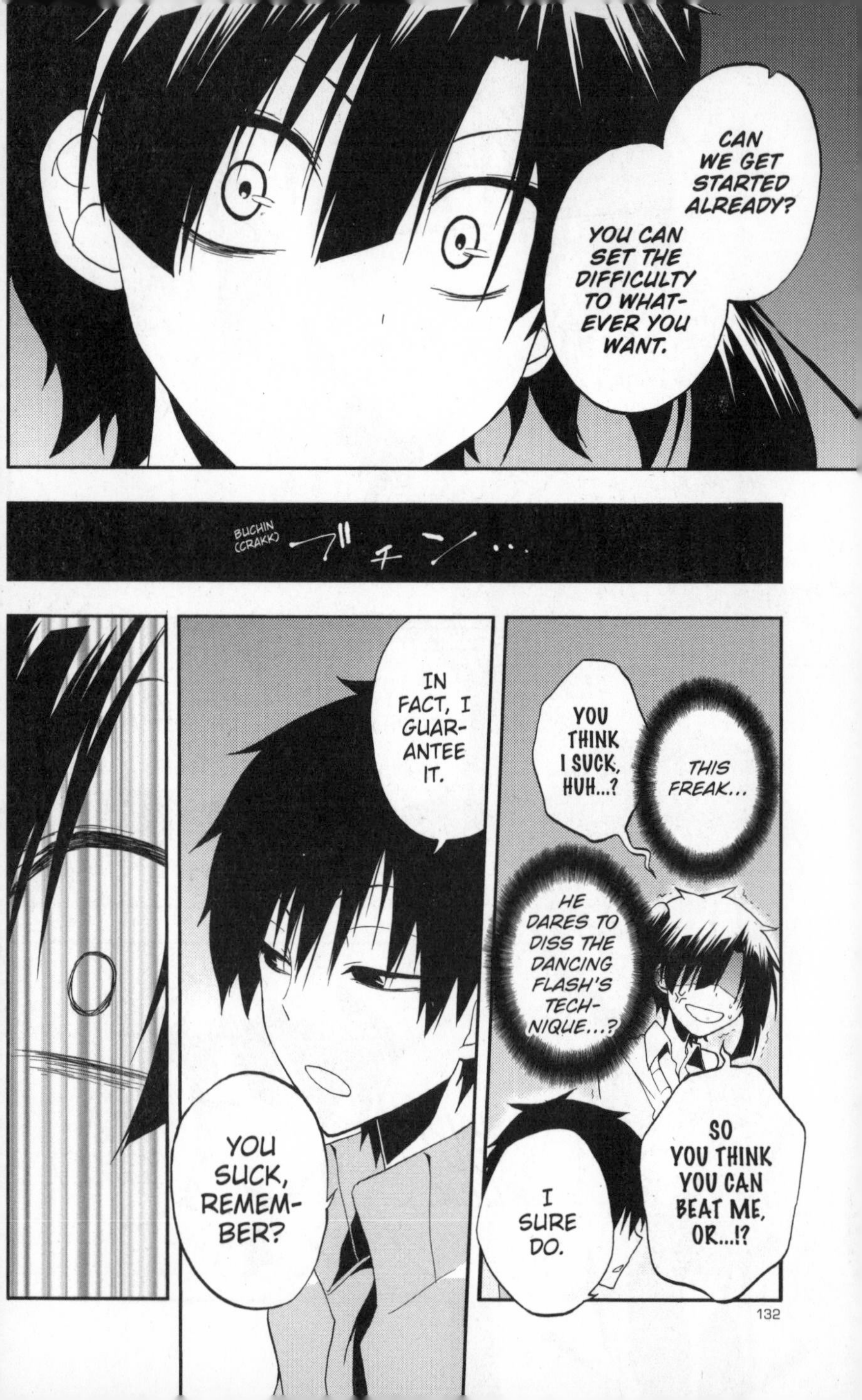
CAN WE GET STARTED ALREADY?
YOU CAN SET THE DIFFICULTY TO WHAT-EVER YOU WANT.
BUCHIN (CRAKK)
ブチン…
THIS FREAK...
YOU THINK I SUCK, HUH...?
HE DARES TO DISS THE DANCING FLASH'S TECH-NIQUE...?
SO YOU THINK YOU CAN BEAT ME, OR...!?
I SURE DO.
IN FACT, I GUAR-ANTEE IT.
YOU SUCK, REMEM-BER?

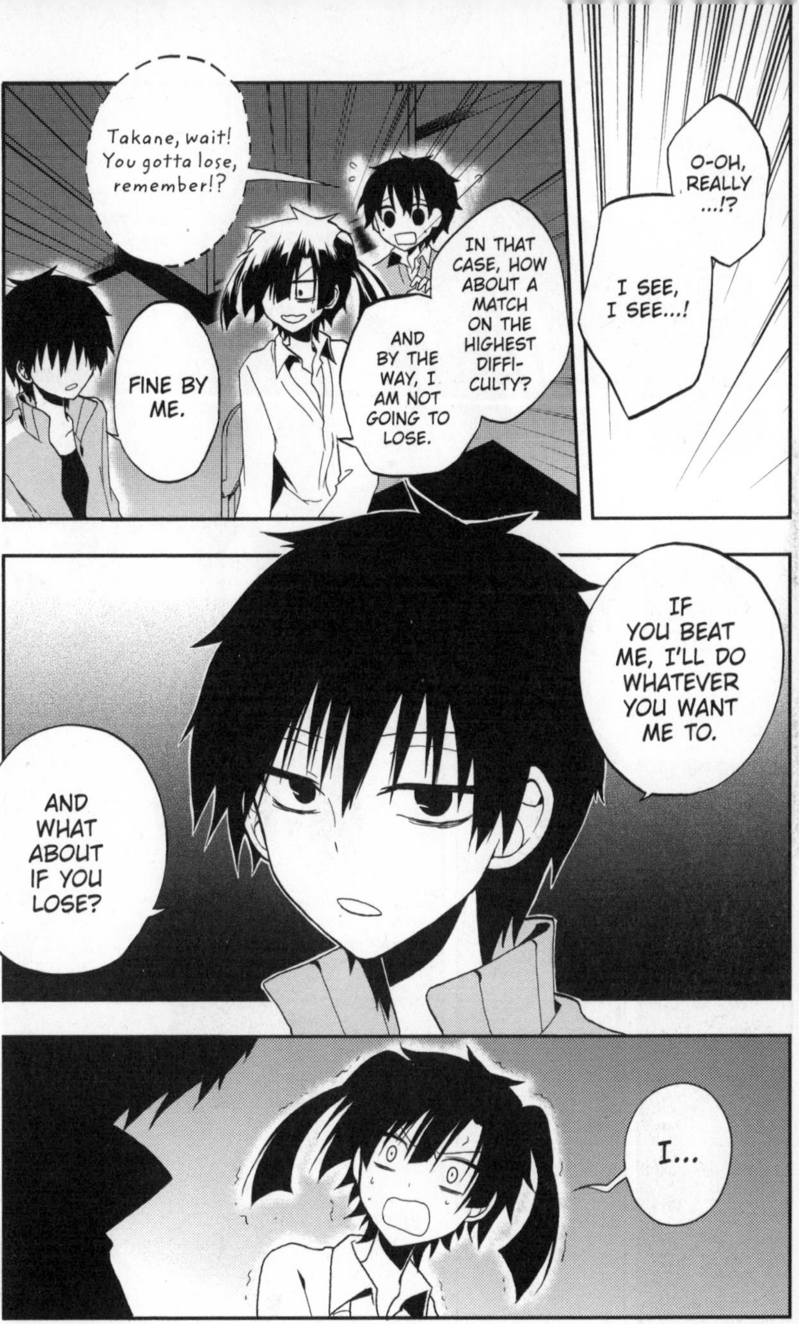
O-OH, REALLY ...!?
I SEE, I SEE...!
IN THAT CASE, HOW ABOUT A MATCH ON THE HIGHEST DIFFICULTY?
AND BY THE WAY, I AM NOT GOING TO LOSE.
Takane, wait! You gotta lose, remember!?
FINE BY ME.
IF YOU BEAT ME, I'LL DO WHATEVER YOU WANT ME TO.
AND WHAT ABOUT IF YOU LOSE?
I...

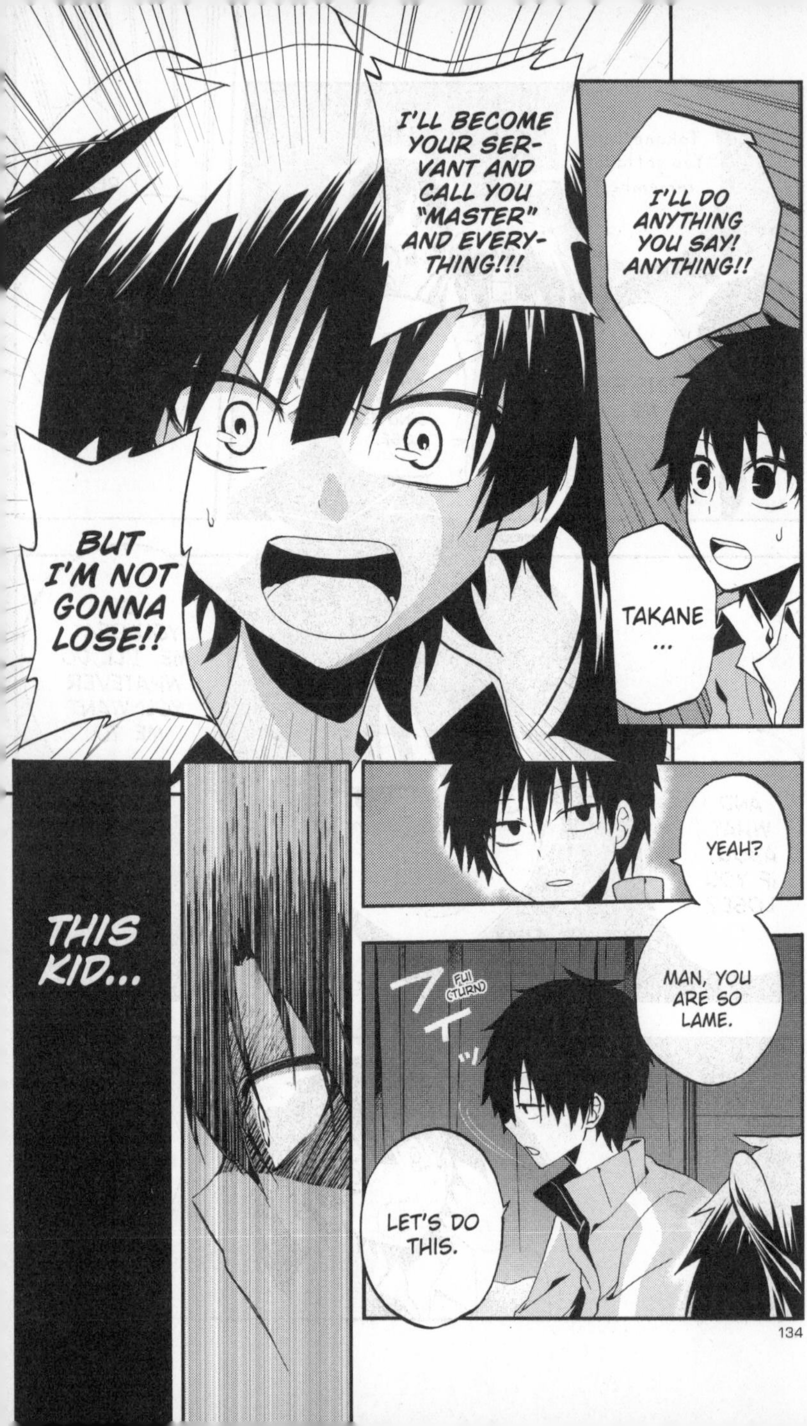
I'LL DO ANYTHING YOU SAY! ANYTHING!!
TAKANE ...
I'LL BECOME YOUR SERVANT AND CALL YOU "MASTER" AND EVERYTHING!!!
BUT I'M NOT GONNA LOSE!!
YEAH?
MAN, YOU ARE SO LAME.
FUI (TURN)
LET'S DO THIS.
THIS KID...

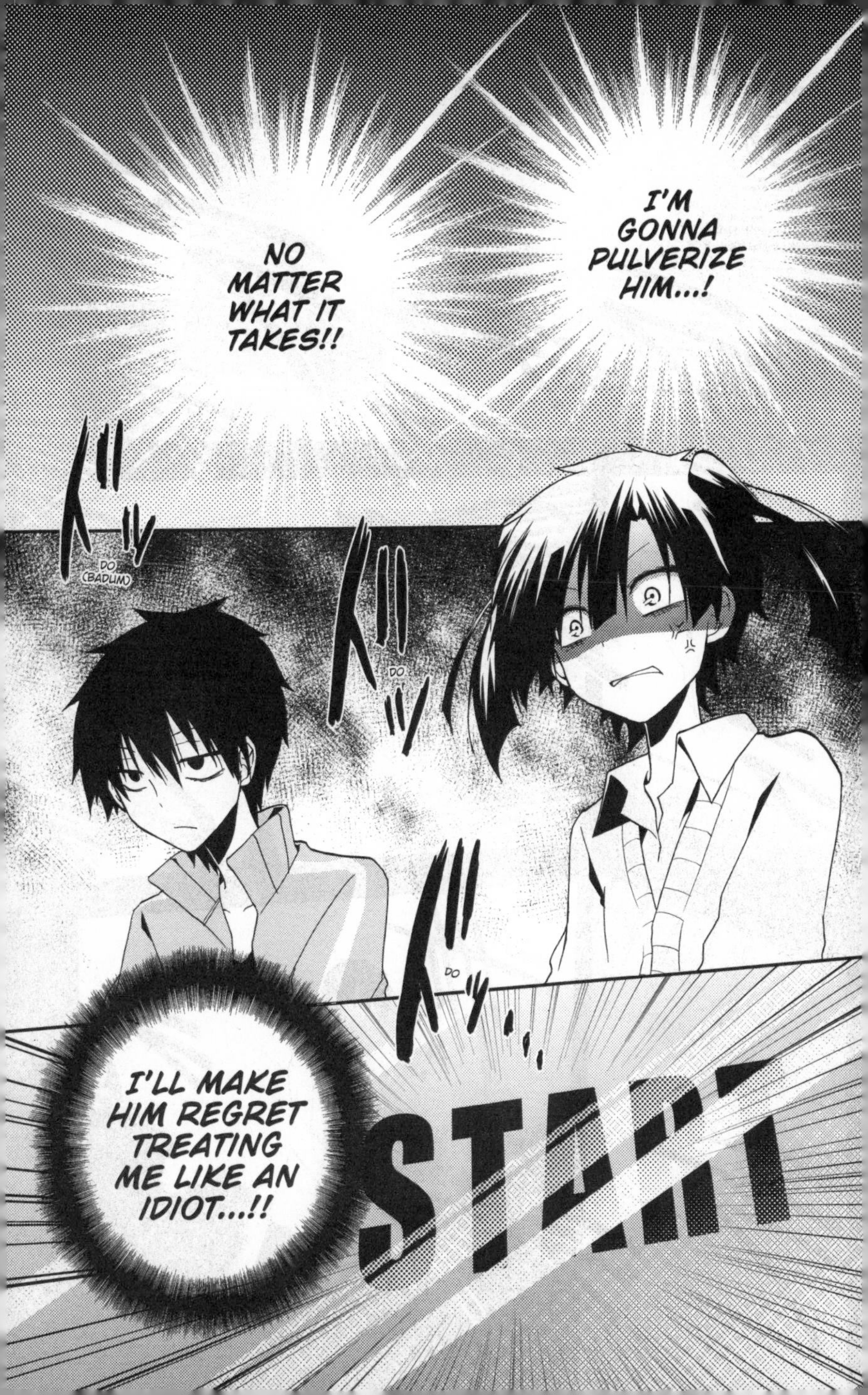
I'M GONNA PULVERIZE HIM...!
NO MATTER WHAT IT TAKES!!
ドッ
DO
ドッ
DO (BADUM)
ドッ
DO
START
I'LL MAKE HIM REGRET TREATING ME LIKE AN IDIOT...!!

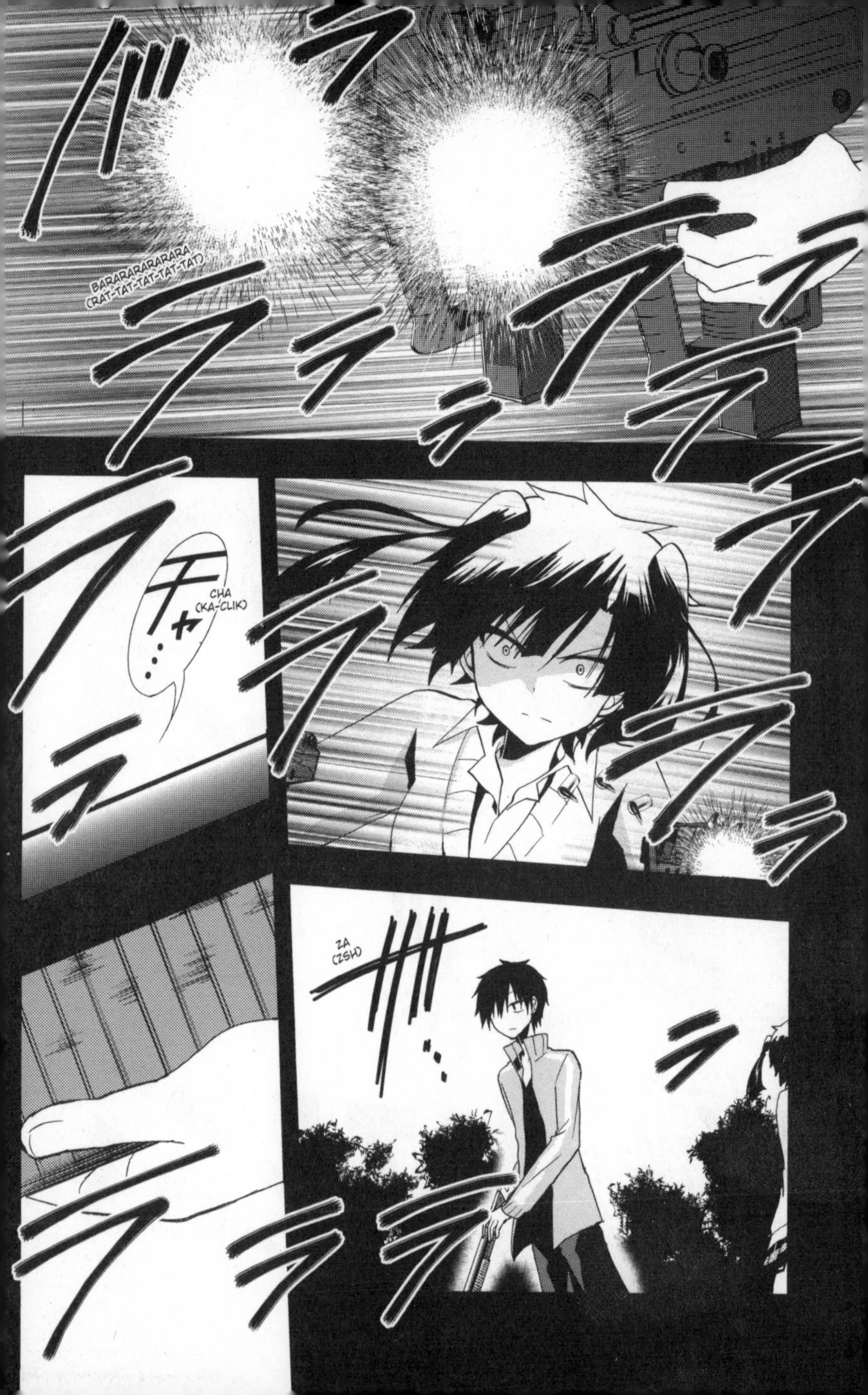
BARARARARARARA
(RAT-TAT-TAT-TAT-TAT)
CHA
(KA-CLIK)
ZA
(ZSH)

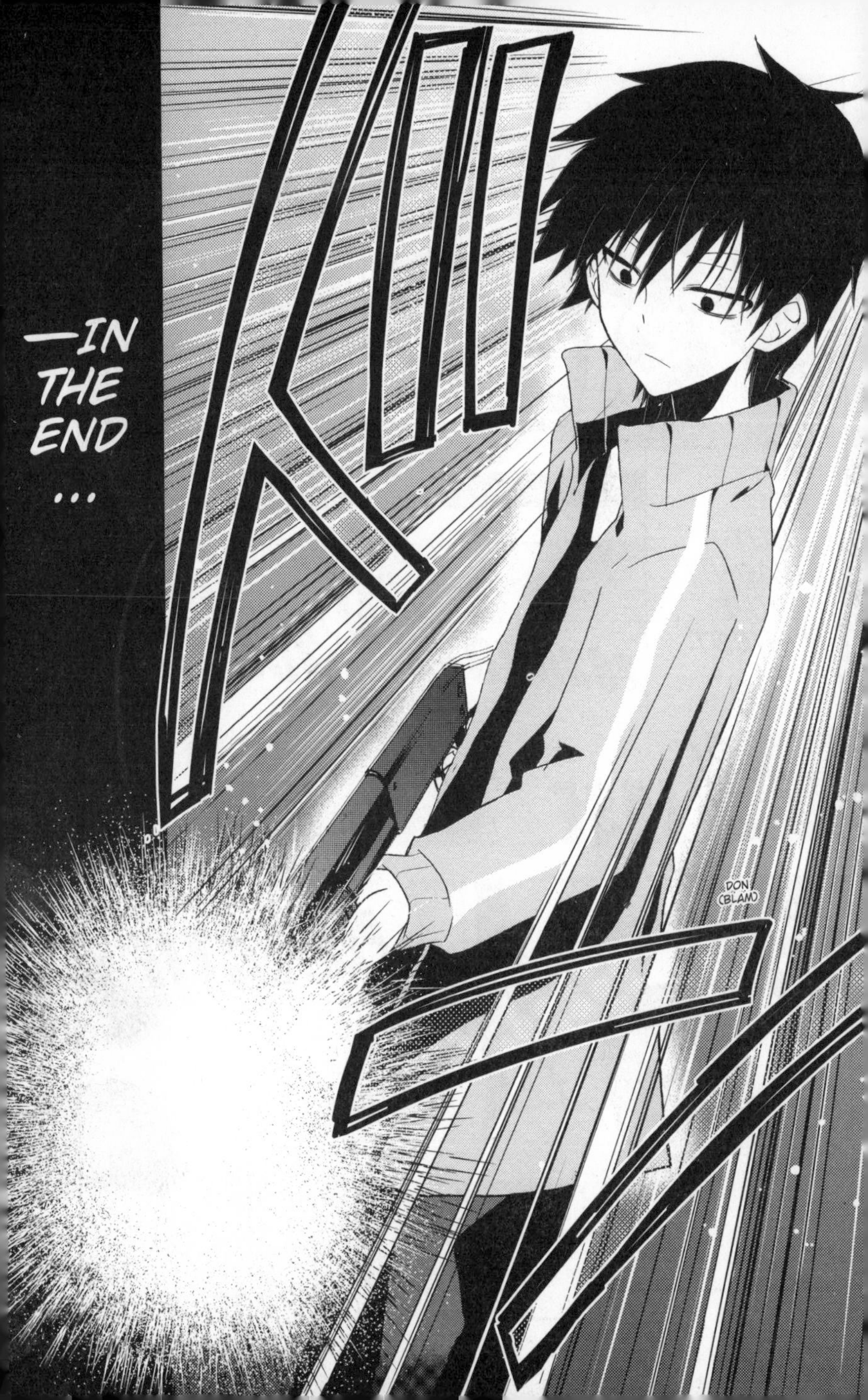
—IN THE END ...
DON (BLAM)

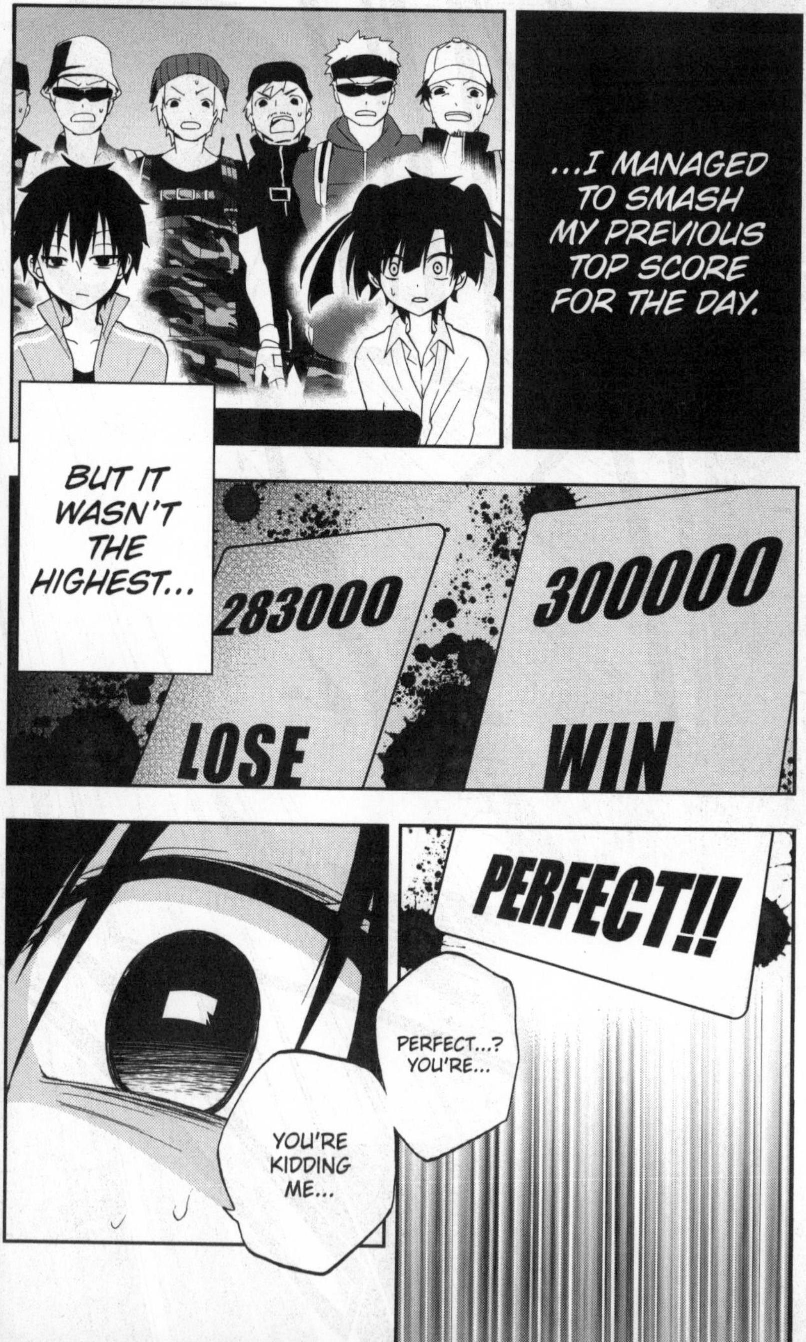
...I MANAGED TO SMASH MY PREVIOUS TOP SCORE FOR THE DAY.
BUT IT WASN'T THE HIGHEST...
300000
WIN
283000
LOSE
PERFECT!!
PERFECT...? YOU'RE...
YOU'RE KIDDING ME...

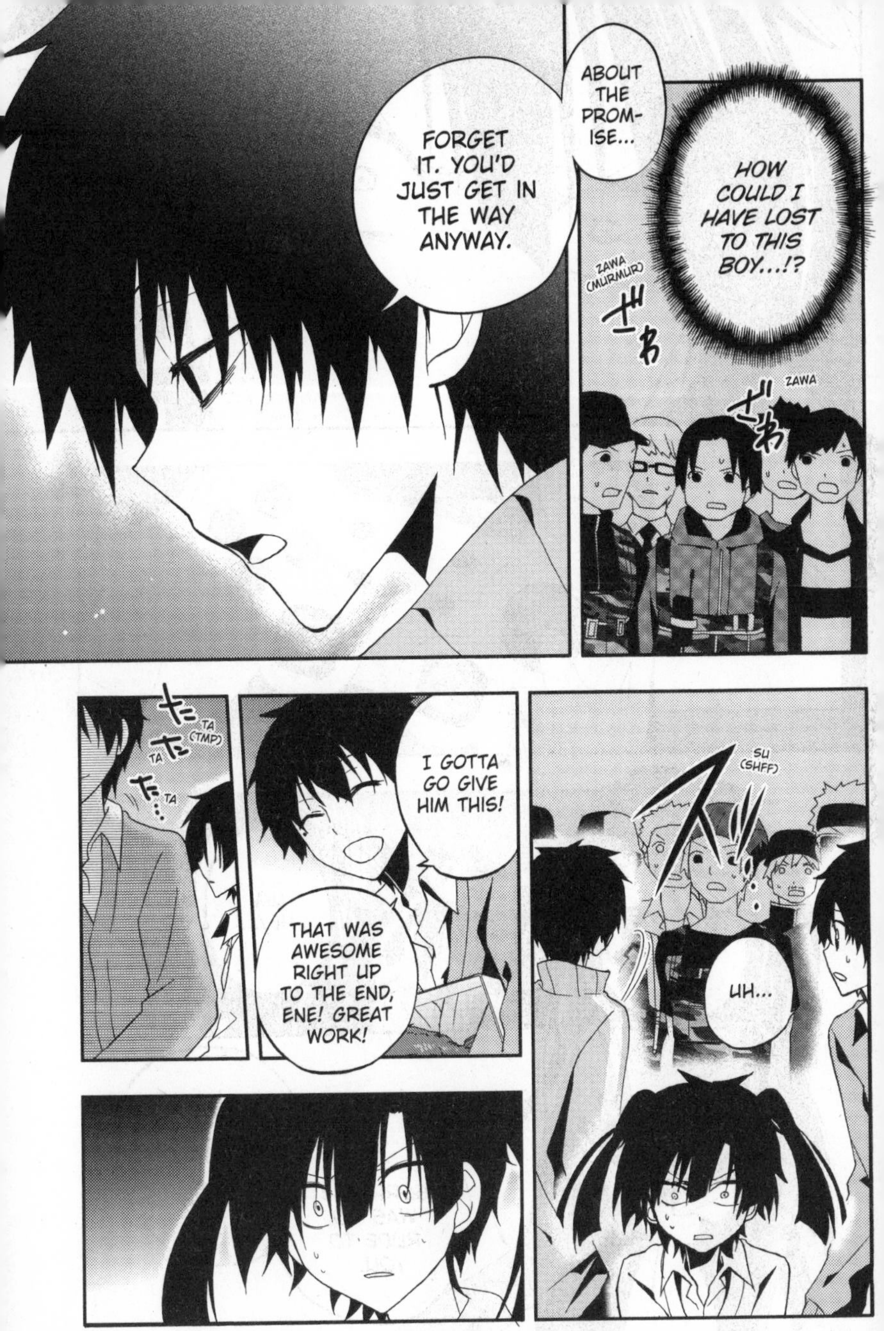
ABOUT THE PROMISE...
HOW COULD I HAVE LOST TO THIS BOY...!?
ZAWA (MURMUR)
ZAWA
FORGET IT. YOU'D JUST GET IN THE WAY ANYWAY.
SU (SHFF)
UH...
I GOTTA GO GIVE HIM THIS!
THAT WAS AWESOME RIGHT UP TO THE END, ENE! GREAT WORK!
TA (TMP)
TA
TA

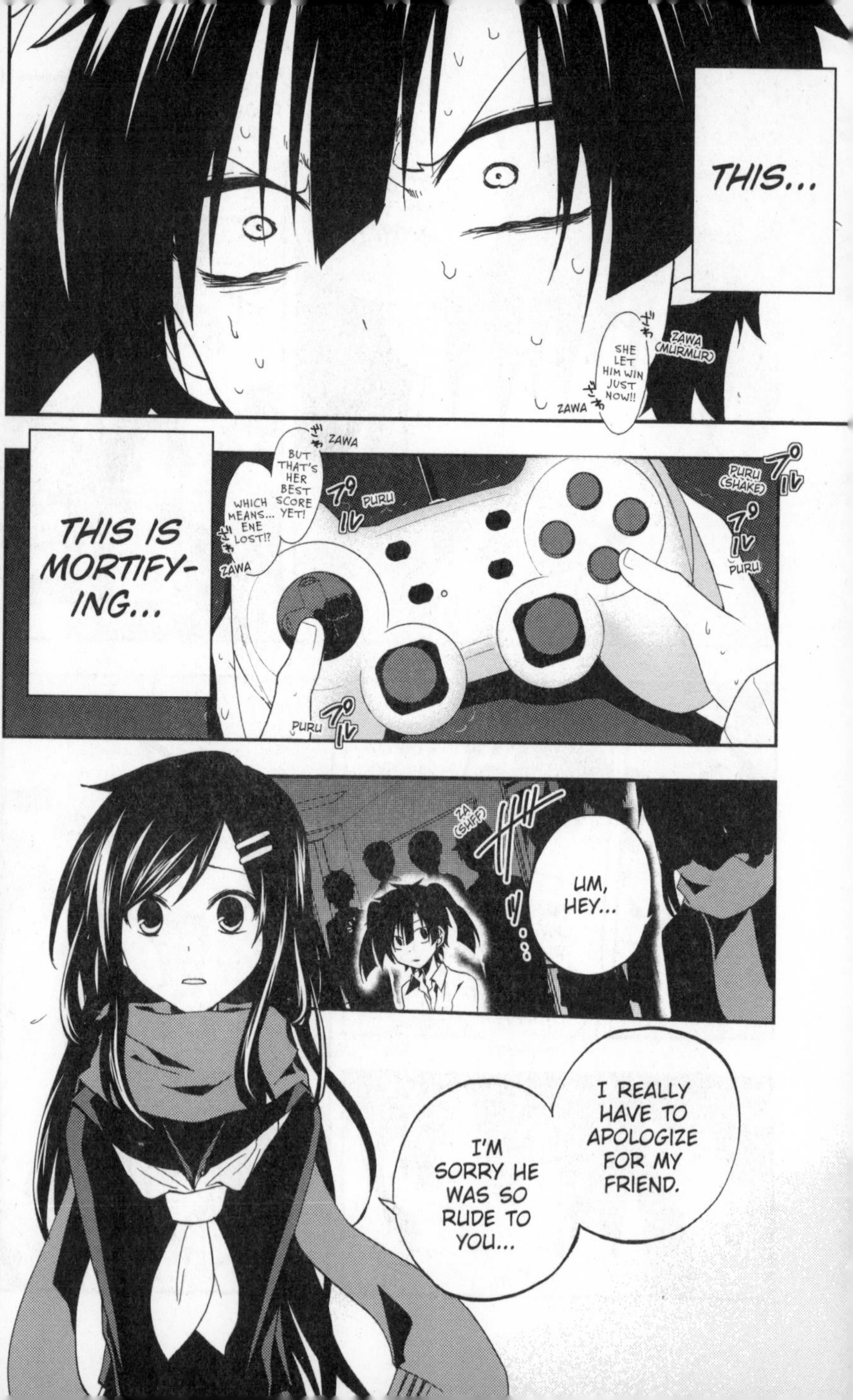
THIS...
ZAWA (MURMUR)
SHE LET HIM WIN JUST NOW!!
ZAWA
PURU (SHAKE)
PURU
PURU
BUT THAT'S HER BEST SCORE YET!
ZAWA
WHICH MEANS... ENE LOST!?
ZAWA
PURU
THIS IS MORTIFY-ING...
UM, HEY...
ZA (SHFF)
I REALLY HAVE TO APOLOGIZE FOR MY FRIEND.
I'M SORRY HE WAS SO RUDE TO YOU...

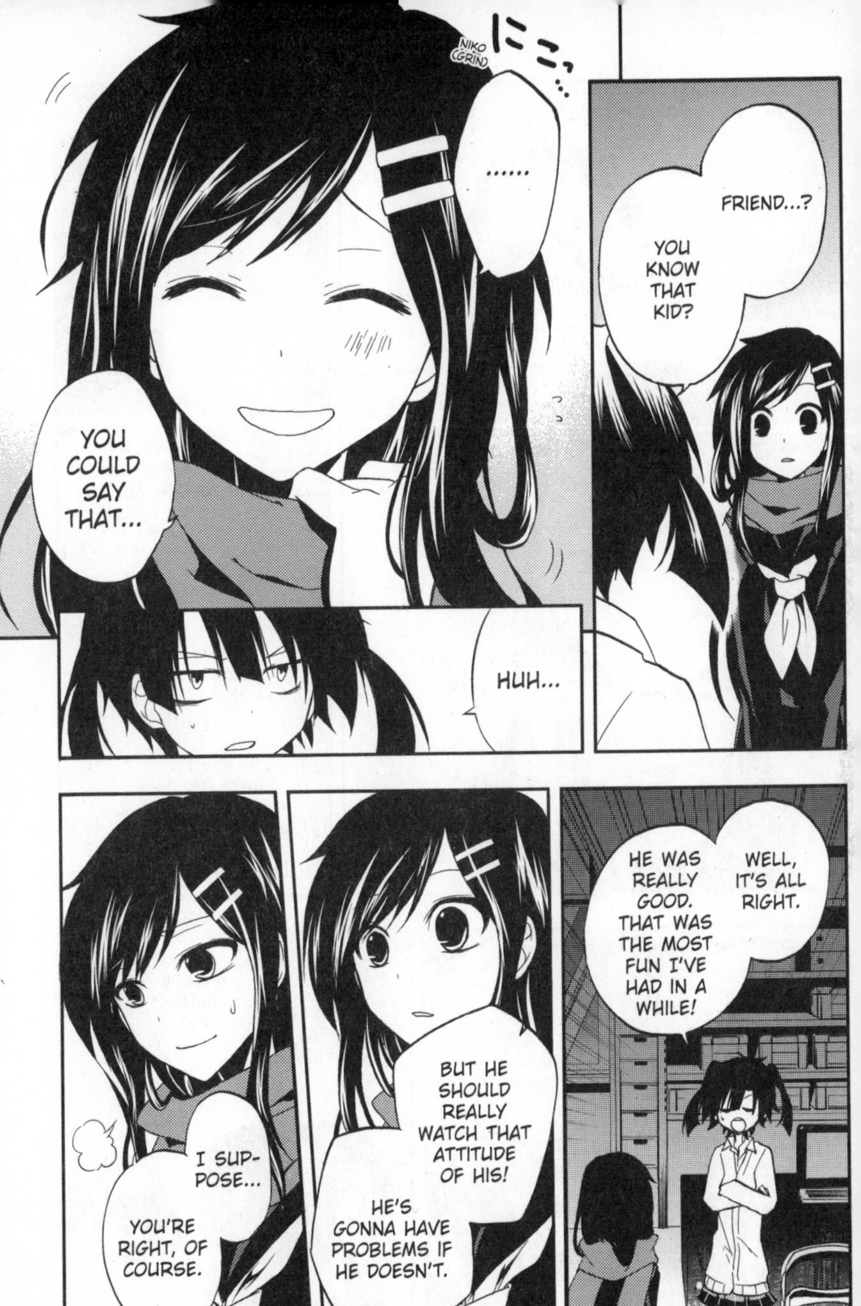
FRIEND...?
YOU KNOW THAT KID?
NIKO (GRIN)
にこっ
......
YOU COULD SAY THAT...
HUH...
WELL, IT'S ALL RIGHT.
HE WAS REALLY GOOD. THAT WAS THE MOST FUN I'VE HAD IN A WHILE!
BUT HE SHOULD REALLY WATCH THAT ATTITUDE OF HIS!
HE'S GONNA HAVE PROBLEMS IF HE DOESN'T.
I SUP-POSE...
YOU'RE RIGHT, OF COURSE.

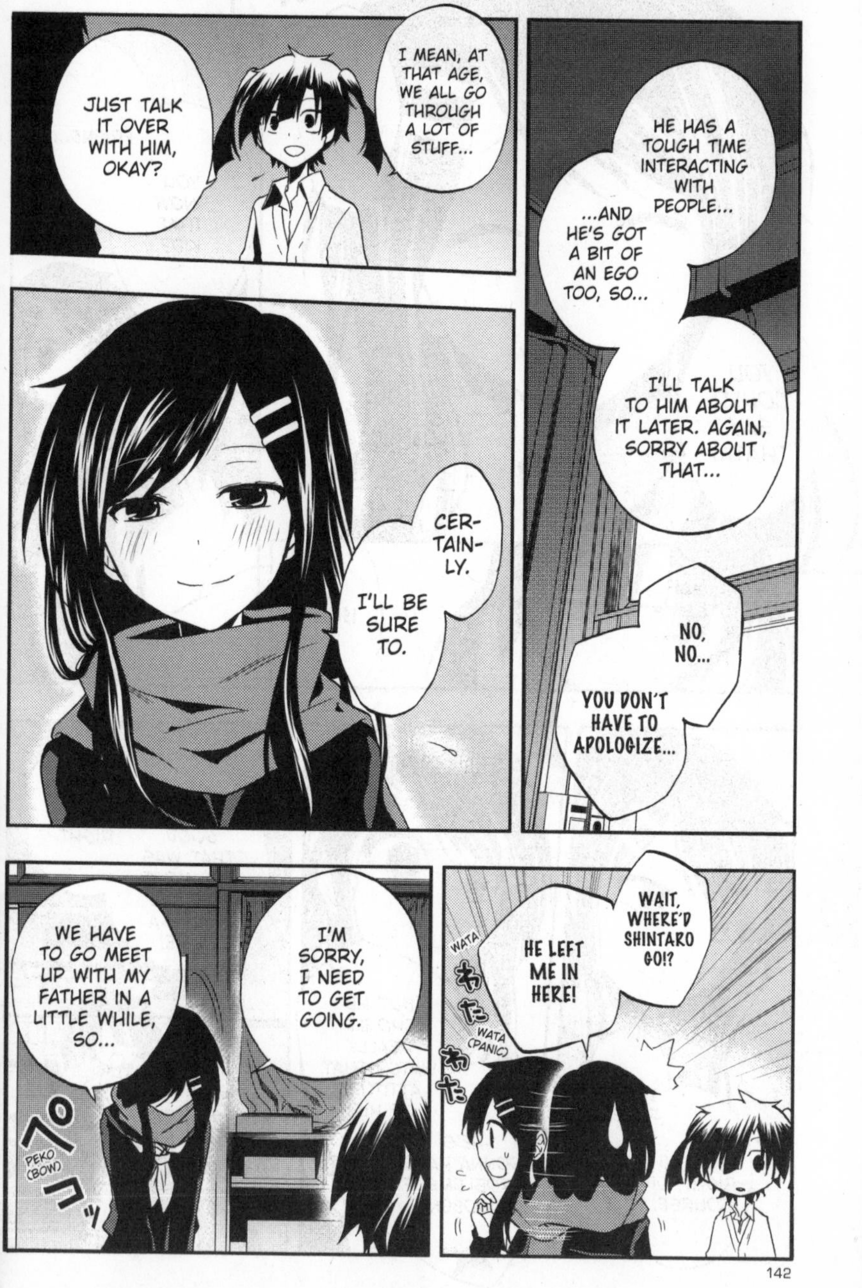
HE HAS A TOUGH TIME INTERACTING WITH PEOPLE...
...AND HE'S GOT A BIT OF AN EGO TOO, SO...
I'LL TALK TO HIM ABOUT IT LATER. AGAIN, SORRY ABOUT THAT...
NO, NO...
YOU DON'T HAVE TO APOLOGIZE...
I MEAN, AT THAT AGE, WE ALL GO THROUGH A LOT OF STUFF...
JUST TALK IT OVER WITH HIM, OKAY?
CER-TAIN-LY.
I'LL BE SURE TO.
WAIT, WHERE'D SHINTARO GO!?
HE LEFT ME IN HERE!
WATA
わた
WATA (PANIC)
わた
I'M SORRY, I NEED TO GET GOING.
WE HAVE TO GO MEET UP WITH MY FATHER IN A LITTLE WHILE, SO...
ペコッ
PEKO (BOW)

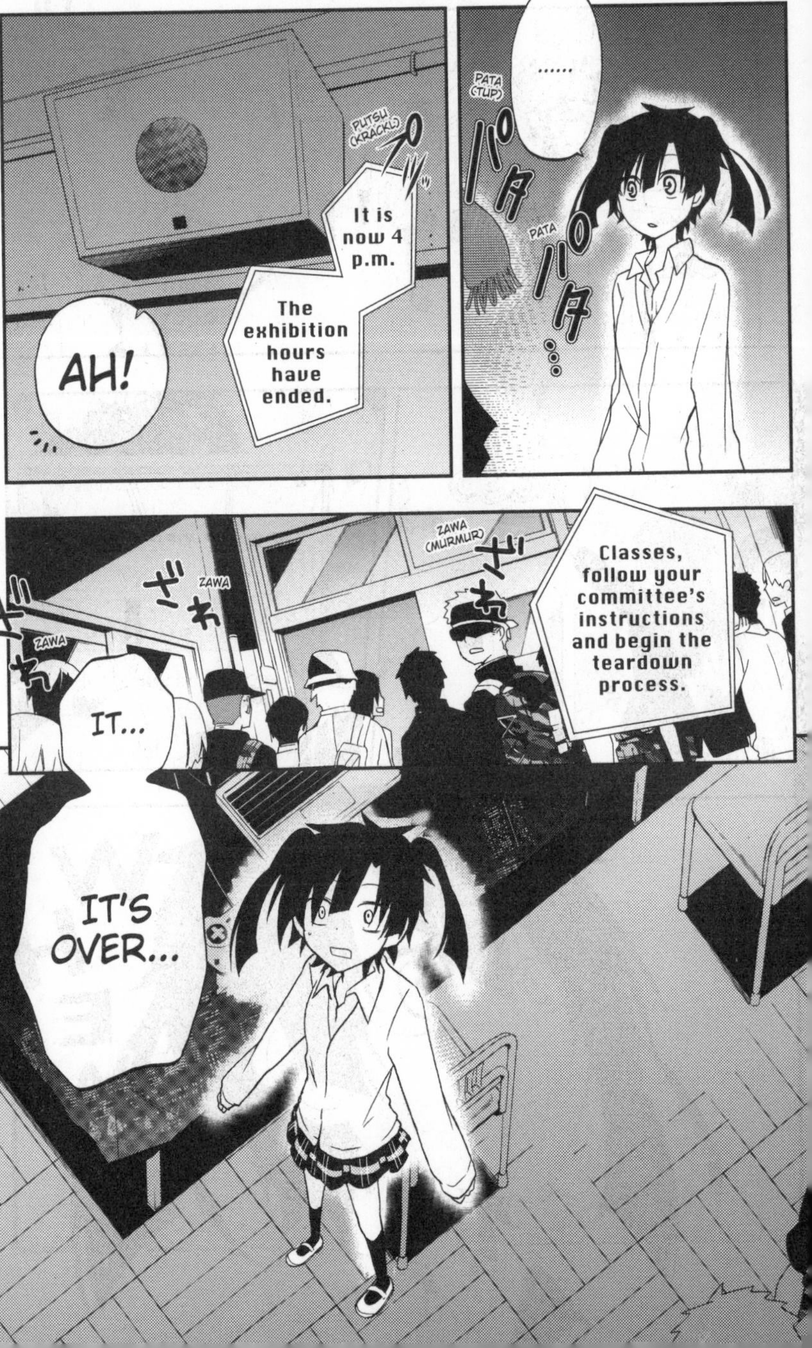
......
PATA (TUP)
パタ
PATA
パタ...
PUTSU (KRACKL)
プツ
It is now 4 p.m.
The exhibition hours have ended.
AH!
Classes, follow your committee's instructions and begin the teardown process.
ZAWA (MURMUR)
ざわ
ZAWA
ざわ
ZAWA
ざわ
IT...
IT'S OVER...

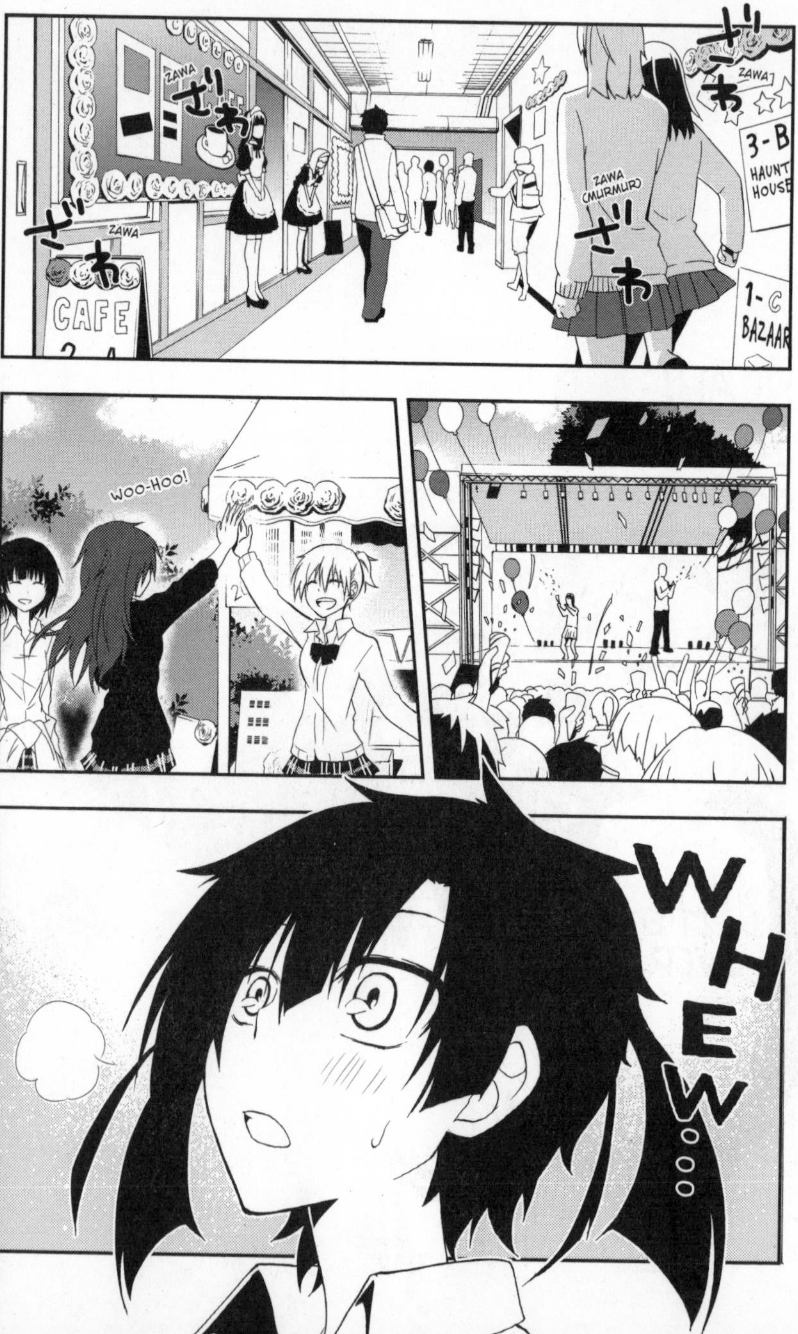

ざーわ
ZAWA
3-B
HAUNT
HOUSE
ZAWA (MURMUR)
ざわ
1-C
BAZAAR
ZAWA
ざわ
ZAWA
ざわ
CAFE
WOO-HOO!
WHEWOOO...

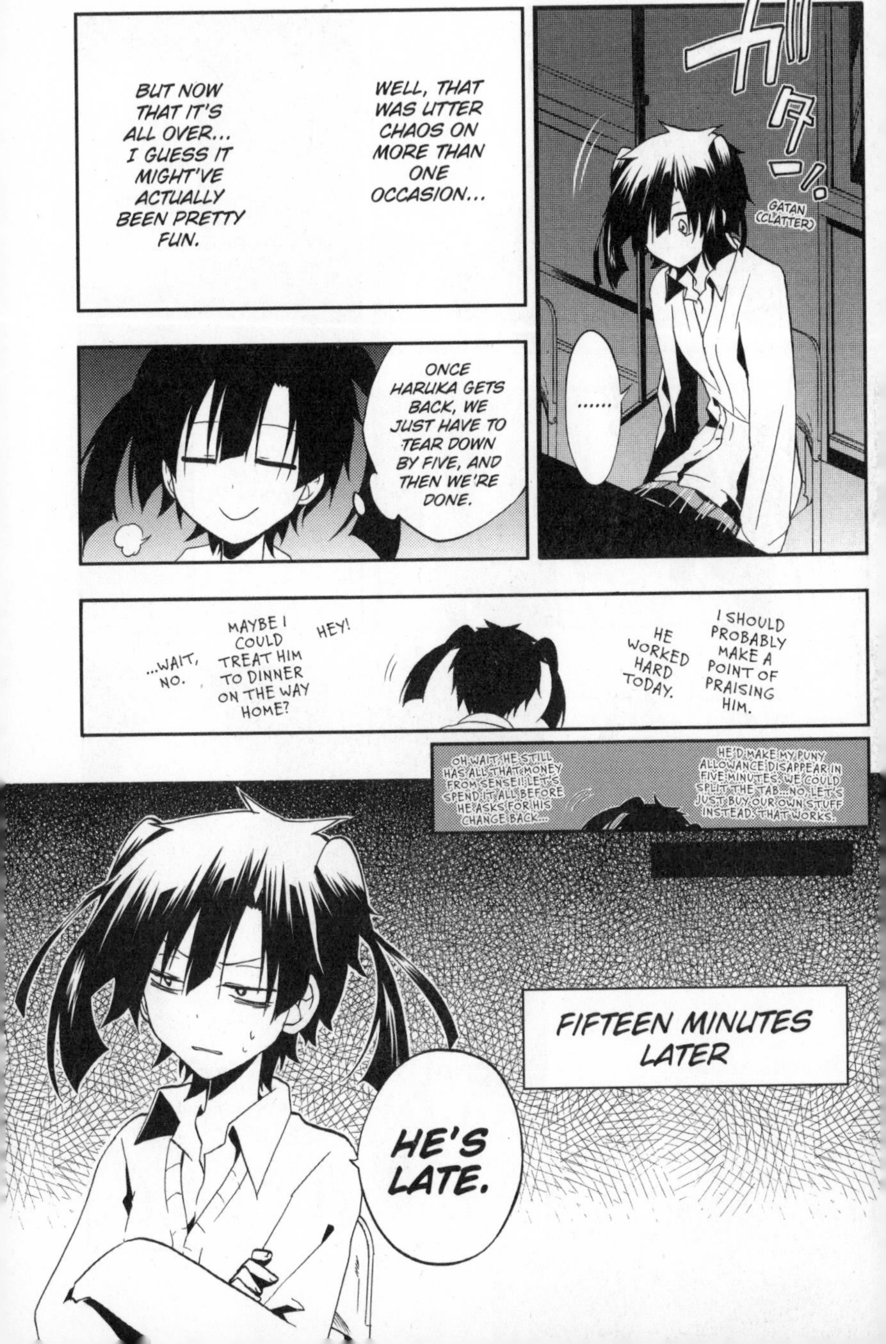
GATAN (CLATTER)
......
WELL, THAT WAS UTTER CHAOS ON MORE THAN ONE OCCASION...
BUT NOW THAT IT'S ALL OVER... I GUESS IT MIGHT'VE ACTUALLY BEEN PRETTY FUN.
ONCE HARUKA GETS BACK, WE JUST HAVE TO TEAR DOWN BY FIVE, AND THEN WE'RE DONE.
I SHOULD PROBABLY MAKE A POINT OF PRAISING HIM.
HE WORKED HARD TODAY.
HEY!
MAYBE I COULD TREAT HIM TO DINNER ON THE WAY HOME?
...WAIT, NO.
HE'D MAKE MY PUNY ALLOWANCE DISAPPEAR IN FIVE MINUTES. WE COULD SPLIT THE TAB... NO, LET'S JUST BUY OUR OWN STUFF INSTEAD. THAT WORKS.
OH WAIT, HE STILL HAS ALL THAT MONEY FROM SENSEI! LET'S SPEND IT ALL BEFORE HE ASKS FOR HIS CHANGE BACK...
[redacted]
FIFTEEN MINUTES LATER
HE'S LATE.

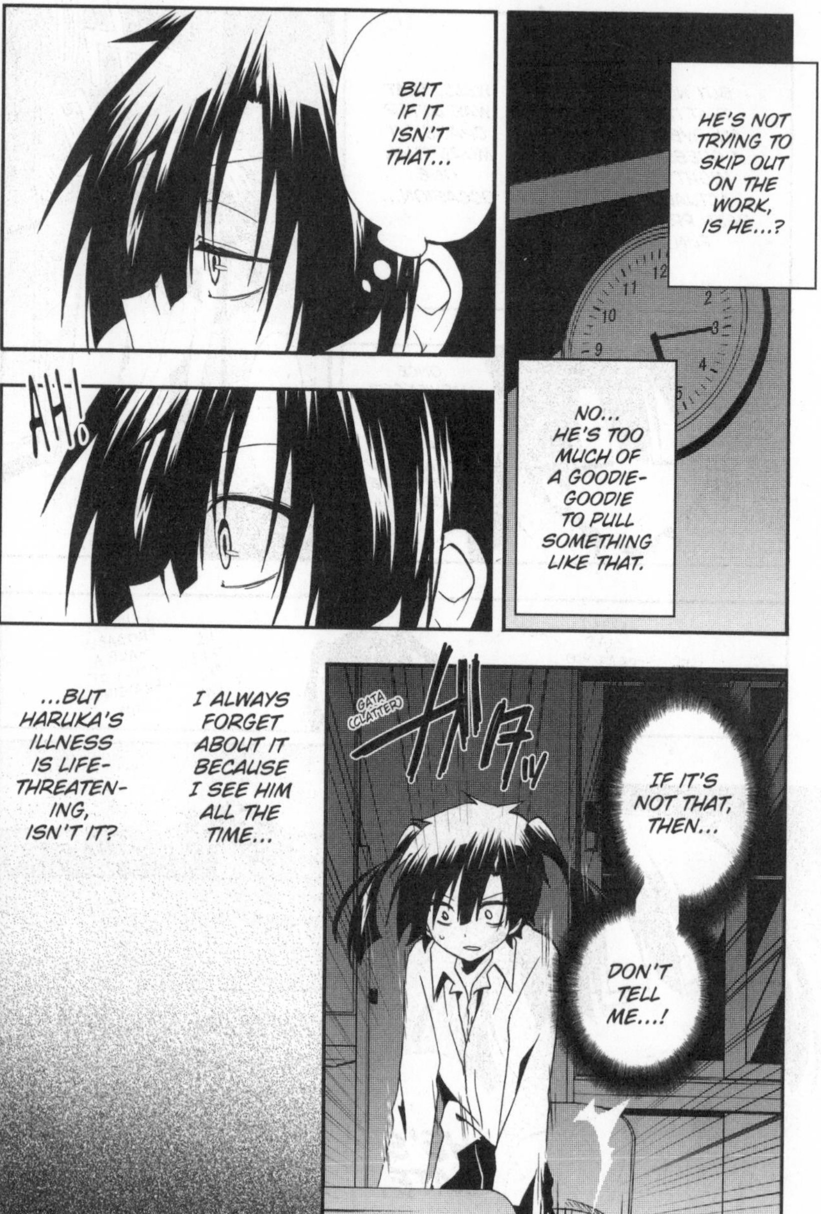
HE'S NOT TRYING TO SKIP OUT ON THE WORK, IS HE...?
NO... HE'S TOO MUCH OF A GOODIE-GOODIE TO PULL SOMETHING LIKE THAT.
BUT IF IT ISN'T THAT...
AH!
GATA (CLATTER)
IF IT'S NOT THAT, THEN...
DON'T TELL ME...!
I ALWAYS FORGET ABOUT IT BECAUSE I SEE HIM ALL THE TIME...
...BUT HARUKA'S ILLNESS IS LIFE-THREATENING, ISN'T IT?

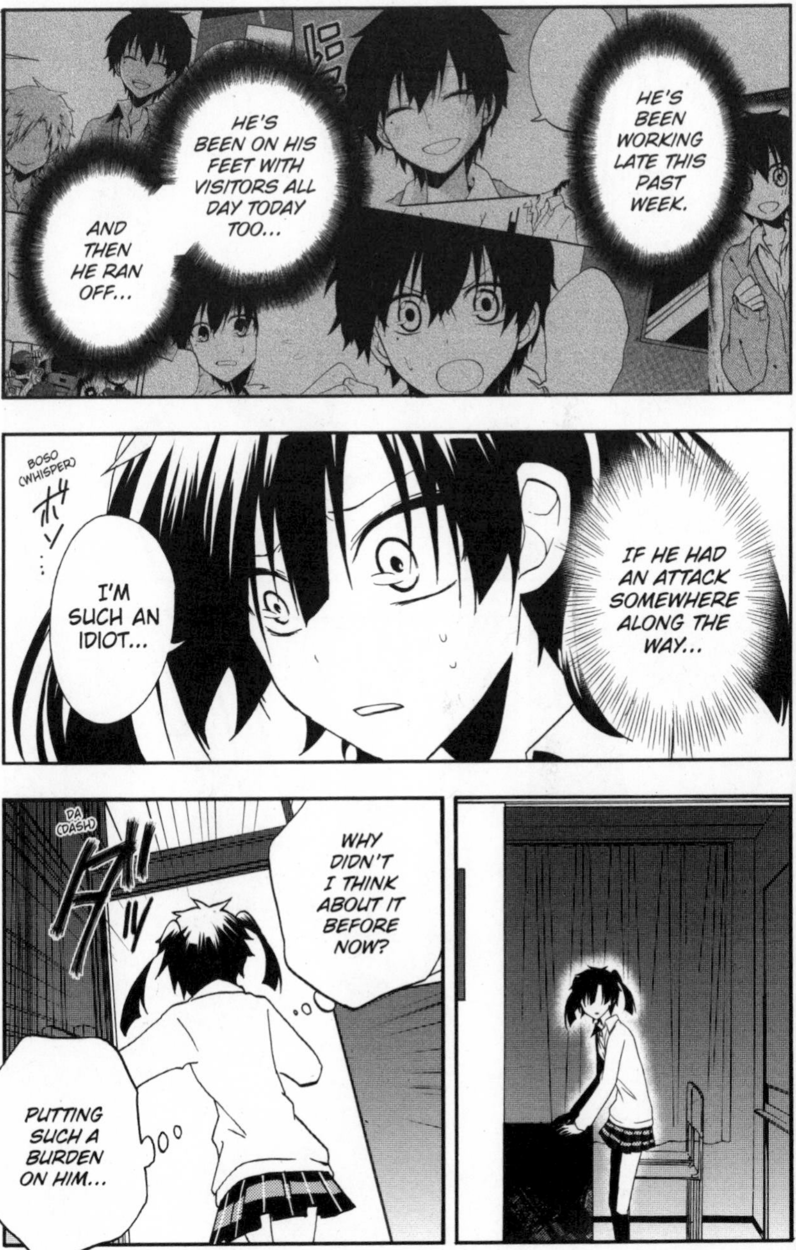
HE'S BEEN WORKING LATE THIS PAST WEEK.
HE'S BEEN ON HIS FEET WITH VISITORS ALL DAY TODAY TOO...
AND THEN HE RAN OFF...
IF HE HAD AN ATTACK SOMEWHERE ALONG THE WAY...
BOSO (WHISPER)
I'M SUCH AN IDIOT...
WHY DIDN'T I THINK ABOUT IT BEFORE NOW?
DA (DASH)
PUTTING SUCH A BURDEN ON HIM...

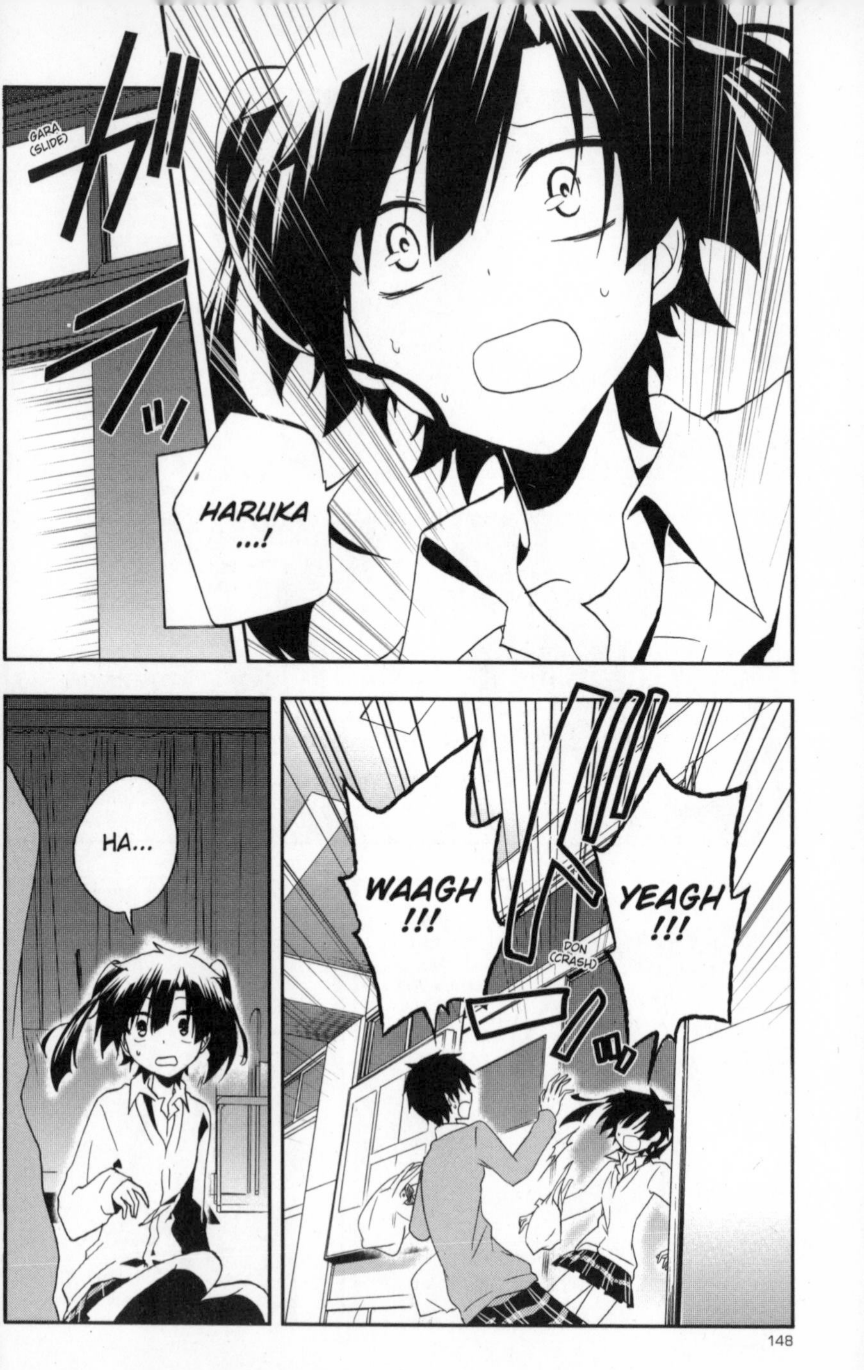
GARA (SLIDE)
HARUKA ...!
YEAGH !!!
WAAGH !!!
DON (CRASH)
HA...

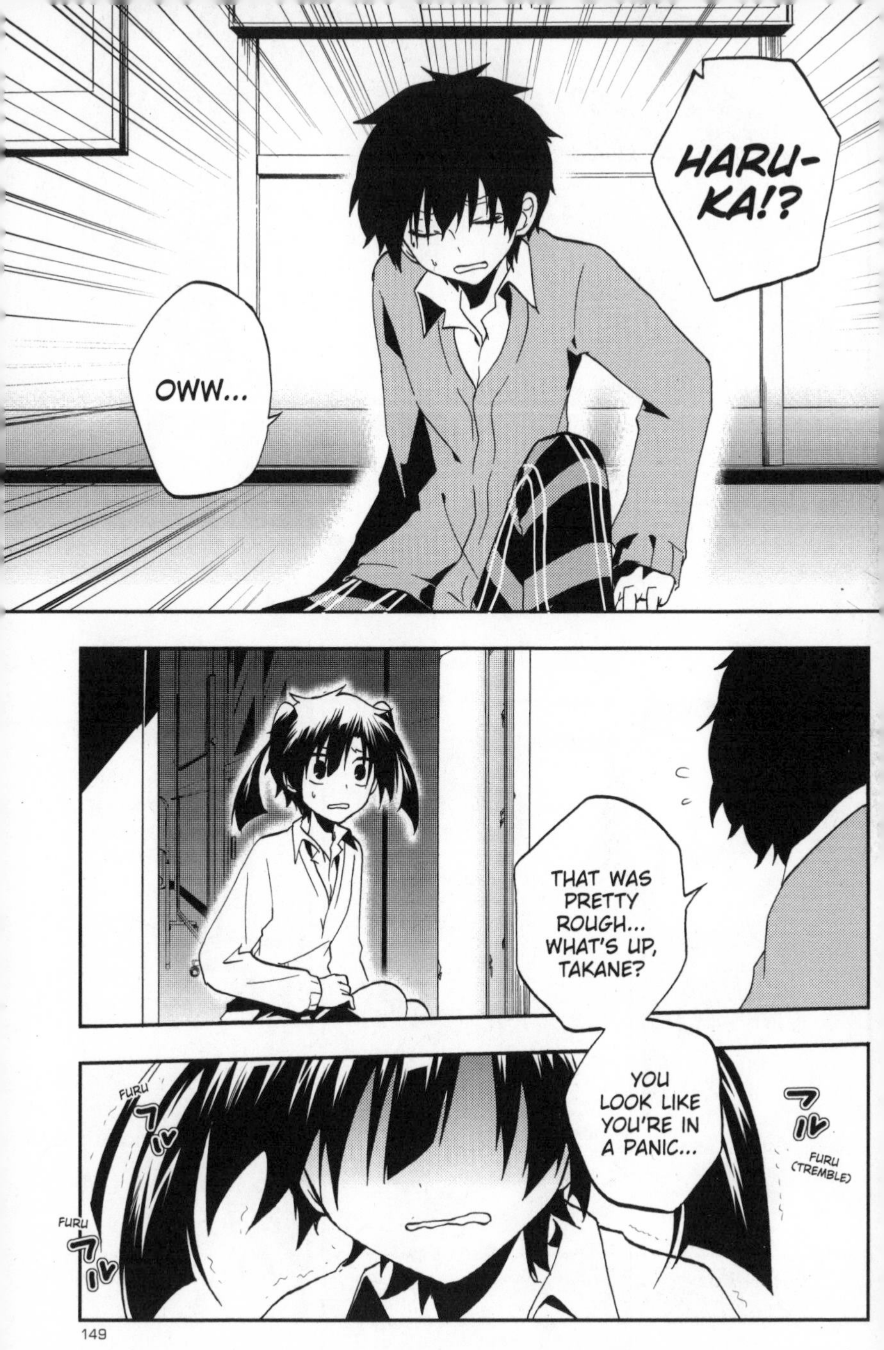
HARU-KA!?
OWW...
THAT WAS PRETTY ROUGH... WHAT'S UP, TAKANE?
YOU LOOK LIKE YOU'RE IN A PANIC...
FURU (TREMBLE)
FURU
FURU

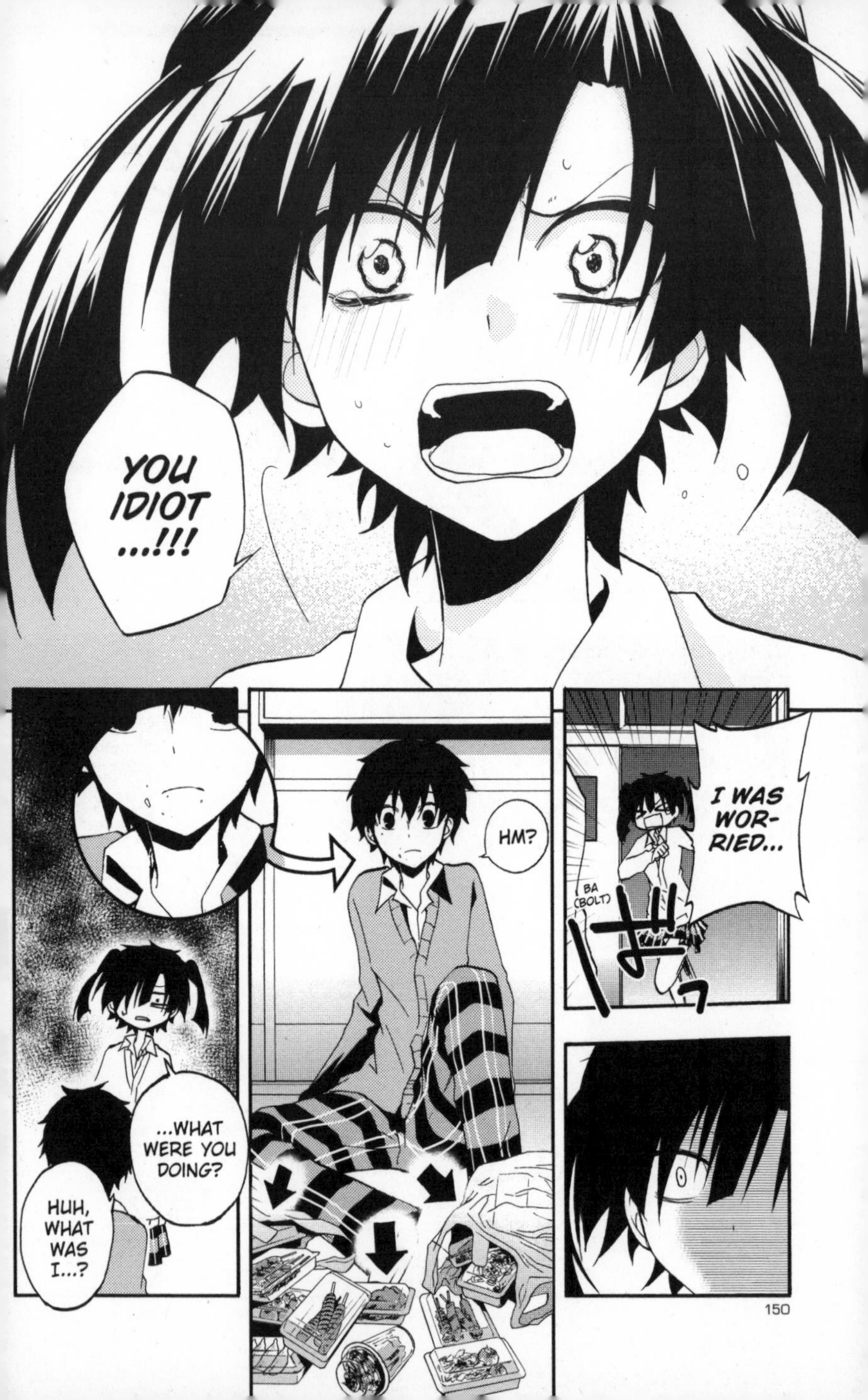
YOU IDIOT ...!!!
I WAS WOR-RIED...
BA (BOLT)
HM?
...WHAT WERE YOU DOING?
HUH, WHAT WAS I...?

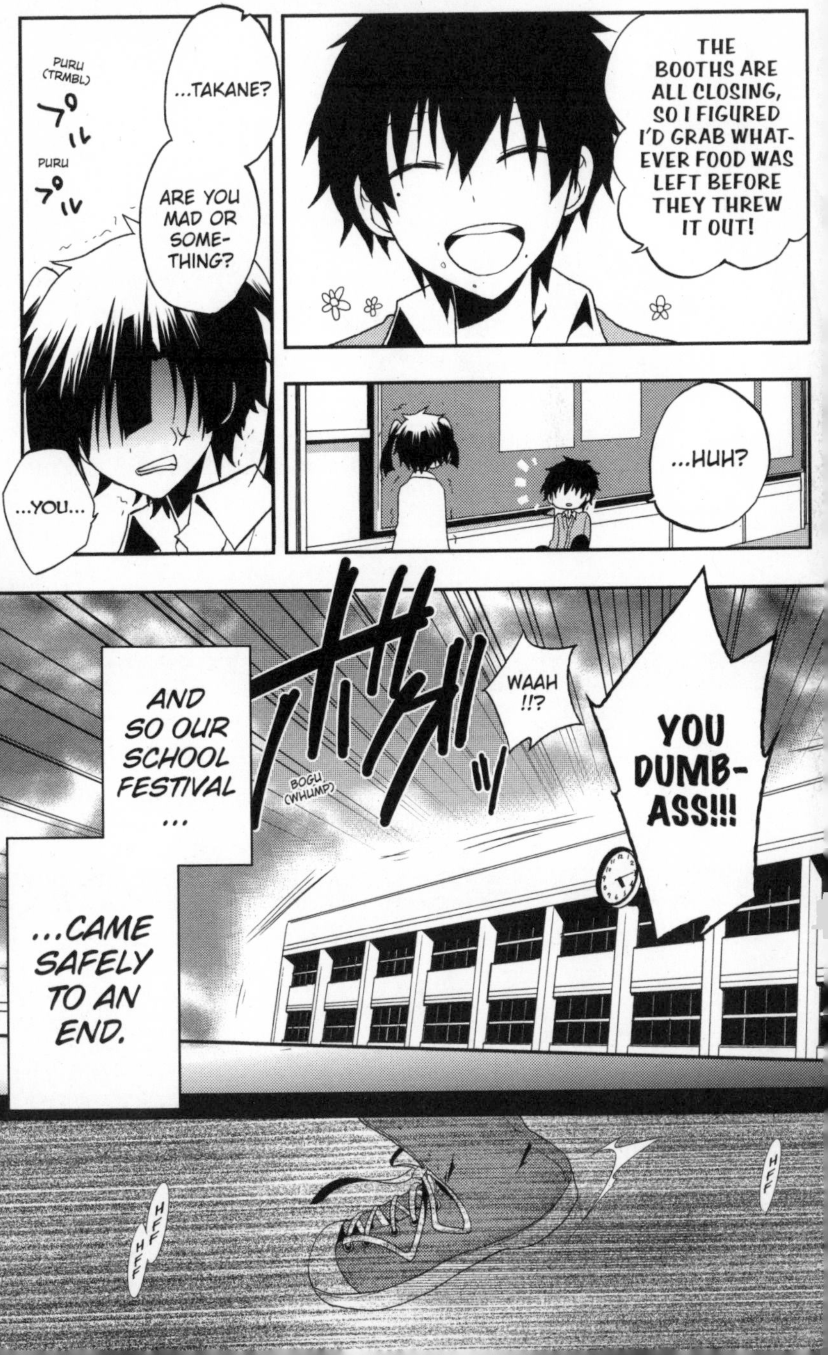
THE BOOTHS ARE ALL CLOSING, SO I FIGURED I'D GRAB WHATEVER FOOD WAS LEFT BEFORE THEY THREW IT OUT!
...HUH?
...TAKANE?
ARE YOU MAD OR SOMETHING?
PURU (TRMBL)
PURU
...YOU...
YOU DUMB-ASS!!!
WAAH !!?
BOGU (WHUMP)
AND SO OUR SCHOOL FESTIVAL...
...CAME SAFELY TO AN END.
HFF
HFF
HFF

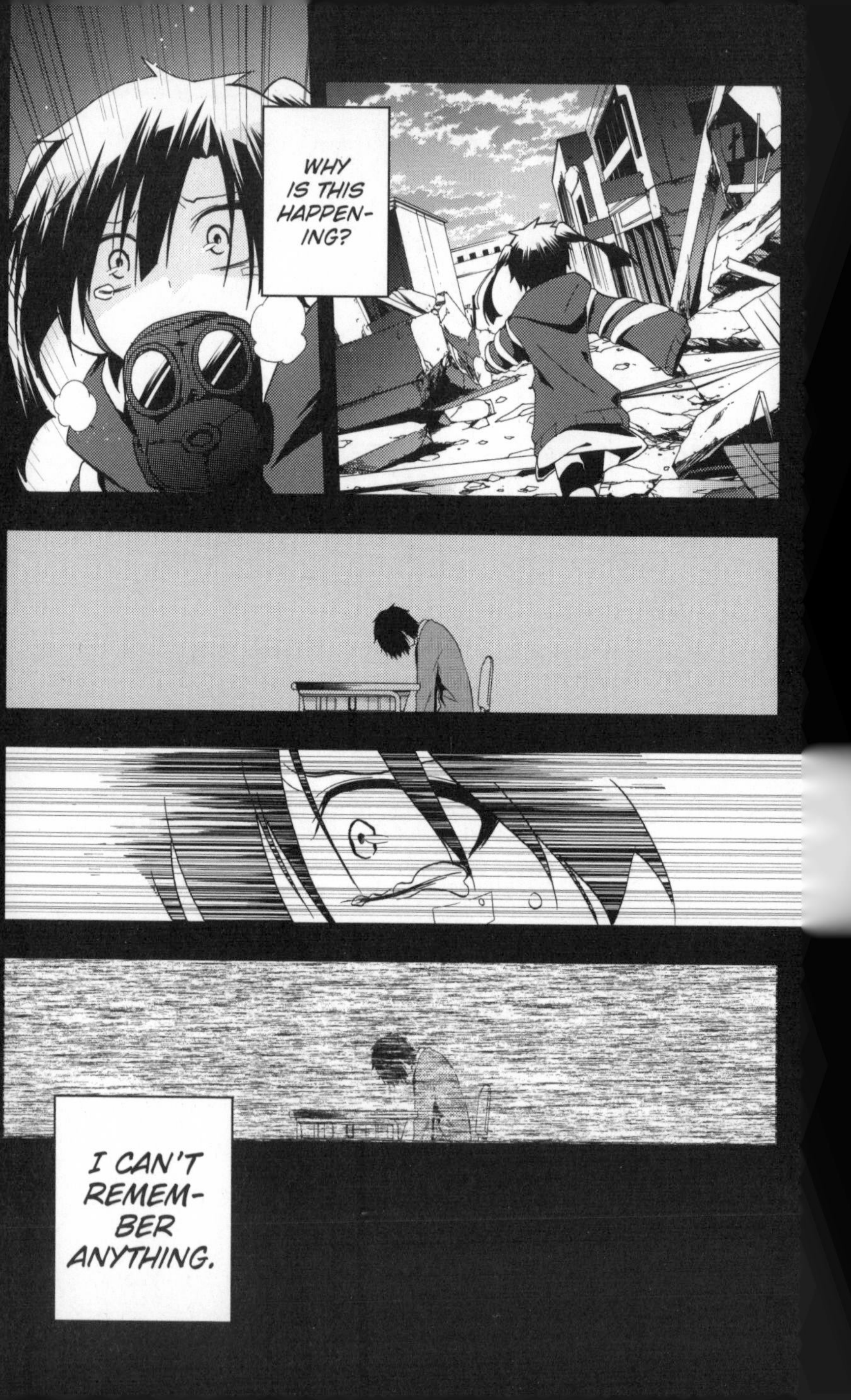
WHY IS THIS HAPPENING?
I CAN'T REMEMBER ANYTHING.

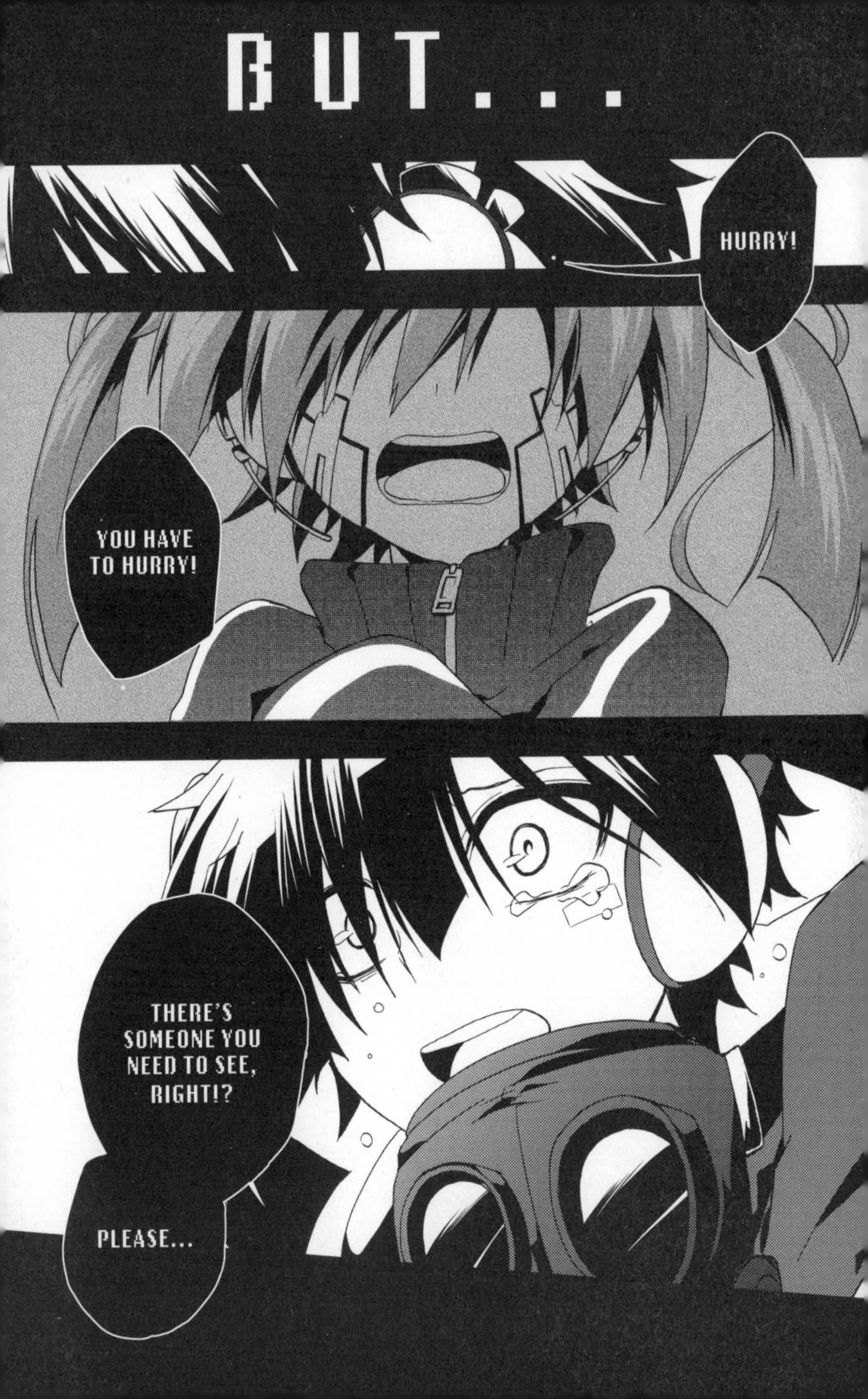
BUT...
HURRY!
YOU HAVE TO HURRY!
THERE'S SOMEONE YOU NEED TO SEE, RIGHT!?
PLEASE...

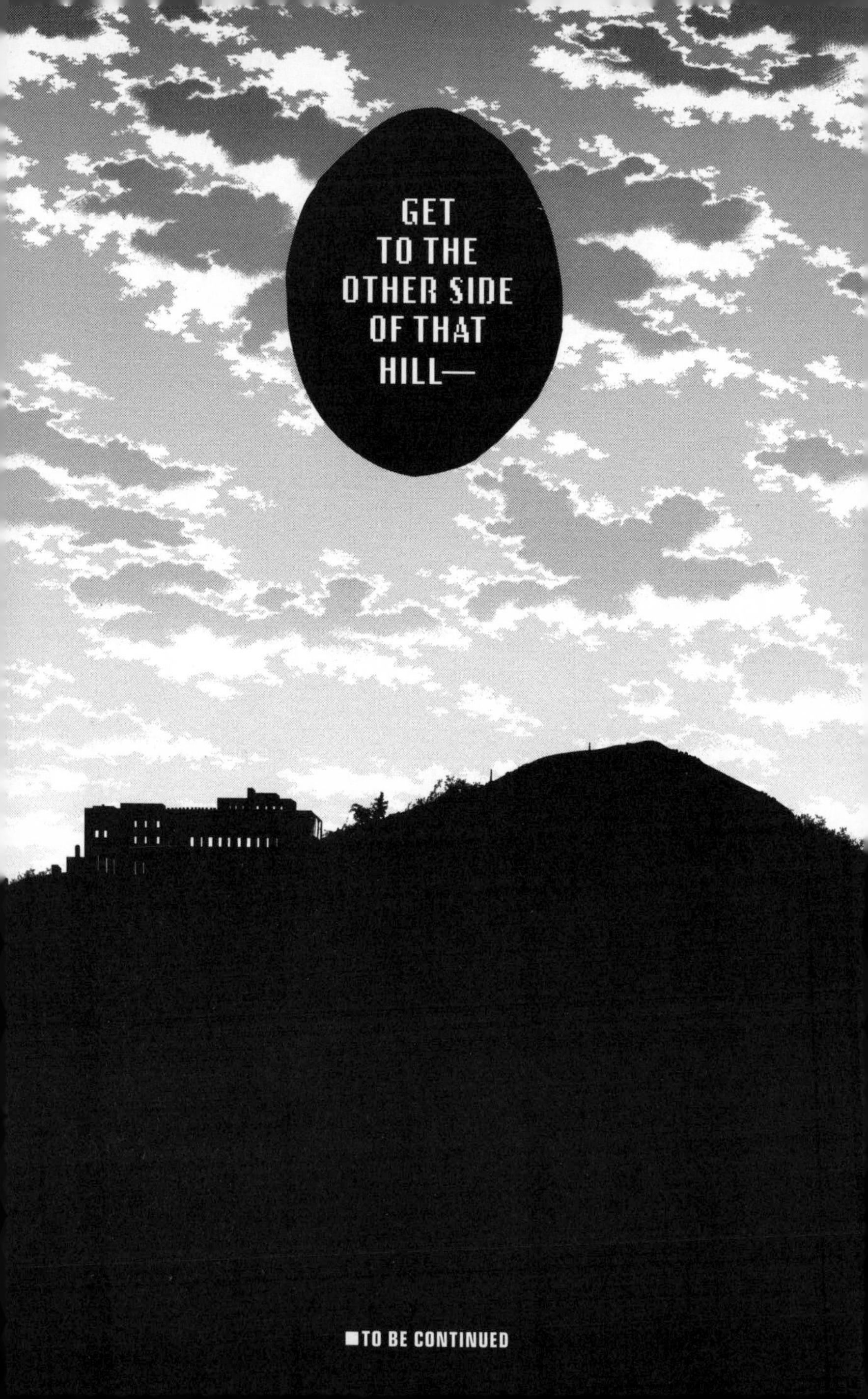
GET TO THE OTHER SIDE OF THAT HILL—
■TO BE CONTINUED

IT'S VOLUME 3!! THANK YOU VERY MUCH!!!

IT'S GONE SO FAST. I'M REALLY SURPRISED. SURPRISED ABOUT WHAT? THE FACT THAT IT'S BEEN A YEAR AND SOME CHANGE SINCE I STARTED DRAWING THIS MANGA. WOW! AMAZING!! AND IT'S ALL THANKS TO EVERYONE WHO'S GIVEN ME SUPPORT! THANK YOU SO MUCH! I REALLY MEAN IT! AND I HOPE YOU'RE LOOKING FORWARD TO WHAT COMES NEXT. HOPEFULLY I'LL SEE ALL OF YOU IN THE NEXT VOLUME!!

MAHIRO SATOU

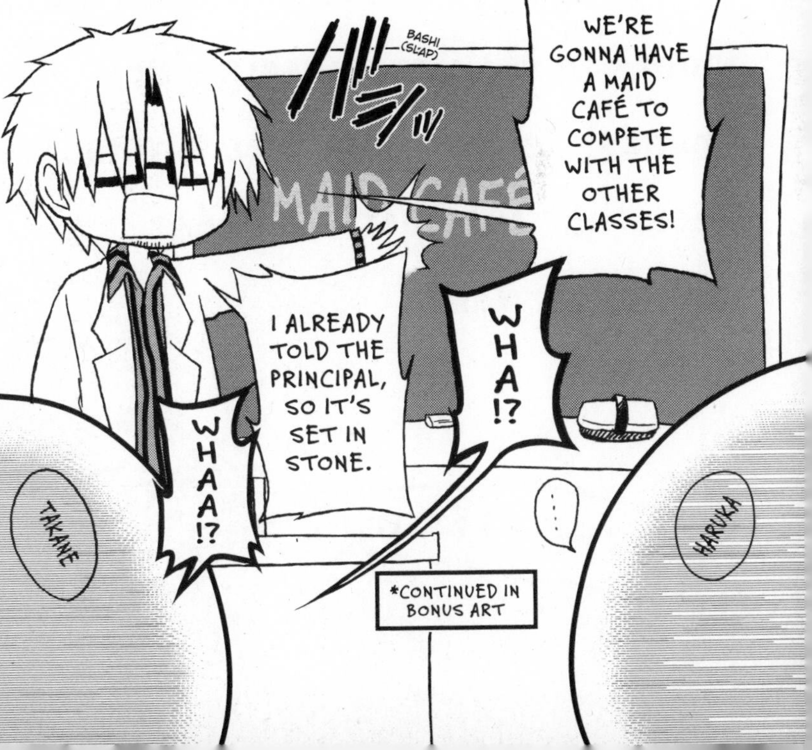
WE'RE GONNA HAVE A MAID CAFÉ TO COMPETE WITH THE OTHER CLASSES!
BASHI (SLAP)
MAID CAFÉ
WHA!?
I ALREADY TOLD THE PRINCIPAL, SO IT'S SET IN STONE.
WHAA!?
...
HARUKA
TAKANE
*CONTINUED IN BONUS ART

Congratulations on manga Volume 3!

Takane is the main hero of this volume, and I was a bit worried about how that icy glare of hers would turn out. Along those lines, I really appreciate how cute she looks in Mahiro-sensei's able hands! I hope he'll keep giving her that cute-yet-cool edge going forward.

WOO-HOO...

じん

Jin

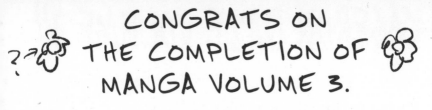

CONGRATS ON THE COMPLETION OF MANGA VOLUME 3.

Number two on my "characters whom I love when Mahiro-sensei draws them" series is Kenjirou Tateyama, Takane's teacher. He looks so, so cool, like this older gent who still has no trouble getting the ladies. Thanks so much for that. I always have a mess of fun reading this.

Keep up the good work.

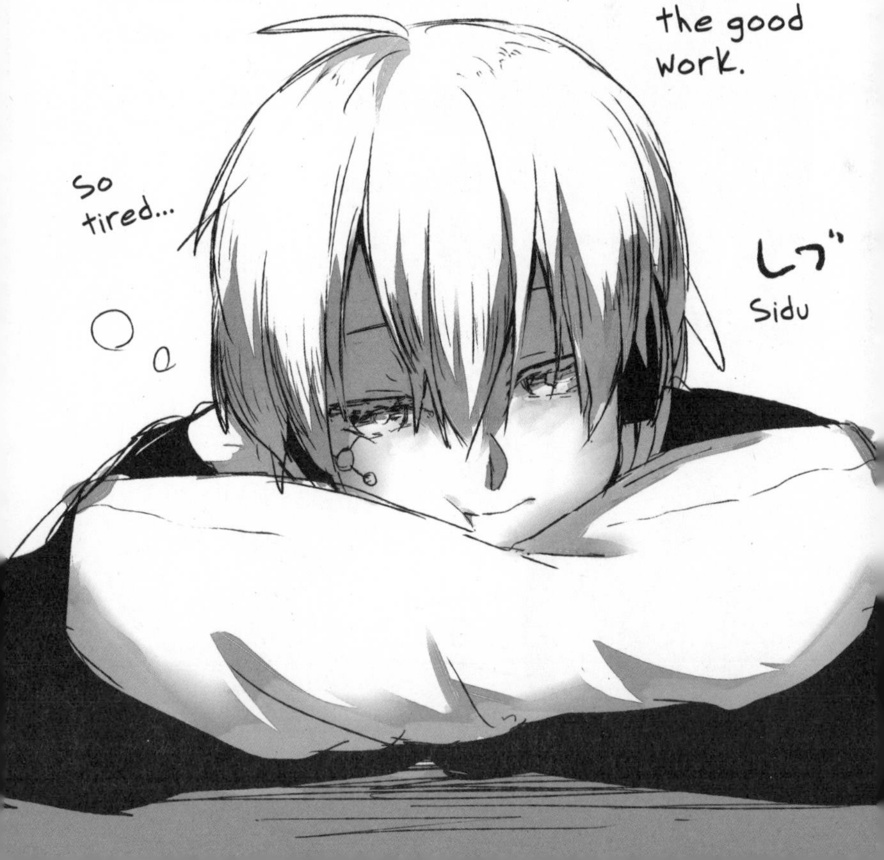
So tired...

しづ
Sidu

KAGEROU DAZE VOLUME 3!!

@わんにゃんぷー
@Wannyanpuu-

Congratulations on getting this volume out!!
This volume is packed to the brim with Takane-chan and Haruka-kun, huh? When Mahiro-san draws them, their angelic qualities really get ramped up. I can hardly stand it!
Seeing Kido-san, Kano-kun, Shintaro-kun, and Ayano-chan in their younger years is really cute too!

Seto...Seto...
Can't wait for the next volume!
Hibiya-kun and Hiyori-chan!
I just gotta see them!

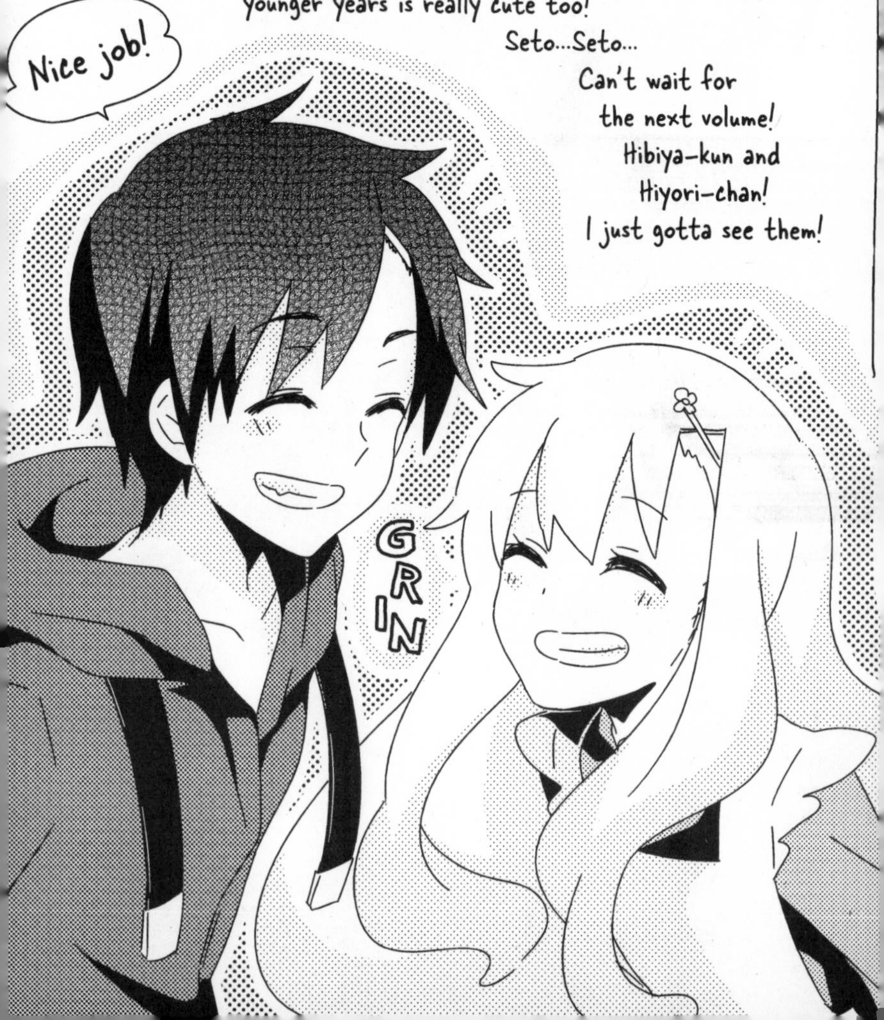
Nice job!
GRIN

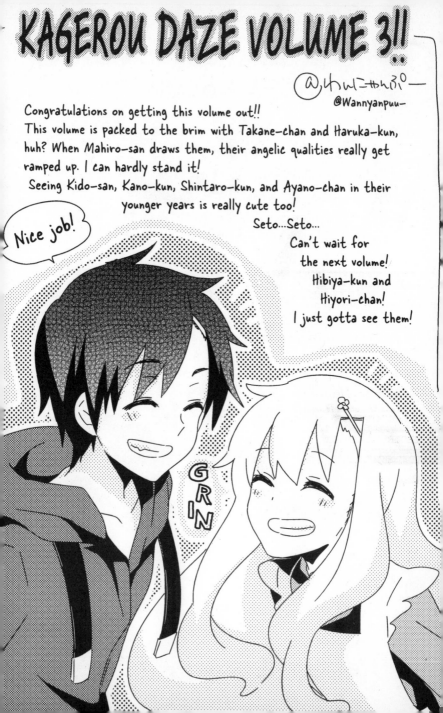